Transitional Justice in South Asia

Offering a comparative case study of transitional justice processes in Afghanistan and Nepal, this book critically evaluates the way the "local" is consulted in post-conflict efforts toward peace and reconciliation. It argues that there is a tendency in transitional justice efforts to contain the discussion of the "local" within religious and cultural parameters, thus engaging only with a "static local," as interpreted by certain local stakeholders.

Based on data collected through interviews and participant observation carried out in the civil societies of the respective countries, this book brings attention to a "dynamic local," where societal norms evolve, and realities on the ground are shaped by shifting power dynamics, local hierarchies, and inequalities between actors. It suggests that the "local" must be understood as an inter-subjective concept, the meaning of which is not only an evolving and moving target, but also dependent on who is consulted to interpret it to external actors.

This timely book engages with the divergent range of civil society voices and offers ways to move forward by including their concerns in the efforts to help impoverished war-torn societies transition from a state of war to the conditions of peace.

Tazreena Sajjad is a Professorial Lecturer in the International Politics Department at the School of International Service, American University, USA. Her research interests include transitional justice, humanitarian intervention, and women and post-conflict reconstruction.

Routledge Contemporary South Asia Series

1 **Pakistan**
Social and cultural transformations
in a Muslim nation
Mohammad A. Qadeer

2 **Labor, Democratization, and
Development in India and
Pakistan**
Christopher Candland

3 **China–India Relations**
Contemporary dynamics
Amardeep Athwal

4 **Madrasas in South Asia**
Teaching terror?
Jamal Malik

5 **Labor, Globalization, and the
State**
Workers, women, and migrants
confront neoliberalism
*Edited by Debdas Banerjee and
Michael Goldfield*

6 **Indian Literature and Popular
Cinema**
Recasting classics
Edited by Heidi R.M. Pauwels

7 **Islamist Militancy in
Bangladesh**
A complex web
Ali Riaz

8 **Regionalism in South Asia**
Negotiating cooperation,
institutional structures
Kishore C. Dash

9 **Federalism, Nationalism, and
Development**
India and the Punjab economy
Pritam Singh

10 **Human Development and
Social Power**
Perspectives from South Asia
Ananya Mukherjee Reed

11 **The South Asian Diaspora**
Transnational networks and
changing identities
*Edited by Rajesh Rai and Peter
Reeves*

12 **Pakistan–Japan Relations**
Continuity and change in economic
relations and security interests
Ahmad Rashid Malik

13 **Himalayan Frontiers of India**
Historical, geo-political, and
strategic perspectives
K. Warikoo

14 **India's Open-Economy Policy**
Globalism, rivalry, continuity
Jalal Alamgir

15 **The Separatist Conflict in Sri Lanka**
Terrorism, ethnicity, political economy
Asoka Bandarage

16 **India's Energy Security**
Edited by Ligia Noronha and Anant Sudarshan

17 **Globalization and the Middle Classes in India**
The social and cultural impact of neoliberal reforms
Ruchira Ganguly-Scrase and Timothy J. Scrase

18 **Water Policy Processes in India**
Discourses of power and resistance
Vandana Asthana

19 **Minority Governments in India**
The puzzle of elusive majorities
Csaba Nikolenyi

20 **The Maoist Insurgency in Nepal**
Revolution in the twenty-first century
Edited by Mahendra Lawoti and Anup K. Pahari

21 **Global Capital and Peripheral Labour**
The history and political economy of plantation workers in India
K. Ravi Raman

22 **Maoism in India**
Reincarnation of ultra-left wing extremism in the twenty-first century
Bidyut Chakrabarty and Rajat Kujur

23 **Economic and Human Development in Contemporary India**
Cronyism and fragility
Debdas Banerjee

24 **Culture and the Environment in the Himalaya**
Arjun Guneratne

25 **The Rise of Ethnic Politics in Nepal**
Democracy in the margins
Susan I. Hangen

26 **The Multiplex in India**
A cultural economy of urban leisure
Adrian Athique and Douglas Hill

27 **Tsunami Recovery in Sri Lanka**
Ethnic and regional dimensions
Dennis B. McGilvray and Michele R. Gamburd

28 **Development, Democracy, and the State**
Critiquing the Kerala model of development
K. Ravi Raman

29 **Mohajir Militancy in Pakistan**
Violence and transformation in the Karachi conflict
Nichola Khan

30 **Nationbuilding, Gender, and War Crimes in South Asia**
Bina D'Costa

31 **The State in India after Liberalization**
Interdisciplinary perspectives
Edited by Akhil Gupta and K. Sivaramakrishnan

32 **National Identities in Pakistan**
The 1971 war in contemporary
Pakistani fiction
Cara Cilano

33 **Political Islam and Governance in Bangladesh**
Edited by Ali Riaz and C. Christine Fair

34 **Bengali Cinema**
'An other nation'
Sharmistha Gooptu

35 **NGOs in India**
The challenges of women's
empowerment and accountability
Patrick Kilby

36 **The Labour Movement in the Global South**
Trade unions in Sri Lanka
S. Janaka Biyanwila

37 **Building Bangalore**
Architecture and urban transfor-
mation in India's Silicon Valley
John C. Stallmeyer

38 **Conflict and Peacebuilding in Sri Lanka**
Caught in the peace trap?
*Edited by Jonathan Goodhand,
Jonathan Spencer, and Benedict
Korf*

39 **Microcredit and Women's Empowerment**
A case study of Bangladesh
*Amunui Faraizi, Jim McAllister,
and Taskinur Rahman*

40 **South Asia in the New World Order**
The role of regional cooperation
Shahid Javed Burki

41 **Explaining Pakistan's Foreign Policy**
Escaping India
Aparna Pande

42 **Development-induced Displacement, Rehabilitation, and Resettlement in India**
Current issues and challenges
*Edited by Sakarama Somayaji
and Smrithi Talwar*

43 **The Politics of Belonging in India**
Becoming Adivasi
*Edited by Daniel J. Rycroft and
Sangeeta Dasgupta*

44 **Re-Orientalism and South Asian Identity Politics**
The oriental other within
*Edited by Lisa Lau and Ana
Cristina Mendes*

45 **Islamic Revival in Nepal**
Religion and a new nation
Megan Adamson Sijapati

46 **Education and Inequality in India**
A classroom view
Manabi Majumdar and Jos Mooij

47 **The Culturalization of Caste in India**
Identity and inequality in a
multicultural age
Balmurli Natrajan

48 **Corporate Social Responsibility in India**
Bidyut Chakrabarty

49 **Pakistan's Stability Paradox**
Domestic, regional, and
international dimensions
*Edited by Ashutosh Misra and
Michael E. Clarke*

50 **Transforming Urban Water
Supplies in India**
The role of reform and
partnerships in globalization
Govind Gopakumar

51 **South Asian Security**
Twenty-first century discourse
Sagarika Dutt and Alok Bansal

52 **Non-discrimination and
Equality in India**
Contesting boundaries of social
justice
Vidhu Verma

53 **Being Middle-Class in India**
A way of life
Henrike Donner

54 **Kashmir's Right to Secede**
A critical examination of contem-
porary theories of secession
Matthew J. Webb

55 **Bollywood Travels**
Culture, diaspora, and border
crossings in popular Hindi cinema
Rajinder Dudrah

56 **Nation, Territory, and
Globalization in Pakistan**
Traversing the margins
Chad Haines

57 **The Politics of Ethnicity in
Pakistan**
The Baloch, Sindhi, and Mohajir
ethnic movements
Farhan Hanif Siddiqi

58 **Nationalism and Ethnic
Conflict**
Identities and mobilization after
1990
*Edited by Mahendra Lawoti and
Susan Hangen*

59 **Islam and Higher Education**
Concepts, challenges, and
opportunities
Marodsilton Muborakshoeva

60 **Religious Freedom in India**
Sovereignty and (anti) conversion
Goldie Osuri

61 **Everyday Ethnicity in Sri
Lanka**
Up-country Tamil identity politics
Daniel Bass

62 **Ritual and Recovery in Post-
Conflict Sri Lanka**
Eloquent bodies
Jane Derges

63 **Bollywood and Globalization**
The global power of popular
Hindi cinema
*Edited by David J. Schaefer and
Kavita Karan*

64 **Regional Economic Integration
in South Asia**
Trapped in conflict?
Amita Batra

65 **Architecture and Nationalism
in Sri Lanka**
The trouser under the cloth
Anoma Pieris

66 **Civil Society and Democratization in India**
Institutions, ideologies, and interests
Sarbeswar Sahoo

67 **Contemporary Pakistani Fiction in English**
Idea, nation, state
Cara N. Cilano

68 **Transitional Justice in South Asia**
A study of Afghanistan and Nepal
Tazreena Sajjad

Transitional Justice in South Asia

A study of Afghanistan and Nepal

Tazreena Sajjad

LONDON AND NEW YORK

First published 2013
by Routledge
2 Park Square, Milton Park, Abingdon, Oxfordshire OX14 4RN

Simultaneously published in the USA and Canada
by Routledge
711 Third Avenue, New York, NY 10017

First issued in paperback 2015

Routledge is an imprint of the Taylor & Francis Group, an informa business

© 2013 Tazreena Sajjad

The right of Tazreena Sajjad to be identified as author of this work has been asserted by her in accordance with sections 77 and 78 of the Copyright, Designs and Patents Act 1988.

All rights reserved. No part of this book may be reprinted or reproduced or utilized in any form or by any electronic, mechanical, or other means, now known or hereafter invented, including photocopying and recording, or in any information storage or retrieval system, without permission in writing from the publishers.

Trademark notice: Product or corporate names may be trademarks or registered trademarks, and are used only for identification and explanation without intent to infringe.

British Library Cataloguing in Publication Data
A catalogue record for this book is available from the British Library

Library of Congress Cataloging in Publication Data
A catalog record for this book has been requested

ISBN 13: 978-1-138-11938-3 (pbk)
ISBN 13: 978-0-415-62997-3 (hbk)

Typeset in Times New Roman
by Sunrise Setting Ltd, Paignton, UK

Contents

Preface		x
Acknowledgements		xv
List of abbreviations		xvi

1	Introduction: examining the justice question in Afghanistan and Nepal	1
2	The legacy of past initiatives	25
3	Ordinary laws	46
4	Through local lenses: the politicization of transitional justice	75
5	A meaning of justice	92
6	Negotiating narrow spaces: National Human Rights Institutions	120
7	Conclusion: toward a theory of the "local"	139

Glossary	147
Notes	153
Bibliography	196
Index	220

Preface

On December 29, 2008, the center-left secular party, the Awami League (AL) swept into power with a resounding victory in Bangladesh, defeating the opposition, the Bangladesh Nationalist Party (BNP). Amongst the many landmark events that marked this victory, including unprecedented political participation of women and youth, was the crushing defeat of the far-right Islamist party the Jamaat-e-Islami (JI), one of the serious contenders for parliamentary seats, and with a long history of being "king-makers" in past elections. The main reason for JI's defeat was attributed to an unprecedented nationwide grassroots movement comprising of victims' families and different sectors of civil society that, since late 2007, mobilized to create awareness about the Liberation War of 1971 and the activities of collaborators of the Pakistani army, many of whom are now the senior leaders of the JI. The mobilization of survivors, civil society members, and those who participated in the liberation struggle to create awareness about political contenders who were widely known to have been involved in human rights atrocities in 1971 was an unprecedented effort, challenging a four-decade old unofficial policy of forgetting and the impunity enjoyed by alleged war criminals in political and social circles since the independence of the country. Their demand was simple – the long-awaited trial for war criminals in 1971, and awareness to be created amongst the electorate about the bloody history that revisionist politicians had participated in, and benefited from. On July 25, 2010, 39 years since the genocide, the special prosecution for the International Crimes Tribunal founded under the International War Crimes Tribunal Act of 1972 filed the first petition seeking direction to show top four Jamaat leaders detained on charges of committing war crimes in 1971.

The developments in Bangladesh and my own experience working in democratic governance and rule of law programs in Afghanistan and Nepal at different periods between 2001 and 2008 made me interested in accountability for wartime atrocities in South Asia, the role of internal politics and amnesty laws, and the role of civil society in demanding individual accountability and efforts, if any, to promote societal reconciliation in the region. I initially began this research to gain a deeper understanding of the efforts of civil society bodies, particularly non-governmental organizations (NGOs), both national and international, to engage with the discussion of transitional justice in Afghanistan and Nepal. I wanted

Preface xi

to examine how national and international NGOs work together to develop a common strategy on transitional justice, the ways in which they maneuver hostile terrain to introduce issues of accountability in society, and the opportunities they create to work in human rights, justice, and reconciliation.

My field observations and interviews generated two conclusions and guided me toward what has become the heart of the book and the central argument it offers. First, in an era dominated by what Teitel termed "transitional justice," where the necessity for justice for human rights violations in war has become an integral component on post-conflict reconstruction efforts, the limited scholarly attention paid to issues of human suffering, civil society's mobilization on questions of justice, the policies of respective governments, and the challenges of instituting a rule of law in post-conflict countries as diverse as Afghanistan, Nepal, Bangladesh, and Sri Lanka was notable. I also observed that there is even a greater dearth in examining these questions within the larger framework of South Asia. Consequently, the literature on transitional justice has been both dominated and enriched by empirical observations from Eastern Europe, Latin America and Africa, but there has been little to no contributions based on the experiences of South Asia about human rights atrocities, the demand for accountability, legal and de facto amnesties, and the work of civil society organizations and NGOs. It followed that early in the research process I was confronted by the reality that outside of anecdotes and a handful of organizational reports, there is very limited writing, particularly of a scholarly nature, tracing the story of how the contemporary transitional justice commitments emerged in the case studies I was interested in i.e. Afghanistan and Nepal. In the Afghanistan case, the exceptions are Semple's *Reconciliation in Afghanistan*; Rubin's *Transitional Justice and Human Rights in Afghanistan*; Niland's chapter "Justice Postponed" in *Nation-Building Unraveled? Aid, Peace and Justice in Afghanistan*; Nadery's article *Peace or Justice? Transitional Justice in Afghanistan*; Kouvo and Mazoori's *Reconciliation, Justice and Mobilization of War Victims in Afghanistan*; and Gossman's chapter "Truth, Justice and Stability in Afghanistan" in *Transitional Justice in the Twenty-First Century: Beyond Truth Versus Justice*. While these important writings capture key events witnessed by the authors who are Afghanistan specialists in Afghanistan and/or have been actively involved in the transitional justice discussion in the country, they are also limited to being specific narratives over specific periods of time, rather than being engagements between the larger questions of wartime accountability, reconciliation, amnesty, and justice, and the specific experiences coming out of Afghanistan, or being entry points to a robust theoretical framework or argument about the issues of peace and justice facing a turbulent society. My own article *These Spaces in between: The Afghanistan Independent Human Rights Commission and its Role in Transitional Justice* and a report I wrote commissioned by the Afghanistan Research and Evaluation Unit (AREU), *Peace at All Costs? Reintegration and Reconciliation in Afghanistan*, make an effort to use Afghanistan to begin to address certain conceptual themes and lay out some challenges in civil society that may have resonance in other contexts, but they too remain constrained by their specific narratives.

xii *Preface*

The scholarly literature on transitional justice in Nepal is even more sparse, save some detailed reports and briefings and with the exception of Pasipanodya's article *A Deeper Justice: Economic and Social Justice as Transitional Justice in Nepal* and Robin's two important contributions *Towards a Victim-Centred Transitional Justice: Understanding the Needs of Families of the Disappeared in Post-Conflict Nepal* and *Transitional Justice as an Elite Discourse: Human Rights Practice Between the Global and the Local in Post-Conflict Nepal.* Similar to what I observed in the case of the writings on Afghanistan, these articles again were constrained by the immediate narrative and challenges of the particular case study and were not amenable to a broader discussion of the critical issues they raised beyond the boundaries of Nepal.

I was convinced that the story of transitional justice of Afghanistan and Nepal needed to be told in an organized and systematic fashion, going beyond the immediate details of each respective case and examining issues and themes that emerged in each. Despite their differences in political history, interestingly both countries began their most recent transitions at around the same period in history, defined by a post 9/11 global environment (the 2000s), and at a time when the discussions and critiques of transitional justice were at their zenith. Both had similar (international) actors involved in the discussion and debate on how to achieve accountability and reconciliation in both societies, within a context where policies of appeasement, both foreign and domestic, have overshadowed questions of culpability (as in the case of Afghanistan) and where the ease of information flow and cross-fertilization of ideas and experiences are facilitated by transnational networks, communications and technology, and the "norm cascade." I must emphasize that in examining these two cases, I do not claim to identify clear causal relationships between independent and dependent variables, or work with cases "most similar" or "most different" but rather tell the story of how two countries in South Asia, marked by deep-rooted socioeconomic challenges, de facto and *de jure* impunity, very weak rule of law, weak centralized authorities, and a civil society landscape dominated and/or influenced by international and elite actors at the helm of many decision-making processes struggle with the discussion of "post-conflict" justice.

In tracing the pathway of transitional justice in both countries, I came to my second conclusion. The criticisms and concerns raised by the different actors interviewed for this research underscored a refrain that has emerged from critiques of transitional justice programs in other contexts, which is that such processes are the product of neoliberal forces and tend to have a "top-down" approach that ignore or marginalize local cultural and religious practices. Individual criminal accountability in the shape of courts have also come under criticism, pointing to its high-level of dependence on the western penological rationale, its inability to try all individuals culpable for wartime atrocities, its overt focus on perpetrators rather than victims, and its limitations in being able to promote reconciliation between antagonistic communities. Socioeconomic and gender justice have also been late entries in the conventional packages to address post-conflict justice. They too emphasize the disconnection between imperatives proscribed

Preface xiii

by international policy-makers and the NGO community, and the realities and nuances of the context in question. While the realization of this disconnect has notably driven greater efforts to integrate "local" actors into consultation and implementation processes (a practice that has become pronounced in fields such as human rights and development programs), what is also evident is that even under such circumstances the power dynamics and hierarchies between decision-makers and recipients of such programs are already established, or further entrenched. Furthermore, the understanding of the "local" that is consulted seems to be a stagnant entity. Consultations with indigenous communities regarding questions of "justice" and "reconciliation" are heavily underlined by societal norms and practices; it is as if the boundaries of what the "local" encompasses begins and ends with understandings of culture and religion. In addition, consultation processes end up being highly selective in terms of which "local" makes it into the exclusive circle of decision-making, leaving others who already occupy marginalized positions in society to remain inaudible and in many instances, irrelevant.

Drawing on the experiences and the narrative of transitional justice in Afghanistan and Nepal therefore, this research engages with the broader theoretical questions of who and what comprises this notion of the "local" and which "local" is consulted and which "local" is not included in contemporary processes of defining human rights, justice, and reconciliation in a given context. I recognize with humility that the effort of tracing the narrative of two moving targets in continually changing and tumultuous contexts is not an easy one, and neither is it possible to capture all the details and nuances of each context. I recognize that in a dynamic region such as South Asia, the currently unfolding events in Bangladesh with its highly flawed international criminal tribunal and the developments and challenges confronting Sri Lanka in acknowledging the deaths of the thousands killed in military operations conducted by the government and the Tamil Tigers (LTTE), create grounds for further inquiry, rather than allow for decisive arguments to be made about the region and how its experiences has bearing on the literature on transitional justice. At the same time, this project hopes to encourage intellectual inquiry about South Asia's experiences with issues of wartime atrocities, the processes and ramifications of de jure and de facto amnesty, the realities of impunity, the socioeconomic challenges facing survivors, the punitive demands for justice, and the ways in which reconciliation has been conceptualization officially and unofficially in the region and in specific countries within it.

As the political turbulence in Afghanistan continues to claim lives, and there is growing concern about the country's future when NATO forces withdraw in 2014, the prospects of transitional justice in the country continues to grow increasingly dim. But the lessons of how the questions of justice for wartime atrocities was approached in the Afghan context, and the opportunities that were lost, are humbling reminders of the continuing limitations of the understanding of what such justice could mean in a country in conflict, and the continued lack of international political will to confront the real questions and challenges facing the country. In Nepal, with the criticisms of the lack of commitment to socioeconomic issues, lack of

xiv *Preface*

progress on robust bills for the Truth and Reconciliation Commission (TRC) and the Disappearance Commission (DC), and the elite politicking that continues to marginalize victims groups, there remain significant questions about the future and relevance of transitional justice. It is with these critical questions in mind that I have humbly approached this project in the hope that there is more research in the field about the South Asian experience, and further questions raised about the "local." Let this be only the beginning.

Acknowledgements

This book would not have been possible without the support of several people. I thank Julie Mertus and Mohammed Abu-Nimer who encouraged me to turn my PhD dissertation into a book manuscript. The sheer challenge of conducting this research in two turbulent countries could not have been overcome without the assistance and cooperation of several individuals in the United States and in Afghanistan and Nepal. I am grateful to Scott Worden and Dr Patricia Gossman who were instrumental in introducing me to some of the key actors in Afghanistan's transitional justice process. On the ground, I am indebted to the Afghanistan Independent Human Rights Commission, Nader Nadery, Wazir Khorami, and many other Afghan friends and colleagues who face tremendous challenges everyday to continue to toil fearlessly in the field of human rights under extraordinary circumstances. In Nepal, I am thankful to Jason and Jannie for opening up their home to me during one of my research trips. I also thank Sushil Pyakurel, Ram Bhandari, Karen Cochran, Mandira Sharma, the staff at Advocacy Forum and the Protection Desk for their time and insight into the transitional justice questions in Nepal. In both countries, I am indebted to survivors and human rights activists who I interviewed and who inspired and humbled me with their stories. I hope this book does their struggle justice.

Finally, I thank my teaching assistant Mithila Deshpande who very ably took on the tedious job of helping me with the manuscript in the final month. Above all, I am indebted to my incredible parents for their unwavering love and encouragement over the years and to Anders, who supported me every step of the project. This book is dedicated to them.

Abbreviations

AAN	Afghanistan Analyst Network
ABP	Afghan Border Police
AC	Afghanistan Compact
ACAP	Afghan Civilian Assistance Program
ACBAR	Agency Coordinating Body for Afghan Relief
ACHR	Asian Center for Human Rights
ACSF	Afghanistan Civil Society Forum
ADB	Asian Development Bank
AF	Advocacy Forum
AF-N	Asia Foundation-Nepal
AHP	Afghan Highway Police
AI	Amnesty International
AIDS	Acquired Immune Deficiency Syndrome
AIHRC	Afghanistan Independent Human Rights Commission
AJP	Afghanistan Justice Project
AL	Awami League
ANBP	Afghanistan New Beginnings Program
ANCOP	Afghan National Civil Order Police
ANDS	Afghanistan National Development Strategy
ANP	Afghan National Police
APF	Armed Police Force
APHRN	Asia Pacific Human Rights Network
APRP	Afghanistan Peace and Reintegration Program
AREU	Afghanistan Research and Evaluation Unit
AUP	Afghan Uniformed Police
AW	Afghanistan Watch
AW-N	Accountability Watch-Nepal
AWN	Afghanistan Women's Network
BBC	British Broadcasting Corporation
BNP	Bangladesh Nationalist Party
CA	Constituent Assembly
CoA	Constitution of Afghanistan
CAP	Conflict Affected Persons

Abbreviations xvii

CAT	Convention Against Torture
CDO	Chief District Officer
CDP	Capacity Development Project
CEDAW	Convention for Elimination of Discrimination Against Women
CERD	Convention on the Elimination of all Forms of Racial Discrimination
CERP	Commander's Emergency Response Program
CCF	Canadian Commander's Contingency Fund
CCDH	Human Rights Consultative Council
CHD	Center for Humanitarian Dialogue
CHR	Commission on Human Rights
CHRP	Commission on Human Rights of the Philippines
CIA	Central Intelligence Agency
CIP	Community Impact Projects
CIVIC	Campaign for Innocent Victims in Conflict
CNPA	Counter Narcotics Police of Afghanistan
COCAP	Collection Campaign for Peace
COID	Commission Inquiry on Conflict-Related Disappearances
CPA	Communist Peace Agreement
CPN-M	United Communist Party of Nepal-Maoist
CRC	Convention on the Rights of the Child
CSHRN	Civil Society and Human Rights Network
CSJ	Committee for Social Justice
CTP	Counter Terrorism Police
CVC	Conflict Victims' Committee
CVSJ	Conflict Victims' Society for Justice
DC	Disappearance Commission
DDR	Disarmament Demobilization and Reintegration
DFID	UK Department of International Development
DIAG	Disbandment of Illegal Armed Groups
DIHR	Danish Institute of Human Rights
DPKO	Department of Peacekeeping Operations
DRA	Democratic Republic of Afghanistan
ECCC	Extraordinary Chambers in the Courts of Cambodia
ECOSOC	Convention on Economic Social and Cultural Rights
EPSP	Emergency Peace Support Program
EU	European Union
FEDO	Feminist Dalit Organization
FIR	First Information Report
FOHRID	Human Rights and Democratic Forum
FSV	Foundation for Solidarity for Victims
GoA	Government of Afghanistan
GoN	Government of Nepal

xviii *Abbreviations*

GTZ	German Technical Agency
HIV	Human Immunodeficiency Virus
HPC	High Peace Council
HRAG	Human Rights Advisory Group
HRC	Human Rights Council
HRPC	Human Rights Promotion Center
HRW	Human Rights Watch
IAGs	Illegal armed groups
ICC	International Criminal Court
ICCPR	International Covenant on Civil and Political Rights
ICG	International Crisis Group
ICJ	International Commission of Jurists
ICRC	International Committee of the Red Cross
ICTJ	International Center for Transitional Justice
ICTR	International Criminal Tribunal for Rwanda
ICTY	International Criminal Tribunal for Former Yugoslavia
IDP	Internally Displaced Peoples
IHCHRP	The International Council on Human Rights Policy
IMF	International Military Forces
INHURED	International Institute for Human Rights, Environment Development
INSEC	Informal Sector Service Center
IO	International Organizations
IOM	International Organization for Migration
INGO	International Non-Governmental Organization
IRP	Interim Relief Program
ISA	Islamic State of Afghanistan
ISAF	International Security Assistance Forces
ISI	Inter-Services Intelligence
JI	Jamaat-e-Islami
KGB	Komitet gosudarstvennoy bezopasnosti/Committee for State Security
KHAD	Khidamati Ittila'at-i Dawlati
LAA	Local Administration Act
LLRC	Lessons Learnt and Reconciliation Commission
LPC	Local Peace Committees
LSGA	Local Self-Governance Act
LTTE	Tamil Tigers
MA	Muluk Ain
MDC	Municipal Development Committee
MOI	Ministry of the Interior
MoJ	Ministry of Justice
MoLSAMD	Ministry of Social Affairs, Labor, Martyrs, and Disabled

MoPR	Ministry of Peace and Reconstruction
MoU	Memorandum of Understanding
MP	Member of Parliament
MPA	Maoist People's Army
MVA	Maoists' Victims' Association
NA	Nepal Army
NATO	North Atlantic Treaty Organization
NBA	Nepal Bar Association
NC	Nepali Congress
NCICC	National Coalition for the International Criminal Court
NCPJ	National Consultative Peace Jirga
NEFAD	National Network of Families of Disappeared and Missing Persons
NSC	National Security Council
NGO	Non-Governmental Organization
NHRC-N	National Human Rights Commission-Nepal
NHRI	National Human Rights Institutions
NMC	National Monitoring Committee
NP	Nepal Police
NPR	Nepali Rupees
NPRC	National Peace and Rehabilitation Commission
NRC	Norwegian Refugee Council
NSC	National Security Council
NTTP	Nepal's Transition To Peace
NWC	National Women's Commission
OEF	Operation Enduring Freedom
OHCHR	Office of the High Commissioner for Human Rights
OHCHR-N	Office of the High Commissioner for Human Rights-Nepal
OIC	Organization of Islamic Countries
OSCE	Organization for Security and Cooperation in Europe
OSI	Open Society Institute
PBI	Peace Brigades International
PD	Protection Desk
PDPA	People's Democratic Party
PHR	Physicians for Human Rights
PLA	People's Liberation Army
POHRF	Post-Operations Humanitarian Relief Fund
PRT	Provincial Reconstruction Teams
PSA	Public Security Act
PTS	Strengthening Peace Program (Proceay-i-Tahkeem-i Sulha)
QIP	Quick Impact Projects

xx *Abbreviations*

RAWA	Revolutionary Association of the Women of Afghanistan
RNA	Royal Nepal Army
RNP	Royal Nepal Police
SCA	States Cases Act
SOCAJ	Solidarity Campaign for Justice
SoFAD	Society of the Families of Warriors Disappeared by the State
SP	Standby Police
SPA	Seven Party Alliance
TADO	Terrorist and Disruptive Activities Ordinance
TCA	Torture Compensation Act
TLO	Tribal Liaison Office
TRC	Truth and Reconciliation Commission
TJCG	Transitional Justice Coordination Group
UDHR	Universal Declaration of Human Rights
UIFSA	United Islamic Front for the Salvation of Afghanistan
UK	United Kingdom
UML	Unified Marxist–Leninist
UN	United Nations
UNAMA	United Nations Assistance Mission in Afghanistan
UNICEF	United Nations Children's Fund
UNDP	United Nations Development Program
UNIFEM	United Nations Entity for Gender Equality and the Empowerment of Women
UNHCR	United Nations High Commission for Refugees
UNOHCHR	United Nations High Commission for Human Rights
UNMIN	UN Mission in Nepal
UNODC	United Nations Office on Drugs and Crime
UNSC	United Nations Security Council
US	United States
USAID	United States Agency for International Development
USD	United States Dollar
USIP	United States Institute of Peace
USSR	Union of Soviet Socialist Republics
VDC	Village Development Committee
WB	World Bank
WDO	Women's Development Office
WHRDs	Women's Human Rights Defenders
WGEID	Working Group for Enforced and Involuntary Disappearances
YCL	Young Communist League

1 Introduction

Examining the justice question in Afghanistan and Nepal

South Asia, comprising of Afghanistan, Pakistan, India, Nepal, Bhutan, Bangladesh, Sri Lanka, and the Maldives, has long been a dynamic and highly volatile region. While today each of these countries are in various stages of experimenting with democracy, conflicts in the region, both inter- and intra-state, have claimed countless lives and left a lingering legacy of human rights atrocities.[1]

In dealing with that legacy, the region has seen a few notable developments, such as the 2010 Lessons Learnt and Reconciliation Commission (LLRC) in Sri Lanka, a number of domestic commissions for human rights atrocities committed in Nepal in the 1990s, the ongoing domestic tribunal for crimes against humanity, war crimes, and genocide committed in 1971 in Bangladesh, and trials of individual Afghans on foreign soil for human rights violations. In general however, despite the dissemination of the accountability norm in international law, South Asia, unlike the African continent, has had very limited experience in pursuing any form of post-conflict justice. Two very recent developments are the main concerns of this book: the National Action Plan for Peace, Reconciliation, and Justice in Afghanistan (henceforth the National Action Plan) and the Comprehensive Peace Agreement in Nepal (henceforth CPA). On December 10, 2006, the Government of Afghanistan (GoA) officially launched the National Action Plan – a national strategy drawn up by the Afghanistan Independent Human Rights Commission (AIHRC) in consultation with other international and national human rights organizations to address the questions of wartime atrocities committed in the country in almost three decades of conflict. Then, on January 31, 2007, the lower chamber of Afghanistan's parliament, the *Wolesi Jirga* (People's Council), passed an amnesty bill forgiving all those responsible for committing war crimes and crimes against humanity. Within a month, on February 20, the *Meshrano Jirga* (Council of Elders) approved the bill by a 50:16 majority. Finally, in December 2009, the Afghanistan's National Reconciliation and Stability Law, also known as the "amnesty law" appeared in the *Official Gazette* (no. 965), thus ending speculation among the international community and national civil society actors regarding the legal status of the bill.[2]

2 *Examining justice in Afghanistan and Nepal*

Two specific events in particular had direct bearing on the passage of the amnesty law. On December 17, 2006, Human Rights Watch (HRW) published a report titled *Afghanistan: Justice for War Criminals Essential to Peace, Karzai Must Hold Officials Accountable for Past Crimes.*[3] The report contained a list of names of individuals allegedly guilty of massive human rights violations during the years of conflict and who today occupy positions of significant political influence.[4] On December 30, 2006, Iraqi dictator Saddam Hussein was executed after a speedy trial by the Iraqi Special Tribunal, which had convicted him on the charge of crimes against humanity for the murder of 148 Iraqi Shi'a in the town of Dujail in 1982. Afghan warlords openly condemned HRW for its "naming, shaming, and blaming" report, and many are certain that the report's publication, and in particular the developments in Iraq, expedited the momentum for the passage of the amnesty law.

While the world's attention was diverted by the Iraq war for much of the early and mid-2000s, a little over two thousand miles away, the land-locked mountainous country of Nepal was experiencing its own political revolution. In November 2006, after a series of failed peace talks, the Government of Nepal (GoN) and the United Communist Party of Nepal–Maoist (CPN–M) finally signed the historic CPA, officially ending ten years of a bitter and brutal conflict. The CPA had three provisions to address abuses that took place during the war: a Truth and Reconciliation Commission (TRC); a National Peace and Rehabilitation Commission (NPRC); and a Commission Inquiry on Conflict-Related Disappearances (COID).

This book tells the story of the discussions and efforts to account for the human rights abuses that were (and are being) committed in Afghanistan and Nepal. The cases also allow us to explore recent attempts at achieving the dual goal of peace (i.e. stability) and justice in "post-conflict" environments.[5] This study is guided by three empirical research questions: to what extent have official commitments seeking justice for those who have suffered the agonies of war ("local" consumers of justice processes) recognized and involved these actors? What concept of the "local" has been operationalized in the transitional justice discussions and processes in Afghanistan and Nepal? And finally, how would the "local" understandings of justice compliment, challenge, and impact the existing discourse of post-conflict justice? Each of these queries generate broader reflections about transitions, weak rule of law, widespread impunity, international compliance in certain political measures at the expense of local demands, and the role of international and national civil society actors that are beyond these two countries and the region of South Asia.

The methodological choice of a comparative case study of Afghanistan and Nepal prompts clarification and explanation. Afghanistan and Nepal are after all markedly different in their political histories, customs, and cultures. In addition, the time frame of their respective conflicts, their *raison d'être*, scale, and magnitude, and the role of external actors in each context are strikingly different. Thus, one may wonder what a comparison of two so unique and disparate cases could yield beyond enriching our knowledge of those specific cases. Comparative

Examining justice in Afghanistan and Nepal 3

case studies are commonly employed for the purpose of identifying correlation between variables with the ultimate goal of demonstrating causal relationships and develop theory.[6] Adam Przeworski and Henry Teune in *The Logic of Comparative Social Inquiry* describe two primary techniques of case selection in comparative analysis.[7] The first centers on selecting "most similar cases" – those that resemble each other with the exception of one specific aspect. The second involves studying "most different" cases – those that are dissimilar but have a single common feature. The purpose of such comparison would, in essence, be to simulate a laboratory environment where certain variables can be isolated and causal relationships can be identified. In reality however, comparative case studies only roughly come close to one or the other of these prototypes and fall somewhere between the two.[8] Recognizing the complexity and fluidity of the social realm, this study does not aim at simulating a laboratory environment, nor does it claim to identify clear causal relationships between independent and dependent variables. The purpose here, beyond making audible marginalized voices, is to construct a plausible account for how transitional justice programming can establish and consolidate power relationships and further marginalize those considered victims of war. In order to achieve that aim, cases were selected not on the basis of "most similar" or "most different," but on the basis of whether they shared certain traits identified as key to engaging with the overarching research question.

First, Afghanistan and Nepal have both experienced atrocities that violate existing international legal norms and defy any established norms of civility. These are atrocities of a kind Hannah Arendt, borrowing from Kant, once labeled "radical evil."[9] Such acts have had scholars scrambling for a moral and linguistic discourse to emphasize their *extraordinary* nature, which simultaneously propels a moral compulsion to act – to prevent and to punish – resulting in a prescriptive package called "transitional justice."[10] Second, they offer an opportunity to engage with the immensely complex issue of facilitating transition from conflict to stability (which some would call "negative" peace[11]) in contexts where extraordinary crimes have been committed, and where the demand for wartime accountability on one hand and antagonistic relationships between different parties on the other have to be reconciled. Third, both these South Asian countries are on parallel trajectories of transition at a time when the "transitional justice" toolkit is at its zenith in its circulation globally. Fourth, they are marked by the absence of strong, centralized governance structures, are defined by *de jure* and de facto impunity, and have relied on the rationale of the political expedience of peace over that of justice at critical moments in their respective political histories. Fifth, years of intensive conflict has left Afghanistan's judicial infrastructure in shambles; further, the combination of French and international jurisprudence, *Shari'a*, and the existing customary practices and tribal laws have made the legal system in the country almost impossible to navigate. Consequently, there is no standardized system of punishment that exists which would have significantly assisted a punitive process. In Nepal, the gaps in law have meant certain *jus cogens* crimes have yet to be criminalized. The overall poor condition of the legal infrastructure has meant little access to justice for the country's poor and marginalized. The screening process

4 *Examining justice in Afghanistan and Nepal*

for elections in Afghanistan has been weak at best, and in Nepal, non-existent. Both cases also provide an interesting study of the consideration of TRCs as a viable prescription for addressing the past. Through offers of pardons and reconciliatory measures, official or assumed, individuals with very poor human rights records in both countries have consolidated their positions in public office.

Afghanistan and Nepal share two additional commonalities. The discussion of post-conflict in both instances emerged within the context of the post 9/11 environment, a global climate infused with hard power, the predominance of the security paradigm, and the eminence of the "war on terror." Subsequently, US rhetoric and the policies were subsequently laden with "violence as an essential agent in the protection of 'civilization'"[12] such that human rights concerns even in protracted conflicts were obfuscated, and the "struggle against impunity was…measured in short-term and military gains."[13] To a great extent, the level of political expedience in international policy calculations toward Afghanistan in this environment has had significant consequences in the political climate that has emerged in the country. A similar argument can also be crafted with regard to Nepal where UK and US support against "Maoist terrorists" strengthened the hand of the Nepali army and provided them with essentially a *carte blanche* in their efforts to "maintain peace and stability" in a volatile context. Second, post-conflict justice processes rarely occur in isolation. The extent of its influence has accelerated, particularly because of the Internet, the proliferation in transnational networks of non-governmental organizations (NGOs) and other advocates (e.g. regional and international bodies, consultants, and policy-makers) who greatly enhance the circulation of information, ideas, and hands-on expertise. In both countries, the United Nations (UN), United States Institute of Peace (USIP), the International Center for Transitional Justice (ICTJ), the World Bank (WB) to name a few, have had notable influence on the discourse and direction of post-conflict justice and reconciliation. The accumulative experiences of these institutions, the cross-fertilization of ideas, and the involvement of local civil society beg for a closer examination of how these actors engage with the justice and reconciliation paradigm in each context.

Plato argued, as did Kant later, that knowledge of all the positions from which people define justice, ethics, good, and evil brings us closer to a true understanding of exactly what is the meaning of human existence. But in a discussion of post-conflict justice, even beyond the narratives of the two case studies selected, the audience is largely its scholars and practitioners; in its implementation, we are no closer to completely grasping who the "local" is, and whether we can honor its demands. Drawing on the Afghan and Nepali experiences and examining the existing literature on the question of post-conflict justice and reconciliation, this study therefore offers the following argument. The reason that questions of justice and accountability are marginalized is because transitional justice programming continues to cede authority to a select few who interpret the "local" in terms of what it means to them. In other words, to the extent that the "local" has gained traction in issues of justice, reconciliation, and peacebuilding, it has been limited to mean cultural practices, rituals, and traditions, which international actors involved in human rights, democracy, and transitional justice promotion assume to be venerable and unchanging i.e. a "static local." This "static local" is increasingly harnessed in recent post-conflict justice efforts to contextualize pre-ordained mechanisms while ensuring they are palatable to communities in question and the international audience i.e. the donors and international civil society actors. This book offers a deeper reflection of this notion of the "local" and makes a sharp distinction between "local" culture and customs, and its more dynamic nature, the "dynamic local," which is too often unrecognized and underutilized in developing mechanisms to account for the past. The following is an in-depth overview of the literature on post-conflict justice, known also as "transitional justice" and its critical components.

Transitional justice as a discipline: from democratic transitions to the search for justice

Democratic transition, the political process through which a framework is established for bargaining and compromise between different political forces and through which pluralist structures are institutionalized, was an area of scholarly examination even prior to what Huntington defined as the third wave of democratization, which began in 1974 and witnessed the change in regimes in about 30 countries in Europe, Asia, and Latin America.[14] Succinctly, it implies a nation's shift from recent history of mass atrocity or violent authoritarian rule to that of a liberalizing democratic state. Particularly since the 1990s, such political developments resulted in the production of extensive scholarly literature on electoral procedures, deliberative democracies, representation, constitution making, the relationship between political and economic transitions, and the role of civil society. Much of the scholarly work however, including Rustow's *Transition to Democracy*,[15] focused on the attributes of democratic states, comparing them to non-democratic countries, promoting the values of democratic peace, and later, critiquing their premise, rather than closely studying the process of transition, emerging democracies and democratization.

In recent times, the study of democracy has focused on violent transitions of states from war to peace, and demonstrated a growing realization that weak transitions to democracy is generally followed by turbulent, fragile political institutions. Mansfield and Snyder for example observe that these transitional democracies are more often than not plagued by "limited suffrage, unfair constraints on electoral competition, disorganized political parties, corrupt bureaucracies or partial media monopolies [that] may skew political outcomes."[16] Even more recently, scholarly examination has gone further, exploring specific mechanisms that assist in democratization processes such as judicial reform, reform of security forces, integration of rebel forces into armed forces, vetting of political and armed actors, all of which constitute tools of neoliberal peacebuilding. Tracing the rise in democratization research, Stacey suggests, "today, the study of democratic institutions has become enough of a scholarly industry that it even warrants (or, at least enjoys) its own neologism: 'transitology.'"[17]

Transitology, in layman's terms, is the branch of political theory that examines the process of change from one regime to another, mainly from an

6 *Examining justice in Afghanistan and Nepal*

authoritarian state to a democracy. Since its inception however, the field itself has been fraught with debates. Critics claim that transitology as an area of study imbues multiple meanings and generates confusion rather than providing clarity to existing scholarship. Some go far enough to draw the conclusion that transitology's mode of analysis is both flawed and hegemonic.[18] Other scholars argue that their concern is with the *way* this field examines political, economic, and social change such that they have a pre-determined beginning and an end.[19] Morse states: "these scholars propose a theory of change based on the notion of overtly open-ended 'transformation,' a formulation that highlights their belief that the word 'transition' is inherently imbued with teleological qualities."[20] Carothers further broadens this debate asking whether countries that have moved away from the authoritarian structure yet do not resemble liberal democracies should be categorized as countries in transit, and considers whether such political systems are in fact in a state of constant equilibrium rather than being a mere stage in the democratization process.[21]

For scholars of transitional justice however, the contributions of transitologists are important because they often provide accounts of how actors actually understand those circumstances, and how they respond within them.[22] It may be suggested however that they do not actually examine the period in which questions of transitional justice arises as a main concern. Elster's definition of transitology is helpful in beginning to understand the development of the transitional justice query since he considers the complexity and the indistinct nature of transitions and sees the latter as "the study of the disequilibrium phenomena that lie between the pre-transitional and post-transitional equilibria."[23] Using this definition, transitional justice in turn, can then be seen to emerge in the very constricted period between Elster's two equilibria; however, since transitologists focus on explanatory and behavioral issues, which occur as a consequence of transitions, there is little attention paid to the normative questions that arise in this period. In contrast, scholars like Huntington, and even Kaufman and Haggard, seem to be of the persuasion that social, political, and economic conditions over determine transitions to democracy and their aftermath and leave no space for even making such inquiries.[24]

Nevertheless, democratic transitions demand normative questions because they pose confusion, choices, and ethical dilemmas. Such questions capture, but are not limited to, the following concerns: how much to remember? How much to forget? Which institutions best serve the needs and demands of survivors as victims, perpetrators, and/bystanders? Who should be punished and who should be set free?[25] Scheper-Hughes best captures the raw tensions that emerge when she writes, "Democratic transitions are best understood as a 'dangerous hour.' With the collapse of authoritarian regimes, there emerge new nations full of needs... and full of rage."[26] Correspondingly, new democracies must negotiate a treacherous path, encompassing difficult and sometimes contradictory ethical, moral, and legal considerations while somehow attempting to achieve some measure of reconciliation and justice. In this debate, realists claim that a retroactive process that deviates from the process of reform (judicial, security-oriented, political, economic) impedes the progress of democratization.[27] Others would argue that the realpolitik of reaching political settlements without regard to a post-conflict justice component is no longer acceptable.[28]

This increasing focus on human rights and justice (including retroactive justice) as core constitutive elements of democratization is of particular relevance to this study. Particularly since the 1990s, on the heels of the Bosnian and Rwandan genocides, international law and human rights norms have exhibited an increasing urgency for the moral obligation to punish and prosecute those who commit *jus cogen* crimes and honor the experiences of those who survived. Redressing the wrongs therefore became not only a legal obligation and a moral imperative imposed on governments; it also began to resonate with solid political logic in the transition from the utter chaos of political violence to democracy. Today, the pursuit of retroactive justice has become an urgent task of democratization, as it highlights the fundamental character of the new order to be established, an order based on the rule of law and on respect for the dignity and worth of each human person. Lundy and MacGovern in *Whose Justice? Rethinking Transitional Justice from the Bottom Up* discuss a concurrent trend by the international community to finance a range of legal initiatives to deal with both retroactive justice and build and strengthen the rule of law in transitional contexts.[29] Correspondingly, it may be argued that the rules of legitimacy in international relations have dramatically changed, particularly with the inception of the International Criminal Tribunal for former Yugoslavia (ICTY), the International Criminal Tribunal for Rwanda (ICTR), and the International Criminal Court (ICC), creating the demand for justice as a new form of "realism." Nevertheless, the realpolitik calculations for stability and "peace" have continued to challenge this new form of realism, insisting that a sequence is necessary in the societies emerging from conflict and authoritarian regimes. In short, pragmatic politics dictates the sequencing of the political demands for peace before the moral demands for justice.

Bertram argues that dealing with past atrocities presents challenging dilemmas for peace builders given that "implications for UN efforts to build democracy and a sustainable peace are ominous."[30] Empirical transitional justice literature comprises of intensive debates of whether to seek peace or to look to a country's violent past to seek justice. Some scholars grounded in a tradition of political realism argue that justice does not lead – it follows i.e. an emerging democracy must first establish political order or enhance the strength of the state by whatever means necessary.[31] Further, authors such as Cobban, drawing on experiences in Africa, insist that prosecutorial mechanisms are not effective means of making societies move forward.[32] Such pragmatists insist that for the establishment of a framework of peace, justice including prosecutorial venues has to wait or, at the most extreme, be permanently compromised to enable a future-oriented political formula to develop. Citing the disruptive nature of particularly retributive justice, the absence of financial and legal resources to undertake the long-drawn out processes of trials, they particularly eschew prosecutions and instead advocate broad amnesties in times of transition.

8 *Examining justice in Afghanistan and Nepal*

Amnesties

Amnesties[33] typically refer to exemptions from criminal liability accorded to classes of individuals before trial.[34] They are implemented in the sensitive period after extreme political violence or in civil wars where those responsible for the abuses are either no longer in power or where they still occupy public office or even have important roles to play in the peace process.[35] In certain cases, amnesties serve as a tactical tool for negotiators trying to persuade human rights violators to relinquish power.[36] They can also be useful for politicians to identify the state's boundaries of permissible political activity and provide a means of enforcing those boundaries.[37] One of the arguments made for amnesties is the importance of making a clean break with the past, thereby creating a common starting point for all members of society from which a better future may be created. Sriram argues:

> [T]here may be self normative reasons for amnesty: should accountability be made a top priority by a nascent, fragile, democracy, a rebellious military could easily end the democratic experiment, and democratic stability and the goods it protects may be viewed as moral goods themselves.[38]

Snyder and Vinjamuri argue in favor of amnesties stating: "...a norm-governed political order must be based on a political bargain among contending groups and on the creation of robust administrative institutions that can predictably enforce the law."[39] They also view the striking of politically expedient bargains and ignoring past abuses as a critical element of atrocity prevention and enforcement of the rule of law through creating political coalitions to contain the power of "spoilers."[40] Proponents of amnesties further offer evidence from difficult cases such as El Salvador, Mozambique, Namibia, and the most well known instance of South Africa where political forgiveness was linked to the TRC to demonstrate that amnesties are in fact a pragmatic formula for the political order that needs to emerge in the post-conflict period. Mallinder, in *Amnesty, Human Rights and Political Transitions* argues that states should be encouraged to make amnesties conditional, and introduce complementary programs to repair social harm and prevent repetition of heinous crimes in the future.[41] In short, amnesties' appeal, in circumstances where there is a history of structural violence, lack of confidence in the judicial system, and a systemic pattern of social scape-goating, lies in its understanding that it serves a catalyst in *transformational* politics. In the long-run, scholars such as Freeman using Spain, Brazil, and Mozambique as examples, argues that amnesties with the widest possible scope "have accompanied, rather than impeded gradual and sustained improvements in democracy, peace, human rights and the rule of law."[42] In other words, an inclusive political framework would allow "disreputable" individuals to become insiders (e.g. South Africa and Spain) in the emerging architecture of a new state and thus occupy, in Schaap's words, the space for politics. According to Schaap, however, such political formulae (political reconciliation) must be both retrospective (in coming to terms with the past) and prospective (in bringing about social harmony) and, therefore, must involve striking a balance between the often-contending demands posed by these differing orientations.[43] Transitional amnesties [therefore] appear to be the precursors to, and coincident with, liberalizing political change,[44] advancing the normative project of political transition, encouraging subsequent political reconciliation and establishing the parameters of peace.

Scholars have criticized the fundamental premise of political pardons/amnesties as the panacea for national healing based on a two-tiered argument – first, based on the developments in international law and human rights law, and second, based on rationale and consequence i.e. the *why* of amnesties and whether they achieve the desired effect. Bell in *The 'New Law' in Transitional Justice* points out that the new law of transitional justice prohibits the provision blanket amnesties that cover serious international crimes i.e. those that violate *jus cogens*.[45] Fundamentally though, for those who demand accountability for crimes committed, the granting of amnesties constitutes the doing of an injustice. Greenwalt argues, "in the general vocabulary of moral considerations, doing injustice is intrinsically wrong, what is called deontological constraint."[46] Hence, when people remark, "the ends do not justify the means," what is meant is that someone should not do what is intrinsically wrong, even to achieve positive consequences. Consequently, while it is possible to accept that the government maybe unable to prosecute, the formal exoneration constitutes an injustice because political expedience itself is not justice. Moreover, critics question the conventional wisdom of using amnesty for societal healing because of its ability to be an instrument for officials of abusive regimes. Sriram for example argues: "the laws of national reconciliation are frequently nothing more than final hour self-amnesties by outgoing regimes, padded with rhetoric about a societal need to forgive if not forget."[47]

Orentlichter and other legal thinkers have further contested that while offering amnesties during peace negotiations may be something of value to those seeking to escape from a culture of atrocity, they also foster a "culture of impunity" and allow the continued commission of atrocities or their resumption after a brief hiatus. Slye argues amnesties have traditionally had the effect of preventing inquiry and denying accountability,[48] and that they are instrumental for laying the groundwork for a new political order:

> Recent history, has shown that pure amnesties, at least in the case of gross violations of human rights, do not in fact achieve the lofty goals of making a clean break from the past; or of creating a common starting point for all members of society from which a better future may be created.[49]

Blanket amnesties, which are still used in many cases, raise a series of questions about possible alternatives: can selective immunity be used effectively to ensure some offenders testify against others? Should prosecutors issue amnesties on a case-by-case basis? Is it possible to at least create venues for some form of minor penalties rather than granting absolute amnesty? Will victims have a legitimate claim against perpetrators despite the amnesty procedure? How and when can such amnesties be revoked? And, can claims against perpetrators be asserted

10   *Examining justice in Afghanistan and Nepal*

legitimately at some point in the future? Any or all of these questions can engender a level of wariness about even selective amnesties in fragile contexts and the extent to which they engender impunity.

Impunity

For rights-based actors and in the realm of law, impunity's existence is very clearly explained – it is brought on by the absence of prosecution. Impunity is seen as the exemption from punishment, culpability, or legal sanction for illegal acts.[50] The production of impunity can take place at any stage of politics. Opotow states:

> Impunity can occur before, during, or after judicial processes, or entirely independent of them. It occurs when crimes are not investigated; suspected offenders are not brought to trial; verdicts to convict are not reached despite convincing evidence that would establish offenders' guilt beyond a reasonable doubt; those convicted are not sentenced or, if sentenced, their punishment is so minor that it is completely out of proportion to the gravity of their crimes; or sentences of those convicted are not enforced.[51]

The discussion of impunity is important because it is the product of not only actions (e.g. of amnesties), individual actions, or lack of retributive measures, but it is also embedded in, and results in certain processes, and even promotes social support among transgressors that ultimately causes extreme psychological trauma and material hardship for victims.[52] In entrenching impunity, it is the *collective* then that becomes important. At one level it is dependent on cooperation and facilitation between those who execute crimes, and the wider network of lateral and hierarchical support and protection transgressors receive; at another, it requires cooperation from horizontal cross-sections of society who are afraid and resigned due to the consequences they might face because they challenge the status quo.

Opotow also suggests that in the impunity hierarchy, those at the top are its architects and strategists, while those lower down the chain become part of the system due to fear and self-preservation.[53] Such collusion can also include other countries, which stand to benefit economically or strategically from a despotic status quo.[54] Subsequently, impunity is of greatest concern when it is institutionalized and widespread – when torture, crimes against humanity, and mass murder are overtly or tacitly condoned and unpunished as the result of amnesties, pardons, indifference, or "looking the other way." This institutionalization and commonality of practice in turn generates the "culture of impunity" in which "government officials, the police and military, and ordinary citizens break the law without fear of punishment, for there is a shared understanding that each person will be silent about the other's abuses as long as the favor is returned."[55]

McSherry and Mejía offer a three-tiered typology of impunity, which looks at its strategic, structural, and psychological dimensions.[56] Succinctly, strategic impunity involves a range of activities – evidence tampering, investigation thwarting, failing to act on reports of disappearances, killings, and torture – basically

Examining justice in Afghanistan and Nepal 11

harnessing procedures to prevent criminal investigation and prosecution. Opotow claims: "structural impunity is the mobilization of official, institutional structures to foster impunity."[57] The result of both manifestations of impunity, feed into the third category of impunity, which is defined as psychological impunity, that is, the manipulation of fear, distrust, and isolation amongst citizens to crush aspirations for freedom, equality, and justice. In accordance with Eugene Walters' analysis of political terror, McSherry and Mejía describe the goal of psychological impunity as a reign of terror that undermines any form of resistance and silences opposition. They further emphasize that psychological impunity ensures that people's demand for social equality and justice is silenced.[58] Using this analysis, it is then possible to understand how violence (both direct and structural) characterizes each level of analysis of impunity from the intrapsychic to state institutions and sociopolitical relationships.

The realm of transitional justice: definition, scale, and scope

Scholars have long struggled with an attempt to conceptualize the magnitude and depravity of atrocities committed during wartime; practitioners have continued to try to seek out ways to eliminate, contain, and prevent such acts that defy any established norms of civility. Arendt's initial exploration of Nazi crimes as "acts of evil," captures a fundamental powerlessness in grappling with the magnitude of such human-made tragedies. She states: "we are unable to forgive what we cannot punish and are unable to punish what has turned out to be unforgivable."[59] Kant's terminology to capture such acts using the term "radical evil" endures because it captures all those "offenses against humanity that are so widespread, persistent and organized that no normal moral assessment seems appropriate."[60] Consequently, this inadequacy in the moral discourse and social evaluation emphasizes the limitations of existing human systems that seem too mundane and *ordinary* to capture what seems *extraordinary*. Perhaps legal jurisprudence has come closest to creating a useful measure based on a central tenet: extreme evil is cognizable by substantive criminal law and because it is egregious, only special substantive categories of criminality – genocide, war crimes, and crimes against humanity – needed to be created to capture it. What sets ordinary crimes apart from what is deemed extraordinary? Aukerman argues:

> [O]rdinary crime – individual conduct that violates domestic criminal law and is undertaken for non-political purposes – concerns individual criminals; [e] xtraordinary evil – massive or systematic human rights violations prohibited by international law – involves individuals committing many of the same actions, such as the unjustified intentional taking of human life, that constitute ordinary crimes.[61]

In terms of substantive categorization however, Drumbl argues, "extreme evil is no ordinary crime."[62] Extreme "evil," Arendt herself noted, "exploded the limits of the law."[63] This did not necessarily imply that evil could not be condemned,

12 Examining justice in Afghanistan and Nepal

or better still constrained, using law, but law itself had to develop and mobilize to catch up with its manifestations.[64] Further, the qualitative categorization of such acts in a class separate from what constitutes as "ordinary" crimes further emphasizes both its "evil" and "extraordinary" nature. In short, they enter the realm of what is now understood to be *extraordinary international criminality*. Subsequently, perpetrators of "extraordinary" crimes have become cast, rhetorically as well as legally, as an enemy of all humankind.[65]

Legal jurisprudence addresses "extraordinary" crimes based on three specific characteristics – scale and scope, intent, and its strategic nature. At the core of the extraordinariness of these acts is conduct – their planning, systematization, and organization – and their target, selected for annihilation or victimization. In international criminal law, these extraordinary crimes are classified under the categories of war crimes, genocide, and crimes against humanity. In turn, each of the three explicit categories – war crimes, genocide,[66] and crimes against humanity – have specific definitions and criteria within international criminal law. Succinctly, war crimes are those that fall outside of the gambit of the ordinary activities undertaken by soldiers during hostilities. Gerwith argues:

> [I]n the broader sense, [war crimes] comprises violations both of the *jus ad bellum* [rarely] and the *jus in bello*: that is violations that consist both in resorting to war on wrongful grounds and in using wrongful practices within war. In the narrower sense, only the latter kinds of violations are war crimes."[67]

Further, war crimes constitute *prima facie* violations of morality.[68] But in contrast to other violations, war crimes have a "criminal status because they transgress restrictions that are designed to protect human rights with regard to the general context of war."[69] Ultimately, genocide, crimes against humanity, and war crimes (under conventional and customary regulation of armed conflicts) have risen to the level of *jus cogens*,[70] generating "the obligation to prosecute or extradite; to provide legal assistance; to eliminate statutes of limitations; to eliminate immunities of superiors up to and including heads of states."[71] Under the auspices of existing international law, these obligations are then considered as *obligatio ergo omnes*, meaning that in the event of commission of such crimes, there is no possibility for impunity.[72] Further, emerging norms of how to respond to widespread atrocities informed by international legal customs, while accommodating pardons for the purpose of political accommodation, nevertheless do not allow for blanket forgiveness in instances of crimes against humanity, and acts of genocide.[73]

Transitional justice explained

Once inhabiting the outer edges of the field of political science, predominantly as a study of regimes in transition,[74] transitional justice has emerged as a core discipline in scholarship and practical policy-making[75] and a recurring motif in the literature on democratization to provide answers for how to deal with extraordinary crimes;

however, as Barahona de Brito noted in 2001 "just 15 years ago, the literature on transitional truth and justice was very limited"[76] and it was not a core area of specialization for either social scientists or the wider academic community until the mid-1980s. In 2000, Ruti Teitel introduced the term "transitional justice" in her groundbreaking work of the same name. Teitel explains transitional justice as "the view of justice associated with periods of political change, as reflected in the phenomenology of primarily legal responses that deal with the wrongdoing of repressive regimes."[77]

Transitional justice today broadly recommends the establishment of a redemptive model of justice through which atrocities of the past are addressed with a view to prevent future violence, a robust and enduring rule of law and a culture of human rights. Since its inception in democratic processes, international donors including UN and specialized organizations such as the ICTJ, have rushed in to promote transitional justice toolkits, "which favors homogenizing jurisdictions and cultures in the guise of developing global governance mechanisms."[78] These toolkits generally consist of programs to establish the rule of law; Disarmament, Demobilization, and Reintegratation (DDR) of former combatants; and vet candidates in election bids. Increasingly, they have also included efforts to create and/or support rights-based civil society actors, particularly NGOs whose core mandate has become the promotion and protection of human rights as defined internationally[79], and to establish a "culture of responsibility" or a "culture of rights."[80] In short, their actions reflect the normative values of a neoliberal ideology. McEvoy observes [today] "transitional justice is a field on an upward trajectory"[81] and has become normal, institutionalized, and mainstreamed,[82] dominating debates on the intersection between democratization, human rights protections, and state-reconstruction after conflict.

Teitel has been criticized for "overvaluing" law and underestimating periods of influx. Rosemary Nagy in *Transitional Justice as Global Project: Critical Reflections* notes: "Teitel rightly provides a normative challenge to Schumpetarian notions of successful transition (marked by fair elections), because she focuses almost exclusively on (re)establishing the rule of law through legal mechanisms – prosecutions, historical inquiry, administrative justice, reparation, and constitutional justice."[83] However, she suggest that while Teitel's argument for law's "independent potential"[84] to shape political change, it does not address customary law, culture, or social justice, which are far more grounded in real experiences of transitional societies.[85] Naomi Roht-Arriaza further observed the limitations of legalism when she noted: "a narrow view can be criticized for ignoring root causes and privileging civil and political rights over economic, social and cultural rights, thereby marginalizing the needs of the women and the poor."[86]

Roht-Arriaza in *Transitional Justice in the Twenty-First Century* widens the context of transitional justice by defining it as "that set of practices, mechanisms and concerns that arise following a period of conflict, civil strife or repression, and that are aimed at directly confronting and dealing with past violations of human rights and humanitarian law.[87] This "thickening of its paradigm" has meant the incorporation of other means to deliver justice, including institutions of accountability for

14   *Examining justice in Afghanistan and Nepal*

past crimes, such as truth commissions and lustration policies; means of promoting restorative justice such as reparations, construction of monuments and public memory projects; and mechanisms of security and peace, such as amnesties and pardons, constitutional amendments and institutional reform.[88]

Rama Mani provides one of the broadest understandings of what she terms "restoring justice within the parameters of peacebuilding."[89] Focusing on low-income, war-torn societies, Mani argues that building peace and building a just society are inseparable processes. Drawing on Johan Galtung's twin objectives of negative peace (cessation of conflict) and positive peace (removal of structural and cultural violence), Mani's argument is therefore premised on the necessity of a holistic approach, which includes a three-fold view of "reparative" justice: restoring the rule of law through reforms to prisons, police, and judiciary; rectifying human rights violations through trials, truth commissions, reparation, and traditional mechanisms; and redressing the inequalities and distributive injustices of war.[90] Mani's work also prioritizes the importance of drawing on local knowledge and culture for sustainable peace, [91] and compellingly argues, "the prevalent liberal–democratic ideal…tends to favor freedom and liberty over equality."[92] "This means," translates Nagy, "there has been a tendency to underrate the gendered and socioeconomic ramifications of violent conflict, which may include HIV/AIDS, widowhood and poverty."[93] However, these important contributions stop short of examining the role of Western states in conflict and draws only from the Western philosophical canon in the conceptualization of justice.[94] Ultimately then, Mani's astute analysis while providing a fundamental lens about questioning the absence of socioeconomic dimensions leaves out the critical analysis of the involvement of Western states in conflict and the relevance of gender in transitional justice. Nevertheless, contributions of scholars such as Mani, Nagy, and others have been critical in broadening the transitional justice paradigm to not only include the concerns of distributive and gender justice, but also generated a push for seeking out the restorative nature of justice i.e. its reconciliatory dimension.

Reconciliation as transitional justice

Leebaw argues, "the idea of utilizing transitional justice to promote reconciliation is relatively new."[95] In its broadest terms, reconciliation involves developing a shared vision of an interdependent society that values different opinions and political beliefs; acknowledging and dealing with the past; healing, restitution, and reparation; building positive relationships; significant cultural and attitudinal change; and substantial social, economic, and political change. It is both an outcome and a process and requires, in the best circumstances, a cognitive change in beliefs, ideology, and emotions.[96]

On the maximalist account, reconciliation implies a transformation of relationships between former adversaries and a need for broad approaches beyond narrow, time-bound programs that are isolated from one another. Lederach argues:

> [R]econciliation requires looking outside the mainstream of international political traditions and operational modalities [and] comprises of four

Examining justice in Afghanistan and Nepal 15

essential components: truth (acknowledgement of wrong and validation of painful loss); mercy (the need for forgiveness and acceptance); justice (the search for individual and group rights for social restructuring and restitution); and peace (the need for interdependence, well-being and security.[97]

Given its multidimensional nature, reconciliation may also be seen as the meeting point between the philosophical–emotional and the practical–material. Gardner-Feldman argues that these components are interwoven because they simultaneously require cooperation and confrontation between the government and societies, involving the tensions between political support and opposition, and including long-term vision and short-term strategy.[98] In the minimalist account, reconciliation is nothing more than "simple coexistence,"[99] which means that former enemies comply with the law instead of killing each other, although the goal is that former enemies respect each other as fellow citizens. Osiel calls this kind of reconciliation "liberal social solidarity"[100] while Gutman and Thompson term it "democratic reciprocity."[101] Under such conditions, former enemies have been offered official pardons, general or individual amnesties.

This premise – the necessary role of the government and the opposition to establish the parameters of a new relationship – brings into focus a far more narrowed understanding of reconciliation, defined as "political reconciliation," which involves processes through which an inclusive platform is created for politics for formerly hostile parties, particularly political institutions and actors. Historically, variant forms of political reconciliation were employed in France, Germany, and the United States after World War II. Economic initiatives have played a significant role in transforming some of these formerly antagonistic relationships; offers of amnesties too have played a critical role including in places like Namibia, El Salvador, Nicaragua, Italy, Peru, and Northern Ireland. Nevertheless, there are certain prerequisites that have emerged in the practices of post-conflict relationship building, even for the most narrowed practice of political reconciliation. Grovier and Verwoerd have suggested that building trust is crucial for political reconciliation "because people are unable to cooperate with each other and work together unless their relationships are characterised by trust."[102] As trust presupposes truth-telling, promise-keeping, and social solidarity, reconciliation in terms of trust provides a tangible way of defining political reconciliation.[103] According to Schapp:

> [P]olitical reconciliation must be both retrospective (in coming to terms with the past) and prospective (in bringing about social harmony) and, therefore, must involve striking a balance between the competing demands of these temporal orientations.[104]

Consequently, "in societies divided by a history of political violence, political reconciliation depends on transforming political enmity into a civic friendship."[105] However, Schaap also recognizes that political reconciliation is related to five issues: confronting polities divided by past wrongs; constitution of political association; the possibility of forgiveness within politics; collective responsibility

16 *Examining justice in Afghanistan and Nepal*

for wrong doing; and remembrance of a painful past. Each of these components echoes with the more expansive understandings of what constitutes a comprehensive reconciliation process and informs the practices of the larger paradigm of transitional justice.

A discussion about reconciliation is inconclusive without recognizing the most common mechanism through which such a process is promoted – the TRC. Scholars, such as Priscilla Hayner and Martha Minow, have promoted such an apparatus, which, as in the South African case, they argue allowed individuals to speak of their roles in politically motivated violence in exchange for amnesty.[106] Minow also points out that the very purpose of truth commissions is healing individuals and societies through restoring dignity to victims.[107] According to her analysis, in addition to catharsis, such truth commissions promote forgiveness. Further, in contexts of mass violence where there are innumerable perpetrators and by-standers, TRCs acknowledge ambiguity, permitting bystanders to take responsibility for inaction and allow the groundwork to be created groundwork for reconciliation.[108] Nagy argues that truth commissions are better positioned to expand the field of transitional justice by addressing the different dimensions of conflict, including, importantly, the marginalization of women and girls because they focus attention on patterns of violations.[109] Ultimately, as in the case of the Sierra Leonean TRC, which included recommendations for repealing discriminatory inheritance, marriageable age, and other customary laws, amendments to laws pertaining to domestic and sexual violence, skills training, education and economic empowerment of women, such commissions can challenge deep-rooted issues of structural inequality.

In recent years, the different tenets of the transitional justice paradigm have come under serious criticism. These concerns have ranged from critiquing the political ideology on which it is based (i.e. the neoliberal paradigm) to questions about the historically heavy reliance on the maximalist position, the tendency of many states to desire a minimalist approach, and to the absence of gender-sensitive approaches in its implementation. The maximalist and minimalist approaches require a brief explanation. The former strictly adheres to the notion that punitive measures serve as a deterrent for the future commission of violence. It also holds that the establishment of the rule of law strengthens democracy. A failure to prosecute, then, results in "a culture of impunity, [that] erodes, the rule of law and encourages vigilante justice."[110] The minimalist approach, in contrast, critiques the assumption that trials will lead to deterrence. Instead, adherents to this approach suggest that trials in fact generate instability because such punitive measures do not take into account the political realities of a given context. Instead, they support the provision of amnesties to best protect the period of transition from unnecessary violence.[111]

However, the widely popular transitional justice rhetoric among scholars and practitioners has, until very recently, been supported more by rhetorical platitudes than solid empirical evidence. Olsen, Payne, and Reiter offer a comprehensive scholarly evaluation of transitional justice using a comparative study. In *Transitional Justice in Balance: Comparing Processes, Weighing Efficacy*, they empirically demonstrate that in general, transitional justice has a positive impact on both human rights and democracy, although they advise caution, warning against over-enthusiasm in such findings. Their study shows that while transitional justice mechanisms in general advance these goals, such an outcome is not immediate and may take over a decade after the transition to manifest.[112] Further, they unveil that neither the maximalist nor the minimalist approach by themselves fare well.[113] A particularly interesting finding in their work is that "truth commissions, when used alone, have a negative and significant effect, [i.e.] a decrease in the measures of democracy and human rights."[114] In *Truth Commissions and Transitional Societies: The Impact on Human Rights and Democracy*, Wiebelhaus-Brahm offers similar findings on the relationship between TRCs, democracy, and human rights. His study concludes, "truth commissions are consistently negatively related to subsequent human rights [and that there is] no statistically significant relationship between truth commission operations or having conducted a truth commission and subsequent democratic developments."[115] Both these recent studies provide impetus for further research as to what kind of truth commissions are the most effective and under what circumstances, and perhaps even raise the question of whether TRCs should be pursued at all. In the interim, the underlying findings of both *Transitional Justice in Balance* and *Truth Commissions and Transitional Societies* effectively challenge a long held perception by advocates of such mechanisms both in scholarly and practitioner circles, which is that victim-centered and less adversarial commissions with its focus on "truth-seeking" and rebuilding fractured relationships are ultimately more effective in delivering justice that is non-adversarial.[116] The studies also underscores that there is a critical place for law and its institutions in strengthening the human rights culture in transitional societies. The following closely examines law's position and its relationship to transitional justice that merits a closer examination.

Locating law in the state

The concept of the rule of law has been seen as a distant aspiration or ideal, while simultaneously being a concrete objective – its serves both as a political goal and a legal institution.[117] From a minimalist or procedural perspective, the rule of law is stripped of its moral and substantive content; it is seen only as a means of protection from the arbitrariness of "rule by man" and an excess abuse of state authority.[118] Thus, it is primarily a rudimentary framework restraining the government while simultaneously delineating specific rules for its constituents. Hayek's definition effectively captures these multiple identities:[119]

> [S]tripped of all its technicalities, this means that government in all its actions is bound by rules fixed and announced beforehand – rules which make it possible to foresee with fair certainty how the authority will use its coercive powers in given circumstances, and to plan one's individual affairs on the basis of that knowledge.

18 *Examining justice in Afghanistan and Nepal*

The maximalist perspective on the rule of law, which may be understood as the "substantive conception of rule of law that posits that laws should contain normative content,"[120] is closer to the natural law position comprising of an umbrella that encompasses structural, procedural, as well as substantive elements.[121] Mani further claims, "definitions within the maximalist perspective would not find it possible to separate substantive justice from formal justice: law *is* about justice."[122] The UN definition of the rule of law, which serves as a guideline for all its programs recognizes it as:

> a principle of governance in which all persons, institutions and entities, public and private, including the state itself, are accountable to the laws that are publicly promulgated, equally enforced and independently adjudicated and which are consistent with international human rights norms and standards. It requires, as well measures to ensure adherence to principles of supremacy of law, equality before the law, accountability to the law, fairness in the application of the law, separation of powers, participation in decision-making, legal uncertainty, avoidance of arbitrariness and procedural and legal transparency.[123]

This definition highlights two aspects of the rule of law. First, it supports the minimalist insistence, outlined by Hayek, on subjecting government and all its institutions to law. It goes further, however, by also extending accountability to individuals and public and private institutions.[124] Second, it adopts the maximalist leaning toward the rule of law, by stipulating "consistency" with human rights norms and standards. Nevertheless, Mani argues, "this definition falls short of actually making the causal and inseparable association between justice, morality and the law that the maximalist view defends."[125]

Since its entrance in policy circles in the 1990s, the rule of law has been considered a critical institutional component of the state building process because it represents both constitutional and development programs for designing the modern nation-state. For transitional practitioners, the rule of law's position in reconstruction has attained the status of orthodoxy given that it is viewed as the crucial ingredient for an orderly, liberal, and economically developed state.[126] The most recent linkage in policy and practice is between the rule of law and security, where the former is seen,

> as a panacea for all troubles – development experts prescribe it as the surest short cut to market-led growth; human rights groups advocate the rule of law as the best defense against human rights abuses; and in the area of peace and security, the rule of law is seen as the surest guarantee against the (re)emergence of conflicts and the basis for rebuilding post conflict societies.[127]

Given its prominence in post-conflict and development efforts, it may therefore be argued that the world is now host to a global rule of law movement.[128] Despite the burgeoning business of the rule of law in post-conflict and transitional societies, the operationalization of such programs confront a host of challenges, stemming from its institutional practice, problems with its conceptual and theoretical development, and its normative underpinnings. First, at the implementation level, rule of law projects are plagued by the realities of ill-conceived training of judges, measures to protect witnesses, poor use of international judges and prosecutors for a coherent approach to criminal justice reform, a lack of coherent strategies, and insufficient knowledge of local conditions, which has sometimes led to overwhelming reliance on adopting the "cookie-cutter" approach. The criticism is then also leveled at the "parachuting" of international experts into a "post-conflict" zone with sometimes little knowledge of local languages and customs, but who play a critical role in designing governing infrastructure. Ultimately, sustainability of many of these projects comes into question given the lack of local ownership of such projects.

Experience also shows that fundamental approaches to legal reform should be approached warily, particularly in cases where new procedural law needs to be learned.[129] Tolbert and Solomon suggest that while a reform process will include the reform of laws, "it should not necessarily change the underlying approach in that system."[130] Rule of law programs often do not acknowledge the actual challenges of non-existing or under-resourced and ill-trained supporting structures, such as the military and the police. Last, but perhaps not least, such programs stop short of recognizing the context within which the legal norms need to be entrenched and how it would be incorporated into social practices and cultural norms.[131]

Reinstitution of the rule of law also comes with conceptual challenges. Democracy specialist Thomas Carothers notes: "…rule of law promoters tend to translate the rule of law into an institutional checklist with primary emphasis on the judiciary."[132] There are several problems with this overtly simplistic formula. First, it amounts to equating rule of law with the mere presence of certain institutions within a state. Second, having a ratified constitution and parchment guarantees means that an assumed independent judiciary is, *ipso facto*, rule of law. Third, there is a flawed assumption that those institutions similar in design produce the same product. The result of this functionalism is a conceptualization that is too thin and divorced from what is happening on the ground.[133] Fourth, some observers have noted that today's world may be characterized by a cross-national formal legal isomorphism as a result of widespread judicial reform, but in reality, rule of law does not exist everywhere because on-the-books reforms have not been translated to reality.[134] The Afghan and Nepali cases clearly demonstrate each of these limitations given that the presence of legal institutions in either country does not directly corresponding to exponential development toward a rule of law state.

The rule of law and transitional justice: a nexus

Campbell and Bell suggest that the complex relationship between law and contemporary transitions is tied to four important global realities, the last three of

20   *Examining justice in Afghanistan and Nepal*

which have direct relevance to this discussion.[135] First, (which is not included for analysis), the post 9/11 environment, shaped by the rhetoric of the "global war on terror," invasions of Afghanistan and Iraq, and the overall exercise of US unilateralism has had significant implications for, and negatively impacted international law.[136] Second, there is an increase in negotiated settlements as the preferred way of dealing with internal conflict.[137] Such settlements necessitate the involvement of levels of compromise, which in turn translated into legal and political institutions, thus premising the location of law in assisting in transitions. Both the Bonn Agreement and the CPA, in laying out the judicial framework in post-Taliban Afghanistan and post-war Nepal respectively, underscore this reality. Third, the centrality of human rights law and its preponderance in transitional negotiations offers increasing opportunities for mitigating the worst accesses of conflict.[138] Fourth, there is an increased interlinking between human rights and humanitarian law to address the excesses of state and non-state actors even in internal conflicts. This in turn leads to greater emphasis on individual responsibility particularly in dealing with past human rights abusers[139] and raises the difficulty of how to reconcile normative legal standards with the pragmatics of making peace.[140]

For transitional justice scholarship, law then provides an entry point, a necessary demonstration of the instantiation of human rights culture, and a tool of analysis to examine its impact in transitional societies. Yet it is law's unique role and position in the period of transition – both because of demands on it to generate legal reform on one hand and to provide answers for the excesses of war and the subsequent tension that result – that calls for a more in-depth discussion. In reflecting on the inherent tension between the rule of law in transition as backward looking and forward looking, Teitel suggests that law's function during transitional periods is "deeply and inherently paradoxical…[since] law is caught between the past and the future…between [the] retrospective and prospective, between the individual and the collective. [Accordingly] transitional justice is that justice associated with this context and political circumstances."[141]

Since transitions imply shifts in paradigms of justice, law's responsibilities are not only to establish order but also to enable transformation. According to Teitel, in dynamic periods of political influx, legal responses generate a *sui generis* paradigm of transformative law.[142] Framed in another way, it is possible to argue that in transitional societies, law must be both the subject and object of change. It must simultaneously both produce change and be changed. In societies such as Afghanistan and Nepal, the responsibility of the newly introduced laws to establish new standards (hence, as a *change producer*) and merge customary laws with more standardized practices (hence, as a *norm merger*) are placed in a unique position to connect the past to the present, and initiate change for the future.

Law's claim to holding transformative potential, however, is stymied when considering how some in the field of international relations recognize and consider the *sequencing* of the rule of law and that of transitional justice. Subsequently, empirical transitional justice literature expounded by those grounded in a tradition of political realism and who assess strategies based on how they promote political stability at the national level, argues that justice does not lead, it follows.[143] In

Examining justice in Afghanistan and Nepal   21

other words, before accountability can be sought in a state that has experienced massive human rights violations, it must first establish political order or enhance the strength of the state, by whatever means necessary. Snyder and Vinjamuri argue:

> a norm-governed political order must be based on a political bargain among contending groups and on the creation of robust administrative institutions that can predictably enforce the law. Amnesty – or simply ignoring past abuses – may be a necessary tool in this bargaining. Once such deals are struck, institutions based on the rule of law become more feasible. Attempting to implement universal standards of criminal justice in the absence of these political and institutional preconditions risks weakening norms of justice by revealing their ineffectiveness and hindering necessary political bargaining.[144]

The existing weaknesses in the legal infrastructure of both case studies will clearly indicate that for punitive justice to be possible, the corresponding laws have to be both available and implemented effectively. Law's transformative potential, however, is certainly challenged where old actors occupy powerful positions within the new order and where local conditions require a far more multidimensional approach than merely technical and institutional developments within and outside of law. In short, Snyder and Vinjamuri's formula for successful transitional justice falls short because "justice does not follow" when the intentions of democracy and state-building commitments confront the complex dimensions of locality. It is to this discussion of the local that the chapter now turns.

Beyond Afghanistan and Nepal: the "local" in transitional justice

This study takes into serious account the criticisms of transitional justice processes and their proffered mechanisms, including the limitations of the rule of law, particularly those that focus on the tensions between the international approach and the "local" context. Succinctly, it argues that the current privileging of the "local" is based on the recognition that the emerging focus on the local has not yet meant a "shift in the underlying assumptions of the field – at most it is a shift in emphasis."[145] Neither has it meant that there has been sufficient critical engagement with the way existing transitional justice practices engage with, incorporate, and, in some ways, limit the understanding of the "locality." The consultation of the "local" particularly to legitimize reconciliatory practices is significant because it deviates from the importance of how local critiques, priorities and practices can demonstrate alternative ways of conceptualizing justice. This limitation, this study argues, is particularly important because thus far there has been greater attention paid to the "static local" in terms of culture and traditional practices, but there has been far less attention, if any, paid to the "dynamic local," comprising of historical experiences and changing sociopolitical dynamics within a given society, and which influence how transitional justice programming may be conceived and

22   Examining justice in Afghanistan and Nepal

operationalized. Furthermore, the "local" must be understood as an inter-subjective concept, filled only with the meaning of those who interpret it. Therefore, it is of critical significance *whose* interpretation of the "local" is consulted in transitional justice processes. Who tells us what the "local" dictates? Is it the warlords? Local elites? International actors? Political strategists? Closely linked to the issue of an inter-subjective "local" is the question of to what extent and whether transitional justice mechanisms can and should take up the fight against impunity, or whether they should recognize that the struggle for accountability requires a different kind of approach, and have a different kind of timetable. As it exists, the manifestations of transitional justice efforts in Afghanistan and Nepal neither have the ability nor the scope to engage with deep-rooted fundamental challenges in these societies.

The terms "local" and "margins," which will be used generously throughout this book, require further discussion. These two terms are not used to denote a descriptive geographical site nor a particular location; they are neither tangible nor inert concepts. The terms are also not used to signify a deviation from accepted social norms and standards. Instead, borrowing from Tsing who uses the term "margin" to "indicate an analytical placement that makes evident both the constraining, oppressive quality of cultural exclusion and the creative potential of rearticulating, enlivening and rearranging the very social categories that peripheralize a group's existence,"[146] the "local" and "margin" signifies the points of entry, engagement, and the central position from which the discussion and activities of transitional justice will be assessed and evaluated. Further, it stresses that the "local" that cannot be categorized within the realm of a singular "culture" or "tradition." The study harnesses Otto, Aponte-Toro, and Farley's uncomfortable term "autistic isolation," used to imply "absent while in the middle of the action"[147] to underscore the situation of the most excluded of the local. Moreover, it argues that *this* "local" is not only the silenced voices, but is in fact also the difficult questions that lurk at the periphery of standardized transitional justice's accepted "local," such as history, domestic processes, politics, realities, and demands of survivors.

The study recognizes that recent efforts have attempted to consult the "local" to inform mechanisms to do "justice," such as Rwanda's integration of the *gacaca* courts for deliberating justice for the genocidaires, Northern Uganda's experimentation with ritual actions such as *mata oput* (drinking the bitter root) and *gomo tong* (bending of the spears) to mark the end of conflict, and the integration of local laws with international legal norms in the Extraordinary Chambers in the Courts of Cambodia (ECCC) to try war criminals of the Cambodian genocide. Such international efforts, however, seem to be missing a fundamental point: that even "culturally informed" programs to promote "justice and/or reconciliation" do not necessarily address the question of a vibrant context, and neither do they *prioritize* the "local." Further, this kind of engagement with the "local" at the level of culture perceives the former as a static entity. Instead, this study suggests that the local is active and evolving, influenced by external and internal forces, sociopolitical factors, and past experiences, resulting in a "dynamic" phenomenon, which, when brought to the center of the transitional justice discourse and practice, has the potential to influence the direction and scope of efforts to "close the manuscripts."

It is the particularities of context, which ultimately inform and legitimize justice claims. Last but not least, a core criticism that emerges from this study is that the paradigm of "societies in transition" approaches transition as a linear process, thereby overlooking its complex and fragmented landscape and the local power relationships that emerge within it. A transitional justice checklist does not take into account the fluid political context in which such programming intends to take place. It follows then that such packages could seem too disconnected from the complexity of a conflict and its aftermath, the power arrangements that emerge, and the privileging of certain local rhetoric and actors over others.

Given these concerns, the study first asserts that the fragmentations, peculiarities, and specificities of the local context should play a more central role in exploring and defining what "accounting for the past" could mean. Second, an overt focus on standardized mechanisms to deliver transitional justice, such as the commissions proposed in Nepal for example, can overshadow underlying and ongoing *ordinary* justice claims against impunity and the demands of immediate needs of survivors. In other words, "transitional justice," unlike the less trendy "justice" may focus on "truth-seeking" and reconciliatory mechanisms, which in turn, encourages states to de-prioritize the identification and punishment of perpetrators or neglect questions of dire socioeconomic inequity. Correspondingly, a state's progress toward "peace" is measured by the ability to stick to a short timeframe to a transition, involve representatives of all warring factions, and transform aggressors into invested political stakeholders; it is rarely focused on responding to deep-rooted questions of *in*justice. In other words, (often internationally designed or informed) commissions with temporal mandates and limited powers neither have the scope nor the ability to deliver on long-term justice concerns or effectively draw the lines between past atrocities and ongoing injustices.

Outline

The story of transitional justice in Afghanistan and Nepal is told in six chapters. Chapter two examines past reconciliation efforts and commissions in both countries, highlighting the influence of these failed legacies on the legitimacy of the transitional justice commitments today. Chapter three focuses attention on *de jure* impunity, discussing existing legal mechanisms, the tensions between customary laws and formal laws, and the challenges facing the legal landscape in both countries. Chapter four looks at the politicization of transitional justice projects, highlighting that the "dynamic local" comprises of domestic politics, power struggles and realities of inclusion and exclusion even within the indigenous civil society and local NGO communities, such that systems of hierarchy emerge and become entrenched in the sociopolitical landscape. Chapter five delves into the justice question, bringing the "local" at the center of the transitional justice discussion, examining the pressing questions that continue to be raised by the voices at the margins. It also lays out what, if any, measures have been initiated to address these demands. Chapter six overviews the innovation and challenges of the National Human Rights Institutions (NHRIs) as an illustration of the domestic

24 *Examining justice in Afghanistan and Nepal*

struggle to create mechanisms to address questions of justice and accountability in Afghanistan and Nepal and the tensions they expose within the local contexts, respectively.[148] Finally, chapter seven provides some issues for reflection, recognizing that transitional justice continues to remain the domain of the elite, including the local elite, and offers concluding thoughts on the need to build on the theory of the local in the transitional justice framework.

Contributions of the study

While the legal literature on transitional justice focuses on the establishment of legal mechanisms and the international relations literature on transitional justice considers how these mechanisms shape state claims to sovereignty, political scientists mainly focus on the political nature of transitional justice, examining winners and losers under various transitional justice proposals. This book is a departure from these approaches. First, it is strongly grounded in the findings of field research in a body of literature, which has been historically abstracted from local experiences. It asks uncomfortable questions about justice and locality in the post-9/11 environment, in contexts where de facto and *de jure* impunity are not only a consequence of the conflict, but has even preceded it. It raises questions about whether criticisms about the preponderance of international criminal law has urged too much of a retreat to generate an overt-reliance on "reconciliatory" means, such that underlying core concerns of societies emerging from conflict remain largely unaddressed. It also challenges the parochial and often simplistic understanding of the local context, with its overt focus on rites and rituals, rather than on processes, societal mechanisms, internal relationships, and hierarchies within a given context.

This book aims to contribute to the literature on comparative studies in transitional justice, and address the glaring gap in the scholarly work on transitional justice in South Asia, particularly with regard to comparative case studies. The focus on two very different South Asian countries offers an important contribution because very little has been written on post-conflict justice in the region, although these and other countries are facing challenges similar to those faced in Africa and Latin America, where the literature is richer and more expansive. By tracing the trajectory of the discussion on transitional justice, identifying the key challenges, domestic demands, and responses, it exposes the complexity of the justice question in the chosen contexts. Simultaneously, it creates the platform for further research to understand what is being ignored in countries that face similar challenges within and outside of South Asia. Finally, on a broader level, this research aims to contribute to the growing scholarly work on the nexus between the "local" and transitional justice, and the nuanced but intricate relationship between "ordinary" justice and "transitional" justice.

2   The legacy of past initiatives

To what extent do legacies of initiatives to "account for the past" bear significance for current initiatives for transitional justice? This chapter is an in-depth engagement with this question, tracing Afghanistan and Nepal's respective histories to confront issues of justice and reconciliation, and highlighting the importance of these experiences as a critical component of the "dynamic local." Framed differently, it argues that current initiatives in transitional contexts should acknowledge how past efforts at forgetting or accounting define and influence the contemporary local context. Such efforts need to recognize how historical experiences of seeking accountability can generate expectations, but perhaps even more importantly, impose limitations on contemporary efforts to address wartime atrocities. Both these arguments underscore the necessity of recognizing history as a core component of the "dynamic local." After all, history is not a static entity, nor a simple account of certain events. Rather, it is a subjective, fluid, and influential factor in shaping understandings and expectations in any given society. It follows then, that history must be harnessed to respond more effectively to challenges that current efforts at transitional justice face in "local" contexts.

In the Afghanistan discussion, this chapter emphasizes the country's historical pattern of appeasement and concessions in the name of political reconciliation that has marked negotiations between hostile parties, while formal acknowledgement of the sufferings of civilians has been largely missing. This pattern of temporary settlements between hostile parties has consequently set the tone and expectations for contemporary political deals. In the Nepal section, the chapter outlines the country's history of experimentations with commissions in different periods of political turmoil when large-scale atrocities were committed against the civilian population. While the ad-hoc commissions differed in their mandate and leadership, all were notable failures both in their inability to achieve their objectives and in their inefficiency in affecting any form of social and institutional change to safeguard human rights. The findings of this research indicate that this history of failed initiatives have made Nepalese, including those in the elite civil society, skeptical of the term "commissions" and promises of such institutions, despite the CPA commitments and elite civil society efforts to create such bodies. Second, this attention to commissions has significantly limited the discussion of

26 *The legacy of past initiatives*

transitional justice to such specific institutions, limiting what accounting for the past means to the Nepalese people.

Confronting history: Afghanistan's past initiatives

Afghanistan has been in conflict for the last 33 years, although some might argue that its descent into chaos began with the overthrow of King Zahir Shah in 1973.[1] Afghanistan's continuing conflict can be divided into four specific phases: the 1978 Saur Revolution and the subsequent Soviet occupation (1979–89); the Mujahideen civil wars (1992–6); the period of the Taliban (1996–2001); and the current conflict which arose after the ousting of the Taliban regime in 2001. Despite the widespread destruction and the heavy loss of civilian lives in three decades, there has never been a formal effort to discuss questions of war crimes committed during each of these periods of intense conflict. Neither is there any documented evidence of a robust state or civil society initiative to bring to the books any individual who committed crimes against humanity or any historical documentation of survivors' claims for the violations they have experienced. Nevertheless, in its different periods of history, Afghanistan has experienced a range of initiatives, termed "reconciliation" in national and international policy circles. In reality, these initiatives have amounted to different forms of deal making for political expedience. This formula has continued to be the only point of reference for what "reconciliation" means in the Afghan experience: attempted negotiated settlements with political overtures, amnesties, and acknowledgement of the political bases of different actors to ensure belligerent actors have loyalty to a new power. In short, these measures reflect the continuum of subjugation, accommodation, appeasement,[2] and capitulation[3] rather than what is understood in peacebuilding literature as "reconciliation" – a complex set of long-term holistic measures designed to be responsive to the multivaried demands of a surviving population. It may even be argued that such efforts did not meet the standard of "political reconciliation," which is premised on fundamental compromises between parties, and more importantly, the establishment of trust between two (or more) opposing sides.

"Reconciliation" in the aftermath of the PDPA and the Soviet Union

During the People's Democratic Party (PDPA) rule,[4] which overthrew President Zahir Shah and which lasted between 1978–92, severe repressions targeted authorities, and opposition and civilians sparked mutinies within the Afghan army in the provinces of Kunar, Herat, Kabul, and Hazarajat that threatened to destabilize its regime. Its ultimate collapse led to several attempts to reach political agreements between different factions who were opposed to the regime. In 1984, Ahmad Shah Masood's[5] Shura-y-Nazar and the GoA signed an agreement, which resulted in the truce for the Panjshir Valley.[6] This arrangement was at best a temporary respite, given that Masood used it to "shift his focus to the northeast and build up his Shura-y-Nazar structure"[7] and the "Afghan Government and Soviets

The legacy of past initiatives   27

derived some benefits in terms of deflecting Masood away from the capital and protecting their supply line through the Salang Pass."[8] In 1985, the Soviet-backed third president of the Democratic Republic of Afghanistan (DRA) Babrak Kamal launched his ten-point "reconciliation" program, which included provisions for dialogue, compromise between oppositional groups, as well as an intention to broaden the regime's base; however, the plan was not effective given the unpopularity of the Soviet regime that brought him to power. Within six months of laying out the plan, Kamal himself was deposed, succeeded by Najibullah.

It is Najibullah who is credited with perhaps the most well-known initiative for "reconciliation" in Afghanistan and which has had the most enduring legacy – *Aasht-i-Milli* (national reconciliation), launched in January 1987. The plan included a power-sharing agreement among political parties in the resistance, the offer to change Afghanistan's status as an Islamic non-aligned state, provision of amnesty for some political prisoners, and a ceasefire. Najibullah's strategy of accommodation, which may be defined as negotiated concessions for the cessation of hostilities and engender a platform of cooperation, was a distinct shift away from his earlier subjugation/co-option model. The latter involved a system where a party could reconcile without being given access to any privileges, namely by supporting expansion of militias into regular armed forces, which in turn constituted a respectable way of renouncing opposition to the existing regime. Semple argues that the relative success of Najibullah's experimentation compared to previous attempts was largely due to the Soviet withdrawal and the effectiveness of the government forces, which undermined the ability of the *mujahideens* to continue to fight.[9] Nevertheless, while the "reconciliation" program staved off defeat temporarily, the absence of international support and dwindling domestic legitimacy of the PDPA regime itself led to its ultimate demise.

The ensuing conflict during this period witnessed several efforts by national, regional, and international actors to resolve it, mainly through offering different kinds of political compromises to the hostile parties. On 14 April 1988, nine years after the invasion, the Soviets finally withdrew from Afghanistan. During the period prior to their withdrawal, they had introduced more selected targets of repression using a secret police, the KHAD (Khidamati Ittila'at-i Dawlati), modeled on the Soviet KGB (Komitet gosudarstvennoy bezopasnosti), which engaged in widespread summary executions, detentions, and torture of suspected *mujahideen* supporters, who were the heart of the resistance.[10] In addition, they engaged in extensive aerial bombardment, which killed approximately one million Afghans and initiated a refugee outflow that reached five million.[11] The Geneva Accords,[12] signed between Afghanistan, Pakistan, United States and the Union of Soviet Socialist Republics (USSR), marked the Soviet withdrawal from Afghanistan. It comprised of several instruments, including a bilateral agreement between Afghanistan and Pakistan on the question of non-interference and non-intervention, the voluntary return of Afghan refugees who fled the indiscriminate rocket launches and bombings that marked the conflict, and an agreement on international guarantees by the USSR and the United States. The agreements also contained provisions for the timetable of the withdrawal of Soviet troops from

28 *The legacy of past initiatives*

Afghanistan. The Geneva Accords finally broke down because it failed to address the power-struggle between various groups in the conflict.

Between 1992 and 2001, national and international actors undertook other "reconciliatory" measures to bring an end to the ongoing political turmoil. On 26 April 1992, leaders in Pakistan signed the Peshawar Accords, which established a transitional government and a timetable for elections and which was an agreement for the *mujahideen* government to be first led by Mojaddedi[13] and then Rabbani.[14] The power of the new Islamic State of Afghanistan (ISA), however, was limited; by the time most of the *mujahideen* parties had agreed to the Accords (the Iran-backed Shi'a parties were excluded, setting the stage for some of the conflict that followed), rival factions had already established a hold on different parts of the capital and its environs.[15]

The UN attempted a third round of negotiations in December 1993 to broker a ceasefire, but the political turmoil within the country, increasing poverty levels, and the regional dynamics of the conflict made the efforts unsustainable. The Organization of Islamic Countries (OIC) tried its hand in making the different parties come to an agreement, but its mission was severely restricted by its own institutional weaknesses, limited financial capacity, and the general absence of political will. The 1993 Islamabad Accord also resulted in a power-sharing agreement between Rabbani and Hekmatyar,[16] with the former taking on the position of prime minister, with an oath in Mecca by the leaders "to adhere to the agreement."[17] However, this also failed due to a number of reasons, including the fact that Masood, Hekmatyar's main rival, was not a signatory to the agreement, there was no specific economic or political roadmap for the country's reconstruction and governance, no provisions for implementation of the operational aspects of the agreement, and due to an absence of regional powers that had a history of intervening in Afghanistan's internal affairs. The Ningarhar Shura in 1993 was yet another major undertaking, which invited all parties to Jalalabad city for political negotiations, but it too collapsed because it did not have the backing of foreign supporters and because of the distrust between Rabbani's forces and the Pushtun shura.

It was during the chaotic post-1992 period that disillusioned former *mujahideen* calling themselves the Taliban emerged under Mullah Mohammad Omar, a former *mujaheed* from Qandahar province, to challenge the constant infighting between the different *mujahideen* factions.[18] The Taliban also consisted of madrassah-schooled students, group commanders in other predominantly Pashtun parties, as well as former Khalqi PDPA members.[19] Their stated aims were to restore stability and enforce *Shari'a* (Islamic law) throughout Afghanistan. The Taliban began their conquest from Kandahar, driving out the feuding commanders who had divided it among themselves. By October 1994, Pakistan began supporting the movement because it saw the Taliban as a means of securing trade routes to Central Asia and establishing a Pakistani-friendly government in Kabul.[20] By 1995, the Taliban controlled Helmand, Ghazni, and Herat and by 1996 they conquered Jalalabad and then Kabul. In October 1997, Mullah Omar renamed the ISA and assumed the title *amir-ul momineen* (commander of the faithful).[21]

In their campaign to win the east, the Taliban signed an agreement with the leadership of Laghman province's Gonapal Valley, which resulted in valley leaders being allowed to have control of local security in return for declared loyalty to the Islamic Emirate of Afghanistan.[22] In Hazarajat, the Taliban approached Ustad Akbari, the local leader, to assist them in successfully establishing their administration in that area. Between 1989 and 1999, the Taliban, again using Ustad Akbari, sought a negotiated outcome with the *mujahideen* in Shahristan, where the former received both acknowledgements of the Emirate of Afghanistan as well as a hundred conscripts, while the latter were allowed to run an autonomous administration without the compulsion of the Taliban's highly rigid policies.[23]

Contemporary commitments for transitional justice

A few weeks after the United States and its coalition partners under the banner of Operation Enduring Freedom (OEF)[24] toppled the Taliban in late 2001, representatives of various Afghan factions (Afghan military commanders, expatriate Afghans, representatives of the exiled monarch, and the country's different ethnic groups) met in Bonn, Germany under the auspices of the Special Representative of the Secretary-General for Afghanistan Lakhdar Brahimi to map out Afghanistan's future.[25] The first discussion of transitional justice arose in these negotiations for the Agreement on Provisional Arrangements in Afghanistan Pending the Re-Establishment of Permanent Government Institutions (henceforth the Bonn Agreement).[26]

The Bonn Agreement laid out the foundations for the general provisions of the interim authority, the special independent commission for the Constitutional *Loya Jirga*, the interim administration, and the general principles of the legal judicial framework, but questions of accountability for war crimes are missing in the final document. As one of the advisers for the UN Special Representative to Brahimi, Barnett Rubin had suggested pre-Bonn that "no one guilty of war crimes, crimes against humanity or gross violations of human rights should serve as a minister in the interim administration."[27] In his account, he recalls the obstacles of screening recruits, especially to the officer corps, because of the absence of any type of credible judicial process to determine eligibility, and second, because of the US-led coalition's decision to arm the Northern Alliance and other commanders, which had already set up a de facto set of new armed forces that did not require them to undergo any vetting processes.[28] Ultimately, the representatives of the four anti-Taliban groups, the UN, and the major powers chose the ministers in the interim administration. Rubin narrates: "they met for 10 days under extreme pressure as a dentists' convention had reserved the same hotel after December 5."[29]

The Bonn Agreement is unlike other peace agreements.[30] Suhrke, Harpviken, and Strand state: "It is merely a statement of general goals and intended power sharing among the victors of a conflict in which their erstwhile common enemy, the Taliban, was suddenly deposed by the intervention of a *deus ex machina*."[31] The distinct features of the Bonn Agreement merit some discussion. First, it was not an arrangement between warring parties to lay down their arms and seek alternative

30   *The legacy of past initiatives*

means of conflict settlement. There was no negotiation about the infrastructure of the government, power-sharing possibilities or mechanisms through which the rule of law would be established. Its final text contained no reference to "transitional justice" or "human rights" except for a reference to the establishment of the AIHRC.[32] Initially, the UN drafters had included a paragraph that the interim administration should not grant amnesty for war crimes and crimes against humanity, but this resulted in significant friction. The two members of the United Front delegation from the party of Abd-al-Rabb al-Rasul Sayyaf[33] insisted that the paragraph be removed because it defamed the struggle of the *mujahideen* and its leaders.[34] Despite efforts by Brahimi during the drafting session to point out the dangers of an amnesty, the audience continued to be unreceptive to the arguments against political forgiveness.[35] Further, as Rubin notes, the phrasing of the term "war crimes" did not translate well into the Afghan context. The actual phrase *janayat-i-jang* translates to mean the crime of waging war, thereby insinuating that the *jihadi* struggle against the Soviets was illegal and immoral and was immediately interpreted as all those who had taken up arms in the *jihad* could be put on trial. Rubin recalls, "some time during the all-night negotiations necessary to clear out the hotel for the dentists, the paragraph forbidding an amnesty for war crimes was struck out."[36] The resistance to the paragraph prohibiting amnesty became thus the foundation of the political struggle that ultimately led to the passage of what has come to be known as the amnesty law.

At around the time of the Bonn negotiations and immediately after, several Afghan ministries, departments, and provincial governors' offices undertook initiatives to accommodate what became termed as the "moderate"[37] Taliban. On December 6, 2001, President Karzai announced broad amnesty for the Taliban. Karzai's efforts could be partly attributed to his "close relationship with many Taliban figures during the 1990s [and] in the aftermath of his election in 2002, [when] his interest in reaching out to the disaffected Pashtuns, who provided the manpower for the defeated Taliban regime, only became more evident."[38] In reality, the International Military Forces (IMF) and government forces continued to harass Afghans and their families for their alleged connections to the Taliban or al-Qaeda, and hunt for, and conduct arrests of former Talibs. The resultant environment did not induce trust amongst the insurgent groups toward the GoA and the IMF.

According to analysts and human rights activists, a huge window of opportunity for "transitional justice" was missed in 2001 partly because of the failed efforts during the Bonn negotiations to discuss accountability for war crimes. Brahimi's proposed strategy for political stabilization and judicial reform did not include any premise for the pursuit of justice. President Karzai was initially supportive of the notion of justice for war crimes at a 2002 UN-sponsored human rights workshop in Kabul stating:

> I believe we must have a truth commission very soon to find out more about the atrocities committed and to address those people who have been violated,

whose relatives have been killed, Afghanistan must find a way to cure those wounds.[39]

"He cried," remembers an interviewee, "when talking about the kind of atrocities Afghans have endured over the years. He seemed eager to learn about the South African TRC as a way to heal the wounds in Afghanistan."[40] Within the same year however, Karzai backpedaled on his position, stating in a 2002 BBC interview, "If we can have justice while we are seeking peace, we will go for that too. So… justice becomes a luxury for now. We must not lose peace for that."[41]

In 2002, at the Emergency *Loya Jirga*,[42] facing the denunciation of warlords particularly from those who were concerned about human rights and from women delegates, Sayyaf declared that criticizing the *mujahideen* amounted to blasphemy. At the same time, international decision to pursue a "cheap, quick peace with a light footprint" further emboldened Karzai's decision to not tackle warlordism. The result was regional commanders taking up some of the key appointments in the government. In February 2003 however, contrary to such political developments, Afghanistan ratified the Rome Statute for the ICC. On September 9, 2009, the Prosecutor of the ICC said he was collecting information on possible war crimes by North Atlantic Treaty Organization (NATO) forces and the Taliban in Afghanistan,[43] although given that the ICC has prospective jurisdiction,[44] there is no possibility of a legal course of action by the ICC for crimes committed in Afghanistan prior to 2002.

In March 2003, at the annual meeting of the UN Commission on Human Rights in Geneva, the UN Special Rapporteur on Extrajudicial, Summary or Arbitrary Executions floated a proposal based on UN Special Rapporteur on Extrajudicial Executions, Asma Jahangir's report, to set up an international commission of inquiry to look into past war crimes in Afghanistan. Dr Gossman, the then project director of the Afghanistan Justice Project (AJP) reflected: "The commission of inquiry was cautiously worded, and did not spell out any particular mechanism, judicial or non-judicial. Instead, it advocated an approach that would involve international experts mapping the major incidents of the past."[45] In general, there was a consensus among those involved regarding the necessity of some form of analysis of sources and existing documentation on Afghanistan, leading to, at some point in the future, the creation of a national record; however, there were certain actors, particularly the United States, who were vehemently opposed to the question of accountability for human rights atrocities in Afghanistan.[46] In the end, due to extreme opposition, the proposal was withdrawn, much to the bitter disappointment of Afghan human rights activists and the new AIHRC.[47]

In April 2003, at a gathering of the National Ulema Council in Kabul, Karzai said a "clear line" had to be drawn between "the ordinary Taliban who are real and honest sons of [Afghanistan]" and those "who still use the Taliban cover to disturb peace and security in the country."[48] Further, he underscored that "no one had the right…to harass or persecute anyone 'under the name Talib/Taliban' from that time onward."[49] This speech could be assessed an announcement, albeit an

32 The legacy of past initiatives

informal one, of the launch of what has come to be known as his "reconciliation" policy toward the Taliban and an effort to classify them as either "good" or "bad" Talibs."[50] Since the announcement, Karzai articulated the issue of "reconciliation" further, essentially stating that:

> ...other than between 100 to 150 former members of the Taliban regime who are known to have committed crimes against the Afghan people; all others, whether dormant or active within the ranks of the neo-Taliban, can begin living as normal citizens of Afghanistan by denouncing violence and renouncing their opposition to the central Afghan Government.[51]

Despite long-standing requests by the Afghan media and politicians to publicise the specific list of the unpardonable former Taliban members, this list was only recently made public. Furthermore, observations of the former President of Afghanistan and head of the Strengthening Peace Program (*Proceay-i -Tahkeem-i Sulha*, PTS) initiative, Sibghatullah Mojaddedi, which were initially supported by Karzai, transformed the issue of who cannot be pardoned into a contentious political problem.[52] According to Mojaddedi, the amnesty would extend to all Taliban leaders, including the head of the regime, Mullah Mohammad Omar.[53]

A particularly important year for Afghanistan was 2005 for the trajectory of human rights and transitional justice activism and for the continued efforts for "reconciliation." That year, the *Peace, Reconciliation and Justice in Afghanistan Action Plan of the Government of the Islamic Republic of Afghanistan* was formalized, thus setting the platform for a broader effort for "transitional justice." Limited to a mandate of four years, it had an impressive framework, identifying five key fields of activity: (i) establishment of national remembrance days, memorials, and museums; (ii) establishing accountable state institutions and purging human rights violators and criminals from the state institutions (through appropriate legislation, establishing a Civil Service Commission, an Advisory Panel for Presidential Appointments); (iii) truth-seeking and documentation; (iv) promotion of reconciliation and national unity; and (v) establishment of accountability mechanisms (using a legal, procedural, and institutional framework to clarify the question of non-amnesty and to ensure that Afghanistan complies with Islamic laws and international obligations such that perpetrators of crimes against humanity are not overlooked). An analysis of the plan indicates that it is a comprehensive effort to address the expansionist position of transitional justice – it takes into account the importance of acknowledgement, the need for reconciliation, the importance of documentation, and the institutionalization of concrete measures to prevent individuals with records of wartime atrocities from occupying public posts. In short, on paper at least, the National Action Plan is a comprehensive arrangement, promising to deliver on justice and reconciliation and recognizing (some of) the demands of victims and the obligations of the state.[54] At around the same time in January 2005, acting within its mandate, the AIHRC, at the completion of the transitional justice consultation, published the *Call for Justice,* which remains, to date, the only comprehensive report on what Afghans understand as justice.[55]

International human rights actors arguing for judicial accountability for war crimes under the doctrine of universal jurisdiction[56] against Afghan rights abusers living abroad also saw some important developments. A UK court convicted Faryadi Zardad, a notorious warlord from the Hizb-i-Islami, of torture and hostage-taking of Afghan civilians between 1991 and 1996, and sentenced him to 23 years in prison. Similarly, on October 14, a Dutch court convicted asylum-seekers Hesamuddin Hesam and Habibullah Jalalzoy, both high-level members of KHAD, Afghanistan's infamous communist-era intelligence service, of engaging in torture and sentenced them to 12 and 9 years in prison, respectively. The first and only war crimes case tried in Afghanistan was that of Assadullah Sarwary, the former intelligence chief and deputy prime minister of the communist government. Sarwary was arrested in 1992 and spent nearly 14 years in prison without a trial.[57]

The publication of Human Rights Watch's *Blood-Stained Hands: Past Atrocities in Kabul and Afghanistan's Legacy of Impunity*[58] laid bare some of the tensions between the human rights community and that of certain international actors, particularly the United Nations Assistance Mission in Afghanistan (UNAMA) regarding the question of "transitional justice" and mainly that of culpability. Several of the interviewees pointed out that the original strategy to build momentum around the demand for culpability was based on an agreement that the UNAMA would release a report drawing on the findings of the Human Rights Watch report and emphasizing the findings in AIHRC's *A Call for Justice*. Anecdotes gathered during this research vary on what exactly happened regarding the report,[59] but the final prognosis was that the UN withdrew from the "deal." Gossman noted:

> The UN got 'cold feet' regarding potential backlash against its workers… but…a lot of people thought that this was not the case…since all of this was [already] published material…the UN report was going to put out something that was already published.[60]

In May 2005, the PTS was established by a presidential decree and headed by Mojaddedi. The objective was to reopen reconciliation talks with the opposition, including the Taliban and the Hizb-i-Islami. Its primary goal was to provide former enemy combatants with an opportunity to recognize the GoA as legitimate, to accept the Constitution, and to lead normal lives as part of wider society.[61] From the start however, the PTS suffered from weak management, insufficient resources, lack of monitoring as well as an overall absence of political will.[62] There was a lack of coordination between local implementers and the International Security Assistance Forces (ISAF) as well as with the disarmament programs, Disarmament Demobilization and Reintegration (DDR) and Disbandment of Illegal Armed Groups (DIAG). It has also been alleged that the PTS has been plagued by corruption, through which Mojaddedi provides patronage to his political and tribal followers.[63] Few believe that those who had been reconciled had been high-ranking or influential actors[64] while many were never "genuine"

34   *The legacy of past initiatives*

insurgents.[65] Such weaknesses led the United Kingdom, in concert with the Dutch and the Americans, to end their support for the PTS in March 2008.[66]

On January 6, 2007, President Karzai issued a public plea to Mullah Omar and Gulbuddin Hekmatyar to end the ongoing insurgency, adding to the National Security Council's (NSC) below-the-radar diplomacy, and several provincial governors' political outreach efforts to insurgents. The same year, both houses of parliament, the *Meshrano Jirga* and the *Wolesi Jirga*, approved a sweeping amnesty bill, officially obstructing national discussion and action on culpability for war crimes. The 12-point "National Stability and Reconciliation Bill" contained four primary clauses dealing with the amnesty issue. First, it called on all opponents to forgive each other and participate in Karzai's national reconciliation process.[67] Second, the opponents (a catch-all phrase that includes communists, *mujahideen*, Taliban, and other antagonists) were promised blanket amnesty as long as they accepted the Afghanistan constitution and committed to abide by all laws of the land. Third, the draft bill proscribed that individuals who were involved in the *jihad* to protect Afghanistan's religion or territorial integrity could not be criticized. Fourth, it rejected the findings of Human Rights Watch's *Blood-Stained Hands*. The bill circumvented several of Afghanistan's international obligations relating to human rights and unleashed criticism internationally and domestically.[68] Consequently, Karzai slightly revised the bill, which then recognized the rights of war crimes victims to bring cases against those alleged to have committed war crimes.[69] Rights-based groups rightly point out that the lack of security and rule of law in Afghanistan makes it almost impossible for individuals to pursue criminal cases against powerful parties involved in the war. In a statement on March 10, 2010, Brad Adams, Director of Human Rights Watch, said, "It is fantasy to think that an individual can take on a major war criminal alone,"[70] adding that the state should not transfer its obligation to prosecute serious human rights violations to individuals.

In 2009, the National Action Plan expired. Despite requests by both AIHRC and civil society to President Karzai to extend its mandate, thus far he has refused to do so. As of writing, there has been very little progress on the Action Plan itself. President Karzai launched the Action Plan more than a year after its formalization on December 10, 2006 to coincide with International Human Rights Day, a delay indicative of its unpopularity within the Afghan Government including with Karzai's trusted advisors.[71] The other requirement met was the establishment of the President Advisory Panel for cabinet appointments. Despite the expiration of its mandate, the Action Plan has a place in recent key policy documents including being used as benchmark in the 2006 Afghanistan Compact (AC) and the 2008 Afghanistan National Development Strategy (ANDS). A 2010 report issued by AREU, however, states:

> ...awareness of the plan within the ministries responsible for its implementation and among some members of the international diplomatic community is weak...[and] although the ANDS reemphasized the responsibility of the Ministry of Justice (MoJ) to implement the plan, government

officials working in the justice field said they were unaware of the plan's existence.[72]

For almost two years, the actual status of the amnesty bill remained unknown to international actors and Afghan human rights activists. In fact, during the period of research, no interviewee could accurately account for where the bill was – whether in the possession of Karzai or in Parliament – and whether it had actually become law. For several of the human rights activists interviewed, the ambiguity of the status of the bill offered cautious hope that "if not too many questions were asked about the bill's status, some progress could be made regarding transitional justice very quietly."[73] This optimism was short-lived. The bill's publication in the Gazette in 2009 dealt a serious blow to the National Action Plan, which for all purposes remains the most significant document that captures the "transitional justice" spectrum for Afghan society. A national civil society actor summarizes this in the following:

> There is no other document that exists today in Afghanistan which outlines the government's obligations to transitional justice…it is pretty comprehensive…the commitments of the GoA are relevant, so the Action Plan is still relevant…this is what we have, and we should continue to demand that GoA meets its obligations.[74]

Indeed the relevance of the National Action Plan has not faded from the international platform (perhaps its expiration date either been not noted or been intentionally disregarded). In fact, the United Nations Security Council Resolution 1868, refers to it when calling on the Afghan Government to "ensure the full implementation of the Action Plan on Peace, Justice and Reconciliation in accordance with the Afghanistan Compact."[75]

As 2014 looms in the horizon, a year earmarked for the withdrawal of international troops from Afghanistan, there is a frenzy of speculation and activities surrounding new peace talks with the Taliban, despite serious derailment caused by the 2011 assassination of former President Burhanuddin Rabbani, head of the Afghanistan Peace Council[76] and even more recently, the assassination of Mullah Arsala Rahmani, a former Taliban minister who was an important go-between in potential peace talks between the GoN and the Taliban in 2012. Policy-makers and supporters of the peace talks argue that making the Taliban formal stakeholders in Afghanistan's future while holding them to Afghanistan's commitments to human rights and democracy is imperative. Yet the realities of a weak central government, the continuing military operations by the Taliban and the Hizb-i-Islami against the IMF, government, and civilian targets, and the state of Afghan's military and police raises concerns amongst many about if and whether progress in the field of human rights, women's rights, and media can indeed be protected under the new regime that will emerge.

Today's fears for Afghanistan's future derive their legitimacy from the country's past patterns of political concessions which, negotiated between national

36   *The legacy of past initiatives*

elites and international actors, resulted in failure time and again. The search for an Afghan sense of reconciliation at the national level ultimately is not an exercise in nuanced understandings of the varying interpretations of justice and peace in the country, but the recycling of an old script of deal-making and political arrangements and at times even capitulation without any integration of the demands of the civilian population.

Accounting for the past: Nepal's commissions

In April 1990, democracy protests reverberated through Kathmandu as part of *Gono Andalon I* (people's movement), resulting in violence and the acquiescence of King Birendra to dissolve the *panchayat,*[77] dismiss the royal cabinet, and establish a constitutional monarchy. Despite the parliamentary elections of May 1991, Nepal began a downward spiral with successive governments marred by no-confidence votes, changes in governments, Supreme Court disputes, and coalition hopping. Emerging from this constant state of chaos, was the Unified Communist Party of Nepal-Maoists (CPN-M), one of the many feuding far left factions whose central aim was to capture state power and establish *naulo janabad* (new people's democracy).[78] In the beginning of the 1990s, practically all of Nepal's communist factions believed in the concept of *naulo janabad* and the idea that it could be attained through a multiparty democracy.[79] Where they differed was about the means to develop such a political formula and how pluralistic the political institutions needed to be to reflect such an objective.[80] On one hand, the moderate Communist Party of Nepal – the Unified Marxist–Leninist (UML) – mobilized around *bahudaliya janabad* (multiparty people's democracy).[81] In contrast, the Maoists were vehemently opposed to the multiparty system towards which Nepal was moving. By 1995, they began a violent insurrection in the rural areas to establish a "people's republic" that would last over a decade. What followed were years of unstable government with frequent exchange of governance authority, dissolutions of parliament, assumption of direct power by a new king,[82] failed ceasefires, collapsed peace talks and declaration of several states of emergency. The government at that time also introduced the Terrorist and Disruptive Activities (Control and Punishment) Ordinance (TADO), granting wide powers to the security forces to arrest people involved in "terrorist activities". Under the ordinance, the CPN-M was declared to be a "terrorist organization"[83] and the King deployed the then Royal Nepal Army (RNA) to quell the growing insurgency. In response, the Maoists increased their attacks on bridges, clinics, dams, electrical supplies, and drinking water facilities, all of which they declared to be part of aid projects backed by "international imperialists."[84]

At the height of their power, the Maoists claimed to control over 90 percent of Nepal, setting up their parallel structures of governance, military, and judiciary, terrorizing Nepali citizens with kidnappings, killings, and extortion. In response, the RNA, the police, and militia groups unleashed a reign of terror across the countryside resulting in thousands of deaths, disappearances, arrests, and innumerable acts of torture and sexual violence. In 2005, the Maoist and main opposition parties began the *Gono Andalon II*, the second people's movement, opposing the King's direct rule

The legacy of past initiatives   37

and to restore democracy. Within a year, the King was forced to step down, and in November 2006, the government and Maoists signed the CPA, declaring a formal end to a ten-year rebel insurgency. In April 2008, former Maoist rebels won the largest bloc of seats in elections to the new constituent assembly, and in May, after formally abolishing the monarchy, the country became the Federal Democratic Republic of Nepal.

While not termed "transitional justice," since 1990, various governments in Nepal have set up commissions of inquiry to investigate specific human rights abuses committed in the years of people's movement I and II and the ten-year insurgency in between; however, such institutions have done little to change the climate of institutionalized impunity. The discussion of the current commissions needs to be understood with these parameters. In 1990, the first post-Panchayat Prime Minister, Krishna Prasad Bhattarai issued an executive order as per the decision of the Council of Ministers to establish to a Commission of Inquiry to locate people who had disappeared during the conflict.[85] The Commission was mandated to examine allegations of human rights violations during the autocratic Panchayat system from 1961–90, to investigate and identify the final places of detention of those who had disappeared, and to identify additional victims. Named the Mallik Commission after the judge who headed it, and comprising of four commissioners, it was quickly embroiled in a series of controversies. As a result, two of the commissioners who were representatives of Nepalese human rights groups, resigned. According to the report, which was completed in 1991, 45 people were killed during the *Jana Andalon* but the Home Ministry contradicted this estimate, putting the death toll at 63 people.[86] Human rights organizations disputed both figures and insisted that the numbers were far higher.[87] The Mallik Commission also acknowledged that there had been gross infringements of human rights, but declined to reveal the identity of those thought to be guilty on the grounds that it would hamper legal actions against them.[88] It suggested that action be taken against the police, administrators, ministers, and members of committees responsible for suppressing the *Jana Andalon*; however, no action was taken based on the report's recommendations. Instead, the then Attorney General maintained, that he "was not able to identify the laws under which action should be taken."[89] The Mallik Commission was dissolved fairly quickly, but it was not until 1994, due to immense pressure by civil society groups, that its report was made public. Today, the report is only available through the parliamentary secretariat and Nepal's national library. Further, in January 1999, based on the recommendations of the Mallik Commission report, a group of bereaved families and 121 lawyers and law students from 38 of Nepal's 75 districts filed a petition in the Supreme Court, demanding action for the killings and injuries during the 1990 *Jana Andalon*.[90] The Court's registrar immediately dismissed the petition.[91]

According to the 2008 Human Rights Watch report *Waiting for Justice,* in the face of rising criticism about their activities, the three arms of the security forces – the Royal Nepal Police (RNP), Afghan National Police (ANP) and RNA – established "Human Rights Cells" as internal bodies to investigate complaints about human rights violations. It notes, however, that "these appear largely cosmetic, although

38   *The legacy of past initiatives*

departmental or disciplinary action has been taken against alleged perpetrators in some cases."[92] Until today, however, no independent investigative mechanisms or prosecutorial measures have been established to look into any complaints of human rights abuses. The army failed to work with the police to investigate allegations of atrocities committed, save for a few instances, such as the Doramba case.[93] Further, the recommendations of the Working Group for Enforced and Involuntary Disappearances (WGEID) have yet to be implemented.[94]

In response to civil society criticisms, several commissions have been established in Nepal to address questions of human rights abuses. Under increasing international pressure, on 1 July 2004, the then Prime Minister Sher Bahadur Deuba established an Investigative Committee on Disappearances to determine the status of reported "disappearances."[95] Known as the Malego Committee, it issued four reports with information about the status of 320 persons in 2004. But the Commission's work barely went beyond consolidating lists of the "disappeared." It also did not possess the necessary powers to compel the security forces to cooperate further, which accentuated its inefficacy.[96] In May 2006, the Office of the High Commissioner for Human Rights-Nepal (OHCHR-N) issued a report documenting the disappearance, illegal detention, and ill treatment of 49 individuals confirmed by OHCHR to be in the custody of the Bhairabnath Battalion of the Nepal Army (NA) at Maharajgunj, Kathmandu. It urged the government to set up an independent commission of inquiry to determine their fate or whereabouts."[97] Unfortunately, the government never provided a detailed response to the OHCHR. Further, the NA did not acknowledge responsibility for any of the documented cases, nor did it take any steps to investigate the 49 cases to OHCHR.[98]

Under pressure for the killings in Doramba, the RNA reluctantly reopened its investigation and on 31 January 2005, announced that the major in charge of the operation would be imprisoned for two years for the excessive use of force.[99] While this was a historic decision – the first clear case of an RNA officer punished for a human rights violation – for national and international human rights activists, the inadequate sentence, lack of transparency of the military trial, and timing made the process highly unsatisfactory. In 2006, after the fall of King Gayanendra's 15-month rule, Nepal created the Rayamajhi Commission, headed by former Supreme Court judge Krishna Jung Rayamajhi, to investigate the violent crackdown during the *Jana Andalon*. The Commission interrogated some of the most senior members of the Nepali Government and even sent questions to the King to clarify his role in the state-sponsored abuses that took place during the pro-democracy movement. The report, which was tabled in the parliament by Home Minister Krishna Sitoula, recommended action against 202 people for the deaths of 25 people and injuries to approximately 9,000 civilians.[100] The names of three ministers who were in the Royal Government were also included in the list.[101] While King Gayenendra was identified in the report, it did not specify any action against him, given that in the Nepalese constitution there was no provision to take action against the Monarch.[102] The report was finally made public six months after its submission after extensive pressure from lawmakers and the general public. A 2009 ICTJ report noted that even as late as September 2006, when a delegation of notable human rights activists met with the prime minister to voice their ongoing concern about Nepal's prevailing culture of impunity, they were told no action would be taken against individuals accused of serious human rights violations.[103] None of the recommendations of the Mallik or Rayamajhi Commissions were ever implemented.

An end to the People's War: Nepal's CPA

If detailed documentation on the actual negotiation process for Afghanistan's Bonn is limited, then there is even less information available on the discussions and negotiations around Nepal's CPA. Consequently, most of the discussion on transitional justice and human rights has been extracted from organizational reports and extensive interviews held in Nepal.

For Nepal's elites, the CPA is a source of pride, given that it is largely a Nepal-initiated peace process. This claim however does not acknowledge the role of international actors who, particularly since 2000, provided critical support and assistance for the ongoing peace negotiations. Of these, the Swiss-based NGO Centre for Humanitarian Dialogue (CHD), the good offices of a UN official, the OHCHR, and the United Nations Mission in Nepal (UNMIN) played prominent roles in promoting dialogues between the different parties. Other actors in the efforts for negotiation included the Carter Center's conflict resolution program, a Swiss Government-appointed special advisor for peacebuilding, Günther Baechler, and South African consultant Hannes Siebert contracted by United States Agency for International Development (USAID) who worked closely with the peace secretariat. Bilateral support was also provided by the United Kingdom, Norway, Denmark, and India.

While much of the donor support was withdrawn as a direct response to the 2005 royal coup,[104] an initiative sponsored by the United States, Nepal's Transition to Peace (NTTP), remained in place. The NTTP served to support political parties and offered a platform where various stakeholders could negotiate a political settlement.[105] The prominent role of Siebert and Baechler need special acknowledgement here because of their strategic partnership in creating a task force comprising of national facilitators, representatives of political parties, and observers, which was affiliated with the peace secretariat and the Nepal Government.[106] This task force was instrumental in raising critical issues about the peace process, including that of transitional justice.

A major push for the discussion on transitional justice came inevitably from Nepal's local civil society, which mostly continued to remain at the peripheries of major discussions and negotiations. Their focus was notably narrow, concerned primarily with questions of impunity and manifest in their demand for prosecution of human rights abusers and the demand for the GoN to ratify the Rome Statute of the ICC.[107] As the political talks dragged on however, cleavages became apparent within the local civil society community. Depending on affiliations with political parties, the Maoists or the government, NGOs and civil society actors sided with either the question of reconciliation or that of criminal accountability.[108] According

40   *The legacy of past initiatives*

to a 2009 ICTJ report, and confirmed in interviews conducted for this book, several civil society members admitted that opportunities were lost on justice-related issues because of the prioritization of political concerns including questions about the configuration of a republic and the Constituent Assembly (CA).[109]

The Baluwatar Accord, an eight-point agreement between the Seven Party Alliance (SPA)[110] and the Maoists signed roughly two weeks prior to the CPA, is the first official document in Nepal to address the issue of human rights atrocities committed in the country. The Accord makes special reference to "a high-level commission to investigate and publicize the whereabouts of citizens that were alleged to be disappeared by the state and the Maoists, a TRC, and compensation for victims' families."[111] But it is the CPA signed on November 21, 2006, which is accredited as the accord that signaled the official end of the conflict.

The CPA called for three mechanisms to address human rights violations that occurred during the decade-long conflict: (i) Article 5.2.5 mandated the establishment of a Truth and Reconciliation Commission to "probe about those involved in serious violation of human rights and crime against humanity...and develop an atmosphere for reconciliation in society;" (ii) Article 5.2.4 calls for a National Peace and Rehabilitation Commission "to carry out works...to normalize the adverse situation arising as a result of the armed conflict, maintain peace in the society and run relief and rehabilitation works for the people victimized and displaced as a result of the conflict;" and (iii) Article 5.2.3 states "both sides also agree to make public within 60 days of signing of the agreement the real name, caste and address of the people 'disappeared' or killed during the conflict and inform the family members about it."[112] Beyond these broad mandates, however, the CPA contains no detailed guidance for how to form each of these investigative bodies or what should be their specific mandate. The following provides a discussion of the genesis of each mechanism in the CPA.

The NPRC

The NPRC was a direct response to the level of destabilization experienced by the Nepali population in the decade-long conflict. An estimated 350,000 to 400,000 Nepalese were internally displaced and millions fled to India to escape from atrocities.[113] In the hill regions of Nepal, where members of the Young Communist League (YCL),[114] took on a public security role since 2007, there were reports of extortion, threats and intimidation, physical assault, ill-treatment sometimes amounting to torture, forced labor, disruption of rallies and meetings, and destruction of property. In the ten years of conflict, Maoist forces were also responsible for killings, abductions, torture, extortion, and the use of children for military purposes.[115] The NPRC was intended to be the primary body responsible for the monitoring and implementation of the CPA under Article 5.2.4, and, in coordination with the TRC and the State Restructuring Commission, was intended to be the "backbone" of the peace agreement. In other words, the PRC was expected to address social and economic disruption, provide relief and rehabilitation to survivors, and in the process address, at least to a limited extent, the deep socioeconomic realities, institutionalized through the caste and patronage system that continues to plague Nepal. In reality, however, despite assurances and rhetorical support of every government that has come to power post-CPA, including the Common Minimum Programme of each post-CPA government in the 23-Point Agreement of 23 December 2007, and clear reference in the 2008/09 budget, the NPRC has yet to be established. In its stead, its responsibilities were handed over to the Ministry of Peace and Reconstruction (MoPR), which as a government agency lacks independence and inclusionary capabilities.

Under the MoPR, between 2008–10, Local Peace Committees (LPCs) were set up in 71 districts with the aim of promoting local conflict resolution and ultimately supporting implementation of the CPA. Although the LPCs have received significant logistical support from the Asian Development Bank (ADB) and USAID, they have faced innumerable challenges brought about by "political disagreements over their composition, confusion over their mandate, and lack of support and local ownership, although by mid-2010 the overall picture appears to be improving."[116] While the involvement of the MoPR has meant external agencies assist in relief assistance such as the contributions of the World Bank (WB) to 17,000 families of those who died or disappeared during the conflict, relief distribution has been subject to substantive criticism.[117] The distribution process has been disorganized, inequitable, and inadequate, contributing to tensions between victims' groups.[118] A civil society actor summarized his observations in the following:

> The MoPR does not have a human rights or a conflict resolution specialist; there are a few people who are well-intentioned within it, but it is a new and weak government bureaucracy which is not independent, and which ultimately does not have the same kind of mandate that the NPRC was envisioned to have.[119]

COID

The need for a COID, often referred to as the "Disappearance Commission" was a response to the large numbers of civilians who were victims of enforced disappearances and whose whereabouts remain unknown. Between 2003–4, Nepal held the distinction of having the highest yearly number of new cases of "disappearances" reported to the UN WGEID in the world,[120] particularly due to the incidents involving torture and disappearances in Bardiya[121] and in Maharajgunj.[122] In total, 1619 disappearances were reported to the NHRC.[123] The vast majority of the disappearances in both instances, as well as in other areas of Nepal, were through abductions, unofficial arrests, secret detentions, and torture of political opposition and marginalized groups. Perpetrators included all three branches of the security services – the Nepalese Police (NP), the Armed Police Force (APF), and the RNA as well as the Maoist People's Army (MPA). Approximately 1000 cases of missing and disappeared people have yet to be investigated.[124]

From the beginning, OHCHR, the International Commission of Jurists (ICJ) and the International Committee of the Red Cross (ICRC) supported the demand

42 *The legacy of past initiatives*

for a disappearance commission echoing the demands of local civil society actors and victims' families. Interestingly enough, the TRC was initially expected to handle the issue of disappearances. Logistical concerns about the feasibility of 60 days given to publish the names of the disappeared and refer cases to the TRC ultimately led to recognizing the need for a separate commission. Subsequently, the Disappearance Commission appeared as a separate mechanism in the CPA.[125]

Thus far, the greatest amount of progress has been around the COID. On July 1, 2007, the Supreme Court ruled to enact a law that would criminalize enforced disappearances in accordance with the International Convention for the Protection of all Persons from Enforced Disappearance. This further consolidated international and national efforts to mobilize around creating drafts for a disappearance bill to ensure that the Disappearance Commission reached stringent international standards. On November 19, 2008, the cabinet approved the draft disappearance bill but, unfortunately, it was not put before the CA in time to be considered during the budget session for the following year. Despite concerns by the human rights community and international organizations, such as the ICJ, about the absence of parliamentary oversight and democratic legislative processes in the effort to pass the bill, the government went ahead and an ordinance on disappearances was among three signed into law by President Ram Baran Yadav on February 10, 2009; however, as of April 2010, the government tabled the Bill on Offences and Punishment of Disappearances 2066. Further, the current political turmoil, which has included the stark absence of a new constitution, has played a significant role in slowing down the progress of the bill. Human rights activists have also expressed concerned that pending legislation for the TRC and the COID has served as justification for not prosecuting conflict-related crimes through the existing judicial system. One of the few exceptions to this has been the work of the Supreme Court. At a February 2009 hearing on writ petitions filed in August 2007, it ordered the NP to begin investigations into the disappearances of five students in Dhanusha District in October 2003.[126]

The TRC

The TRC is in many ways the most ambitious of the three commissions, and responsibility for conceiving and implementing its framework has been given to MoPR. The general principle behind it is to find the "truth" about the approximately 13,256 Nepalese killed in the decade-long conflict and the human rights violations committed during that period, including illegal detentions, rapes, and murders of female civilians.[127] It would also have the mandate to investigate the role of the RNA, which frequently ignored the Supreme Court habeas corpus orders and even staged killings to appear as "armed encounters," threatened witnesses to sign exonerating statements, took staged photographs, and publicized false accounts of circumstances of death.[128]

Several people interviewed in the course of this study expressed surprise at seeing the TRC as a separate mechanism mentioned in the CPA, particularly because most were unaware of what such an institution would actually mean and how it would operate in the Nepali context.[129] From the beginning, the support for the TRC came from the Nepali Congress (NC) who wanted a mechanism to address past violations and who considered the Maoists as being mainly responsible for human rights atrocities committed during the conflict. The Maoists in turn, were less receptive to the idea, focusing their attention on the need for prioritizing the publication of the names of the disappeared. While one of the earlier versions of the CPA draft had referred to a Truth, Justice, and Reconciliation Commission, due to pressure from political parties, the term justice was ultimately omitted.[130]

In June 2007, the Supreme Court made a landmark ruling on enforced disappearances.[131] In May 2007, the MoPR formed a Working Group mandated to draft legislation necessary to establish a TRC. These initial efforts, however, met with substantive criticism from civil society actors, who feared it would be another "amnesty" commission. In 2008, similar to the bill on disappearances, the TRC bill was not put before the CA in time to be considered during the impending budget session for the upcoming year; however, unlike the passage of the disappearance commission bill as an ordinance, there has been little official movement on the commitment to a TRC by the Nepal Government.

The most amount of activity around the TRC bill has been with regard to the drafting of the legislation where Nepali civil society actors and international human rights organizations have demonstrated a significant level of commitment. The government and even some elite civil society actors have insisted that consultations on the TRC have been widespread and far-reaching, but others reflected that the voices of the most marginalized (and hence the most affected) were not taken into consideration in drafting versions of the bill. Human rights activists and international organizations such as the ICJ, OHCHR-N, and ICTJ have also publicly offered criticisms and recommendations on several of the versions of the TRC bill drafted by the government, pointing out that the procedures and content did not adhere to international human rights standards, both in terms of its administrative and technical nature, as well as its content. For example, serious criticism was voiced about the lack of transparency, independence, and impartiality and ambiguity in the appointment process of the commissioners, staffing, funding, powers of the commission, and dissolution of the commission in the earlier drafts.[132] They also vehemently protested provisions that allowed the omission to recommend amnesty for serious crimes "that were committed in the course of one's 'duty' or for political purposes during the armed conflict, without further clarification,"[133] those that allowed for de facto amnesty, placing primacy of reconciliation over prosecution in the case of those perpetrators who were not recommended for amnesty. Last, criticisms were directed at the fact that the drafts did not grant the Commission sufficient mandate to investigate the underlying causes of conflict and patterns of violence, nor include an expansive understanding of the definition of victims.[134]

These criticisms resulted in several revisions of the TRC bill. The current draft continues to contain an amnesty provision, which allows the TRC to recommend amnesties, but this has been further clarified. Amnesties under this draft can only be granted on the condition that the applicant fully discloses information about

44   *The legacy of past initiatives*

their own activities during the armed conflict,[135] and only for certain crimes. Amnesties however will not be granted to anyone responsible for "(a) any kind of murder committed after taking the person into custody (whether State or non-State); (b) murder of an unarmed person; (c) torture; (d) rape; (e) disappearance of a person; and (f) abduction and hostage taking."[136] The current bill also allows for the Commission to consult victims before making a recommendation for amnesty, but according to human rights actors, this should be a mandatory, not a discretionary requirement. Further, they demand that the provisions should provide detailed information about the procedural, financial, and logistical details of how such consultation will take place, they should be facilitated, and that the TRC should outline guidelines for victim consultations and the circumstances under which amnesties will be granted.[137]

The current TRC bill also includes specific provisions for reconciliation, including providing the Commission with the mandate to facilitate personal reconciliation between victims and perpetrators.[138] There is, however, reservation that such a measure assumes that "the perpetrator will be easily identifiable as linked to a particular crime and a particular victim."[139] The provision also gives the Commission the authority to compel the perpetrator to provide reasonable compensation as part of the reconciliation process.[140] Some have underscored that this suggests that the payment of compensation depends on the Commission facilitating the parties to reconcile while generating the risk of creating inequality in the amount of compensation received by victims who have suffered similar violations because this would then depend on the identification of the perpetrator, the decision to undertake a reconciliation process, and the perpetrator's ability to provide a compensation.[141] Finally, the current TRC bill uses the term *melmilap* (reconciliation) but still does not provide a definition of the term. The ambiguity of what the term means in the Nepali context, and how it can actually be achieved both at the individual and social process in the long-term rather than being "enforced" through a particular commission, continues to raise questions of how such a mechanism will in fact promote a functional relationship between the victim and the perpetrator. As of 2013, given the continuing political turmoil, there has been stilted progress on the TRC and indeed on any of the bills on transitional justice, and human rights actors, national and international, continue to decry the continuing climate of pervasive impunity in the country.[142]

Conclusion

In exploring the historical background and the contemporary efforts for transitional justice in Afghanistan and Nepal, what emerges is a singular narrative of striking similarity – consistent failure to deliver either in the fronts of sustainable "reconciliation" or on the questions of culpability. In other words, the legacy of past institutions and negotiations and their corresponding shortcomings have cast long shadows in the efficacy and legitimacy of proposed programs for transitional justice. In its stead, these legacies have created a historical framework of unaccountability and generated little confidence in the contemporary transitional justice discourse.

The legacy of past initiatives   45

Afghanistan, for instance, is no stranger to what appears in mainstream discourse as "political reconciliation," which in fact has been a euphemism for various kinds of concessions, short-term power-brokering, and capitulation. These measures have never, except for extremely short periods of time, yielded a stable political platform or privileged the underlying causes of the conflict, or indeed the interests of the civilian population. It is within this particular context that current political bargaining and challenges to transitional justice need to be understood. A climate of impunity where only the powerful have been privileged has generated little space for the promises of the National Action Plan and any subsequent efforts to gain significant traction; the result has been that international and local civil society actors committed to human rights and justice continue to struggle for space to address questions of accountable governance in the country.

Nepal's discouraging history of creating commissions to seek accountability for civilian deaths have been a showcase for the country's weak political will and institutional vulnerabilities to external manipulation, rather than illustrations of the country's commitment to seek accountability and peace for the disenfranchised. Going forward, the outcome of such efforts depends on how, and to what extent, the establishment of the promised commissions can challenge the legacy of the past initiatives.

Both the Afghan and Nepali illustrations emphasize a critical point: historical legacies of past failures account for not only diminished expectations of future efforts to address questions of accountability, justice, and peace, but just as importantly, to cripple political space and institutional capacity for the search for such goals. This influence of history, in turn, this chapter argues, is a critical component of what has been defined as the "dynamic local." What has been done in the past informs different understandings of concepts such as "reconciliation" – it is not enough to know *what* has been done, but also to know how what has been done *means* to various actors in society. Framed in another way, local history is not only a summation of facts and figures or an objective account of actors and decisions, but also a critical and *active* component in the politics and processes of a given context, influencing and even restricting the understanding and prospects of discussions of governance. Narrating history is a selective process and one heavily dependent on perspective. Consequently, when engaging with the legacy of the past, it is important to know whose interpretation of the past is adopted as "the" legacy. We must acknowledge that there are multiple legacies of past experiences and that history – the old idiom of 20/20 hindsight notwithstanding – changes over time. The experiences in Nepal and Afghanistan clearly underscore that in order to engage with discussions of governance, including that of justice and peace, the historical legacies of past efforts need to be understood and analyzed to inform, and perhaps even legitimize, contemporary efforts. Otherwise, stripped of context, such discussions remain ahistorical, disengaged from the continuing reality of a given situation and fail to accommodate people's experiences and the lessons learned from institutional limitations of past efforts.

3 Ordinary laws

While atrocities committed during conflict are considered *extraordinary* by their very intent, scope, and magnitude, the societies within which they have been committed only have the *ordinary* modality of punishment to respond to such crimes, better suited to respond to "ordinary" civil and criminal violations.[1] International lawyers assert normative differences between extraordinary crimes and ordinary common crimes, insisting that the nature of the former is more serious because they enter "into the realm of *extraordinary international criminality*. The perpetrator of extraordinary international crimes has then become cast, rhetorically as well as legally, as an *enemy of all humankind*."[2] Correspondingly, since the twentieth century, there has been an effort, halted by the period of the Cold War and re-energized in the 1990s, to create legal institutions to adjudicate mass violence.[3]

In the 1990s, spurred by international outrage, the active engagement of a post-Cold War United Nations and the tireless efforts of human rights and women's rights activists, two *ad hoc* tribunals were established – the International Criminal Tribunal for Former Yugoslavia (ICTY) and the International Criminal Tribunal for Rwanda (ICTR) – to seek punishment for all those who violate international humanitarian law. These two *ad hoc* tribunals set a remarkable precedent for other international, hybrid, and local legal responses to crimes of war, ranging from the hybrid courts of Sierra Leone, East Timor, and Kosovo, the current Extraordinary Chambers in the courts of Cambodia (ECCC) and the establishment of the permanent International Criminal Court (ICC) in The Hague.

The extensive literature on punitive punishment for wartime atrocities today also includes a new regime of scholarship that critiques these institutions for their reliance on the Western penological rationale of domestic criminal law, for individualizing complex social norms and factors that produce instances of mass violence and reducing them to frameworks generated by deviance theory and pathology, subsequently overriding local legal codes and interpretations of justice.[4] It also raises critical questions of how, despite claims that such tribunals may strengthen domestic jurisprudence, they remain far removed from simultaneous local struggles to develop (or revive) systems of criminal adjudication. After all, while international criminal law continues to grapple with the enormity of war crimes, crimes against humanity and genocide, fledgling legal institutions in transitional contexts face severe constraints in adopting and implementing domestic legislation for civil and criminal violations even for "peaceful" times. Consequently, on one level, a paradox emerges given the juxtaposition of the "ordinariness" of the legal codes and the "extraordinariness" of the transitional period. On another level, tensions emerge between Western-derived legal norms and existing local (and customary) laws. In both Afghanistan and Nepal, the discussion of transitional justice and legal reform exposes the tension between the need for *retroactive* justice for large-scale atrocities and *proactive* justice that would address the commission of ordinary peacetime crimes. Further, it reveals the struggles in both countries to create a comprehensive legal framework that pulls together multiple legal codes to adjudicate over matters of criminality.

This chapter explores the juridical states of Afghanistan and Nepal, delving into the local legal infrastructure in both contexts, teasing out the tensions between international legal commitments, legal codes, and customary laws, and laying out the multi-layered challenges that face the process of legal reform. A key finding in this research is that not only are both countries plagued by de facto and *de jure* impunity, but they are severely disenfranchised because of a lack of equality *before* the law (both in customary and formal systems). Further, in both instances, the sociopolitical dynamics have generated a consistent disregard for existing legal norms. Consequently, crimes of the present, from the mundane to the extraordinary, continue to go unpunished or remain outside of the boundaries of *nullen crimen sine lege* – the principle of legality. Nevertheless, in both contexts, the law remains a site for mobilization for human rights actors in their struggle against impunity. This research also stresses fundamental distinctions between the two case studies. While Afghanistan continues to grapple with how best to merge customary and the Islamic *Shari'a* with international legal norms, Nepal's challenge is how to use the transitional period to harness international legal norms to strengthen and expand on its existing legal framework. Finally, in both contexts, the role of law in checking impunity and preventing further violations underscores that the line between *retroactive, proactive,* and *successive* justice continues to be blurred.

From theory to reality: the challenges of "ordinary" laws

For the last ten years, justice reform in Afghanistan has continued within a complex landscape of legal pluralism defined by historical efforts to modernize its laws, the country's current international legal commitments, a traditional Islamic society administered by a council of elders long resistant to certain forms of social and political change, customary laws of different ethnic groups, and the dictates of the *Shari'a.*[5] Such tensions play out within the context of armed political confrontation, which in turn "affects the solidity of the internal political order, the establishment of a transitional justice phase, and thus the effectiveness of any successful legal and justice reform."[6] Further, Tondini soberly issues the reminder that in Afghanistan, what is being witnessed is "not a post-conflict but an in-conflict justice reform."[7] Nepal's challenges in the legal realm are strikingly

48 *Ordinary laws*

different from those that face Afghanistan, although its legal code too generally acquiesces to international legal standards. The country's legal system, however, faces significant challenges that arise from trying to address the extraordinariness of the transitional period using the existing legal framework, which has yet to criminalize certain types of violations.

Some international practitioners who have worked in both contexts suggest that the Afghan context is a much easier one to grasp than the realities in Nepal.[8] They claim that because the legal system in Afghanistan has been more heavily influenced by Western legal philosophy, there is a clear criminal code and the laws are more neatly codified. Further, one international legal expert asserted: "Efforts for working with the *jirgas* has somehow meant a chain of interconnectivity and what got addressed by whom."[9] In contrast, while Nepal, at least in theory, has judicial independence and a singular legal code, the country's legal system is not uniform. A rule of law consultant noted:

> [T]he body of law that exists was started by one of the early kings and since then later monarchs have added to it; ministries and a judiciary created by a King moved at its pace which was different from how things ran at the local level...[further] some of the laws have been the result of aid agencies getting very excited about funding them, which then passed through the Parliament, but are in fact terrible laws...and in the end, all of this patchwork of laws took place in an atmosphere of very little transparency and entrenched caste and power systems.[10]

Consequently, such a context did not generate any confidence in independent human rights entities or in the rule of law itself. Keeping these distinctions in mind, the following section examines the status and challenges of the legal systems and their challenges in Afghanistan and Nepal, respectively.

The Afghan legal system

Afghanistan's contemporary legal tradition can be traced back to 1923, when its first constitution was written under King Amanullah's rule. Before 1923, the country's legal system consisted of a mixture between different interpretations of the *Shari'a*,[11] including their sectarian strains and their corresponding ethnic manifestations. Hence, while the *Hanafi* jurisprudence, which governs the Sunni population in places as diverse as Turkey, the Indian subcontinent, and Central Asia, has always been prominent, the *Jafariyya* school of jurisprudence has also been influential particularly among the Hazara community who are predominantly Shi'a. These bifurcations become even more complicated when considering that Islam in Afghanistan has been integrated within tribal as well as ethnic frameworks, resulting in the customary laws of the *Afghaniyat, Islamiyat* and tribal practices of the different regions, such as the *Pashtunwali*. Consequently, there is a constant overlap and infusion between what is tribal and what is Islamic.[12] Despite interactions with Western colonial powers, European legal philosophy[13] never

Ordinary laws 49

completely dominated the Afghan legal landscape, although the latter has been influenced by "Western legal thought (mainly French), moderate Islam (Turkey), radical Marxism and again radical Islam."[14] Today, the country's legal landscape continues to be a meeting point and a battleground for three separate, although at times overlapping, components: (a) the provisions of the current constitution (the state legal code), which is constrained by the limited reach of the *de jure* government, and which does not represent the de facto norms that govern the lives of the majority of Afghans; (b) *Shari'a*; and (c) the customary laws of the different ethnic groups. Before engaging with the legal specificities in Afghanistan, it is critical to gain an understanding of the basic principles of Islamic law.

Islamic law in Afghanistan

Islamic law is derived from four main sources: the Qu'ran, the *Hadith* (sayings and actions of Prophet Muhammed), *ijma* (consensus of legal scholars on specific cases similar to opinio juris), and *qiyas* (cases decided by analogical reasoning).[15] It differs significantly from statutory law not only because it is interpreted by the *madhab* (private schools of jurists), but also because Islamic culture does not recognize the separation of powers. Instead, the *ulema* (legal scholars) are responsible for interpreting legal norms, acting as judicial authorities for settlement of disputes, and when necessary, issuing *fatwas*.[16] Professor of Islamic History, Dr Wael Hallaq explains the role and authority of the *ulema* in Muslim societies in the following:

> The authority of the [Islamic] jurists…must not be confused with any notions of worldly power, since they wielded none. Nor was their authority of the charismatic or even moral type, though these types of authority were not entirely precluded. Nor, yet, was their authority purely religious, for the Islamic scene witnessed a number of learned religious classes who, despite their impressive erudition and intellectual output, were entirely devoid of legal authority. The jurists' authority was predominantly, if not essentially, epistemic. Their very learning and erudition bestowed on them the authority that they enjoyed, in the first place the authority to interpret the law, but also the authority to command what is morally good and forbid what is morally bad, to lead and administer society and its civic institutions, to collect taxes, to represent the orphans and the downtrodden, to run educational institutions and law schools, and to supervise charities and public works.[17]

The philosophical legal orientation which grants special status to the *ulema* demonstrates that in Islam, "law is epitomized not in a system of objective, formal, general, public, compulsory rules, but in the unique decision of an individual conscience (*ijtihad*) applied to the evaluation of a concrete act."[18] Furthermore, in Islamic law, the principle of *stare decisis* (judicial precedent) is considered unfair "because people are different and even the same individual's situation vary from moment to moment."[19] Accordingly, "judg[ing] without considering context

50   *Ordinary laws*

would be to violate all sense of justice."[20] Summarily then, Islamic law is based not on "law sources" but "legal authorities,"[21] and the *ulema* are the "lawmakers of Islam."[22] Consequently, at different points in history, efforts at codification of statutes have generated tension between the state and the *ulema,* who opposed the codification of statutes, viewing such initiatives as a threat to their authority and position in society. In addition, for many *ulema*, codifying *Shari'a* amounts to imposing human limits on the Divine.[23]

Shari'a's engagement with criminal offences is vastly different from the Western penological system. *Hudd* (Islamic crimes) for example, are distinct from each other based on the penalties exacted upon their commission. The realm of penalties in turn has two separate classifications. *Hudud* punishment (restrictive prescriptions decided by the divine i.e. Allah, and explained in the Qu'ran) are pre-determined and are given for crimes of alcohol consumption, fornication, rape, adultery, highway robbery, and theft;[24] they are not subject to the judge's (*qadi's*) discretion. The second category of punishment, the *tazir* (discretionary punishment determined by the *qadi*) are meted out for crimes such as bearing false witness, prostitution, extortion, forgery, fraud, and in cases of *hudud* offences where the case against the defendant could not be made with adequate evidence.[25] In the case of *qassass*, or *quisas* (intentional crimes) when individuals are targeted for *lex talionis* (retaliation), victims or their families have the option of forgiving the perpetrator who is required to then offer *diat* or *irsy* (financial compensation or property respectively).[26]

The fundamental philosophy of *Fiqh* (Islamic jurisprudence) and its distinct practices then clearly demarcate the distinctions between the *Shari'a* and the Western legal philosophy and their corresponding penological systems; however, in practically all Islamic countries, there is coexistence between statutory laws and the *Shari'a*. Muslim countries like Iraq, Kuwait, Morocco, and Egypt organized their legal system drawing from both the French codes and the civil law legal tradition;[27] former British colonies such as Bangladesh, Indonesia, Malaysia, and Pakistan co-opted the British common law system while developing a statutory legal system.[28] A general practice in many Islamic countries is that the "*ulema* and state authorities (government and parliament) share jurisdiction over applicable law."[29] In the event that the *ulema* have social and political prominence or when there is a monarchy, "Islamic law may bind state authorities in their legislative power."[30] In some Islamic societies, *Shari'a* plays a critical role both in the constitutional review of laws and in their interpretation.[31] In other instances, Islam is the state religion and no revision of laws based on Islamic principles is permitted.[32] There are a few exceptional cases to both these patterns: Uzbekistan, Turkey, Albania, and a few other former Soviet republics do not mention *Shari'a* in their respective constitutions. In Islamic states (not necessarily in all Muslim countries), while family law falls under the jurisdiction of the *ulema* as in the case of Saudi Arabia, in countries like Pakistan, Egypt, and Bangladesh, statutory norms regulate commercial and administrative law, while the state adjudicates over civil and criminal law.

In Afghanistan, King Amanullah's modernization efforts were reflected in the 1923 constitution, which stressed the principle of complimentarity.[33] The constitution that followed in 1931 reflected the hostile response to Amanullah's modernization efforts (discussed shortly) and established the *Shari'a* as the primary source of laws. The 1964 constitution, perceived as the most liberal constitution until then and which served as a template for the current constitution, was however conservative about matters of law.[34] It confirmed "the subsidiary principle (courts would apply *Shari'a* principles in the absence of statutory law), but also the stronger principle of repugnancy."[35] Suhrke and Borchgrevink explain,

> the repugnancy principle established *Shari'a* as the foundational law and positioned the *ulema* as the ultimate authority on the constitutionality of a given code. Th[is] meant "'the government defines the *qanun* [statute],' but the religious authorities 'interpret and control the *fiqh*.'"[36]

Despite the subsequent political developments in Afghanistan since the 1960s, the corresponding power shifts and efforts at modification, Islamic laws continued to be privileged. The constitution crafted during King Daoud's reign (1973–1978) confirmed respect for Islam and recognized a subsidiary role for *Shari'a*, particularly to be applied in contexts where statutory law was absent. Comparable provisions can also be found in the PDPA's interim constitution. Further, Afghanistan's 1987 Constitution recognized Islam in the preamble and in Article 2, which stated: "The sacred religion of Islam is the religion of Afghanistan and no law shall run counter to the principles of Islam."[37] Summarily, the repugnancy tenet was re-established, but a caveat was introduced through the complimentarity principle that was in Amanullah's constitution.[38] Finally, Article 3(1) of Afghanistan's current constitution clearly acknowledges *Shari'a*'s place in the country in its pronouncement: "in Afghanistan, no law can be contrary to the beliefs and provisions of the sacred religion of Islam."[39]

The ulema *in Afghanistan*

The Afghan *ulema* are a fundamental component of the country's legal system. They are not monolithic in structure[40] and based on their level of responsibilities and education, are significantly distinct from ordinary village *mullahs*.[41] Some are organized as the *shura-e-ulema* (councils of religious leaders), which exist at the local, provincial, and even national levels. The *ulema* in Afghanistan have always been responsible for issuing *fatwas* on religious issues and social matters. Until Afghanistan's emergence as a modern state in the late nineteenth century, the *ulema* had a free reign of the legal system with little or no interference from the state's legal system. Consequently, as in some other Islamic and Muslim countries, the *ulema* in Afghanistan were also historically opposed to codification and homogenization of the *Shari'a*. In addition, the Afghan *ulema* have long been the source of significant controversy. As custodians of Afghanistan's religious

52 Ordinary laws

institutions, they have also historically shared a complex relationship with the Afghan state. Dr Mohammed Hashim Kamali, an Afghan legal scholar and former professor of Islamic jurisprudence, elaborates:

> The religious leaders in Afghanistan have historically been recipients of government grants and subsidies…the *qadis* [judges], *muftis* [jurists] and *mutasibs* [religious superintendents] were keen enforcers of *Shari'a* [Islamic law], which was the authoritative law of the land. The rulers proclaimed themselves to be patrons of the faith to whom allegiance was declared as a religious duty by the congregate on leaders in their Friday sermon of khutba. In sum, so long as the government avoided radical measures against the religious leaders and did not attempt a direct clash with the principles of Islam, the religious leaders were, unlike the tribal chiefs, in potential alliance with the political authority.[42]

It is because of these reasons, argues Ahmed, that the *ulema* in countries like Afghanistan have become increasingly suspicious of codification measures, and views them as efforts by foreign powers to subjugate Islamic law and religious actors to secular authorities.[43]

Afghanistan's customary laws

Barfield defines customary law as "the means by which local communities resolve disputes in the absence of (or opposition to) state or religious authority."[44] While systems of customary law are found throughout the 34 provinces in Afghanistan, they are not uniform in philosophy or practice. Despite these distinctions, one of the most important characteristics of customary law is the use of respected community members or outsiders selected by disputants to adjudicate over individual or community disputes. While such practices have been historically successful in its use of mediation and arbitration of conflict, they have not always had effective enforcement mechanisms and have required state intervention for criminal offences. Certain customary practices have also been critiqued for not subscribing to contemporary human rights standards and for not being responsive to women's rights. Further, depending on context, they can be subjected to internal and external manipulation by shifting power structures, contestations, and interests of the existing authority.

In Afghanistan, the Pashtuns are the largest ethnic group, consisting of 42 percent of the population.[45] Consequently, of the codes of customary laws that are dominant today, the *Pashtunwali* (the code of conduct for the Pashtuns), is amongst the most researched. Similar to other customary laws, the *Pashtunwali* is an oral tradition that comprises of *tsali* (general principles and practices), applies to "every aspect of life, have quasi-legal status, and are considered an essential part of Pashtu 'elegance.'"[46] The principles of *Pashtunwali* in turn comprise of "*Seyal* (equality), *Seyali* (applying equality through competition) *Namus* (protection of female family members and wealth), *Ezzat or Nang* (honor), *Ghairat* (heroism/personal honor), *Gundi* (rivalry), *Patna* (feud), *Qawm* (ethnicity, tribe, social network), *Qawmi Taroon* (tribal binding) *Hamsaya* (protection of neighbors or outsiders living with a family or in a village), *Jirga, Pur/Ghach/Enteqam or Badal* (revenge) and *Nanawati* (forgiveness/harmony)."[47] Traditionally, it is said that disputes among Pashtuns arise from the three 'Z's: *Zar, Zan,* and *Zamin* (gold, women, and land)[48] – the foundations of wealth and honor in the agrarian but tribal society.[49]

The *Pashtunwali* focuses on the principles of compensation and restorative justice that fundamentally attempts to restitute the victim (to the extent possible) to the situation he or she was in prior to the incident. It also attempts to make the offender publicly and personally accountable for his deeds.[50] This in turn provides an opportunity for the wrongdoer to apologize to the victim and pay the *Sharm* (payment such as sheep*)* or the *Poar* (blood money) that seeks to honor the victim and recognize the harm done. Once the *Sharm/Poar* has been paid and accepted, the victim's family slaughters the sheep and invites neighbors, the village mullah, and the offender and his family to the subsequent feast.[51] This event also provides the offender the opportunity to make a public apology, which signals the end to the conflict and the restitution of harmony in the community.

For crimes that are of a serious nature (murder, rape, kidnapping, possession of weapons), the *Poar* demanded is contingent upon the severity of the violation. In fact, it follows an established criteria focused on the specificity of the crime such as murder without intentional abuse, torture, or murder and abduction of a married woman. The *Poar* system can include, among other forms of exchanges, the gifts of girls for marriage to the victim's family. In addition to *Poar* and the *Nanawati*, the principle of *Enteqam/Pur/Badal* (revenge) is extremely important in such instances. In fact, the following Pashtun saying captures the essence of the responsibility for *Badal*: *Ka cheeri Pakhtun, khapal badal sal kala pas ham wakhle no beya ham-e-bera karay da,* which translates to "if a Pakhtun gets his revenge after 100 years, he is still in a hurry."[52] In *Pashtunwali*, a son, grandson, great grandson or a cousin can exact "revenge" even after several generations.[53] In short, it is the victim's right and responsibility to seek retribution for a crime committed against him or his kin group. Since it is also a matter of honor, failure to seek retribution is understood to be a demonstration of moral weakness not only of the individual who has been wronged but also of his entire kin.[54] It is this right and expectation of retaliation that lies at the heart of the *Pashtunwali*, and while the community does not take collective responsibility for judging and punishing the perpetrator, "public opinion plays a large role in structuring how, on whom, and where one may take revenge legitimately [and] it also lays out mechanisms for resolving such disputes through mediation or arbitration."[55] In cases of blood feuds, communities are also responsible for exerting considerable social pressure through measures such as using external intermediaries, establishing a truce to enable negotiations and to ensure that the cycle of attacks do not continue, or ensuring that a truce is established.[56]

In *Pashtunwali,* heavy emphasis on personal autonomy means that consensus is at the heart of leadership.[57] Public deliberations take place through the

54   Ordinary laws

jirga, an open forum at the village level, where the (voluntary) members, the *Marakchi,* are older and/or respected men, responsible for making decisions on behalf of the entire community, and set policies or adjudicate over a misdemeanor. Because *jirgas* are highly deliberative and "democratic" in nature, the focus is on nominal equality, with the participants sitting in a circle, and binding decisions are reached through common consensus. In the case of dispute resolutions, the *Marakchi* decide on the price, which varies depending on the extent of the damage done.[58] Women are almost entirely excluded from participating in the *jirga* either as members or as disputants; in matters that involve a woman, a male relative generally represents her.[59]

The size of the *jirga* depends often on the scale of the injury. In instances where the parties are from the same lineage and do not have complicated claims, two local elders are generally invited for offering a resolution. In cases where the dispute is more complex and when disputants are more distantly related, "as many as 10 elders may be invited to be judges or *markachian* in the *jirga.*"[60] It is the responsibility of these elders then to carry out an independent investigation and propose a resolution. In case the issue is not resolved, or in the instance that one of the disputing parties disagrees with the conclusions, the next course of redress is the appeals-level *maraka,* which is similar in structure and process to the original *jirga,* but there are more *marakachian* involved including at times a religious figure.[61] If, however, the decision from this appeals-level *maraka* is not considered acceptable, disputants can demand for a *tukhum,* which includes not only representatives from other lineages but also from other Pashtun clans.[62] Generally, although the *tukhum,* like the *jirga* and the *maraca,* does not have enforcement powers, the cost of organizing such a body alone exerts pressure significant pressure for disputing parties to accept the resolution offered in such deliberations.[63]

The *Pashtunwali,* of course, is not the only system of customary law in practice within Afghanistan, and even within its practices there are distinctions regarding rituals of apology and forms of *Poar* within different Pashtun tribes. Barfield, Nojumi, and Thier point out that among the Central Asian Arabs of Kunduz, "the customary law system established links between the villages and governments through the post of the *arbab.*"[64] Selected by either state officials or the local community, the *arbab* is responsible for acting as a mediator between the formal and informal systems through influencing state authorities in cases of criminal violations and helping reduce or even eliminate charges.[65] Similar yet distinct practices of circles of deliberation and consensus building, punishment and forgiveness, and compensatory measures also exist among the Hazarat (known as *Majelisi Qawmi*), the people of Nuristan, and the ethnically diverse provinces of northern Afghanistan among the Tajiks, Uzbeks, Turkmen, and Arabs known as *Shura-I – Islahi/Shura-Qawnii/Majles-Eslahy/Jirgas* and *Mookee Khans*).[66] These traditional mechanisms are not only different in terms of their historicity but often in structure, the type of crimes over which they deliberate and the kind of compensation and forgiveness they proscribe. In *Shura-i-Islahi,* the local clergy plays an important and active role, but the final remedy does not have to

Ordinary laws 55

correspond exclusively with the *Shari'a*.[67] Members in the *shura* include respected community members such as the *wakil* (local government representative), local prominent leaders, and members of the clergy. Similar to *Pashtunwali* practices, in such traditional mechanisms too, women are generally represented by their male relatives. In northern Afghanistan, where Pashtuns, Uzbeks, Turkmen, Tajiks, and Hazaras live in the same village or share land and water, the *shuras* represent the ethnic diversity in the community. A striking difference between *Hazarat* practices of the *Bad* (blood money) and the *Pashtunwali*, is that the former rarely asks for the giving over of girls from one family to another to settle a dispute, particularly when the conflict is between individuals. Unlike in *Pashtunwali*, in *Hazarat* practices, the consent of a woman is also considered critical in the event of marriage. Finally, the Afghan Ismaili Shi'a resolve their differences through the *shura-i-jamaatkhana* (gathering in a place or house) through a *mukhi* (cleric) who acts as an informal judge but who has no law enforcement authority.[68] The *mukhi* is responsible for mediating in matters of family issues but in external and important matters, the head of the village plays the role of the mediator.[69]

Three specific observations emerge in the examination of Afghan customary laws. First, current internationalized efforts have made an effort to consult "Afghan culture," to advance the discussion of transitional justice and legal reform in the country; however, there is no single entity called "Afghan culture," and an overt simplification of a complex historical, social, cultural, and legal landscape does not generate the kind of culturally sensitive understanding that is sorely needed to legitimize external assistance and involvement in Afghanistan. Further, the international focus on the *Pashtunwali* privileges Pashtun customs above the practices of other ethnic groups. Second, while international actors legitimize reconciliation through its exploration of the *jirga* and practices such as *Nanawati*, one might ask where is the equitable attention to *Peor* and *Badal*? How will the questions of justice and restitution be resolved within a framework that privileges forgiveness above all other local considerations? To what extent are the limitations of the traditional practices of the *jirga*, which includes the systematic exclusion of women, and which allows for bartering of women for blood money, be addressed to promote reconciliation? Should Pashtun-based systems take priority over customs of *Nanawati* when trying to mediate between different ethnic groups even when there are notable ethnic and religious tensions between them?

Finally, one could critique the extent to which existing understandings of the *jirga* is limited to examining it as a static entity. Since the 1980s, the relative independence of the *jirgas* was severely constrained by the presence of military commanders whose goals were to control and manage populations through exerting influence through such a mechanism. Further, Nojumi, Mazurana, and Stites claim that during this period, "the practice of customary law was overwhelmed by numerous different interpretations of *Sharia*, led by a new generation of clerics trained in Pakistan."[70] This trend was especially prominent during the Taliban regime given the increasing number of young Afghan men from tribal areas were enrolled in the madrassah in Pakistan. The direct control of the Taliban on the *jirgas* through replacing customary laws with their interpretation of the *Shari'a*,

56 Ordinary laws

constant interference with their functioning and decision-making processes, replacing the word *jirga* with the Arabic term *shura* (council), and appointing the village mullah as the head of the *shura*, further eroded the independence of this traditional practice.[71] Since 2001, *jirgas* have continued to come under the influence of warlords and militia commanders.[72] These developments underscore the critical importance of contextual factors, and underscore that the *jirga* has become potent instruments for powerholders to deliberate on matters in their favor.

Formal legal code, customary laws and the fiqh: *a case of tricky configuration*

Since Afghanistan's establishment as a nation-state in 1747, the central authority has been heavily challenged by the prevalence of competing legal systems, particularly in the outlaying provinces.[73] The resultant scenario has been "a patchwork of differing and overlapping laws, elements of different legal systems and an overall incoherent collection of law enforcement and military structures with extensive diversity and internal dissonance within individual branches and ministries of the Afghan state."[74] The complex pluralism in the legal system has had two obvious consequences. First, it generated general uncertainty among legal practitioners about applicable and procedural laws, knowledge about the organization of the court system and overall deficiency in legal procedures. Second, it resulted in a fragmented complex and confusing legal education system (provided by religious and secular faculties), which in turn produced under-qualified legal practitioners ill-prepared to be in legal practice and prone to providing arbitrary legal decisions. The subsequent struggle has to be appreciated within the context of three broad exigencies: (a) tensions produced because of, and between "legal implants" i.e. "Western" law versus the *fiqh* and customary laws; (b) power struggles between local authorities, tribal councils, and the state-sanctioned uniform criminal code; and (c) the country's record of decentralized government, factionalized politics, localized political authority, discontinuous and violent political regimes, and above all, ongoing conflict.

Since 1919, when King Amanullah attempted to cut back reliance on traditional leaders and increased support for educational reform, the existing and resistant legal system and Western-based secular jurisprudence were set on a collision course. Weinbaum states: "secular law [was] expected to be in harmony with the *Shari'a* and to supplement it, and both overlay indigenous tribal codes or *adat* (customs)."[75] In reality, the secular/Western legal system and the *Shari'a* collided with jurists because of their inability to converse with one another.[76] This clash of competing legal codes was even more pronounced between the urban and rural society, and between the state and the autonomy of local powerholders, particularly the *shura-e-ulema,* amongst whom centralization was never popular. The experience of state-sponsored authoritarianism also generated a lack of distrust for the central government.[77] Furthermore, among local Afghans and traditional authorities, the formal legal structure soon developed a reputation for being elitist. Those who ventured into the system experienced long delays in administrative procedures and were victimized by practices of bribery and corruption. Faced with such obstacles, many Afghans were unwilling to interact with state judicial institutions. Instead, they continued to rely on the traditional institutions of informal justice, a practice that continues till today.

In the 1950s and 1960s, like many other decolonized and decolonizing countries, subjected to the global influx of foreign aid for the purpose of "development,"[78] Afghanistan received significant external funding for education and legal reform that subsequently played a significant role in modernizing the justice system and marginalizing the *Shari'a* significantly.[79] In receiving countries such as Afghanistan, "Euro–American sociolegal norms came to be perceived as Trojan horses of neocolonial projects as brave new forces promoting liberalizing, civilizing processes in the darker corners of the world."[80] In his study of American development lawyers working in Latin American countries in the 1960s and 1970s, James A. Gardner presented a bold criticism of American development lawyers, describing the latter group by the term "legal missionaries."[81] He argued that American-trained lawyers' parochial definitions of law in non-US jurisdictions, lack of consultations with local actors, and inexperience in interacting with the multiplicity of legal actors and layers of law in post- and neocolonial settings was the writing on the wall for the American law and development movement. This "naïve" view of funneling resources to poor countries for immediate development severely neglected social and cultural complexities.[82] In Afghanistan, the normative underpinnings of such efforts also created the grounds for an inevitable confrontation.

The reforms of the 1960s, under King Zahir Shah using foreign funding, witnessed the birth of a "modern" constitution and were influenced by the US Bill of Rights and the Universal Declaration of Human Rights (UDHR).[83] Even though *Shari'a* remained a secondary source for law in the 1964 constitution where Article 69 states "in area [s] where no such law exists, the provisions of the Hanafi jurisprudence of the *Shariaat* of Islam shall be considered as law,"[84] the new constitution included guarantees for fundamental freedoms, including thought, speech, association, and press.[85] It also guaranteed the right of freedom of association[86] and affirmed several basic economic and social rights, among them free education.[87] Further, it prohibited coerced confessions, arbitrary detention, torture, and other forms of punishment incompatible with human dignity, provided guarantees against arbitrary search and seizure[88] and prohibited government surveillance of private communications without a court order.[89]

Initially, the reforms of the 1960s did not alter the traditional moral authority vested in the mullahs and khans in the countryside, or even challenge the existing rural power structure and established agrarian relations. During the entire period of the New Democracy Period[90] and under Daoud, tribal leaders participated in *Loya Jirgas* and they were allowed autonomy to manage local affairs.[91] This changed drastically after the PDPA's seizure of power because one of its main objectives was to instrumentalize the legal system and its affiliated institutions to promote its social and political agendas for a complete social transformation. In particular, the PDPA aimed to "curb the power of local jurists and the authority of Islamic legal reasoning through secularizing administration of the law."[92] It deployed a range of different tactics to achieve this goal – in the rural areas, it imposed radical reforms through

58 *Ordinary laws*

decrees, challenged the local religious leaders' control over family matter and systems of social organization, and even instituted, often by force, new regulations on rural land ownership and tenancy, debt, and customs regulating marriages and bride price.[93] Further, the PDPA regime established "popular committees," under the control of state bureaucrats, to resolve legal disputes about land ownership.[94] Such unpopular measures inevitably led to a series of revolts across the rural countryside, with rural, tribal, and religious leaders joining forces with urban-educated Islamists and non-Pashtun minority leaders to "reject the imposition of alien concepts of state and religion that threatened their power."[95] This clash between the "secularist" PDPA and the "traditionalists" was not simply a "clash of civilizations" or merely a response to overt government intervention in matters of rural society, but also a response to the harsh and brutal response of the PDPA regime to these revolts. Resistance to external forces and ideas, however, did not necessarily mean that there was uniformity between and within the religious civil society in Afghanistan. In the 1980s and the 1990s, a growing polarization emerged between the "modernists" – products of the University of Kabul and in turn influenced by Egyptian (and Pakistani) Islamism and/or inspired by the philosophies of the Al-Ahzar University in Cairo – and the traditionalist" *ulema*, the product of private, home-grown madrassahs.[96] This bifurcation along ideological and political lines was repeated as recently as 2001, with the schism between government supporters (perceived by other *ulema* as political opportunists) and government skeptics (whose main interest was the independence of the *ulema* from government interference).[97]

Under the Taliban regime a new, perverse legal system emerged as a consequence of what could be termed as an "idiosyncratic" interpretation of Islamic law intermingled with the *Pashtunwali*. Under the Taliban legal practices, there was no distinction between criminal and military jurisdictions.[98] They frequently held summary trials and exacted specific penalties (e.g. amputations) for violations of the Islamic penal code for *hudd* crimes and established the infamous Ministry of Enforcement of Virtue and Suppression of Vice (*al-Amr bi al-Ma'ruf wa al-Nahi 'an al- Munkir*), for enforcing all decrees regarding moral behavior, including decrees against imported videos, music, improper haircuts, and women travelling alone, to name a few.

By the time of the Taliban's collapse, the Afghan court system was sharply divided between the *Shari'a* courts and the special courts to deal with matters of the state administration and the economy. This division was also reflected within the legal personnel – judges, lawyers, prosecutors – regarding where they obtained their formal legal education, at the Islamic Law Faculty or the Law and Political Science Faculty at Kabul University.[99] The body of law to be applied depended on the training of judges, except in the case of special statutory courts where judges were trained in the Western legal system and applied statutory law.[100] Judges who were trained in the *fiqh* applied Islamic jurisprudence.[101] While in the 1960s, there was some concerted effort to integrated these two parallel legal systems with a focus on judges' training, little progress was made on this front,[102] and with the beginning of the war in 1978, such efforts were inevitably abandoned.

Ordinary laws   59

Afghanistan's rule of law post-Bonn

The fall of the Taliban and the subsequent Bonn Agreement presented Afghan lawyers and international practitioners of legal reform with a unique opportunity to standardize legal practices in accordance with universal legal norms. In early 2002, based on the "lead" nation model, which allowed for the management of reconstruction activities within a single sector of responsibility by specific countries,[103] Italy was given the responsibility for judicial sector reform. Tensions in the reform project began early. To draft the law, the Italian expert drew extensively for the Italian code without consulting with Afghan officials, who resented their exclusion. In response, they requested President Karzai not sign the draft.[104] To add insult to injury, the Italian Government fully supported their expert and instead threatened to withdraw funding for related projects unless the draft was approved.[105] The struggles of justice sector reform not only exposed the serious weaknesses of a "lead nation approach," but also the inability of Afghanistan to absorb fast-flowing assistance and Italy's own limitations[106] especially given its focus on Western legal tradition and little engagement with Islamic legal norms.[107] Evaluating five years of aid to the justice sector, legal scholar Cherif Bassiouni concluded that "internationally supported rule of law programs tend to ignore or avoid issues of Islamic law [and] this negatively impacts the acceptance of these programs by Afghan society."[108]

There continues to be serious conflict between Western-based laws and the country's customary practices. The country already had a large body of codified laws including the 1975 Afghan Civil Code, the 1976 Criminal Codes, the Amended 1973 Law of Criminal Procedure, and the 1973 Law of Police.[109] It also signed and ratified a number of international legal documents including the Geneva Conventions of 1949, Genocide Convention of 1948, Convention on non-applicability of Statutory Limitations to War Crimes and Crimes Against Humanity of 1968, International Covenant on Civil and Political Rights (ICCPR) of 1966, Convention on the Elimination of all Forms of Racial Discrimination (CERD) of 1966, Convention Against Torture and Other Cruel, Inhuman Degrading Treatment or Punishment (CAT) of 1984, Convention on the Rights of the Child (CRC) of 1989 and the Convention on the Elimination of Discrimination Against Women (CEDAW) of 1979.[110] However, since the Afghan constitution recognizes the pre-eminence of *Shari'a* in all legal matters, the country's secular commitments constitute a formidable challenge when it comes to, for example, the confrontation between CEDAW and CAT. There are other areas of contention. In cases of murder, the *jirga* may recommend *badal* or the marriage of a woman from the par (perpetrator's) tribe to the victim's close relative, which is a serious violation of both the *Shari'a* and international human rights law. Under an interpretation of the *Shari'a*, a rape victim needs to produce four male witnesses; for the commission of a crime, a perpetrator's limb needs to be cut off. These practices are in direct conflict with Afghan state laws and its international legal obligations.

60 *Ordinary laws*

Additional challenges

A critical component of the rule of law, the Afghan police, also face significant challenges. As of June 2010, ANP forces numbered at 104,459.[111] It comprises of several distinct entities operating under the direction of the Interior Ministry including the Afghan Uniformed Police (AUP), responsible for general police duties, and the specialized police organizations of the Afghan National Civil Order Police (ANCOP), the Afghan Border Police (ABP), the Afghan Highway Police (AHP), the Counter Narcotics Police of Afghanistan (CNPA), the Counter Terrorism Police (CTP) and the Standby Police (SP). By 2002, it was evident that a vast majority of the police force was untrained, ill-equipped, illiterate, and loyal to warlords and local commanders.[112] Further, many were former mujahideen whose past experiences of acting with impunity should have, in an ideal setting, disqualified them for being too poorly equipped to act as officers of the law. Further, the police are also heavily implicated in the country's struggle against the explosion of organized crime and drug cartels. A 2007 extensive study on the ANP conducted on the Afghan police by the AREU found that police were routinely accused of being corrupt and operating on an "arrest, bribe and release" basis; of violating human rights through arbitrary and illegal detentions; cruel, inhuman, and degrading treatment of prisoners, including torture; and of being involved in criminal activities including theft, kidnapping, extortion, and drug trafficking.[113] At a June 2008 USIP event in Washington DC, Afghan Attorney General Sabbit summarized the pressing problems of corruption and the realities of impunity in the following:

> [W]hat makes it difficult for us to strengthen the rule of the law in the country is the corruption – corruption in the law enforcement agency – in the police and even within the Prosecutor's Office. Corruption has helped a lot of criminals, a lot of terrorists, a lot of drug dealers to get away with their crimes they have committed. But this is not the only challenge. We do not have a complete rule of law in Afghanistan... because, we have warlords, who consider themselves above the law, they do whatever they want to do and we cannot touch them... it is always an exercise of their will, not of law.[114]

Finally, a few words on Afghanistan's legal infrastructure are necessary. Many of the Afghan courts are non-functional; a vast majority of them are understaffed and ill-equipped. The Ministry of Justice and the University of Kabul do not have complete sets of Afghanistan's main statutory laws, and judges, lawyers, educational institutions, and even most courts even do not have access to them[115] The challenges of corruption, low salaries and delays in salaries for legal professionals have not dissipated, thereby failing to generate any form of confidence in the official legal system. The existing legal system is "highly fragmented with little or no contact between the judiciary, the police, the prosecution, and the prison/correction service."[116] Last, but not least, many of the training programs and facilities for legal practitioners continue to be concentrated in the capital, leaving most of

Ordinary laws   61

Afghanistan outside of the formal legal structure, and subsequently engendering their continued dependence on informal mechanisms of justice and arbitration.

Nepal: from customary laws to a secular legal code

An understanding of the Nepali legal system requires an examination of the historical trajectory of the Nepal state, the role of the Hindu monarchy, the *dharmadhikara* (the owner of justice), and pundits in codifying its legislation.[117] In fact, similar to Muslim societies in their situating the place of *Shari'a* in society, laws in Nepal were considered to be a branch of religion.[118] Like Afghanistan, Nepal's engagement with a Western-based code is fairly recent. Until about half a century ago, its laws were primarily based on a complex interplay of social customs, values, cultural practices, Hindu legal texts, and royal edicts.[119] Thapa states: "Traditional concepts of fairness and impartiality under the laws of religion were the basic rules of justice."[120] Nepal's official legal system, however, has precedence over its customary practices, and unlike in Afghanistan, its secular legal code did not encounter the same kind of resistance. A second difference between the two countries is the position and importance attached to customary practices in the constitutional framework. While Article 3(1) of the CoA establishes the pre-eminence of Islamic laws above all others, Nepal's contemporary claim as a secular state privileges international legal standards above that of domestic laws. Third, there is significant literature today on the *Shari'a, fiqh,* and in the case of Afghanistan, about the *Pashtunwali.* Much remains to be known about the complex legal customs in Nepal, home to 61 ethnic groups and 45 indigenous populations living within a complex hierarchy of caste and ethnicity, and within a context of Hindu, Buddhist, Islamic, Kiranti, Jainism and other religious beliefs and their corresponding sociocultural norms.

The development of the Nepali state took place in three phases: (i) the Shah and Rana periods (1768–1846 and 184–1951, respectively); (ii) the Panchayat period (1960–90); and (iii) the period of multi-party democracy (1990–onwards).[121] During the period of Prithivi Narayan Shah, under whom Nepal was united as a political entity in 1768, the king was considered to be the source and foundation of law and justice and Brahmin (highest caste) pundits were responsible for their implementation.[122] The Shah also first initiated an aggressive policy of Hinduisation and centralization of state power. Under this policy Hindus were afforded the highest status in society and the premier posts of the state were the exclusive preserve of the *Tharghar* (comprising of the groups of *Pande, Pant, Bohara, Aryal, Khanal, and Rana*).[123] This deeply political move formalized the historically and categorically problematic Brahmanic philosophy and practice of law and justice where the *Brahmin* and *Chetris* were privileged,[124] and officially ensured that the concept of equality did not exist in legal and judicial practices. This had (and continues to have) severe implications for people of the "lower" castes and for women. Brahmanic principles, particularly relating to family laws, are singularly and blatantly patriarchal, for example, it strictly prohibits women from owning property, having access to inheritance or, for example, the

62   Ordinary laws

remarriage of widows. For *Dalit* women, Brahmanic laws have constituted a double discrimination leading inevitably to less access to education, health care, and employment opportunities.[125]

The Rana system that emerged since 1846 first introduced some form of Western influence on the multiple legal practices and customs in Nepal. In 1851, impressed with the English and French legal infrastructure, Jung Bahadur Rana appointed an *Ain Kausal* (Law Council) to institute a unified legal code, comprising of royal decree orders, *seals, sanad, sawal, rokka, istihar*,[126] customs, and traditions. The formal country code that resulted in 1854 came to be known as the *Muluk Ain* (MA).[127] In his 1979 landmark study, Hofer argued that the code was "in order to protect the truncated state from British menace, security screen against the outside world…to relegitimize the identity of Nepal and to motivate the solidarity of her citizens."[128] The code also provided a social order as a basis for a centralized agrarian bureaucracy while simultaneously cementing the privileges and authority of the state elites.[129] Finally, it drew the lines between Nepal and other "foreign societies and cultures by defining it as a specifically Nepalese 'national' caste hierarchy," with a political objective of creating a homogenous society.[130] Finally, according to Hofer, the code's overall conservative and authoritarian tone was instrumental in strengthening the Rana rule.[131]

Overall, the MA "provided provisions relating to administrative law, land law, regulation for the management of revenues administration, and land survey."[132] It also tried to define the legal relations in terms of *Kul* (Kin group), *Santan* (family lineage), *Jat* (caste) and *Linga* (sex).[133] The 1854 MA conformed to the principle of ethnic purity, which has its roots in the Hindu *Manusmriti*,[134] and accordingly gave legal sanction to the "hinduization" of indigenous nationalities, despite their more egalitarian traditional social structures, and brought them under the ambit of Hindu laws, customs, and ritual purity. In short, the MA was the first and most comprehensive effort to codify diverse legal customs pertaining to ethnic groups and caste-based practices based on Hindu jurisprudence, resulting in an institutionalization of untouchability and caste hierarchy.[135] In reality, Hoffer argued, the claim of the MA as the ultimate homogenous legislation for the entire political entity of Nepal could be open to question because different groups were either openly or tacitly given a certain degree of autonomy, and local traditions including those relating to marriage, kinship, sexuality, residence, and inheritance were given the status of customary law with jurisdiction in the hands of village councils.[136] The 1854 MA also laid out varying degrees of punishment for the same offence based on caste affiliation such that, for instance, while *Bahun Chhetris* were protected indigenous communities, *Dalits* and women were severely punished for the commission of the same crimes. Cultural practices of indigenous groups were further denigrated by the upper caste.[137] In keeping with the effort to institutionalize caste hierarchy, any *Bahun Chhetri* who married a "low caste" woman was punished by being deprived of his property and, "after being forced to eat pork, was demoted to the alcohol-drinking *matawali* caste."[138]

The collapse of the Rana Regime in 1951 provided the first real opportunity to revise several of the laws within the MA. In 1963, the new MA emerged "based on the principle of legal equality and removing caste and religious considerations."[139] It not only provided a common criminal and civil code for Hindus, Buddhists, Muslims, and other groups of different religious persuasions but also finally addressed family matters such as in marriage, adoption, inheritance, and succession. It simultaneously abolished the premises of discrimination and "untouchability" and recognized the customary practices of certain indigenous communities;[140] however, the new code continued to perpetuate gender segregation and gender-based discrimination.[141] Gilbert, in particular, compellingly argues that first, the existing MA grants or denies rights based on women's social and familial status and affinities, and generates a social climate where women are unable or unwilling to threaten their long-term interests as members of families with specific roles in a subsistence economy.[142] Arguably, the newest revision of the code introduced the concept of a single system of family law, which allowed for some progressive and radical changes, such as the enforcement of laws against traditional practices as child marriage, bigamy, marital battery, arbitrary divorce, denial of support, and loss of custodial rights to minor children.[143] The MA not only discriminates against non-Hindu communities, but also:

> directly discriminates against women by establishing property and kinship relationships that emphasize the rights of the agnatic[144] kin group over the women affiliated with it, by treating women as peripheral and dependent members of such groups, and by limiting the rights of women to important property forms such as *aungsa* (ancestral property).[145]

Second, the code reveals Nepali society's overt emphasis on women's sexual and marital status. Gilbert outlines that women are categorized based on *kanya* (virgin), *bihe nagareko* (never married), *bihe gareko* (married), *liyaeko* (brought but not formally married), *bahira rakeko* (kept secretly and outside the home), *poila gaiyo* (having eloped), *satya dagaune* (unfaithful), *vidhva* (widowed), *sadhya* (married, with a living husband), *buhari* (daughter-in-law) and *vidhva buhari* (widowed daughter-in-law), *amma* (mother) or *chora hune* and *chora nahune* (with or without sons).[146] Each of these terms defines and limits the level of access, control, and authority women have over property, family status, and inheritance. Third, according to Gilbert, because property ownership is defined by gender and family status rather than the consequence of human labor, women's labor under the code is rendered invisible.[147]

Nepal's constitutions have also undergone significant changes during its different periods in history, thereby institutionalizing secularist principles within legal practices. Since 1948, Nepal has had six constitutions, including the Constitution of 1962, which dismissed the parliamentary system and introduced the far less democratic four-tiered Panchayat system,[148] and the 1992 Constitution, which introduced multiparty parliamentary democracy but recognized Nepal to be a Hindu Kingdom. But it is the Interim Constitution of 2007, which followed the success of the People's Movement II, that has most comprehensively recognized the complex and varied demographics in the country. Article 3 of the

64 Ordinary laws

Interim Constitution of Nepal declares: "Having multi-ethnic, multi-lingual, multi-religious, multi-cultural characteristics with common aspirations, and being committed to and united by a bond of allegiance to national independence, integrity, national interest and prosperity of Nepal, all the Nepali people collectively constitute the nation."[149] Further, Article 4 consolidates the place of secularism and inclusivity in stating Nepal is now "an independent, indivisible, sovereign, secular, inclusive and fully democratic State."[150]

Customary laws remain prevalent across Nepal, particularly among indigenous communities of Nepal who practice a communal system of ownership known as *Kipat,* one of the fundamental pillars of a tribe's autonomy. Such laws influence matters as wide-ranging as resource ownership, management and allocation, systems of governance, dispute resolution mechanisms, traditional methods of food, drink and spices preparations, medicinal practices, hairstyles, meat-cutting techniques, preservation of natural and genetic resources, dietary restrictions, languages, care of historical sites, resources management and distribution, knowledge-sharing, grazing, animal tracking systems, weather patterns, and environmental and biodiversity conservation.[151] The following section takes a more in-depth look at such practices.

Traditional dispute resolution

While there is notably limited literature on the different forms of traditional dispute mechanisms in Nepal's highly diverse ethnic communities, a discussion of justice nevertheless merits an exploration of such practices. While the decade-long People's War had a direct impact on both state and customary laws, in several cases forcing their retreat, certain customary traditions, functioning as unwritten law, continue to govern the lives of different ethnic communities in Nepal.

Among tribal communities in the country, there is a strong pattern of kinship groups with a particular emphasis on lineage. The lineage generates a wider social group, the clan, which in turn constitutes the tribe, comprising of people belonging to different lineages but speaking the same language and following the same traditions.[152] The leader in each group is selected based on seniority, knowledge, and his leadership quality, and he is accountable to the leader of the clan, who in turn is accountable to the tribal assembly and the tribe. The *Choho* and *Bang* (members and chief) of the tribal assembly are elected annually. The *Bang* and tribal assembly "control territories including meadows, farmland, forests, lakes, waters and other property of the group, allocates land for slash and burn (swidden) agriculture, arbitrates disputes and imposes punishment to control the behavior of group members."[153] Consensus building plays a critical role in matters of punishment and reconciliation, and group relations determine a series of well-defined rights and obligations for members of the group. Customary laws themselves are a product of the combination of religious and magical beliefs, notions of collective responsibility, and fears of ridicule and ostracism. Observance of all traditional norms is secured through a system of sanctions that may vary according to the degree of kinship, and forms of punishment can range from censure, to fines, to

Ordinary laws 65

ostracism or even expulsion from the group. The fear that the spirit of ancestors will unfailingly punish offenders also ensures compliance with society's rules. Where an offense has already been committed, legal compensation is urged to avoid the spiritual retribution that could befall the offender.

The concept of collective responsibility is particularly important to systems of customary law sanction. Under collective responsibility, all clansmen are responsible for one another's actions and each is bound to protect the others. Thus collective responsibility serves to deter unnecessary wrongdoing because of the inherent belief that any offense committed by a clansman may be avenged against any member of the clan. In addition, it increases the deterrent effect of expulsion as a form of punishment because an offender who has been expelled can no longer count on the support and protection of his ethnic group. Finally, collective sanctions put the offender out of status such that he is not in a position to participate in communal activities until his offense has been purged and his status restored. Under the notion of collective responsibility, all these sanctions are not limited to the individual but can apply also to his children, spouse, relatives, and even his clansmen.

Historically, in Nepal, dispute resolutions have taken the shape of mediation by community leaders, decision-making processes by community leaders, and the practice of *Divya Pariksha* (Ordeal).[154] Each of these was a flawed process, in that privilege, power, and decision-making authority were in the hands of exclusively male higher-caste pundits and local landlords. Traditional dispute mechanisms can range from addressing matters such as irrigation practices and questions of land, to family and other disputes, in which case they adopt a more mediation-based role; however, unlike the traditional *jirgas* and *shura* in Afghanistan, Nepal's experience with "community-based" mediation on a more egalitarian platform and on a diverse range of issues have been externally introduced, and have been donor-driven and designed.[155] In general, such traditional mechanisms are particular to specific ethnic groups, religious communities and even people of different castes. In the Banke District, in the mid-western development region of Nepal, which comprises mainly of the Tharu community, the informal dispute resolution mechanism that handles communities' security and justice concerns is the *badghar*; however, Muslims in the same district rely on the *maulana* for the resolution of any conflict. Jumla, an ancient Khas state[156] and today one of the poorest districts heavily affected by the conflict, widely uses the *kachahari* system. It consists of a village "court," traditionally presided over by the village elder(s), usually male, where cases are presented and decisions are made and announced to the assembled villagers. Nowadays, *kachahari* elders also consult other sectors of the community when making their decision, including women's groups and political parties.[157] In the Kailali district, while the Tharu communities use the *badghar*, the Raji communities seek to resolve disputes on justice and security through the *bhalmansa*; both rarely approach formal justice system for assistance. In the Siraha district in the eastern development region, where there is a significant Dalit population, most people, because of questions of geographical distance and because of the biases of the formal sector, turn to

66 *Ordinary laws*

their *mukhiya* (village leader) or political leaders to resolve their family and land disputes. In Nawalparasi, the southern part of the western development region, the Muslim communities have their own traditional justice mechanisms, while non-Muslim communities rely on the village elder for dispute resolution. In each of these districts, the role of paralegal organizations and NGOs in dispute resolution has become increasingly prominent, underscoring Nepalis continual distrust of formal state mechanisms. In Banke, local communities rely on the services provided by paralegal communities, community mediation centers, NGOs working on violence against women such as SAATHI, which provides counseling and shelters for women survivors. The formal justice sector remains the place of last resort. Similarly in Jumla, people look to paralegal committees, the women's groups set up by the Women's Development Office (WDO) and village-level peace groups because they are cheap, accessible, and responsive while having local legitimacy. Women in particular seek out women's groups for issues of their concern because they find state mechanisms highly inaccessible.[158] Similarly to Kailali, in Nawalparasi, outside of the village elder, people turn to NGOs or *amma samuha* (mother's group); in Siraha, outside of NGOs and women's groups, people also seek assistance from Women's Human Rights Defenders (WHRDs) and women's security pressure groups.[159]

Increasingly, there has been effort to incorporate such traditional dispute resolution mechanisms within the local government. In some civil cases, the Local Self-Governance Act 1999 (LSGA) has elaborate provisions for mediation and arbitration to be carried out by Village Development Committees (VDC) and Municipal Development Committees (MDC), although the decade-long conflict, conflict, pressure by the CPN-M to stop community-based traditional dispute resolution mechanisms, and political developments since the CPA have slowed such efforts.[160]

Clearly, on certain civil matters, there is still much to be learned about how traditional dispute mechanisms can continue to enhance and support the formal legal structure in Nepal; however, in matters of criminal justice relating to killings, arbitrary executions, torture, rape, and displacement during the period of war, questions remain about how much mechanisms could be harnessed to pursue the goals of transitional justice, particularly that of reconciliation. Nevertheless, given Nepal's history of power hierarchy and the disenfranchisement of Dalits, the landless, the *janajatis*, and women in traditional practices, its recent history with the CPN-M's arbitrary and often dangerously flawed People's Courts, and its current politicization of grass-roots peace committees, there is justifiable concerns about to what extent such traditional mechanisms can effectively deliver on justice.

Criminalizing human rights violations: the glaring gaps in the formal legal code

The *Nepali Brihyat Sabdhakosh*, the root dictionary for Nepali, does not recognize the term *dandahinta* – which, according to human rights activists, is the Nepali synonym for impunity.[161] *Dandahinta* itself is fairly new and gained currency with the explosion of human rights activism in recent years. A few terms could

Ordinary laws 67

possibly come close – *ucchrinkal* (meaning one unfettered by rules and discipline, or out of control) and *uddhanda* (insinuating one who seeks to exert control over others even with the use of force and does not fear retribution).[162] Neither term, even collectively, captures the depth and magnitude of its equivalence in English. Impunity continues to be a challenge for Nepali society where the powerful and the connected have always been privileged.

Ironically, however, Nepal is a country of formal laws, with a history of eagerly engaging with and adopting international human rights treaties, even while its citizens lack a widespread understanding of, and are denied the benefits from, the international human rights discourse. As a fledgling democracy in 1990, Nepal ratified all major international human rights treaties, including the ICCPR and its first Optional Protocol, the Convention on Economic Social and Cultural Rights (ECOSOC), the CAT, the CRC and the CEDAW. Nepal's parliament passed the 1990 Treaty Act, which stipulated that international human rights treaties ratified by Nepal should be applied as national law. But unlike Afghanistan where international laws and *Shari'a* need to be in conformity for their application, Nepal's Act instructs that international laws can supersede national laws if the latter are inconsistent with the former.

One could argue that what Nepal mainly suffers from is not necessarily a lack of laws, but the absence of their implementation. A representation of a local NGO, the PD, put this succinctly in the following observation: "We are signatories to many laws but very weak in their execution…so its very contradictory – signing conventions but not holding the laws to those standards."[163] But outside of implementation, there are serious gaps that merit attention. One of the major problems Nepali human rights organizations and victims face is that several of the human rights abuses detailed in First Information Reports (FIR) have not been prohibited in the Interim Constitution; further, existing Nepali criminal law does not specify some of these abuses as distinct crimes. A representative of the Kathmandu-based public interest NGO, Human Rights and Democratic Forum (FOHRID) reflected: "Such *lacunae* not only limits the reach of law and the activism of legal practitioners, but also meets with political apathy and issues a *carte blanche* to authorities for not investigating and prosecuting such crimes."[164] The absence of criminalization of enforced disappearances is a good illustration of this.

A second legal *lacuna* is with regard to torture. Nepal ratified the CAT on 14 April 1991, just after the restoration of parliamentary democracy in 1990. The 1990 Constitution enshrined the freedom from torture as a fundamental right of the citizens. Article 14(4) of the 1990 constitution expressly prohibited "physical and mental torture" and "cruel, inhuman or degrading treatment," the first time this principle was recognized in the Nepali Law.[165] This constitutional provision also required that "persons subjected to torture shall be compensated in a manner determined by law."[166] Further, the ratification of CAT in 1991 created some important obligations including provisions that no exceptional circumstances, whether a war or a threat or war, internal political instability or any other public emergency, may be invoked as a justification of torture. Further, an order from

68 Ordinary laws

a superior officer or a public authority may not be invoked as a justification of torture[167] and all acts of torture are offenses under its criminal law and should be punishable by appropriate penalties that take into account their grave nature.[168] Despite these constitutional and international legal obligations, the practice of torture in Nepal is not only rampant, but also significantly increased between 1990 and 2005. Since 1991, the UN Committee Against Torture received only two reports from the Nepali Government. The first is the preliminary report on December 16, 1993;[169] the second was a periodical report on January 14, 2005.[170] Most recently, in 2007, the Committee Against Torture again reminded the GoN of the most basic obligations that it had failed to meet since 1991 in the following statement:

> The State Party should adopt domestic legislation which ensures that acts of torture, including the acts of attempt, complicity and participation, are criminal offences punishable in a manner proportionate to the gravity of the crimes committed, and consider steps to amend the Compensation Relating to Torture Act of 1996 to bring it into compliance with all the elements of the definition of torture provided in the convention.[171]

Nepal has yet to meet these basic requirements. Torture still does not violate criminal law and no one to date has been prosecuted for committing torture. The only existing recourse for victims is the provision of "physical assault" in the MA, which stops short of covering torture used by security forces, who continue to be one of its main users.[172] The 1996 Torture Compensation Act (TCA), the formal parliamentary enactment initiated by the GoN following the CAT ratification and the 1990 constitutional ratification, has been of little relevance in the practical protection of human rights, mainly because fear and intimidation faced by victims' prevents them from going to the courts for compensation. One of the examples cited by Amnesty International (AI) shows that, "during 1998, 12 people claimed compensation. Of these 12 people, six later withdrew their cases because of intimidation and fear for their safety."[173] Moreover, even if compensation is provided, it occurs in exchange for impunity.[174]

The existing legal system in Nepal is further undermined both by the glaring absence of clear statutes and the subsequent absence of any means of inquiry to look into cases of "wrongful" deaths or inhumane treatment. The State Cases Act (SCA) is a prime example. While the Act lays out the procedures for the investigation and prosecution of cases where a state authority is a party to a case filed, it does not specify the necessary measures for state authorities when security forces are implicated in the case of a "suspicious" death. Consequently, the police, public prosecutors, and other agencies can leave serious crimes uninvestigated, often in limbo, for years using specious justifications. This continues to be one of the main reasons why Nepal has not yet been able to ensure independent investigations in many cases of wrongful or suspicious deaths. Further, in the absence of an inquiry procedure under an independent authority, such as a legal or court officer, victims' bodies can "disappear" without any post-mortem examination.[175]

Ordinary laws   69

A significant source of concern for the Nepal human rights community continues to be the excessive use of force used by security forces. From a legal standpoint, proponents of the need for force argue that the security forces are not breaking the law. The 1971 Local Administration Act (LAA) provides the legal framework for the use of force by state apparatus including the use of lathi (batons), blankshots, tear gas, and water canon depending on the situation.[176] If the crowd does not disperse, the police may open fire upon a written order from the Chief District Officer (CDO) after issuing a warning to the crowd.[177] It also permits the CDO to direct the police to prevent any gatherings likely to result in a breach of public order.[178] During the April 2006 *Jano Andalon*, such actions by security forces were well documented by organizations such as OHCHR-N.[179]

At the height of the state of emergency between November 2001 and August 2002, the RNA extensively invoked the TADO. TADO allowed the use of "necessary force or weapon" for a range of situations including if "any person or group with or without weapon hinder security force(s) while obeying their duty."[180] The Police Act of 1955 is another example of a law that provides immunity for CDOs or for any police personnel "for action taken...in good faith while discharging... duties."[181] It contains no provisions that establish individual criminal liability for extrajudicial executions, disappearances, arbitrary detention, torture, or ill treatment. HRW states:

> the only provision that comes close addressing responsibility for human rights abuses is section 34(n), which makes a police official liable for up to five years of imprisonment and up to one year suspension of salary if, "he unjustly harasses any person through arrogance or intimidation or causes loss or damage to the property of any person."[182]

There are two additional acts that local and international human rights organizations have identified as significant areas of concern that provide protection to perpetrators rather than protect the rights of civilians – the Army Act of 1959 and the 2006 new Army Act. In fact, neither the 1959 Act nor any other law stipulates that the army is required to release full and complete details of court-martial proceeding, including information about any FIR, criminal investigations or any judgment. HRW's 2008 report *Waiting for Justice* explains that although "the 1959 Army Act has a provision requiring a court of inquiry board and a court martial for any violations of the Act,"[183] which allows, in principle, making soldiers accountable for human rights abuses, this has only been evoked for a few cases such as the killings at Doramba and the torture, disappearance, and Maina Sunuwar's death in custody.[184] The Public Security Act (PSA) of 1989 is another illustration of the existing weakness in the legal system. The Act was used extensively during the April 2006 *Jano Andalon* to arrest thousands of suspected members and sympathizers of the CPN-M and members of mainstream political parties, but it has yet to be revised or even amended despite criticisms by human rights lawyers and activists in the country.

70   *Ordinary laws*

Nepal's current MA also has significant weaknesses. Under it, judges do not have the adequate authority to ascertain that security forces and other state organs cooperate wholly with the courts. Habeas corpus cases particularly have suffered because of existing defects in Nepal's law on perjury and contempt of court. For example, "while witnesses can be liable for perjury under Section 169 of the MA, government officials are not considered witnesses; [consequently] state officials, including security forces personnel, cannot be sanctioned if they fail to tell the truth."[185] Furthermore, given that habeas corpus petitions can only be filed at Appellate Court or Supreme Court level, the stark absence of sufficient courts and the remoteness of areas where atrocities took place, relatives often have to travel for days before they can lodge a petition. This has special bearing in cases of "disappearances" because district courts are not mandated to hear habeas corpus writs.[186]

Auxiliary forces: the NP

One of the continuing sources of concern regarding impunity in Nepal has been the security sector, both the army and the police. These concerns have related to the result of deploying armed forces in areas to quell the conflict, but in Nepal, apprehension about the armed forces stems also from their code of conduct during "peace" times. The NP in particular has come under severe scrutiny in this regard. It continues to have a reputation of unprofessionalism marked by high levels of corruption in recruitment,[187] endorsement of transfers,[188] misuse in the provision of opportunities to travel, failures in case registration, collection of evidence, interrogation, arrest, and in the presentation of cases to court.[189] In some instances, the NP has been recorded offering money and bribes to victims' families to drop charges rather than filing FIRs through the proper channels. In other cases, even if FIRs were registered, there has been no progress on investigations. The politicizing of police institutions has ultimately undermined the capacity of the police to operate effectively or within the limits of the law and has contributed to institutionalized impunity.[190] This political interference has more than often resulted in offenders being granted amnesty in peace times, and also for the crimes committed during the period of conflict.[191]

An overview of developments as recently as 2009 indicate that an overwhelming number of cases show continuing obfuscation and failure by state authorities to initiate meaningful investigations relating to past grave human rights abuses. The Maina Sunuwar case is a rare exception where the authorities filed charges, and then only under the pressure of sustained campaigning and litigation, but to date the police have not arrested the suspects.[192]

The Nepali military has its own sphere of influence when it comes to ordinary law enforcement. In fact, according to International Crisis Group's (ICG) 2009 report, an important factor for the lack of effective investigations is the *esprit de corps* between the army and the police.[193] Other reasons include instructions from higher police officers not to investigate cases involving soldiers; fear that the government might change and the army might again seize power, putting police officers at risk; and considerable difference in rank between the junior police officers often responsible for these investigations and senior army officers named in the FIRs. Additional structural factors echo not only Afghanistan's experience but that of societies transitioning out of conflict: low reporting of incidences, lack of confidence in the system, insufficient capacity, lack of accountability, and weak monitoring mechanisms. The lack of incentives and the absence of vertical and horizontal coordinating mechanisms among the police stations, government attorneys, police, civil society, and the media serve as a deterrent to the rule of law. There is also the lack of cooperation in the presentation of evidence before court, insufficient record keeping, poor management and communication, poor laboratory services, and the lack of compliance with judicial orders. Since the signing of the CPA, the lack of progress on security sector reform continues to be one of the main threats to the Nepali peace process.

Technical challenges

Nepal's legal system also has a range of other formidable challenges. First, the statute of limitations serves as a serious impediment to seeking justice, particularly in cases of rape and sexual violence. Second, there are inadequate measures to protect witnesses. Nepal is also plagued by corruption within the judiciary and law enforcement forces that makes justice a commodity that goes to the highest bidder. In Afghanistan, warlords and militia commanders are beyond the reach of the law, whilst in Nepal, politicization of the judiciary and its auxiliary branches continue to be a significant hindrance to legal access. A spokesperson from the directorate of Public Relations of the Nepali army reflected: "the police are overtly politicized; they can get promotions depending on who they know within political parties; such parties also provide protection to criminal gangs...all of this means a very weak enforcement of law and order."[194]

Finally, there are too few judges, lawyers, and law enforcement agencies outside Kathmandu. Consequently, "people in remote areas either cannot access the legal system, or cannot access it on time to file a FIR (because of the statute of limitations) resulting in a dependence on parallel structures of justice."[195] The limited number of lawyers and judges, many of whom are poor quality, do little to inspire confidence in an already fragile and often ineffective legal system. A rule of law specialist with Asia Foundation-Nepal (AF-N) summarized his analysis as follows:

> The lawyers here are so bad. They are keen to take as long as possible on any case so as to make as much money as possible. The sort of negative stereotype of divorce lawyers, its all over here. It's a sad state of affairs. Using mediators is a much better way to resolve disputes than through the court system in this country.[196]

Ordinary laws in extraordinary times: a site for mobilization

Given the scope and magnitude of impunity in both Afghanistan and Nepal, the law has become a critical site for mobilization for greater protection for the civilians. This kind of activism is motivated by a terse logic – more laws mean greater

72 Ordinary laws

accountability; and the philosophy of inverse proportionality – the greater the number of laws, the lower the possibility of impunity. A significant site for mobilization for both Afghan and Nepal human rights actors and lawyers has been the Rome Statute for the ICC. Since February 10, 2003, Afghanistan has been a signatory to the Rome Statute, and in recent years, this has brought together Afghan lawyers and civil society actors to push the GoA for compliance with its international commitments. In Afghanistan, the local Afghanistan Watch (AW) has taken its leadership role seriously, acting as the Afghan member of the international coalition for the ICC in this regard. Although in its infant stages, AW in its first major activity held a comprehensive consultative meeting in October 2009, bringing together the AIHRC, representatives of the Afghanistan's judicial sectors, including representatives of the justice sector and Taqnin, the legislative department of the Ministry of Justice (MoJ), civil institutions, legal experts, and representatives of international human rights organizations. The focus of the meeting and the ensuing discussions on compliance with ICC has not been with a focus on the question of "transitional justice" per se, but rather on amending national criminal laws. Thus, for example, Afghan lawyers have been pushing their government to take on the legal responsibility to investigate and prosecute the crimes listed in Articles 6, 7, and 8 as per the requirement of the Rome Statute. They also look to the standards of fair trial outlined in the Statute to push for a revision of the national laws dealing with prosecutions.

A significant gap in Afghanistan's legal system today is the right of suspects and accused persons detailed in Articles 66, 67, and 85, the protection of victims and witnesses outlined in Paragraph 3 of Article 68 and their right to compensation in Article 75 of the Rome Statute. According to Afghan law, these specific legal *lacunae* demand immediate attention to strengthen Afghanistan's criminal procedural law, criminal law, law governing crimes against Internal and External Security of the Country, and the Law of Detecting and Investigating Administrative Offences.

In contrast to Afghanistan, Nepal has yet to sign the Rome Statute. But the current transitional period has provided a unique opportunity for Nepali legal actors and general human rights activists to push for Nepal's accession to the ICC community. While there is recognition that the Rome Statute will not have an retroactive effect, since its establishment in 2001, the National Coalition for the International Criminal Court (NCICC), a loosely established coalition of human rights NGOs, media, lawyers, and academics coordinated by the local Informal Sector Service Center (INSEC) and the Nepal Bar Association (NBA), have been actively involved in putting pressure on the Nepali Government to ratify the Statute. The NCICC in particular has conducted educational and promotional campaigns to build support for the ratification, which have included working with members of parliament (MPs), bureaucrats, and other stakeholders. The ratification, both NCICC and NBA argue, would strengthen Nepal's existing laws in accordance with international standards. More importantly, the ratification would ultimately bring about changes in the legislative process that would "promote accountability, place the Nepal Army personnel under the jurisdiction of civilian courts, criminalize torture and ensure that blanket amnesties are not granted for serious human rights violations."[197]

A striking distinction between Afghanistan and Nepal is the state and strength of civil society, particularly when one refers to contemporary official non-state organizations as opposed to more traditional associations and networks. Rights-based advocacy organizations have had a longer history in Nepal, particularly since its first democratic shift in 1990. The resultant professionalization, specialization, and advocacy skills has meant that the human rights movement in Nepal has been, even in times of conflict, notably strong. It is also this reality that has allowed for a significant mobilization around "transitional justice" by Nepal's human rights community. In particular, human rights and legal NGOs have particularly mobilized around the commitments made in the CPA – the Disappearance Commission and the TRC – and for the criminalization of torture, providing recommendations on the draft laws for the commissions and pushing for anti-torture legislation, while simultaneously filing FIRs on behalf of victims of conflict.

Conclusion

This chapter discussed a component of justice – the law – and examined its relationship to transitional justice. Fundamentally, it underscored that the law's position in transitional contexts is unique because of the dualistic roles they are expected to fulfill i.e. *retroactive* justice to underscore the criminality of war's excesses and *proactive* or *successive* justice to create a new set of rules to determine the impermissibility of certain acts even during times of peace. The blurring of the lines between past and present justice stressed that because law derives legitimacy from past events, inherits problems from the past and strives to fulfill past promises, justice cannot be simply an auxiliary component of the peacebuilding process but is one of the fundamental pillars of the transitional process.[198] The chapter also presented some crucial distinctions between the two emerging legal systems: Afghanistan where the tensions between parallel legal codes often overshadow the functionality of the courts and impede justice deliverance, and Nepal where legal *lacunae* has consistently ensured that those in power use excessive ways to suppress the Nepali population. These distinctions are critical because they question the formulaic prescriptions of "rule of law" and "transitional justice" offered to countries trying to emerge from conflict.

Finally, the local contexts in both countries are neither unitary entities nor static institutions. The resistance to "legal implants" in Afghanistan was not simply a consequence of rejecting a Western-styled framework, but also a response to the brutal ways in which the PDPA attempted to secularize the legal–political system. It was also a result of the severe rifts between capital-centric elite and the agrarian society. Both are components of the "dynamic local." Further, the vulnerability of the *jirgas* to manipulation by military commanders, and later the Taliban and warlords, underscore that traditional practices are not ahistorical or independent of political factors at play, but rather that they may be manipulated to

74 *Ordinary laws*

serve the interests of powerholders. Finally, the chapter also highlighted that in a context where there are deep-rooted tensions between different ethnic groups, the overt focus on *Pashtunwali* processes, as a unitary cultural code at the expense of understanding other systems, does not provide an in-depth grasp of the multiple manifestations of justice within and among Afghan cultures. Nepal's history of the monarchy, the *Panchayat* system, and the institutionalization of caste hierarchies indicate that what is considered local and customary are not unchanging as contemporary understandings of the local imply. In both instances, traditional mechanisms' inability to incorporate voices of women and minority communities highlight why official and secular codes of law have their appeal.

This chapter ultimately underscored that law, writ large, is limited in its ability to challenge impunity or address every dimension of injustice experienced by Afghan and Nepali populations. The politicization of the law and the process of transitional justice are also critical areas that require a deeper examination, as does a clearer understanding of what "justice" actually means in both the case studies. Next, this study turns to the larger questions of de facto impunity and the political environment within which the transitional justice question has arisen in both contexts.

4 Through local lenses

The politicization of transitional justice

In the aftermath of conflict, victims' multifaceted demands, echoed by the human rights community, fundamentally assert the universal value of justice. These are the expected demands of punishment, access to basic needs, and acknowledgement of having been wronged. But among victims of atrocities, there is also an understanding of the need for reconciliation and forgiveness, although not for the worst perpetrators, and a strong rejection of amnesties.[1] This universal demand to "right the wrongs" calls into question the legitimacy of the new trend within transitional justice practices of coating some of the most difficult questions (e.g. how to address the issue of perpetrators) facing societies in transition with the "dressings" of reconciliation (i.e. framing warlord/perpetrator bargaining as a process of reconciliation, claiming legitimacy from local customs and values). In other words, despite the strides made in institutionalizing transitional justice processes, serious questions about accountability and the power exerted by warlords and elites in political bargaining continue to be too often evaded with superficial measures. These realities of *ongoing injustice,* as a consequence of the political order that emerges, blur the line between the past and present. The trend of consulting the "local" when designing and implementing a transitional justice package can then be understood as not a matter of objectively infusing static local practices, but of *selectively infusing subjective interpretations of the local.* The question is, then, whose subjective interpretations of the local – which in any case is dynamic and evolving – are prioritized? What do such tensions reveal about *which* local is heard and prioritized, and for whom is transitional justice performed? Finally, does situating the local within a preordained transitional justice framework necessarily make it responsive and legitimate in particular contexts?

This chapter argues that engaging with the local is not only complex, but, in certain circumstances, could be merely symbolic and even futile if the main goal is to fit the "local" into a pre-existing standard. Further, the local becomes acceptable so long as it does not challenge some of the underlying normative assumptions and the ordained good that transitional justice toolkits offers, and is deployed only to bolster the legitimacy of a transitional justice package. It may even be argued that at times this strategic deployment of the local serves to inculcate a more authentic cultural flavor to such practices and mechanisms of transitional justice, as is the case particularly in the exercises for "reconciliation." Framed differently,

76 *The politicization of transitional justice*

the fashionable trend to situate the "local" in transitional justice with its overt focus on how indigenous communities "do" reconciliation obfuscates the imperative and importunate claims against ongoing injustices. In the case of Afghanistan for example, there has been focused international attention on how to use the *jirgas* to explore issues of peace and reconciliation, while moving away from a concerted discussion of justice with the victims.[2] In Nepal, the sufferings of the Nepali population have legitimized the focus on political justice supported by rule of law programs and peacebuilding activities promoted by international organizations, in coordination with local partners, but day-to-day injustices suffered by Nepal's poor and issues of socioeconomic injustice remains unchallenged. In both contexts, unanswered questions about social and economic injustices and the challenges of impunity remain. Ultimately then, the standardized toolkit with its "kinder, gentler" formula stops short of being able to deliver on the very front from which it purports to derive its legitimacy: the voices of survivors.

In continuing the discussion of the "dynamic local," drawing on the experiences from Afghanistan and Nepal, this chapter offers yet another dimension of the "local" in transitional justice processes – its politicization within the very fluid, non-linear, and often confusing period termed as "transition." It begins with a close analysis of the politicking within the elite in Afghanistan about the transitional justice process and lays out the incisive criticisms offered by local actors about the mistakes made and the elite bargaining processes that ultimately sidelined the real questions of justice at a critical moment in the country. The chapter then turns attention to the ways in which politics played out in determining the scope of transitional justice in Nepal and delves into the nature of politicization that mars Nepal's civil society landscape today, and which hinders effective mobilization on questions of justice on behalf of the victims. The chapter concludes with reflections on the TRC and offers a critique of not only the limitations of the model in contexts such as Afghanistan and Nepal, but also how understandings of norm diffusion in such instances ignore questions of power politics and interests of elites in the national sphere at one level, and the shortcomings of such models to address questions of impunity which define sociopolitical realities in both contexts.

What's in a name? The search for a term for "transitional justice" in Afghanistan

In post-2001 Afghanistan, the term "transitional justice" quickly became polarizing and provocative, dragging the UNAMA and other international actors into a direct confrontation with key warlords and militia commanders, who quickly rose to prominence soon after the signing of the Bonn Agreement. Subsequently, instead of being able to define a clear agenda for culpability for the past and accountability for the future, these organizations quickly found themselves in a defensive position, unable to control the growing vitriol emanating from these political actors. In 2005, when the momentum was building around the National Action Plan, the now more politically powerful warlords and militia commanders were

The politicization of transitional justice   77

quick to conflate the discussion of accountability with that of a Western-led agenda to legally prosecute "holy warriors" who had fought for Islam and Afghanistan against the Soviet invasion. By 2007, when the "amnesty bill" was first introduced in the Afghan parliament, they were dictating the rhetoric significantly, and organized perhaps one of the largest public rallies held in Kabul since 2001, comprising of 25,000 people, to show support for the draft legislation.[3] Accounts and analyses of the event vary, but what was evident was the momentum around the demand for blanket amnesties for all those who fought in the decades of war. USIP Rule of Law advisor Scott Worden summarized his observations of that time in the following:

> [F]or the thousands of people who came out in support of the amnesty law, transitional justice meant prosecution of holy warriors, and even more important, removal of their patrons on behest of the infidels...they had the advantage of using the religious language because these warlords define themselves as mujaheeds who had fought for Islam against the Russians, and they gloss over the fact they have killed thousands of their own country men who are also "good" [quotes with fingers] Muslims.[4]

This "hijacking" of the project by warlords and militia commanders, particularly the harnessing of religious language, provides insight into several emerging dynamics: (i) the increasing strength of the warlords; (ii) their ability to harness nationalist sentiments, particularly given the growing frustration and resentment among the Afghan civilian population toward the international military forces; (iii) the heavy-handed approach of international presence and their failure to deliver on their promises to the Afghan people; and (iv) the "peace at all costs" rhetoric gathering strength in Karzai's speeches and among several international stakeholders such that "transitional justice" quickly evolved into "a code word for prosecuting warlords or ushering western liberalism or both."[5]

The immediate reaction from the international community working on human rights and transitional justice to these political developments was to scramble for a new term that would be both less antagonistic by implying a shift away from punitive measures. Local human rights actors interviewed for this research saw the knee-jerk response as a confirmation of what they already feared – the UN's growing reluctance to take a firm stand on political negotiations between international actors and warlords to ensure that the latter would have a significant stake in the new political order. This hesitation was in accordance with UNAMA withdrawing from the commitment to publish a report that would have supported the findings of HRW and the AIHRC.[6] Its subsequent eagerness to seek a less minatory term underscored its intention not to "ruffle feathers" and challenge accommodating policies that would inevitably destroy the momentum around the National Action Plan.

According to some of the local human rights actors and Afghanistan specialists interviewed, the energy and focus on trying to find a literal translation of the term "transitional justice" that would not be considered antagonistic was an almost

78 *The politicization of transitional justice*

ineffectual endeavor. First, such an effort ultimately highlighted the already weak position of the international human rights community in Afghanistan. Second, such a term, even in the best translation, does not either capture the realities in Afghanistan, nor does it reflect the fundamental demands for justice in the country. Rina Amiri, formerly with the Open Society Institute (OSI), captured these contradictions best in the following reflection:

> When translated into Farsi the words transitional justice [at best] sounds awkward. In Farsi we say *adalate (justice) taqqalli (transition),* which literally means 'justice in transition.' But the reality is that we don't even have current justice in Afghanistan. We don't even have rule of law. There is still tremendous impunity...there is still gross violations of human rights and the rights that have been accorded to the population in the constitution is only on paper. Why are we even talking about transitional justice when we don't even have current justice? And what does it mean for us to be advocating for justice in transition?[7]

Other local actors questioned whether a name change would necessarily pull the wool over the eyes of those most opposed to any mechanism for accountability. "I think that you can call it whatever you want," noted an Afghan rights activist, "no one is going to think its something different once you start talking about reform and removing war criminals from power. Frankly speaking, I don't understand how the name change helps at all."[8] An issue of even greater concern among some of the local actors interviewed was the depiction of "transitional justice" as a Western agenda and how quickly the international community assumed a defensive position, as if corroborating the existing accusations emanating from the warlord camps that the *raison d'être* for demanding accountability itself was borne out of Western sensibilities, rather than local realities.

Interestingly, in 2007, when the *Wolesi Jirga* circulated the draft bill for amnesty, Afghanistan's highest body of *mullahs* (clerics) criticized the legislation, stating that under *Shari'a* only the victims of crimes, not the state, have the right to forgive the perpetrators. This doctrine of *Haqqul Ibad* is based on the principle that in Islam, sins against men are forgivable only if the offended pardons the offender.[9] Islamic clerics' engagement with the amnesty bill highlighted the fact that blanket amnesty against war criminals is as much a violation of international legal norms as of Islamic jurisprudence, and that justice for war crimes may be approached from the standpoint of Islamic rules of conflict, which clearly delineate what may not be hurt or destroyed in war.[10] Further, Afghan traditions, infused by various injunctions in the *Shari'a,* uphold that those with blood on their hands should stand in the back row, as much in the mosque as in government. Both these doctrines – one that clearly asserts the moral authority of victims to address their sufferings, and another that pronounces moral opprobrium on perpetrators – are powerful articulations of Islam's position on victims' prerogative to justice claims, accountability, and forgiveness. They also speak to the "local" that has been obscured by the existing power dynamics and hierarchies between and amongst

The politicization of transitional justice   79

local actors, and local actors and the international community. It may be speculated that an emphasis on *Haqqul Rab* might have allowed for a deeper exploration of how victims were articulating their demands and certainly created the scope for developing mechanisms for compensations and/or reparations. Islamic and Afghan chastisements on criminal acts could have strengthened the standardized practices of vetting that took place, although not necessarily effectively, during the parliamentary elections of 2005.[11] While such a scenario is speculative, the actual developments between 2002 and 2007 indicate that the window of opportunity to privilege the "local" and allow it to be the centripetal force driving questions of justice, accountability, and reconciliation was undeniably lost.

A discussion about the local cannot take place in a vacuum; it needs to engage with the religious and cultural contours of the context. Chapter three provided an in-depth discussion of the complexity of parallel legal systems, an outcome of the attempted synthesizing of Western laws, *Shari'a,* and customary practices, and how the resultant complementary, and at times contradictory, laws challenge international legal norms. For example, specific injunctions both in Islamic and Afghan cultural practices necessitate the deliverance of swift justice, which compliment international humanitarian law's position on war crimes and crimes against humanity. They clearly allowed for a unique opportunity to explore the commonalities of both Afghan legal tradition and cultures on the one hand, and the official legal code in the discussion around transitional justice on the other. Concurrently, engaging with local norms and practices can challenge standardized practices. An extreme example is the continuing conflict between the death penalty in the national laws of many countries and the prohibition of such a form of punishment in international law. Even sincere enthusiasm to incorporate the local does not iron away such fundamental differences; these tensions are particularly significant when neoliberal assumptions of "human rights" and "justice" collide with local communities' understandings and practices of the same.

A local civil society actor assessed that "international law's position on criminality is too lenient, and might not necessarily be palatable amongst many Afghans who adhere to strict codes of justice and punishment."[12] Several of the local human rights and transitional justice activists interviewed also questioned the wisdom of international organizations trying to locate transitional justice's position in Islam. They pointed to the absurdity of seeking accountability for extraordinary crimes in a context that is neither in a clear state of transition nor has a culture of effective justice. A local human rights actor passionately captured this dilemma in the following:

> I don't think justice contradicts any religion. I don't think transitional justice needs to be analyzed from the point of Islam. If you want justice, I don't know any part of the *Qu'ran* and any part of the *Shari'a* that discourages people from seeking justice…I think this discussion of cultural relevance of transitional justice in Afghanistan is a whole lot of excuses that the international community makes. When they wanted to bomb us they never consulted our culture or the Islamic perspective. When they send troops they never ask

80   *The politicization of transitional justice*

> if it is contradicting our culture or our religion. But when it comes to the issue of justice, then they raise the question of whether we should do it and does it contradict the religion.[13]

External actors' search for the "right" answers in a possible intersection between Islam and "transitional justice," concluded some of the local actors interviewed, is more of an intellectual exercise and detracts from addressing the urgent problems in Afghanistan – the issues of ongoing impunity, poor governance, and poverty. Such careful cherry picking could be seen as privileging certain interpretations of justice and reconciliation over others. In a geopolitical landscape, where there is a history of hostility between different ethno–political communities as well as between "secular" institutions and more "traditional" communities, some expressed concern that such naïve efforts could mean new fault lines would be drawn or old fault lines could be deepened. Some also considered that an overzealous but naïve effort to delve into the specificities of Islam's philosophy of justice would be a waste of time and resources, particularly given that the Afghans' insistence on justice claims already mirrored what the universalist position on justice promises to deliver. An important question to ask in such a pursuit would be how to deal with a potential fall-out when such an endeavor did not result in the answers that international actors were necessarily looking for. An Afghan human rights activist framed these very critical questions in the following reflection:

> I have mixed feelings about consulting Islam for transitional justice and not particularly good ones. For you to say you want to encourage a native discourse on Islam and an Afghan-based Islam and transitional justice – you are playing with fire. Do you really want to have a discussion about Islamic principles and justice and accountability amongst religious clergy many of whom are quasi-literate? This question is not about indigenous dialogue so don't force it. What you will do is paint your efforts with an Islamic veneer and say now we have an indigenous discourse. And what if you start getting answers you don't like? Are you prepared to face the fact that you don't have legitimacy and authority in this area at all?[14]

Such questions about legitimacy and authority, and of appropriate interpretations, bring back the questions on which this research is premised – where is the "local" situated in the lofty transitional justice goals? In the case of Afghanistan, its position seems to be still at the margins, available only to be gainfully employed as and when it would fit the international political agenda. This assertion holds true when considering the discussions around the possibility of a TRC in particular, and of reconciliation in general in Afghanistan.

Today, international think tanks, policy-makers, researchers, and academics are churning out research papers and policy proposals examining Islamic/Afghan-based models of "reconciliation" for *afwa* (forgiveness)*, sulh* (arbitration), and *jirgas* for dispute resolution. While culturally sensitive and informed mechanisms for promoting ways to reconcile hostile parties are undisputedly critical, the privileging of the discussion of reconciliation, its basis in Islam, and the absence of any discussion on justice raises some questions. For those who have been involved in the human rights field under dire circumstances, the focus on "reconciliation" as a singular technique, a "magic bullet" that will attain societal healing through certain culturally bound exercises, diminishes it as a progression, and undermines it as an outcome of some extremely difficult, long-term processes.[15] For these actors, this overt focus on "reconciliation" signals a softer, resigned approach and an ultimately futile route that international stakeholders seem comfortable pursuing.

Some critics recognize that if done the "right way" and used as a "basket of carrots and sticks" with the threat of prosecution, reconciliation could have potential. But without a functional judicial system and a rampant system of corruption, "the stick" has little leverage. "In the offer of reconciliation," noted an Afghan human rights actor, "it is almost seen as a mechanism, that is only enabled when certain reformative measures are taken...[thus] the space for transitional justice, and reconciliation gets reduced to mere "window-dressing."[16] Ultimately, the possibility of a truth commission, if it ever were to happen, remains suspect for those who question the effectiveness of a mechanism, particularly if it is premised on amnesty provisions.

Nepal's accounting for the past

The CPA's detailed engagement with "transitional justice" may be commended for outlining specific mechanisms for the specific needs that emerged in Nepal as a consequence of war; however, these very specifications with their respective mandates raises deep-seated concerns, including questions about a South African-styled TRC and the appropriateness of such a model in the Nepal context. In retrospect, Siebert's particular contribution in bringing a discussion of a South African-styled TRC to the forefront of the deliberations of a transitional justice process is indeed notable. Subsequent visits of Nepali politicians to South Africa and several visits by South African experts to Nepal also underscored the heavy influence of a handful of actors in pushing forward a particular style of TRC to address the demands for justice and reconciliation in the country. In the negotiating room, support for the South African-styled TRC was uneven among the different political actors. The NC was in favor of such an approach because it considered the Maoists to be mainly responsible for human rights atrocities committed during the conflict. The Maoists were less receptive to the idea and focused their attention on the need for prioritizing the publication of the names of the disappeared. According to a 2009 ICTJ report, although one of the earlier versions of the CPA draft had referred to a TRC, due to pressure from political parties the term "justice" was ultimately omitted.[17] Interviews revealed that international actors also brought the Peruvian Truth Commission to the attention of the negotiating parties with support from the NTTP, and there were field visits to Peru to learn about the Peruvian institution, but "these visits did not mitigate the overwhelming primacy of the South African example."[18]

82   *The politicization of transitional justice*

The deliberate introduction of the South African-styled TRC and the corresponding visits to South Africa and Peru had not gone unnoticed by those in the Nepal human rights community and to casual observers of the peace process. They were seen as evidence that the transitional justice discussion was driven by external actors who are either not cognizant of, nor interested in the Nepali context. For such critics, these efforts also undermined the complex intersection of multiple cultures, caste, ethnicity, a feudalistic societal structure, poverty, and lack of privilege that determine the country's social realities. They raised questions of a South African-styled TRC and its ability to address Nepal's challenges, which are the result of a complex history of feudalism, caste-discrimination, and the revolutionary shift from a monarchy to a federal republic. It also raised the issue of a Christian model of public apology and forgiveness alienating a population of Hindus, Buddhists, Sikhs, Jains, Muslims, and people from other religious persuasions. Further, a lack of understanding of the genesis, purpose, and outcome of a TRC model discussed in policy and elite political circles underscored the inaccessibility and unfamiliarity of such a mechanism for the ordinary Nepali citizen. One civil society actor pointed out that the TRC is, at times, confused for a mediation program, and similar to the ones that already exist in the country.[19]

Local actors who have long been active in human rights activism in Nepal also pointed to the historical, structural, and political distinctions between Nepal and South Africa. The South African challenge, after all, was to overturn the abhorrent practices of the apartheid regime, change a constitution based on discrimination, and delegitimize state practices that drew clear lines between "whites," "blacks," "coloreds," and "Indians." The struggle was therefore about racial equality. A long-time prominent human rights activist and civil society actor noted:

> In Nepal, everything comes at once – the need for restructuring the state, feudalism, abolition of the monarchy, a dire need for social security reform, of dealing with the caste system, of basically reconfiguring an entire political entity…and yet, we don't have a system, a complaint structure, anything to build on, as they did in South Africa, so the context is very, very different here.[20]

Richard Bennett, head of OHCHR-N reflected on the specific mention of the TRC:

> [O]ne could look at it in two ways…a different reference to the TRC [at one level] means that a TJ mechanism is formally introduced in the agenda, which spells good intentions, if also ignorance about what it means…but there are two problems…there is already a description of a mechanism, rather than of a process, which is what TJ needs to be…and [second] there is a view here, cynical but not inaccurate, that the TRC was promoted by those who wanted a vehicle to provide amnesty…and the South African model with its configuration of truth for amnesty was very appealing.[21]

The politicization of transitional justice   83

As in Afghanistan, human rights activists, local and international, have made an effort to find terms to capture both the meaning of "transitional justice" and the mechanisms specified in the CPA. *Sankramankaalin Nyaya*, the coined term for "transitional justice" has its limitations. First, it is unable to fully capture the meaning of the term "transitional," and effectively laying out to *what* there is a transition. Second, it fails to express how this *nyaya* (justice) is different from the justice that has been demanded in Nepal's ongoing struggles against socioeconomic cleavages and caste system on which the Maoist war was primarily premised. "People don't know what to really expect from transitional justice," noted an interviewee, "...after all, they never saw justice at work in this country."[22] Some of those interviewed pointed to the confusion the term also engenders because of the general association of Nepal's transition to the new constitution i.e. that the transition would end as and when the country formalizes its new constitution.

The COID, or *Bepatta Aayog*, has had better fortune in translation because it captures the *raison d'être* for its establishment and is a direct response to people's demands to track down the missing and the dead. But by far, it is the *Satya Nirupan Tatha Mil Milap Aayog* (the Nepali term for the TRC), that has been the most difficult to define, and has been the subject of both confusion regarding what reconciliation means at the individual and societal level, and criticism because of the perception that it is a vehicle for institutionalizing amnesty. This is because of two reasons – first, as mentioned above, the confessional–forgiveness mechanism informed and advocated by an Anglican bishop (Desmond Tutu) is seemingly at odds in a predominantly Hindu country. Second, the formula of amnesties in exchange for confessions is met with hostility and suspicion in a country that continues to struggle against institutionalized impunity. The following excerpt from an interview perhaps best summarizes the inherent skepticism that Nepalis interviewed expressed toward the possibility of a TRC:

> [Y]ou know we don't have the word sorry. We don't confess. If someone brings us a cup of tea, we don't say thank you. It is understood implicitly. If someone bumps you, they don't say they are sorry. It's the way he looks at you that you know he is. But can you really say this is the general culture in Nepal? It's people's decision if they want justice or forgiveness, but this kind of commission...it just seems to be an external way of addressing grievances.[23]

Finally, the term and possibility of reconciliation in and of itself was seen to be the most provocative. The term *melmilap* does not actually mean reconciliation; its translation is closer to amity or friendship. Therefore, it indicates a closer relationship between antagonistic parties, with which victims by and large are not comfortable. Interviews with civil society actors, and conversations with Nepalis in general, indicated that reconciliation was a pronouncement of resignation and defeat to the existing and ongoing conditions of impunity and abuse of

84 *The politicization of transitional justice*

power, class, and caste, and succinctly stated, a legitimization of the status quo. A representative of PD shared:

> [P]eople want to move on, but they will understand reconciliation to be too much…at the most they will work with a philosophy of forgetting…but before that, they will say first we want some justice, some compensation, then only we can have reconciliation, then we can forget.[24]

Nepal's victims' network landscape is no stranger to politicization; one could argue that a significant factor in its marginalization and its corresponding invisibility is generated because of the politics between and within the different victims networks. Within this, the ones that claim to be the most legitimate in voicing the concerns of the victims and survivors, correspondingly insist they are the most marginalized as a direct consequence of the level and extent of local and elite politics. There are grounds for such claims. Smaller, less informal networks, and particularly those outside of the capital and without elite recognition, have been largely absent from formal decision-making processes on peace and justice and the democratic process in Nepal. Indeed, representatives of victims were starkly absent in the peace negotiations. In June 2006, only five representatives of civil society were invited as observers to the peace talks. While they had no formal function, they were at times able to provide some input and play a role in breaking deadlocks.[25] Finally, victims' networks and human rights NGOs have been generally skeptical of the level of involvement of victims in the actual peace negotiations and, in particular, for the bills on transitional justice. "There was little interest to involve victims overall," noted a civil society actor, "and a genuine opportunity to engage with the bills was denied to the large number of victims' representatives who desperately want to have a say in how they want justice done."[26] While intense lobbying by a few victims' groups together with pressure from human rights NGOs ultimately resulted in the MoPR conducting several consultations on proposed bills, this did not take place to the same extent with regard to the disappearance commission. Critics (both from the victims' networks and those civil society members sympathetic towards their struggles) pointed out that victims in many instances were handpicked, and did not always represent diversity; instead, access was often directly related to political affiliation and patronage.

Consider, for example, the Society of Families Disappeared by the State, later known as the Society of the Families of Warriors Disappeared by the State (SoFAD), which was the first collective voice of victims in the country, and established in 1999. From the beginning, SoFAD's potential to be the organization for all victims was intuitively curtailed because its focus was only on those who were victimized by state security forces. By definition, it excluded all those who were impacted by the Maoist forces. SoFAD was, in essence, a political extension of the CPN-M, drawing on the party for its leadership, membership, and direction. As such, its identity was derived from the politics of exclusion, and prevented any scope of a collective campaign based on the claim to victimhood itself. The political nature of SoFAD was further emphasized with the larger political developments in the

The politicization of transitional justice 85

country – at the completion of CA elections, which won seats for the CPN-M in the government, most of the leadership in SoFAD became members in CPN-M. With CPN-M's rise to political prominence, SoFAD's activism and leadership in campaigning for victims' rights experienced a corresponding decline. By May 2009, its events had diminished significantly and the few that were organized were fully under CPN-M's control and dominated by a single political party agenda.[27]

During the second period of political upheaval that led to the People's War, a second victims' network appeared in the civil society landscape. Self-identified as the Maoists' Victims' Association (MVA), its focus was on survivors of Maoist atrocities. But the MVA, like SoFAD, followed a similar pattern of exclusion when it came to organizational membership. Its leadership was largely derived from the NC and a few other political parties, and it does not officially recognize the victims of state security forces or lobby on their behalf. An interview with a senior member of the MVA revealed the following:

> Yes, there are victims on the other side…at least, there are many such claims…but advocating for their behalf is not our responsibility. If they want to mobilize for their rights, they are welcome to it, but our duty is to speak for those of us who have suffered in the hands of the Maoists…the Maoists have committed so many violations…pushed us off our lands, extortion, torture, beatings, killings…it is not possible to forget or forgive. So they can mobilize on their own and fight for their rights, but we should concentrate on our demands. There is a lot of bad feeling between the two sides…it will not happen that all victims come together…they wouldn't be welcome here…[28]

In 2006, the first victim-initiated advocacy group – the Conflict Victims' Committee (CVC) was formed in the Bardiya district, in the mid-western region of the country, where the number of disappeared during the height of the People's War was the highest, not only in Nepal but in the world.[29] To date, CVC remains the largest victims' network in Nepal. In addition to a diverse range of activities, such as making public the whereabouts of the missing and disappeared during the People's War, awareness-building about legal provisions about disappearances, and coordinating efforts of national and international organizations to push for whereabouts of the disappeared, CVC also actively provides internal counseling, community therapy, and a "safe space" for survivors to share their narratives of war and loss. It has been able to reach out to regional victims' associations and work in coordination with the ICRC, the British Embassy, and OHCHR-N through local programs to work with survivors in different communities.[30] CVC has also coordinated with Peace Brigades International (PBI) on matters of security, as well as worked with the ICJ on documentation of wartime atrocities.

In 2008, Nepal's elite civil society began the initiative to create an umbrella network for the different victims' networks that began appearing across Nepal. Termed the Conflict Victim Society for Justice (CVSJ), the initiative was registered in Kathmandu, with a network in 20 districts.[31] At around the same time,

86 *The politicization of transitional justice*

victims' families also demanded an umbrella network that would represent all their interests. Through putting pressure on ICRC, the newly developed Network of Families of the Disappeared and the Missing (NEFAD) was established in the eastern region of Nepal. While the ultimate goal of NEFAD is to function as a comprehensive network for all victims, its agenda was focused narrowly on the issue of the missing and the disappeared. Today, NEFAD has five regional structures and a secretariat in Kathmandu, and collaborates with CSJ and CVC. In addition, drawing on the genuine concern about the need for a network that would coordinate activities and push for the larger issues of transitional justice, the Solidarity Campaign for Justice (SOCAJ) was established in coordination with NEFAD in 2010 to include all actors of transitional justice within a singular network. The work of SOCAJ is still in its development stage.

Today, in Nepal, there are 17 different victims' networks. Progress on victim activism, however, continues to be slow and potential for collaboration is greatly compromised because of the tensions between and within efforts to create umbrella networks for comprehensive programming. The cleavages between the different networks are not only due to the stark discrepancies between SoFAD and MVA but also because of power relationships between and among the different NGOs and elite civil society actors that have determined the legitimacy of certain networks over others in advocating for the rights of victims. Consider a specific example regarding tensions between CVSJ and local victims' networks. Soon after its establishment as a local initiative by the well-established AF, CVSJ became the site for significant criticism from grassroots victim networks and its leaders. Criticisms ranged from the lack of transparency in decision-making processes and agenda setting, limited access of actual victims to formal processes, to lack of independence. In short, CVSJ in the different districts is being viewed by victims both inside and outside of the CVC as being divorced from the actual victims. A victim leader also pointed out, "CVSJ sees many of the strong district victims' organizations such as the CVC in Bardiya as a direct competitor that potentially threatens its relationship with international donors."[32]

The relationship between the state, international and local NGOs are marked by complex dynamics, particularly in transitional societies. At the institutional level, the relationship between international and national NGOs can be determined by effective networking but also by the dependency syndrome. This is often manifested through foreign donors determining the agendas of local NGOs and constricting local creativity.[33] Palpable tensions also arise when NGOs become competitors with their governments (and with each other) for funding. In Nepal, there is competition between the elite NGOs as well as between victims' networks seeking legitimacy. As the CVSJ example clearly illustrates, severe competition and hostile relations are manifest even between some in the elite NGO community and grassroots victim organizations. Victim representatives repeatedly stated how, because of competition and distrust, they generally receive little to no support even from the NGO community. Further, despite the widespread belief among victim networks that they best represent victims' interests, donors focus on how elite

The politicization of transitional justice 87

NGOs select and present victim agendas in institutionalized settings, and seem most interested in supporting them in their representation of "victims' voices."

The current reality of Nepal's victim networks is marked by the absence of an institutional framework based on transparency, coherence and a commitment to victims' perspectives in the transitional justice process, continued lack of access to information, mechanisms and forums for participation, and the level of politicization of civil society. The vast number of victims from impoverished and socially marginalized communities lack powerful political connections and leverage to the powerbrokers in the peace process on one hand, and direct access to donors for support for a range of different necessary activities, including livelihood support, professional opportunities, and structures that allow for cross-district and cross-border sharing of experiences and skills, on the other hand. Victims' networks over and again repeated that donor attention to their needs would make a significant difference in the efficacy of their advocacy. It is in these specific areas of marginalization, they observe, that the level of exclusiveness and disparity between elite "local" actors and themselves have become the most apparent and constitute a formidable barrier to their struggle for justice.

Concerns about the TRC: reflections on Afghanistan and Nepal

The concerns about transitional justice in Afghanistan and Nepal merit one final discussion. At the macro-level, the privileging of TRCs should be assessed carefully. In transitional justice literature, TRCs have increasingly been promoted as the vehicles for democracy deliverance and the promotion of democratic values.[34] Because such mechanisms have the mandate to offer recommendations on legal and institutional reforms and strengthen accountability norms, their influence is seen to be more positive and less antagonistic than retributive measures particularly trials. Further, it is believed they could play a constructive role in promoting a "societal consensus."[35] Hayner asserts that making a TRC's findings public could produce "a more knowledgeable citizenry [that] will recognize and resist any sign of return to repressive rule."[36] Other scholars have asserted that there is a positive relationship between TRCs and human rights protection.[37] In short, the retroactive and the forward-looking measures shed light on past human rights abuses, attempt to end the pattern of impunity, and assist survivors in accessing reparations and symbolic structures of acknowledgement of the atrocities.

Despite these claims, TRCs remain a field of ongoing research. In general, TRCs have a mixed record of being able – or allowed – to complete their mandate without interference. There is also a mixed record about the extent to which the recommendations they offer are actually institutionalized. In some instances, they have challenged democratic processes when victims have "resorted to vigilantism when unsatisfied with the limited accountability of the TRC."[38] Ultimately, it is important to keep in mind that such mechanisms are responses to contingent causes. Their temporary nature and limited powers will not necessarily generate substantive sociopolitical changes, particularly if the context in which they operate

88 *The politicization of transitional justice*

has not undergone significant political shifts, such as a complete regime change or a comprehensive effort to institutionalize their recommendations.

Given the ongoing conflict in Afghanistan and continuing political turmoil in Nepal, to what extent does "transitional justice" reach out to the very people whose lives it commits to improve? In both contexts, the discussion of who leads the process and the kind of negotiations and politicking that takes place is limited to not only the capitals, but to a small circle of elites within government and civil society. This inevitably creates the perception that "transitional justice" is an elite-driven process. A local human rights actor also remarked on this point, emphasizing how alienated Kabul is and how removed from the realities of the lives of the majority of the Afghan population in the 34 districts of the country. "Most people," she remarked "had no idea even about the whole amnesty discussion and were so upset and confused about how these warlords got into parliament and how they had amnesties. It was to add insult to injury."[39]

In Nepal, Kathmandu's monopolization of the "transitional justice" discussion and processes was an inevitability of the privileges endowed upon a capital in any developing context – access to resources and the site for congregation of the movers and shakers of society. The outcome consequently is that only a few determined what was included in the CPA regarding "transitional justice" and what was left out. This observation is particularly striking when considering how the slow but emerging support for the TRC is developing in Nepal. In 2007, the USIP developed a 73-minute documentary called *Confronting the Truth: Truth Commissions and Societies in Transition*. This documentary, which lays out the experiences of South Africa, Peru, East Timor, and Morocco has been used in working groups to inform both local civil society actors and the general public about how truth commissions work and how they are effective. The influence and impact of this kind of information-sharing is best summarized by a local human rights actor who reflected: "the people demand trials, punishment and compensation, but then we explain what a TRC does and what reparations are, and then they want that too."[40]

Constructivists would argue that the acceptance of the TRC, and indeed the larger transitional justice framework and language by Nepal, is a reflection of the power and influence of international norms and structures, which by definition are "collective expectations about proper behavior for a given identity."[41] These norms are also persuasive, such that states are "persuaded" to join the international society for legitimacy and approval, based on the fact that "normative claims become powerful and prevail by being persuasive."[42] In other words, Nepal's response to the pressure to accept the TRC framework can be explained as a product of exogenous forces of global norm transfusion based on global expectations of human rights and democracy, which compels states to comply because they may consider that their legitimacy could be at stake.[43] In short, there is a socially constructed pressure for states to absorb and reflect cultural models of appropriate statehood[44] to which Nepal has responded. The evolving norm of "accountability for wartime atrocities" therefore becomes not only an ideal but also an organizing principle of behavior and a standard for all regimes. Further,

The politicization of transitional justice 89

this type of norm transmission i.e. TRC as the most effective and valid response to wartime atrocities in Nepal, is a clear demonstration of the efficiency with which powerful actors can influence the scope of post-conflict justice because such norm entrepreneurs are those able to "frame" normative ideas in a way that they resonate with relevant audiences.[45] This explanation goes far to explain how international NGOs such as USIP, advocacy networks, and even the donor community have influenced and informed the transitional justice discourse in Nepal, where the demand for justice and human rights from local actors dovetailed with the questions of *how* to address these questions. This analysis is emphasized by Meyer and Scott who argue International Organizations (IOs) and International NGOs (INGOs) do not directly play the role of actors but "instruct and guide putatively self-interested actors in the widest variety of matters: how to organize the good society, how to live safely and effectively in the natural world, how to respect the human members of society, and so on and on."[46]

Such explanations of norm diffusion, however, do not explain the desire of political elites to seek a solution that does not include penalties for their actions. Neither do they highlight how elite-driven processes can displace, and often marginalize the grassroots primary concerns. In the end, both in Afghanistan and Nepal, "transitional justice" and its specific mechanisms do not, and will not, address some of the most deep-rooted challenges in society relating to poverty, discrimination, and *de jure* and de facto impunity. Richard Bennett, who has served both in Afghanistan and Nepal, recognizes this disjuncture between the need for mechanisms for addressing impunity and the processes required for "transitional justice" and the conflation that happens between the two:

> [W]e talk about impunity and transitional justice in the same breath as if it is the same thing, as if TJ mechanisms are the only way to address impunity and that's questionable. I don't think we should put them together. There is a range of objectives for dealing with an internally damaged society – physically, emotionally, legally, but impunity is different. In Nepal impunity preceded the conflict, it exists now after the conflict, its something that TJ can have a part to play in addressing but it won't deal with it wholly. Impunity requires its own strategy.[47]

This question of a strategy for addressing impunity ultimately remains one of the biggest challenges for both Afghanistan and Nepal. In Afghanistan, as preceding chapters have underscored, "political reconciliation" continues to be both an international and national policy, but there is no discussion on the issues of impunity. In Nepal, Phuyel best summarizes the extent of impunity in the country in the following:

> In the CPA, the Maoists got benefits. The Nepal army, security forces, the police – they had no threat to their jobs. They even have good positions in UN peacekeeping. Who suffered? The victims. They suffered in the hands of the army and the Maoists and they still did not get anything. And when

90 *The politicization of transitional justice*

the Maoists came to power, they tried to politicize the disappearance issues. And with the army becoming strong, it will be very difficult to establish the disappearance commission…and the TRC will become even more difficult to establish because we will need the political consent of the Maoists and the army…[48]

Phuyel's questions give the conversations about "transitional justice" and the importance of commissions in post-CPA Nepal pause, and are also relevant for Afghanistan. Ultimately, any "transitional justice" mechanism is as good as the conditions in which it is allowed to operate. Until questions of politics and politicization of the processes themselves are recognized and addressed, negotiations at the elite level, as in the Afghanistan and Nepal cases, will continue to ensure that victims' voices will be effectively and inordinately marginalized.

Conclusion

This chapter examined the internal and external politicization around the transitional justice process in Afghanistan and Nepal, situating the *local* within the dynamics of these political tensions. These realities cause problems for the new trend within transitional justice of framing warlord/perpetrator bargaining as a process of reconciliation, claiming legitimacy from local customs. In the discussion on Afghanistan, it traced the emergence of the transitional justice discourse and outlined how it quickly became a polarizing topic in a tenuous landscape, pitting a weak civil society and human rights community against an increasingly powerful group of warlords and extremely influential international decision-makers. It laid out how in the intense focus on arriving at a term that explains transitional justice without antagonizing the perpetrators, the space was created for warlords to dominate the rhetoric, and ultimately narrowed the scope for activism on questions of culpability. It then highlighted how local civil society actors perceived the focus on trying to find a less provocative term for transitional justice, which they viewed as disengagement and reluctance on the part of the international community to address victims' calls for justice. Finally, and perhaps most importantly, it provided insight into how the overt focus by international actors on reconciliation resulted in it being considered a strategy, rather than a process, that could only truly begin once concerns of survivors and the Afghan population could be addressed.

In Nepal, South Africa's TRC, which provided the blueprint for the truth commission, raised questions about the incongruity of a Christian-based forgiveness model functioning adequately in a predominantly Hindu society. The chapter also discussed the experiences of Nepal's civil society, particularly the victims' networks that continue to remain mostly in the fringes of the discussion of justice and peace. Finally, it concluded with reflections on the limitations and potential of the TRC within the contexts of Afghanistan and Nepal. In both instances, the detailed discussion underscored how the current trend within transitional justice of coating some of the most difficult questions facing societies in transition with the "dressings" of reconciliation (i.e. framing warlord/perpetrator bargaining as a process of reconciliation through claiming legitimacy from local customs and values) does not reflect the voices of survivors. Instead, by providing clout to perpetrators through labeling what essentially amounts to elite alliances, the opportunity of implementing processes of accounting for the past may be lost, as those who are opposed to such efforts become increasingly entrenched in the structures of power.

5 A meaning of justice

What constitutes justice in Afghanistan and Nepal? Do the existing commitments of transitional justice and its discussion in elite circles reflect the understandings and expectations of justice in the two countries? This chapter is an in-depth examination of the justice question in both the case studies in consideration. It identifies four specific refrains of justice that emerged during the research: (i) retributive punishment; (ii) marginalization of perpetrators of human rights atrocities; (iii) socioeconomic demands; and (iv) the rights of women. It underscores that in poverty-stricken contexts undergoing transition with long histories of institutionalized impunity, neatly arranged transitional justice packages are markedly incomplete frameworks, particularly when they confront the raw and unrelenting demands for punishment and for subsistence. As such, they fail to capture the needs and expectations of those who have paid the heaviest price in the ongoing conflict and the transitional period. This failure matters because it calls into question the beneficiaries of transitional justice and who it ultimately marginalizes. Finally, it underscores that beyond the pressing demand for a response to extraordinary atrocities, there remains the persistent claim of the marginalized for "ordinary," every day justice.

Contextualizing impunity: examining Afghanistan and Nepal

Any discussion on justice in Afghanistan and Nepal has to begin with a thorough understanding of the extent to which impunity is a sociopolitical and psychological reality in both contexts. Such structures of impunity are sustained by cooperation and facilitation; the fear and insecurity they subsequently produce ultimately ensure that no action is taken to challenge the status quo.

In Afghanistan, many of the *jang salar* (warlords) who were directly and indirectly involved in the three decades of conflict and were complicit in the commission of large-scale human rights atrocities, emerged as some of the country's most prominent political actors after the fall of the Taliban. Today, while Kabul remains the center for government bureaucracy, de facto political and administrative control is exercised by regional power holders who operate relatively freely without state supervision and who impose their own taxes on those who fall under their authority.[1] The September 2005 parliamentary and local elections, which signaled the end of the Bonn process, were marked by a notable number of warlords and war criminals running for political office, many of who won parliamentary seats and took positions in the different ministries.[2] Well-known human rights violators serve as officials in Afghanistan's defense or interior ministries, in the judiciary, as public advisors to President Hamid Karzai and/or "function as provincial drug lords or regional strongmen in Kabul and elsewhere.[3] Many of these warlord–governors are also responsible for entrenching corrupt practices. In the upper house, where President Karzai appoints one-third of the seats, a majority of the appointees have had a serious record of human rights violations.[4] The Kabul Government also created space for mid- and lower-level commanders to become prominent political and economic actors, often with the acquiescence of external donors.[5] Anger toward the international power brokers for paving the way for current circumstances is palpable because of their complicity to accommodate some of the worst perpetrators in the political processes, when many argue they could have been at least marginalized at key moments in the transition. "Today's entrenchment of the warlords," argued an expert, "involving drug cartels, cutting deals with criminal gangs and the Taliban, is largely a consequence of Pentagon's policy."[6]

Stedman's spoiler framework asserts international actors can, "as custodians of peace, manage spoilers; where international custodians have failed to develop and implement such strategies, as in the case of Afghanistan, spoilers have succeeded at the cost of hundreds of thousands of lives."[7] Interviewees in this research noted the silence among international powerbrokers about the developments surrounding the amnesty bill in 2007 as a sign that when it comes to human rights and accountability in Afghanistan, the international powers don't care. Several also asserted that, rather than playing the role of "custodians of peace," international actors in Afghanistan have acted as "enablers" of the spoiler syndrome.

Why bring in the discussion of spoilers in a chapter focused on justice? Certainly, the role of de facto impunity, brought about both by international calculations and state compliance have instituted a political culture where the "paper tigers" of 2001, have gained considerable power, access, and legitimacy. Jose Zalaquett, the renowned Chilean philosopher and activist astutely observed, "one could not expect morality from politicians, only accountability."[8] Afghanistan's current political culture clearly indicates it is impossible to expect progress on issues of accountability from Afghanistan's "spoilers of peace." The promise of transitional amnesties in places as diverse as Spain, Brazil, and Mozambique have, according to some, resulted in the promotion of human rights, democracy, and the rule of law; however, developments since 2001, and indeed earlier in Afghanistan's history, demonstrate that both the promise of transitional amnesties and that of reconciliation have consistently failed to deliver on democratization goals. Instead, they have disenfranchised Afghans of their claims to due process and functional governance.

Of the innumerable wartime atrocities committed in Nepal in the decade-long war, a few incidents are notable for serving as catalysts for mobilization

94   *A meaning of justice*

for the human rights community. One of the best documented and most significant illustrations of RNA impunity was the case of the killing of 21 people in the village of Doramba, Ramechhap district, on August 17, 2003, the very day that the third round of peace talks got underway after a three-month hiatus. In response to the killings, the NHRC established a high-level inquiry team, comprising of a leading forensic doctor, two former Supreme Court judges, and a prominent publisher to investigate the events described by the military as "Maoist ambushes." The inquiry concluded that 21 people, most of whom were Maoists or sympathizers, "had been detained for several hours before they were marched a further two hours, then executed, most with shots to the head from close range while their hands were bound."[9] The Doramba massacre was more than just a violation of the law of armed combat; it unambiguously demonstrated that the military were given a *carte blanche* to use mass executions as a deliberate strategy. The Maoists too continued "targeted killing and torture of members of the security forces, government officials, politicians civilians, and journalists,"[10] as well as "recruiting children as soldiers, executing party cadres suspected of disloyalty, and engaging in widespread extortion and abduction against the civilian population."[11] Both RNA and the People's Liberation Army (PLA) were guilty of severe breaches of Common Article Three of the Geneva Conventions that governs internal armed conflict. Placing Nepal at the top of the list of priorities for the Commission on Human Rights (CHR) AI's representative at the UN in Geneva, Peter Splinter reiterated, "Nepal is on the verge of a human rights catastrophe – basic human rights have been suspended; impunity is rampant. The international community must take immediate and decisive action to pull Nepal back from the verge."[12]

The torture and disappearances at the Maharajgunj barracks illustrate that all three branches of the security services – the NP, the APF, and the RNA – were responsible for human rights violations. In theory, the battalion commanders who managed the barracks were accountable to their brigade commander but, "given their location and the sensitivity of their work, they were almost certainly reporting directly to army headquarters."[13] Further, major military operations required authorization from higher powers, including the palace.[14] According to a 2010 ICG report,

> ...a decision to load a group of detainees onto trucks and take them to be executed, as many former Maharajgunj detainees believe happened on December, 20, 2003, would not have been taken by a battalion commander on his own initiative, given the disciplined army hierarchy.[15]

Further, the same report states: "the systematic torture carried out in Maharajgunj required the participation of entire units, including numerous medical officers who were charged with keeping detainees alive so that they could continue to be tortured."[16] Soldiers in the RNA developed their own slang for certain techniques, such as the use of electric shocks.[17] Interviews for this research emphasized that there is substantive evidence from other cases to suggest that soldiers were well aware of established torture techniques and used them frequently. The 2004 Maina

Sunuwar case has become a case of symbolic significance. Following substantial domestic and international pressure after her disappearance, the army established a court of inquiry. Even though it confirmed that her death resulted from torture, the subsequent court martial of three officers found them responsible only for a botched cover-up (improper interrogation and disposal of her body) and passed very light sentences.[18] Under further pressure, another investigation was conducted for the exhumation of the body. In February 2008, arrest warrants for four of the army officers involved in her disappearance were issued, but the army did not hand any of them over to civilian authorities.[19]

Stedman's analysis is also helpful in understanding the role and complicity of international actors in consolidating impunity in Nepal. The most serious army abuses uncovered to date took place at the same time as the United States, United Kingdom, and India stepped up military aid to the Nepali state, and in particular to the RNA to support the state against the "terrorists."[20] As late as the February 2005 palace coup, this assistance was largely unconditional and was accompanied by strong political support to the state and the military. At the same time, "the UN Department of Peacekeeping Operations (DPKO) also steadily increased Nepali participation in peacekeeping operations, continuing to do so even after the palace coup."[21] These UN missions served both as internal patronage systems (creating opportunities for senior personnel to reward or punish officers by granting or denying postings) while continuing to be a main source of income and prestige for the army.[22] The stark negligence of the evidence of systematic state crimes and the unwillingness of the RNA to impose any internal accountability, underscore not only the accommodative politics of international backers, but also their role as enabler of human rights violations, in the global climate of "fighting terrorism." This duality of message – one of systematic ignorance of the dire human rights situation and direct and indirect support to the Nepal military on the one hand, and relatively weaker calls for an end to the abuses on the other – translated ultimately to the weakening of both moral and political leverage of international actors for most of the duration of the long drawn out conflict. It is within such a context of impunity that the discussion of justice in Afghanistan and Nepal needs to be understood.

Ordinary or transitional justice? Afghan and Nepali concepts of justice

In January 2005, the AIHRC released *A Call for Justice*, the only comprehensive report to date that documents Afghan people's understanding of justice. Of the total 4,151 respondents included in the interview, 69 percent identified themselves as being direct victims of a human rights violation during the more than 23-year-old conflict.[23] The analysis of 50 focus groups used in the study identified the following as fundamental rights:

> the right to live and the right to its necessary components of food, shelter, clothing, and basic health care; Islamic rights; the right to security and

96 *A meaning of justice*

justice; and the right to an occupation and employment; freedom of thought and speech; ethnic, religious and gender equality; political rights such as the right to participate in free and fair elections; and the right to education.[24]

Over 76 percent of all respondents indicated that they thought bringing war criminals to justice in the near future would increase the security in Afghanistan;[25] 61 percent of the respondents rejected the idea of amnesties or pardons for anyone who confessed their crimes before an institution created for transitional justice;[26] and 90 percent of respondents favored the removal of perpetrators from their positions and wanted to prevent perpetrators from gaining political power in the future.[27] The survey results further indicated that almost 40 percent of all respondents understood justice as criminal justice in the courts, although in the research the participants expressed a more holistic view of justice.[28] The report states: "Some of this preference may stem from a lack of familiarity with other mechanisms, but it is clear that for many, a transitional justice strategy without a *criminal* justice component is likely to be viewed as unsatisfactory."[29]

In March 2008, the ICTJ and the local AF released *Nepali Voices: Perceptions of Truth, Justice, Reconciliation, Reparation, and the Transition in Nepal*. Of the 811 surveys conducted, the respondents defined human rights primarily as:

> the right to live without intimidation and fear (22 percent); civil and political rights, such as the right to life, freedom of speech and expression, and freedom of movement (14 percent); and socioeconomic rights, such as food, shelter, clothing, and employment (13 percent); [approximately] a fifth of respondents could not define the term; among female respondents, 'don't know' formed the single largest category of responses.[30]

In the survey, 24 percent of the respondents equated the understanding of justice with the ability of individuals to gain access to justice, 12 percent as punitive punishment, 8 percent as compensation, 7 percent saw justice as the fulfillment of victims' demands, 6 percent saw justice as establishing the truth about human-rights violations and 6 percent saw it as a means of equality.[31] Sixty percent of the respondents across ethnic and gender groups consistently defined peace as the absence of conflict.[32] Eighty percent of the respondents defined reconciliation as living in peace and harmony with everyone but only less than 1 percent equated reconciliation with forgetting the past[33] and 77 percent said that human rights perpetrators should not receive amnesty for their crimes.[34]

The methodologies of both studies are open to criticism. *A Call for Justice*, for example, is not adequately comprehensive. The report does not do justice to Afghanistan's diversity; nor does it engage in-depth about how its different groups perceive the questions of justice, reconciliation, and amnesties. In addition, it does not provide explanations as to why there could be regional variations in responses to questions regarding, for example, trials, or that of amnesties. It also fails to pay detailed attention to gender variations regarding the question of peace, justice, and reconciliation. It makes no mention of the question of Internally

A meaning of justice 97

Displaced Peoples (IDP) and refugees, nor of persons with disabilities, both of which are significantly marginalized voices in Afghanistan's demographic landscape. Finally, given the poverty levels in the country, a substantive gap in the report is the lack of a greater engagement with the socioeconomic dimensions of justice.

Nepali Voices likewise raises several questions, in particular about the selection of respondents and its reliance on quantitative methods. Indeed, it is well recognized that a survey-based methodology has limitations, in part because it is restricted to answering the set of questions asked. Robins observes: "the nature of the qualitative work that preceded the survey is unclear, but without an understanding of the issues that concern victims, a quantitative methodology to find the views of the victim population is flawed."[35] Pham and Vinck state: "[p]rior ethnographic research [...] [is] critical in informing the type and content of the questionnaire," but there was "no interaction with victims to guide the topics and emphasis of the questionnaire."[36] In addition, the sampling procedure failed to adequately represent the traditional marginalized communities in Nepal – the *janajatis,*[37] *madhesis,*[38] the lower castes particularly the *dalits,*[39] and women. Finally, the report fell short of recognizing that poverty inevitably would determine the priorities of those surveyed. Hence, when asked an open question about their priorities, victims overwhelmingly responded in terms of basic needs, with only 3 percent prioritizing judicial process. Considering that a root cause of the Nepal conflict was systematic socioeconomic marginalization, *Nepali Voices'* limitation in delving further into socioeconomic justice is worth noting. Further, as Robins points out, the report "represents the supremacy of a legalism that sees transitional justice narrowly, as a primarily legal exercise rather than as something which can begin to address the broader consequences of violations during the conflict."[40]

A 2009 study of victims in Nepal confirms that while victims want retributive justice, their demand for subsistence comes first.[41] In 2010, a joint collaboration of six organizations published *Security and Justice in Nepal Districts: Assessment Findings,* based on the results of their research in six districts – Banke, Jumla, Kailali Nawalparasi, Siraha, and Sunsari. The understandings of justice varied between districts based on ethnic, caste religious and social–economic groups, yet overall, there were certain striking commonalities in the six districts particularly in the following areas: (i) the absence of access to security and justice sectors for women; (ii) lack of representation of minority groups and of women within the police forces and a lack of trust of the police forces because minorities and those from lower castes tend to be most often harassed and arrested; (iii) lack of resources for adequate training and equipment for law enforcement agencies; (iv) the role of socioeconomic status as significant barriers to travel to formal judicial institutions and the cost of affording legal support; (v) the subsequent reliance on informal justice and dispute mechanisms, and when available, on service providers such as NGOs, particularly women's organizations and networks; and (vi) chronic poverty and its associated economic insecurity particularly amongst marginalized groups.

The 2010 study is an examination of justice and security in only six of Nepal's 75 districts. For all intents and purposes, AIHRC's *A Call for Justice and Nepali*

98 *A meaning of justice*

Voices represents the first and most comprehensive efforts of their kind to document victims' understandings of and demands for justice. Second, despite their shortcomings, these two projects underscore fundamental realities in both contexts – the dire need for socioeconomic compensation, a demand to address questions of ongoing impunity, and lack of access to judicial institutions and political machinations. Strikingly, a significant majority of respondents in both countries decried amnesty for perpetrators of the worst violations and demanded punitive punishment, a means for recording history and the truth of the atrocities they endured.

Of perpetrators amidst politics: justice as retribution

Overtly accommodative politics in Afghanistan and in Nepal have engendered a systemic prevalence of de facto impunity in both contexts. *A Call for Justice* and *Nepali Voices* underscored that while those interviewed wanted some form of conciliation and conflict resolution between antagonistic parties, their primary association with justice was based on punitive measures. Several hypotheses can be offered for this. First, punitive responses to crimes committed, the minimalist approach to justice, is the most commonly known way to address questions of accountability. The universality of its appeal, its scope of individualizing criminality, its intricate association with punishment i.e. "just dessert" for a past crime makes it the most dominant recourse. The question of individual culpability is important – the need to identify perpetrators by names and their crimes and hear the pronouncement of judgment is a universal demand. Punitive punishment is perhaps the closest form of "vengeance," where those who commit crimes are held responsible through the concerted efforts of a larger community – whether it be an immediate social network, or perhaps better still, the state, whose responses publicly declare the illegality of an atrocity. In instances such as Afghanistan and Nepal, however, trials and prosecutions also speak to what law represents, and the emblematic significance of justice – a clear statement of a break from systematic exemptions enjoyed by those in power and the continuing exploitation of those who are vulnerable. In the interviews held in both Afghanistan and Nepal, the symbolic nature of trials and their potential to serve as a deterrent for perpetrators were recurrent themes. Afghan human rights actors are well aware of the limitations of their legal system, but maintained that without isolating some of these individuals and publicly forcing them to face their crimes, the Afghan Government's very legitimacy is called into question. An Islamic scholar and elected delegate in two of Afghanistan's *jirgas*, voiced:

> From the start we needed to have a strong central government, not the puppet American one we have now, …and we needed to punish 6, 7 or 9 of the biggest criminals in Afghanistan either directly or indirectly… it would have been a kind of teaching for others and paved the way for bringing all those other criminals to trial in the future. This is something that the central government should have done.[42]

For human rights organizations in Nepal, the idea of trials is compelling because it is about identifying individuals known to have committed atrocities during the conflict and who now exercise political, military, and/or social power in the aftermath. They argue that it would send a strong signal that the state has both the political will and the ability to respond to the impunity that plagues Nepal. AF has taken a lead on this issue, gathering evidence, filing FIRs and lobbying for tougher laws, in conjunction with other local organizations, which would greatly assist in the criminal prosecution of human rights abusers. A voluntary civil society network called Accountability Watch-Nepal (AW-N)[43] now serves as an umbrella for efforts in Nepal's long-standing battle against impunity and promoting the platform of transitional justice. Members in AW-N include some of the best and most prominent human rights activists with significant experience in human rights monitoring, investigation, lobbying, and advocacy. They routinely challenge the government on meeting the CPA commitments, push for Nepal's ratification of anti-torture and ICC legislation, and for constitutional provisions on the statute of limitations of crimes.

AW-N's network of members, despite being united on the question of strengthening the rule of law and promoting criminal justice, have different understandings of how to move forward on the question of punitive measures. According to constitutional lawyer Hari Phuyel, for example, at least 10–20 people directly responsible for the atrocities committed in the decade-long conflict should be tried and their isolation from political offices and the military should be enforced because "accountable governance without impunity in Nepal is just not possible."[44] Mandira Sharma, also an AW-N member determined that five to six cases, such as the massacres in Doramba and Bhairabnath, could serve as the "emblematic cases" and would require OHCHR-N, NHRC, and ICTJ to work in concert for them to reach trial. For these local elite actors, the act of taking emblematic cases to court is in fact an act of defiance – against the current political climate in Nepal, the dismissiveness of international development agencies at the prospects of trials and their outcomes, and the general skepticism many hold in Nepal about what is feasible.

There is, however, an emerging body of literature critical of such processes. They support existing arguments against Afghan and Nepali activists' insistence on trials as deterrence and the significance they attach to "emblematic" cases.[45] The most common argument against the rationale of deterrence is that the threat of prosecutions alone has never been an effective measure to prevent individuals from committing future crimes, particularly those that are committed in the context of war.[46] Elster emphasized the concerns raised by the lead prosecutor of the Nuremberg trials, Robert Jackson, when he observed: "even if violations are harshly punished now, how can future would-be violators know that they, if overthrown, will be treated in the same way? Incentive effects presuppose stable institutions, which almost by assumption do not exist."[47]

Scholars have also debated whether deterrence theory is more effective or less in the case of *jus cogens* crimes as opposed to that of ordinary crimes. After all, in a functional criminal justice system, there is the imminent threat of

100　*A meaning of justice*

punishment if a perpetrator is apprehended. In contrast, argues Aukerman, "in the transitional justice context, 'getting caught' usually has little to do with the risk of detection; indeed, many atrocities are committed in plain view."[48] Furthermore, the reality that only a few perpetrators actually face trial effectively undermines the logic of deterrence.[49] Reflecting on the track record of international law regarding the prospects of punishment, Minow acknowledges, "[n]o one really knows how to deter those individuals who become potential dictators or leaders of mass destruction …one hopes that current-day prosecutions would make a future Hitler, or Pol Pot, or [Bosnian Serb leader] Radovan Karadzic; change course, but we have no evidence of this."[50]

Drumbl categorically dismisses the unbridled faith in international criminal law and the transformative potential of criminal trials: "there is a sense that conducting more criminal trials in more places afflicted by atrocity will lead to more justice so long as those trials conform to due process standards."[51] To that the end, "justice is not a recipe and due process is not a magical ingredient."[52] At the least, the reality on the ground is far more complex; consequently an overt reliance of international institutions on a predetermined formula of due process fails expectations, particularly of survivors of atrocities. Finally, the question of deterrence also hinges on the personality and rational choices of the perpetrator of extraordinary crimes. Cassel asserts that against certain dictators, like Milošević, threats could be effective,[53] while others, like Hitler (and Idi Amin),[54] might be undeterrable. Unfortunately in the end, whether in the context of conflict or during times of "peace," and irrespective of the nature of the crime, deterrence is not uniformly effective on offenders.

Despite these criticisms, the call for criminal justice prevails and is particularly favored by many legal scholars and human rights practitioners. Orentlicher states: "[t]he fulcrum of the case for criminal punishment is that it is the most effective insurance against future repression."[55] Kritz reiterates this faith in criminal procedures, noting the imperative of prosecuting key figures, without which "[it will] encourage new rounds of mass abuses in the country in question but also to embolden the instigators of crimes against humanity elsewhere."[56] Deterrence theory therefore provides a valuable rationalization for selective prosecution, allowing, as Ackermann argues, "for a cost/benefit analysis in which one assesses whether the advantages of preventing crime through prosecution outweigh the costs to democracy and human rights that might result if trials lead to political instability."[57]

In *The Justice Cascade: How Human Rights Prosecutions are Changing World Politics*, Sikkink examines the question of punitive punishment to understand to what extent, and if, in fact, criminal prosecutions actually impact the human rights situation in a post-conflict society.[58] Using quantitative analysis and case studies, she asserts that while human rights prosecutions can be disappointing in their inability to deliver on the lofty expectations of survivors and even rights activists, there is strong evidence to support that they do in fact promote democracy and reduce human rights repressions in states where they are implemented. She acknowledges the argument offered by trial skeptics that retributive justice is possible in "consolidated" democracies rather than transitional democracies, but offers that:

> some Latin American countries like Argentina, Guatemala and Peru chose to hold prosecutions before their democracies were consolidated, and there is no evidence that this choice undermined their path toward a stronger democracy One could even argue that prosecutions helped consolidate democracy by warning spoilers of the possible costs to them of another coup and an authoritarian interlude.[59]

Supporting (yet with different emphasis) evidence for the relevance of trials is offered by the quantitative research conducted by Olsen, Payne, and Reiter in *Transitional Justice in the Balance: Comparing Processes, Weighing Efficacy,* who assert that their findings indicate that trials in isolation do not have a statistically significant impact on human rights improvements, but when combined with amnesties, increase the likelihood of positive change.[60] While these arguments do not provide the sole grounds for advocating for criminal punishment for wartime atrocities in Afghanistan and Nepal, they do provide grounds for serious reflection and challenge the conventional wisdom offered by international actors and elite actors in both instances, who remain convinced that "reconciliatory" measures would be the only means of addressing the past in the volatile and turbulent contexts in Afghanistan and Nepal.

Justice as marginalization: of might and men

The sociopolitical realities in Afghanistan and Nepal ensure that punitive measures against alleged war criminals will not take place any time in the near future. Even if local measures are taken, serious questions will be raised about whether and how these mechanisms will meet international standards of justice, fairness, and overall due process. Nonetheless, national actors interviewed in Afghanistan and Nepal iterated the importance of removing war criminals from political processes. A systematic process of marginalization, they stressed, while it may not directly punish such actors, would at least "clip their wings."[61]

In Afghanistan, the closest effort at systemic marginalization came from vetting, but its process and guidelines did not make them particularly effective. For example, the 2004 CoA is in line with the international instruments of human rights, including the elections standards outlined in both the UDHR and the ICCPR. Stipulations for candidates for presidential or parliamentary elections include that they cannot have been convicted for crimes against humanity or any criminal act. Article 15(3) of Afghanistan's electoral law provides the most significant vetting provision, stating that people "who practically command or are members of unofficial military forces or armed groups cannot run for office."[62] Nonetheless, both due to lack of international and national political will, and challenges of the legal system, no one has been charged for any violation of laws.[63] The existing vetting provisions were implemented for the parliamentary elections of 2005; however, even though the

102 *A meaning of justice*

secretariat identified 1,100 candidates with links to illegal armed groups (IAGs), most candidates were not disqualified because there was insufficient evidence to prove culpability. There was also concern that their disqualification would pose a security threat.[64] The 2010 ICTJ report identifies three specific reasons for the failure of the vetting process in 2005: (i) the inadequacy of the legal criteria to disqualify candidates based on their links to armed groups; (ii) lack of resources in institutions to properly implement vetting procedures; and (iii) lack of political will in the GoA and the international community to ensure a fair vetting process was starkly absent.[65] These weaknesses ultimately meant that many militia commanders could (and did) run for political office. If, however, *A Call for Justice* can be seen as an indicator of Afghan sentiments, and the *Victims' Jirga* as a voice of what "ordinary" Afghans want, then the single most important message to the international community was to end the rule of these individuals and to stop issuing *carte blanche*.

The rhetoric of listening to the local but failing to deliver on the message not only signals a need to revise political calculations, but betrays a certain discomfort with concepts of justice regarded as being rooted in non-Western philosophy. In fact, for Afghan civil society actors interviewed, this disregard for the fundamental demands for justice amounted to an exercise in some form of perverse cultural relativism, where the need to tackle the difficult questions of accountability are marginalized by what they consider as a "flawed and perhaps even a false" appreciation for local customs and cultures of reconciliation. An Afghan civil society actor bluntly accused international power holders of hiding behind the cultural façade to guise pragmatic interests:

> [I]n Afghanistan, we are talking about justice and accountability, and the need to link between justice and reconciliation. Yes, the *Shari'a* its important, but ultimately its not religion nor culture nor the tribal parts that are the problem…it is the same as in any other country in the world whether it's Muslim or not – there is corruption, there is no effective government, no judiciary…And Islam is neither going to help nor hurt these problems. Yes, it is a conservative Islamic country but…listen, at the end of the day justice is justice and right is right…[66]

One may ask then, who are these conciliatory measures, packaged as reconciliation, intended to benefit? Trying to locate reconciliation in a context of *injustice* and in a culture where justice, both because of religious beliefs and cultural practices, emphasizes on questions of equity and fairness, it may be even suggested, is a self-defeating exercise. An international Afghanistan analyst expressed his frustration with this overt focus on what reconciliation means in Afghanistan and the absence of the question of what kind of justice Afghans want in the following passage:

> [T]here has to be a message sent that people like Fahim, Sayyaf, Mohaqqiq. Say we are investigating these guys. Travel ban. And let it be done through the EU. We are not going to let Sayyaf travel. You send the message and Afghans can say why can't this guy go? What has he done? And some people will be upset…You just had to start marginalizing [them]. So while I think

A meaning of justice 103

you have to pay attention to local sensitivities and you have to recognize the Islamic context, at the end of the day, the question is, why is the corrupt guy there? Get rid of him! It's that simple.[67]

De facto impunity signifies a simple reality – those who have exploited in the past will, given the opportunity, continue the same abuses in the present. This is particularly true in Afghanistan where warlords and militia commanders exert tremendous political and military authority and continue to undermine the country's fledgling rule of law. Such concerns also exist in Nepal, relating to political parties and the increasingly powerful NA. This basically means that the lines between the "past" and the "present," so cleanly drawn in the transitional justice toolkit, are not only blurred, they are often times non-existent. Additionally, this kind of dynamic also lays bare the limited extent to which standardized transitional justice packages are equipped to deal with questions of impunity. Both these observations should compel a deeper examination of the tensions and complexities in a given context, and inform the efforts of closing the books such that transitional justice does not remain a lofty goal with trials and commissions as mechanisms through which certain goals are reached. Rather they need to creatively address questions of *ongoing* injustices that dominate current realities. Attorney General Sabbit challenged the idea that transitional justice alone can, in Afghanistan, address questions of impunity and indeed have the answers to some of the most pressing problems in the country:

> [O]ne could postpone transitional justice and uphold justice for today. For example, consider Dostum. He killed a man in his clan and he brought in supporters to plead his cause saying he was a valiant fighter during the years of conflict. But his valiance does not mean he should not be punished for his present crime…There is no equality before the law in Afghanistan…But still, what is possible right now is to focus on the crimes of current days such as the drug mafia who are committing crimes today. If the rule of law is strong and criminals are arrested for what they do today, it may happen that 30–40 percent of the concerns of the national act of reconciliation and transitional justice could be addressed. It is therefore more of an issue of management and how you put it forward – that's what matters…[68]

Succinctly, Sabbit's argument captures a fundamental shortcoming in the transitional justice paradigm in its emphasis on punishment for extraordinary crimes. Instead, what the current context in Afghanistan urges is a thorough examination of the link between past crimes committed during wartimes, and those being committed post-Bonn, and scrutinize to what extent the same perpetrators are, in many cases, continuing to exploit both the political scenario and the civilian population. Such a framework, at least in the Afghan context, could in theory contain the lofty expectations and assumptions of transitional justice, and focus attention on what in fact could be done to assist the country's effort in transitioning to some form of a rule of law state.

104   *A meaning of justice*

If the urging from the Afghan population is about marginalizing certain actors, what has been the discussion about the possibility of such a process in Nepal? As far as anyone can recall, official vetting procedures were never systematically used, if at all, in Nepal's political history.[69] Vetting did not figure in any official policy during the historic elections of 2007. The UN, which often leads the vetting procedures in transitional societies, did not take on a similar role in Nepal. According to some of those interviewed, including OHCHR-N officials, the reason for this was that the UN was invited to Nepal, particularly around the negotiations of the CPA, but were given too limited a mandate and was in too precarious a position to push for any kind of process that leading negotiators would object to. A few others have criticized this position, noting that the UN had an opportunity to negotiate its terms and should have pushed for a stronger mandate.[70] As it stood, removing perpetrators from powerful positions was not a priority, even after the elections. In fact, noted a Nepal human rights actor, "for the peace process, 346 crime cases were withdrawn – all of these cases related to the question of impunity."[71]

An exception to this frustrating status quo was in 2006 when, under tremendous pressure, General Thapa, the Chief of Army, finally stepped down, handing over his post to General Kutuwal. Thapa's resignation was a victory for Nepalese civil society because of his role in the atrocities committed by state forces during the conflict. But the pressure to marginalize or even to vet others continues, underscoring a commonly held maxim in Nepal, "impunity is never punished, it is often rewarded." Indeed, such a pronouncement seems to hold true; none of those in command responsibility in Nepal during the conflict has ever faced public or legal censure. In fact, NA personnel in positions of command responsibility during the time that human rights violations were being committed at the Maharajgunj barracks have been recommended for promotion or extension. "When the scale and depth of magnitude of impunity is so immense," observed an interviewee, "one individual's resignation does not mean the system from above has changed… there are always others to take his place."[72]

Shadow justice

The failure of the official legal system and the climate of general impunity in both societies have in the end generated a perverse sense of law and order – parallel systems of adjudication, or "shadow justice," which are at times brutal and harsh, but expedient. The Taliban, for example, has taken advantage of the absence of state presence in many of the provinces. Their methods of "swift" justice have often included immediate killing or maiming of the offender for both punishment and deterrence. In a climate of chaos and impunity, what many Afghans experience therefore is the most raw form of *adalat* (justice), which some might contend is a perverse interpretation of the *Shari'a* or at the very least, a form of vengeance killing. In an in-depth interview about the prevalence of the Taliban-styled justice in the country, an Afghanistan analyst pointed out the difference between the *act of democracy* and the *premise of justice*:

A meaning of justice 105

[T]here is an oversimplified understanding promoted that life will get better if there is democracy, and [in reality] it hasn't...so people supposedly have democracy, but they don't have *adalat*. I rarely heard people say that the Taliban are my biggest problem. People say that the reason the Taliban are here is because they have a corrupt police officer and although you and I thoroughly disagree with their method of justice, they do things that are perceived as justice by Afghans. Because they immediately deal with the corrupt officer or person who had done wrong. You know, in some places that resonates.[73]

When considering today's realities in Afghanistan, where the promise of a post-Taliban democratic nation has yet to be realized, and where the reality is dominated by the emergence and strengthening hands of warlords, corruption, and a drug economy in the midst of poverty, the question of transitional justice seems too far removed. The immediate concerns instead are about the demand for ordinary justice because of ongoing injustices and acts of impunity that communities are confronted with on a daily basis. A long-term observer perhaps best summarized the blurring of the lines between past and present in an active conflict, like in Afghanistan, when he noted: "If there is a transition, it's a transition away from peace to war...for transitional justice, you need the transitional piece, you need a clear break from the past...here its not about transitional justice...it is about justice, period."[74]

In Nepal, years of corruption and institutionalized caste systems made access to justice virtually impossible for the poor and the marginalized. The divorce between the state-level legal system and the people has been so great historically that during the decade-long conflict, it was easy for the Maoists to quickly fill the administrative vacuum in rural areas with their own *ad hoc* arrangements, including "people's courts" that administered prompt justice not according to the law but according to "conscience." In 2006, the BBC reported that Maoists had used this parallel justice system "to combat caste discrimination and secure equal rights for women, for instance, reducing polygamy."[75] While this parallel system of justice was severely criticized for using popular laws, harsh methods of punishment, and adjudicating on matters outside the realm of existing Nepali laws (e.g. family and social matters), such practices constituted a threat to the government because these systems, in their expedient delivery of justice, systematically challenged the state's legitimacy and were preferred for the deliberation of issues as widely diverse as killings and property inheritance for women.

Since the signing of the CPA, the GoN has been under significant pressure from the realities of ongoing extrajudicial killings, particularly those carried out by Nepal's armed forces on innocent civilians. Recent reports also indicate that the people's courts have started reappearing in some areas in Nepal to deliver on social justice in particular because the official legal system continues to be seen as being too corrupt, slow, and expensive.[76] While these courts are in violation of the CPA and there is pressure to hand over their cases to the police, their rebirth highlights the continuous demand for ordinary justice in remote areas of the country, and underscores the consequences of a continual judicial vacuum.

106 *A meaning of justice*

Achilles' heel: the socioeconomic dimension of justice

The absence of an in-depth discussion of economic justice in the CPA and in the Action Plan is particularly glaring given the criticism that transitional justice continues to generally neglect survivors' demands for basic economic and social rights and for development. This parochial approach is particularly problematic when considering that economic justice is one of the singular concerns for countries transitioning from conflict.

The poverty levels in Afghanistan and Nepal are strikingly high. Thirty-one percent of the Nepali population is estimated to live below the poverty line, but the distribution of poverty among social groups is unequal. While the highest castes i.e. *Brahmins, Chetris,* and *Newars* are the smallest groups in the poverty bracket, the poverty levels amongst *Dalits* (46 percent), hill *Janajatis* (44 percent) and Muslims (41 percent) are formidably high.[77] In Afghanistan, 36 percent of the population is below the absolute poverty line, and 37 percent just above it.[78] Summarily, Afghanistan and Nepal are two of the poorest countries in the world. Schabas compellingly argues that given the pre-existing conditions of poverty in many of the societies emerging from conflict, survivors cannot grasp the legal concept of reparations and compensation because their demand is not about restoring their pre-conflict realities.[79] It follows then, that a transition, and a corresponding transitional justice process, opens up a unique opportunity, as Mani has argued, to create and institutionalize a new socioeconomic configuration that is far more equitable.[80]

According to international law, states that violate their duty to protect their constituents have a legal responsibility to repair.[81] Particularly since the programs for reparations were established in Argentina, Chile and South Africa, there has been increasing attention paid to examining the role and types of reparations that are offered to communities emerging from conflict. In its narrowest forms, reparations include economic and material compensation in the form of cash payments or pensions, and can even include free or discounted social services such as scholarships, housing, health benefits, skills training, and provisions of sustainable livelihoods. They can also be symbolic, individual, or community-based and could take the shape of public apologies, museums, memorials, commemorations, or public acknowledgements of responsibility. Individualized reparation schemes, could, in the best circumstances, also include medical, psychological, and legal services, monetary compensation for financially assessable losses, and economic redress for unquantifiable harms restitution of lost, stolen, or destroyed property.[82] Irrespective of their manifestation, however, Minow insists that the "core idea" behind reparations is compensatory justice, summarily evoking the principle "wrongdoers should pay victims for losses" to wipe the slate clean.[83] The following section examines how, and to what extent the role of compensation and/or reparations have played out in the Afghan and Nepali contexts.

The National Action Plan in Afghanistan does not delve into details of reparations and overall socioeconomic justice, and there has been no official conversation about monetary compensation and reparative measures. According to the only comprehensive report on addressing victims' restitution released in 2009, the record for compensation for victims post-2001 is irregular and demonstrates both unequal distribution and lack of cohesion between the different parties involved in the conflict.[84] Ironically, the members of ISAF have by far had the most engagement on the issue of those Afghans who have been affected since the US invasion in 2001. For example, ISAF provides medical assistance in military bases, mobile medical centers, Provincial Reconstruction Team (PRT) compounds, and "walk-in" medical clinics.[85] ISAF's Post-Operations Humanitarian Relief Fund (POHRF) and projects taken on by PRTs, historically used for natural disasters, are now used for community-based projects such as rebuilding infra-structure, providing emergency relief and other forms of non-monetary aid with funds from voluntary donations of ISAF member countries. US troop command-ers have access to the US Commander's Emergency Response Program (CERP) for "community impact" projects (CIPs) in their zones of operations.[86] Similarly, the Canadian contingent draws on the Canadian Commander's Contingency Fund (CCF) for "quick impact" projects (QIPs)[87] in the community. CIPs and QIPs projects range from building schools, developing and/or repairing infrastructure, supporting local governance and even include providing funds for "condolences" for conflict-ravaged communities; however, there are no common ISAF funds for compensation for victims;[88] neither is there a standardized ISAF policy outlining how member countries can assist civilians affected by troop activities.[89] Instead each country's national laws or decisions of individual command structures generally guide this kind of initiative. Technically speaking, most of the "com-pensation" payments are not exactly compensation; rather, they are voluntary, non-legally binding "ex gratia" ("out of kindness") payments for unintentionally causing harm.[90]

In addition to international assistance through military forces, the 2009 CIVIC report identifies one program funded by the civilian branch of an IMF country specifically targeting the needs of conflict-affected civilians: the International Organization for Migration (IOM)-implemented Afghan Civilian Assistance Program (ACAP).[91] The program created by the US Congress provides tailored, in-kind assistance to civilians harmed by IMF since 2001. Finally, the Afghan Government has taken some steps to offer compensation to victims. The office of President Karzai, for example, has established a fund titled "Code 99 Fund" to provide monetary support (approximate US$2,000) to families who have lost a member in the ongoing conflict and who have to those with conflict-related injuries (approximately US$1,000).[92] In addition, it promises that in cases where someone is killed, a member of the family will be sent on the religious pilgrimage (Hajj) to Mecca. Finally, the Afghan Government runs two separate funds – the Fund for Martyrs and the Fund for the Disabled, both through the Ministry of Social Affairs, Labor, Martyrs, and Disabled (MoLSAMD).[93] The Fund for Martyrs resembles the pension system, with those killed either before or after 2001 being considered *shahids* (martyrs), enabling their surviving relatives collect monthly financial assistance.

The MoLSAMD Fund, at least in theory, is aimed at providing social solidarity to those injured during conflict, and the rate of compensation varies depending on

108 *A meaning of justice*

the extent of their injuries. In reality, this kind of assistance from the IMF, foreign governments and the Afghan Government is plagued with challenges and tempered by controversy. At the operational level, all three are limited and sometimes compromised by corruption, tribal politics, inadequate delivery services and channels, security, lack of adequate information on the side of survivors' about where and how to navigate available sources, insufficient information about victims, and the challenge of determining genuine claims. Since its inception, such assistance has also been criticized for their lack of transparency, inconsistent administration, their *ad hoc* nature (particularly regarding ex gratia payments), lack of coordination within ISAF countries and between ISAF and other contributing partners, and most often, for existing in theory, but not in actuality.[94]

At the conceptual level, these efforts muddy the waters for any discussion on transitional justice, fall outside of the National Action Plan's ambit, and do not address the needs and concerns of victims and survivors prior to 2001. While it is impossible to evaluate what the long-term impact will be of these programs, it is possible to claim that military forces determining, assessing, and disbursing monetary compensation and reparative measures cannot have a beneficial long-term impact. The temporary nature of a foreign military's engagement in a conflict, and uncoordinated and *ad hoc* "knee-jerk" responses to conflict-based claims can also undermine the authority of an already weak state. Further, payment for damages in an existing vicious cycle of conflict generates a dangerous precedent for creating unhealthy and unsustainable dependence on a foreign (military) force. Increasingly, ISAF and PRT involvement in civilian reconstruction work has also come under heavy criticism for crowding the "humanitarian space," in its deployment of militarized humanism, and subsequently usurping the roles of human rights, development, and more broadly, civil society actors, and obscuring the boundaries between military operations and development assistance.[95]

The legitimacy of the Maoist insurgency drew heavily on the culturally and politically institutionalized socioeconomic disparity that defines Nepali society. The CPN-M heavily recruited from poor and marginalized communities, and consequently they experienced the heaviest brunt of excessive force unleashed by state security forces. In theory, at least, it would follow then, these groups targeted by both the GoN (for allegedly supporting the CPN-M) and the Maoists (for bribes, recruitment, etc.) would be priority groups for compensation and reparations; however, six years since the formal end of the conflict, Nepal's record for compensation and/or reparations continue to be irregular and fragmented. A common complaint from victim networks, underscored by several of the more elite civil society actors, was that the Nepali Government has consistently neglected victims' networks and victims as active agents, and instead seen them as "passive" recipients of aid. Through the World Bank (WB), the GoN had been offered US$44.96 billion as part of the bank's Emergency Peace Support Program (EPSP) to provide compensation for conflict victims. The NHRC recommended that 100,000 Nepalese rupees (NPR) (US$1,500) or NPR150,000 (US$2,350) should be paid in cases where a person's right to life had been violated.[96] The Home Ministry also had a tariff and budget for the payment of compensation, but the parliament was not bound to apply the same level tariff.[97] While a parliamentary probe committee awarded record amounts of compensation – NPR1 million (US$15,500) – to the relatives of Sapana Gurung and the six killed during the subsequent demonstration against her murder, this case did not generate the momentum for assisting other victims of the war.[98]

Between 2008–09, the GoN published three policy documents on the Interim Relief Program (IRP).[99] These guidelines introduced the term "conflict affected persons" (CAPs) to those entitled to benefit from the IRP.[100] The measures in the IRP are committed to providing NPR100,000, approximately US$1,430, to families of those who died or who disappeared in the conflict and NPR25,000 to the widows of men who were killed in the conflict.[101] Other provisions in the guidelines included skills development programs, economic assistance to people and institutions whose properties were damaged during the war, scholarship for orphans, and medical treatment for the injured and disabled. In December 2009, the cabinet repealed "Measures for Financial Support and Relief for Convict Victims" and introduced "Procedure for Relief, Compensation and Financial Support for Citizens," which extended scholarship provisions for children of the disappeared. Women's activists and victims' representatives, however, have emphasized that none of the guidelines recognize victims of torture, assault, rape, and sexual violence. Overall, Nepal still does not have an overall policy for granting compensation to conflict victims and a reparations program has yet to be instituted.

Victims' networks and individual victims have also been critical of the government-initiated and externally supported MoPR, which was mandated to create Local Peace Committees (LPCs) as a temporary measure to facilitate the peace process at the local level until the new Constitution was adopted.[102] While the terms of reference for LPCs include the mandate to monitor the MoPR's implementation of programs and support its Task Force, there is however no explicit reference in the IRP to certify conflict victims. Despite the fact that 72 LPCs have been formed since February 2011, many of these committees have not yet held their first meetings.[103] Although functioning LPCs require that four of its 23 members should be victims, in reality these four often represent political parties rather than victims. They have not been offered any role in decision-making about programs in the LPCs and there has been no effort to consult with them. In fact, a common observation from human rights NGOs and allegation of victims' representatives was that unless victims are affiliated with a political party, they get no support from LPCs. Some victims even alleged that they were directly denied support because they did not patronize a politician or a political party where initiatives such as the LPC serve as "bargaining sites of political parties and not a venue for victims' voices."[104]

The monetary assistance offered to Nepalis has been held hostage to unequal and highly politicized relief distribution, ineffective government outreach, technical challenges, lack of recognition of human rights violations even during relief distribution, and victims' own inability to articulate their claims and their rights.[105] In the interim, *Tharus*, the *Dalits*, and women have seen little improvement; in many instances, their situation has worsened. The local demand for justice has,

110   *A meaning of justice*

consequently, centered on urgent and immediate compensatory relief. A local civil society actor, voiced a common frustration:

> Right after the conflict, the demand was very much about justice, justice against perpetrators, for the rights of victims, for the missing. As time has gone by, there is a shift – there is still a demand for justice, but there is a more pressing demand for compensation…after all, most of these victims are very poor, they need to bring up their children, they have to keep themselves alive. When that is taken care of, the other things can come…sometimes it seems like if the government could just send a letter acknowledging that someone was killed in your family they would be satisfied.[106]

A fundamental concern that may be raised in both the Nepali and Afghan contexts is whether, and to what extent immediate monetary compensation and long-term reparations, individual and/or collective in nature, are sufficient to address the struggles of conflict victims. Some scholars and practitioners claim that there needs to be a stronger nexus between transitional justice and the broader development infrastructure. Aguierre and Pietropaoli, for example, insist "the right to development is the closest legal manifestation of the rights of marginalized people to participate in development."[107] In addition, they assert that transitional justice and the right to development is linked because it allows for a connectivity between development and human rights law, underscores the interdependence and universality of human rights in relation to development, and also helps create a rights-based framework for development and transitional justice for state action.[108]

Taking into account the realities in Afghanistan and Nepal, where the poorest have also constituted the largest numbers of conflict victims, such an argument certainly has strong resonance. Consider for example, the question of land in both countries. Land conflict is a complex reality in Afghanistan. Land is both a homestead and a source of income, given that Afghanistan is a largely agricultural and pastoral country. Given illegal land possessions by warlords and competing claims of land ownership by returning refugees and IDPs, according to a 2009 AREU report, the highest frequency of land disputes is about questions of property ownership rights relating to inheritance and that of occupation.[109] Despite being an agriculture-based country, the feudal system in Nepal has historically denied lower caste people land ownership and ensured their continued position as "servants" who worked the land. The system of landlordism as it exists today evolved out of non-farmer elites accruing land holdings over time as a means of attaining both security and elevated social status. According to a 2009 UK Department of International Development (DFID) report, the land tenure system introduced in Nepal in 1951 has afforded tenants little protection other than for those with money.[110] The 1964 Land Act, which terminated the practice of offering vast land grants to royal favorites, failed to address entrenched inequalities in land ownership and distribution.[111] In a 2001 government census, a little over a million out of over four million families in Nepal did not own land; five million mostly

A meaning of justice 111

belonging to members of the *Dalit* and other Terai communities were landless.[112] The staggering statistics not only reflect Nepal's poverty, but also its institutionalized caste structure, urging the need for land reform. Expressing his frustration at the current state of affairs and the central question of land within the broader framework of socioeconomic justice, an analyst vented:

> This is a country governed by the rich for the rich at the expense of the poor. And it's very frustrating that you don't have many of the systems in place that actually vindicate the rights of the poor. There is a ton of development speak but none of these actually help the poor. There is no real system of land tenure and there seems to be no way that the actual poor can have any leverage.[113]

Certainly then, socioeconomic reconfiguration is imperative to address some of the fundamental premises of inequity in both countries. Scholars, such as Pablo de Greiff in his critique of a "juridical" approach to reparations that aims to re-establish the status quo ante by proportionate compensation for harms, proposes a "political" framework of reparations programs that measures their effectiveness in terms of social justice, which in contexts such as Afghanistan and Nepal would encompass distributive justice including land reform.[114] Others, however, would urge caution in blending two different agendas – that of reparations and that of development. Verdeja for example, argues:

> While most of society would benefit from an increase in development, there is a question of whether the specifically normative dimension of reparations risks subsumption under general development and distributive programs, clouding the normative distinction between reparative justice aimed at victims per se and more general state policies to combat poverty."[115]

Further, in contexts where victims were specifically targeted (in Nepal, the *Tharu* population and the *Dalits* assumed to be part of the Maoist movement, and in Afghanistan, political affiliations assumed of communities based on ethnic and ideological identities), they were considered, as Arendt described, as "objective enemies."[116] For victims then, the question is not only that of financial compensation, but also the *moral* reaction of the state.

In Afghanistan, while victims' demands vary, the 2009 CIVIC report stated that "beyond requests for formal justice, more civilians told us that some sense of redress could be achieved through a simple apology from those responsible for their loss...interviewees noted whether troops had apologized to them, publicly or personally."[117] The report also quotes Anja de Beer, the head of Agency Coordinating Body for Afghan Relief (ACBAR) as stating: "The [IMF] are not straightforward on a human level to say that they're sorry and in Afghanistan that is important...Compensation is important in Afghanistan...but showing you're sorry is also important."[118] In Nepal, victims and local human rights organizations interviewed stressed the distinction between immediate "interim relief" provided or promised and the broader scope of justice that they demanded, particularly

112   *A meaning of justice*

relating to questions of punishing perpetrators, knowing the whereabouts of the disappeared, and sustainable rehabilitation. Otherwise, a victim's group representative argued, it becomes "a lump sum of money being thrown at you and then the government and civil society forgetting about your every day struggles."[119] In both Afghanistan and Nepal, what emerges is that even when poverty levels are so dire, people demand to be recognized for the damages endured. It is this universal claim to human dignity that local voices continue to claim in both contexts.

Where are the women? The gender dimension of transitional justice

The question of gender cuts across the discussion of justice. Since its inception, transitional justice practices have not included the experiences and needs of women in accounting for the past. Criminal prosecutions, particularly in the earlier years, fell short of delivering justice for gender-based atrocities and it is only until recently that they have begun to treat the rape of women not only as inhumane and an attack on "honor and dignity" but also "with the same fervor as are the war crimes which happen routinely to men."[120] The discussion of women's involvement and their experiences during and after the war has also engendered greater scholarly rigor in trying to understand how they can engage with different transitional justice mechanisms and how such efforts can actually have relevance in their lives. In *Does Feminism Need a Theory of Transitional Justice?* Bell and O'Rourke ask, "where are women in transitional justice?"[121] This query exposes both the absence of women in formal negotiations for transitional justice and the glaring absence of their diverse experiences during and after conflict in the nature and design of the transitional justice mechanisms.[122] Both these inquiries compel an incisive critique of the transitional justice discourse in Afghanistan and Nepal. They also help broaden the discussion of not only the need to recognize women's experiences with sexual violence during the period of conflict, but also their social, political, and economic experiences in the period following the official cessation of hostilities.

Applying a feminist lens to *A Call for Justice* and *Nepali Voices*, as well as to Afghanistan's National Action Plan and the CPA provisions, raises serious concerns about the stark absence of women and their specific concerns. *A Call for Justice*, for example, which, while involving women in focus group discussions and in the interviews, does not include specific sections that relate to gender-based violations or the views of women on the subject. *Nepali Voices* too has been critiqued for its limited engagement with marginalized populations, particularly women, and women of lower castes, ethnicities and religious persuasions, their experience with gender-based violations and what could constitute redress for such crimes.[123] In the same vein, Afghanistan's National Action Plan only makes passing reference to the question of gender-based violations and has, according to a 2009 ICTJ report, "made little substantive headway in addressing the fundamental social and political imbalances that have permitted abuses against women."[124] Nepal's CPA makes no specific reference to women either in relation to their role as combatants or as victims of the decade-long conflict. Their relative absence in the respective surveys of what survivors demand in the aftermath of conflict, and certainly their absence in national platforms of action is a reflection of the status of women and their lack of access in both societies. The following section takes a closer look at women's realities in Afghanistan and Nepal.

Afghan women's experiences under the Taliban are well documented. During the height of their rule, through the *al-Amr bi al-Ma'ruf wa al-Nahi 'an al-Mun-kir* (Ministry of Enforcement of Virtue and Suppression of Vice), particularly in the cities, they enforced decrees that regulated "moral behavior," particularly of women, which included "edicts restricting movement, the denial of the right to work, beatings and other physical abuse, arbitrary detention, and a near ban on post-pubescent girls' access to education."[125] Even minor infractions of the rules could lead to public beatings, threats, and imprisonment.[126] Deaths frequently occurred due to lack of access to medical facilities; illiteracy, unemployment, and poverty among the female population skyrocketed; sexual violence was commonplace; and women were targeted for summary executions and extrajudicial killings when accused of adultery, "immorality," and violating the strict edicts issued. Subsequently, the use of the rhetoric of "liberating Afghan women from the Taliban" became a politically salient way to legitimize the 2001 invasion of Afghanistan. But gender-based violence was not unique during the period of Taliban rule. During the civil war between 1992–8, and particularly during the Afshar Operation,[127] the AJP reports that rape was first majorly used as a weapon of war, with Ittihad forces[128] raping an unknown number of Hazara Shi'a women, and Wahdat forces[129] raping Pashtun women. The 2005 AJP report notes: "every mujahideen group fighting inside Kabul committed rape with the specific purpose of punishing entire communities for their perceived support for rival militias,"[130] thereby establishing the use of rape and sexual violence as not only a weapon of war, but also an instrument of ethnic cleansing. An interview with an international analyst about the possibility of seeking retributive justice for sex-based crimes during wartime revealed the rift between cultural dictates and certain notions of universalism:

> It gets so terribly complicated when it comes to the question of women's experiences during the conflict and the possibility of trials. Under what laws should such trials operate? Strict interpretation of the *Shari'a* calls for producing four male witnesses in a rape case. Who would come forward to testify for rape during conflict? Given the highly conservative culture, would women even consider coming forward to give testimonies? How would punishment be meted out for rape crimes?[131]

An international or a hybrid trial would not necessarily address the multidimensional complexity of such a theoretical enterprise. Lack of substantive evidence, access and limited testimonies and reluctance of survivors would inevitably be significant obstacles. Nevertheless, this overt focus on the *Shari'a*, some of those interviewed argued, could be seen to avoid specific violations committed against women during the ongoing conflicts and what women continue to experience

114 *A meaning of justice*

today. Even if some of those trials were symbolic, and held sometime in the future, some of those interviewed believed they would serve as an acknowledgement of the specific experiences of Afghan women in almost three decades of continuous conflict.

Punitive measures for sexual violence during conflict are only one fragment of the justice when approaching the question of Afghan women. For the 48.9 percent of the Afghan population who are women,[132] gender justice in every aspect of life continues to be a far cry from reality. While Afghan women now occupy some seats in both the *Meshrano* and *Wolesi Jirgas*, hold provincial council seats and civil servant positions, have participated as voters as well as candidates in the presidential and parliamentary elections of 2004, 2005, and 2010, overall they continue to suffer extremely low social, economic, and political status. They rank among the world's worst off for most indicators, including life expectancy (46 years), maternal mortality (1,600 deaths per 100,000 births), and literacy (12.6 percent of females 15 years and older).[133] Women and girls continue to face restrictions on their mobility; many still cannot travel without an accompanying male relative. Along with social and political rights, the right to education is also being eroded at a frightening rate. Attacks on girl students, schools, closing down of educational institutions, societal resistance to equal access to education for girls, and a lack of resources has meant that the majority of girls in the country continue to remain out of school.

The general lawlessness and insecurity in Afghanistan continue to make women all the more vulnerable to sexual violence. Widespread poverty has increased the practice of the sale by parents of their daughters, putatively as brides but in practice as prostitutes.[134] Although Islamic law prohibits selling girls, ambiguity around local laws is such that according to a local Afghan jurist "nobody would ever be charged for selling a daughter."[135] The AIHRC continues to register a rise in the cases of violence against women, including that of forced marriages, rape, and self-immolation. Provisions operationalized by the Karzai Government have also been significantly regressive. Today, restrictions against Afghan women include curtailing educational opportunities, forcing chastity examinations, imprisoning women for refusing to marry or for leaving a marriage, and blocking redress in cases of state-orchestrated sexual assault.[136] The Vice and Virtue Patrol, which established a record of arbitrary abuses, notably for beating and harassing women and girls for traveling without male guardians and for even slight infractions of stringent dress requirements, continues to operate under the new Ministry of Justice and under the aegis of the Department of Islamic Instruction.[137] In June 2007, Karzai sent the Afghan parliament a proposal for reestablishing the Department for the Promotion of Virtue and the Prevention of Vice. In November 2007, parliament debated the possibility of closing the Ministry of Women's Affairs. In response to women's rights activists decrying the increasing stronghold of the warlords and expressing concern about the current efforts to "reconcile" antagonistic parties, Arsala Rahmani, the recently assassinated member of the Afghanistan High Peace Council (HPC) and a former Taliban government official, reportedly said,

Afghan women's rights activists are being close-minded and neglecting a mother's duty to always try to unite their sons. The Taliban only wants to protect women. Yes, it's for your own good, young women, that Taliban fighters burn down your schools in areas they control and force you to marry them at, oh, age 13 or 14 if they like what they imagine is under your burqas.[138]

Such a position reflects the sentiments of several of Afghanistan's national lawmakers, generating a hostile environment for women. It follows then that the question of gender justice in current efforts to jumpstart a new reconciliation process in Afghanistan underscores the deep cleavages between an elite understanding of what such processes would mean and for the voices at the margins. While several women leaders interviewed expressed the importance of reconciliation to end the conflict, many women civil society actors continue to be extremely concerned about Karzai's current efforts, supported by the international community, to bring parties together for negotiations. Without strong international support for certain non-negotiable issues such as women's rights, they fear elite political dealings could make compromises that would ultimately be a step backward in the strides made in the last 11 years. Women's groups also expressed their reservations about the current reintegration and reconciliation strategy in the run-up to the 2010 London Conference.[139] They raised them again at the Dubai Women's Dialogue,[140] which exposed the exclusion of gender in the London Conference's agenda and the clear absence of women representatives in the Afghan delegation.[141] For advocates for Afghan women, until concerns of systemic marginalization and lack of participation are adequately addressed, the justice question, beyond that of the transitional justice framework, remains an elusive project.

A Hindu kingdom until 2007, Nepal's socio–cultural framework infused by Hinduism has historically been a deeply patriarchal society. A verse from *Ram Charit Manas*[142] best captures this with its proclamation, "drums, idiots, outcasts and women are fit only for beating."[143] Despite the fact that Nepali women constitute 50.05 percent of the population, traditions and cultural practices of patriarchy have ensured that there is very little scope for women to be decision-makers both in the private and public realms. Only 11 percent of Nepali women have any land ownership, 72 percent of women versus 48 percent of men work in agriculture, and 60 percent of women work as unpaid family laborers.[144] The executive director of the Feminist Dalit Organization (FEDO) summarized the conditions of *Dalit* women in the following:

[W]e have had systematic marginalization and exclusion of women…and then during the conflict they were also raped and tortured… *Dalit* women have very few rights to begin with; they do not have marriage registration, they do not have citizenship, and they don't have birth registrations of their children…which means, without official records, their children cannot go to school. If a husband leaves his wife, she has no right to his property.[145]

116 *A meaning of justice*

While the decade-long conflict resulted in rape and sexual torture of thousands of Nepali women,[146] the destruction of their homes and families, widowhood and rendered thousands of civilian women refugees and IDPs, the People's War also provided a unique opportunity for many women, especially from impoverished and marginalized castes, to actively participate in the frontlines of war. The United People's Front, the Maoists' political wing, summarized the fundamental social disruption brought on by the Maoist ideology in its statement: "Patriarchal exploitation and discrimination against women should be stopped. Their daughters should be allowed access to paternal property."[147] The Maoists also encouraged social reform, promoted remarriage for widows, inter-caste marriage, revoked *chaupadi*, the strict taboos concerning women's menstrual periods [and] opposed child marriage and polygamy.[148] Their calls to arms and the crisis situation that emerged particularly broke new grounds and created intended and unintended spaces for women's participation and challenged traditional caste and gender hierarchies; women comprised 40 percent of the Maoist cadres in combatant roles, including in female-only squads and platoons.[149]

The euphoria of the conflict period, however, did not translate seamlessly in official efforts to end the war. The negotiations between the political parties in the lead-up to the 12-point Letter of Understanding of November 2005 and subsequent negotiations for the formation of an interim government did not include a single female representative.[150] Other mechanisms formed during the peace negotiations similarly had no women participants. A National Monitoring Committee (NMC) created to monitor the implementation of the 12-point Letter of Understanding only had two women among its 31 members.[151] The Interim Constitution Drafting Committee initially comprised of six men, but later included four women in response to a campaign led by women's organizations.[152]

There is a deep social stigma attached to their participation in the frontlines of war. Women also struggle with the realities of social and economic inequity and sexual violence experienced during and after the formal cessation of conflict. A significant challenge they have is related to the legal and social status of widowhood, which they cannot claim being family members of the "disappeared." Married women who have lost their husbands may continue to wear the *sindhur* (the red powder in their hair that denotes marriage) and wear bangles, but without exact knowledge of the status of their partners, and conducting the rituals of death, their social status remains unclear. Without the fulfillment of these last rites for their partners, they are denied the purification rites to pass through onto widowhood. A local human rights actor explains,

> In Nepal, disappearances are tied to not only emotional suffering, but also to the question of economics…so many of those disappeared belonged to the lower castes and came from the poor and marginalized communities…. this means main breadwinners were now gone and women survivors don't know if they are widows or they will find their husbands…a skewed power relationship then emerges within the family they have married in to, and they remain socially, culturally and economically ostracized.[153]

These realities of gender justice raise questions about the existing framework for transitional justice in Nepal. Overall, women were latecomers in current transitional justice activism and it was only recently that organizations such as AF, FEDO, United Nations Entity for Gender Equality and the Empowerment of Women (UNIFEM), and the National Women's Commission (NWC) became involved in trying to advocate for the rights of women within the existing framework. Thus far, there have been some fledgling improvements as a consequence of such mobilization. The proposed TRC bill as it stands, for example, finally recognizes women and girls who experienced sexual violence as victims; the category of "serious violations of human rights" now includes rape and sexual violence;[154] and rape is included as one of the categories of crimes for which "no recommendation for amnesty shall be made to a person involved."[155] Yet despite demands of survivors of sexual violence for compensation from the state,[156] and recognition of the criminal nature of such crimes, the current draft gives powers "to the TRC to 'cause reconciliation' for certain crimes, including sexual violence."[157] The reference to recommending amnesty still remains, which again human rights and women's rights organizations consider as being extremely problematic for victims of sexual violence. Further, the 2010 AF and ICTJ report states:

> According to the Bill, recommendation for amnesty involves submitting an application for amnesty and 'repenting for the misdeeds carried out' in a way that is 'to the satisfaction of the victim.' However, the victim does not necessarily have a voice in this process, as the Commission 'may' consult the victim before making a decision, but such a consultation is not required. Thus, even though the Bill requires the victim's satisfaction, it does not have in place measures to ensure that this satisfaction element is attained.[158]

There still remain unanswered questions about the appointment of commissioners and whether statement taking, hearings, and outreach processes would be more gender-sensitive. The Disappearances Commission Bill thus far has failed to recognize the gendered dimension of enforced disappearances and there was no consultation with women's organizations in drafting the bill. The struggle for visibility in the official processes of justice and reconciliation for women in Nepal are far from over.

Conclusion

Opotow contests the assumption that justice is "firm, stable and unwavering" and insists, "in reality...justice is sensitive to contextual contingencies."[159] This chapter was an effort to illuminate challenges of the concept of justice as it pertains to the local realities of Afghanistan and Nepal, and illustrate how, contrary to Opotow's claims, in reality, the pursuit of justice remains *in*sensitive to the contextual contingencies.

This chapter began the discussion with a close examination of impunity as a socioeconomic and political reality that constraints and undermines prospects of

118 A meaning of justice

democratic governance and a functional rule of law. It then turned to four specific concerns of local justice, which has emerged in both contexts. In doing so, it first recognizes that each of these questions – retributive justice, justice as marginalization, socioeconomic demands, and gender justice – are in and of themselves significant fields of in-depth study. These claims encompass the need to address the extraordinary crimes committed during conflict, "ordinary" crimes, and existing sociopolitical and economic inequities.

The discussion on retributive justice, highlights that justice as punishment has appeal, both symbolically and tangibly, to make a break from the cycles of impunity that has so entrenched itself in both societies, a priori, during and even after the cessation of hostilities. Further, contrary to reservations about trials for war crimes, Sikkink has demonstrated that prosecutions do in fact contribute significantly to reduced levels of human rights repression in states where they have been implemented, even if they do not deliver on the lofty expectations that generate the demand for retribution. In places like Afghanistan and Nepal where warlords, politicians, and military personnel continue to occupy powerful public positions, they serve as a reminder of the legacies of war, and as catalysts for a climate within which "ordinary" crimes continue to be committed without any fear of retribution. Ultimately, the very reason why a TRC was considered for Afghanistan and indeed for Nepal, i.e. a weak rule of law, was the reason why activists believe that a more stringent mechanism is required to send a "strong message"[160] to other violations.

The practice of vetting might have only emerged recently in transitional justice literature as standard practice, but as the example in Afghanistan clearly illustrates, "those with blood on their hands, should stand at the back of the mosque," resounds with the traditional philosophy of social ostracization and an emphasis to remove anyone from a position of authority who has caused human suffering. If indeed culture, the "static local," continues to be the point of reference for transitional justice packages, then the question must be raised, where, in the efforts to legitimize practices of societal healing and conciliatory measures, is the issue of accountability? Certainly, both the Afghan and Nepali contexts clearly illustrate that the local concerns about social, economic, and political marginalization of those with power would constitute as justice.

Finally, the chapter took a critical look at socioeconomic justice and gender justice, both of which are important missing elements in the formal commitments for transitional justice. Both Afghanistan and Nepal are poor countries, which simultaneously face deep-rooted questions of economic inequity on one hand, and lack of equal access and security for the female population on the other. The *ad hoc* nature of providing monetary compensation and other forms of relief by international military forces in Afghanistan, for example, undermines the Afghan state and generates a dangerous precedent for creating unhealthy and unsustainable dependence on a situation out of which there is currently no clear exit strategy. In Nepal, GoN and WB efforts to provide monetary compensation to victims have not reached the large numbers of survivors, nor have they adequately addressed the need for communal reparations or, equally importantly, questions the nexus between transitional justice and development. Afghan and Nepali women's limited access to formal and informal judicial mechanisms, land ownership, educational and social services, and other discriminatory laws are a humbling reminder of the absence of a gender-sensitive approach to issues of justice, truth, security, and reconciliation in both countries.

In short then, the formal commitments to transitional justice in Afghanistan and Nepal have largely failed to capture the needs of the "voices from the margins." This failure underscores that even beyond the pressing demand for a response to extraordinary atrocities is the persistent claim for ordinary justice by the voiceless.

6 Negotiating narrow spaces
National Human Rights Institutions

On February 10, 2010, Wahid Omar, spokesperson for the president of Afghanistan, was quoted in *Hasht-e-Sob* as stating: "Governments do not implement transitional justice," suggesting that it is up to civil institutions to find ways of doing it.[1] In Afghanistan, and also to a great extent in Nepal, the reality reflects this very same pronouncement – a handful of national and international actors have valiantly fought to keep the discussion of accounting for the past alive, even if at the absolute margins. This state of affairs reflects a complex picture of the states in question, the priorities and limitations of the respective governments, the challenges facing national and international actors, and the politics and politicking between them.

In Afghanistan and Nepal, a discussion of local actors and their engagement with "transitional justice" is incomplete without recognizing the role of two very specific national actors – the AIHRC and the NHRC.[2] These two national actors, independent of NGO actors, networks, or associations that emerge or disappear based on funding availability, donor decisions and sometimes leadership, occupy a unique position in human rights programming and increasingly, in transitional justice, given their permanent legal status, the scale of their programmes, their mandates to act as a bridge between local concerns and their respective governments while also serving as an umbrella for local human rights actors.

This chapter begins with an overview of the role of NHRIs particularly in societies emerging from conflict to better understand their specific mandates relating to questions of human rights and transitional justice. It then focuses on the significance of the AIHRC and NHRC, their specific experiences, contributions, and their challenges in the ongoing efforts in transitional justice Afghanistan and Nepal, respectively. It concludes that NHRIs such as AIHRC and the NHRC, despite all their imperfections, are uniquely positioned to link the issues of past injustices (the *raison d'être* of transitional justice) to that of current injustices, thereby challenging the somewhat false dichotomy between "ordinary" and "extraordinary" crimes in societies' struggling to make a transition from war to stability.

Enter NHRIs: an overview[3]

NHRIs are state-sponsored entities set up under an act of parliament or by the constitution with the broad objective of protecting and promoting human rights.[4] They have quasi-judicial competence, and key elements of their composition are independence and pluralism.[5] According to the Paris Principles,[6] NHRIs are required to monitor violations of human rights; advise the government and parliament on issues related to legislation and compliance with international human rights violations; audit laws; train personnel; educate the public; report to international bodies; hold inquiries; handle complaints; relate to regional and international organizations; and assist in formulating educational human rights programs. In short, they are the "practical link between international standards and their concrete application,"[7] and, irrespective of their mandate, represent government efforts to "embed international norms in domestic structures."[8]

The International Council on Human Rights Policy (IHCHRP) reports that NHRIs are established in one of three circumstances: in countries making the transition from conflict, such as Northern Ireland, South Africa, the Philippines, Spain, and Latvia; in countries where a commission is established to consolidate and underpin other human rights protections, such as Australia, Canada, and France; or in countries that come under pressure to respond to allegations of serious human rights abuses, as in Cameroon, Nigeria, Togo, and Mexico.[9] Bell writes that "NHRIs signal a stamp of democratic legitimacy on the deal arrived at: they constitute part of the politically correct approach to constitutionalism."[10]

Contemporary history is replete with examples of how NHRIs are being incorporated into peace negotiations. Both the 1995 Dayton Peace Accords and the failed NATO-led Rambouillet peace proposal of March 1999 included the establishment human rights ombudsmen for Bosnia and Herzegovina and Kosovo, respectively. The Lomé Peace Agreement of 1999 included provisions for the establishment of both a human rights commission and a TRC in Sierra Leone, and the Northern Ireland Peace Agreement included provisions for creating human rights institutions on a bilateral basis in both Ireland and Northern Ireland. Recent discussions about the expanding responsibilities of NHRIs have included their contributions in "transitional justice" processes.[11] They can raise awareness about various transitional justice mechanisms and lessons learned worldwide; engage civil society and institutional actors in the transitional justice discourse; facilitate national consultations; ensure the participation of victims, women and vulnerable groups; assist in the establishment of transitional justice initiatives; and facilitate follow-up on the recommendations of various transitional justice mechanisms.[12]

During transitions, NHRIs may play a critical role in ensuring accountability and combating impunity by documenting and archiving past and present violations of international human rights law and international humanitarian law.[13] They can also promote an environment conducive to establishing transitional justice

122 *National Human Rights Institutions*

initiatives most suited to local context.[14] The establishment of NHRIs, however, does not automatically lead to building good governance and protecting human rights. They may be established with the best of intentions, but such commissions can often become "window-dressing." As such, they might provide opportune moments for fledgling governments who want to give the appearance that they are taking concrete steps to address human rights concerns, but in fact affect very little real change. Cardenas asserts:

> NHRIs are being created largely to satisfy international audiences; they are the result of state adaptation. These international origins, however, have the following paradoxical effect: most NHRIs remain too weak to protect society from human rights violations at the same time that they create an unprecedented demand for such protection."[15]

It is within this complex interplay of legal, political, financial and social tensions, between what is ideal and what is real that the domestic struggle for long-term justice by NHRIs, and in this case AIHRC and NHRC, needs to be understood.

The AIHRC

Established by the 2001 Bonn Agreement and the Presidential Decree of 6th June 2002, based on UN General Assembly 134/38 in 1993 and the Paris Principles, and institutionalized by Article 58 of the Constitution of the Islamic Republic of Afghanistan, the AIHRC was, for the longest time, the solitary institution claiming to lead the transitional justice movement in Afghanistan. Chaired by Dr Sima Samar, who was then the Minister of Women's Affairs in the Interim Administration, its eleven members included five women and representatives from each of the major ethnic groups. Many observers have lauded the AIHRC commissioners for their independence and their commitment because many were former civil society activists who had long been working in Afghanistan under very difficult wartime conditions, but some have noted their lack of experience in working in human rights.[16] A current commissioner concurred: "...none of us were human rights experts...we were all human rights activists but had no idea how to run a professional national commission so it was really a challenge for us."[17] Furthermore, their independence meant that they lacked the political clout of the more politicized bodies with influential members.[18] Despite these concerns, the Presidential Decree, which established the commission, made it a powerful mechanism for human rights protection. Today's AIHRC's position is aided by quasi-judicial powers, including the ability to summon anyone living in Afghanistan as witnesses and to "compel them to produce documentary or material evidence in their possession or under their control."[19]

In early 2002, the United Nations Development Program (UNDP) supported the UNAMA and the UNOHCHR to facilitate four Afghan Working Groups, which included human rights education, transitional justice, human rights for women, and monitoring and investigating human rights violations.[20] This in turn resulted in six programs: human rights education; women's human rights; children's rights; monitoring and investigating human rights violation; research, policy, and media; and transitional justice.[21] Later on, it added its program for people with disabilities.[22]

The AIHRC quickly positioned itself to tackle some of the most complicated human rights concerns in a country devastated by more than thirty years of civil war and protracted violence, and despite several constraints, with the cooperation of organizations such as the UNDP, it has made significant logistical progress. With more than 600 staff members distributed amongst its eight regional and six provincial offices, the commission has conducted training and workshops in women's rights, children's rights, and human rights education in Kabul and in the regions and provinces where it has a presence. It also produces and broadcasts radio-based and TV programs on human rights. In addition, AIHRC chairs the Human Rights Advisory Group (HRAG).

Given its unique mandate, the commission regularly receives complaints on human rights related issues from right to due process, land grabs, alleged use of torture to extort confessions from detainees, to abuse of power from all over the country. In the absence of government presence in many areas of the country, including judicial structures, people commute, often on foot, to file their complaints with the institution in the hope for some government action.[23] The commission has also been active in documenting rights violations by US-led coalition forces in Afghanistan that have included alleged beatings, arbitrary detention, and damage to homes, and has publicly decried the lack of respect for Afghan culture during coalition raids. It has also been at the forefront of publicizing incidents of "collateral damage" due to NATO and US bombing campaigns. Other activities have included monitoring prisons and creating sustained pressure on the government for human rights commitments, which led to the establishment of human rights units in the Ministries of Interior, Justice, Women's Affairs, Education, Defense and Foreign Affairs. Today, the AIHRC is increasingly integrated into the human rights monitoring and investigative work of the UN and works in close collaboration with the human rights focal points at UNAMA and the Danish Embassy.

AIHRC's responsibilities in transitional justice are clearly enunciated in the commission's mandate.[24] Those responsibilities have been interpreted to include investigation, recording, and publication of the human rights violations defined as such in international law, Islamic principles, and Afghan tradition.[25] Accordingly, it began a two-pronged approach for this project: (i) documentation of human rights abuses; and (ii) a national consultation to learn how the Afghan people would want justice for human rights violations committed during the decades of war.

In January 2005, at the completion of its transitional justice consultation, the AIHRC published *A Call For Justice.* In December of the same year, a joint collaboration by OHCHR, UNAMA, and AIHRC resulted in a conference on truth seeking and reconciliation in Kabul. The main outcomes of the conference included emphatic support for a comprehensive approach to transitional

124 *National Human Rights Institutions*

justice, which emphasized the need for a truth-seeking process and a reconciliation platform that did not compromise the search for justice. The conference also outlined the need for administrative reform, improvement in security conditions, measures to remove human rights abusers from positions of power, and urged the creation of an environment conducive to other transitional justice activities. The importance of including women in the truth-seeking process was strongly emphasized. With strong international support from the UN, the European Union (EU), The Netherlands, and Canada, and drawing from numerous consultations, the AIHRC, in coordination with other notable international human rights and transitional justice groups, began work to draw up the Action Plan for Peace, Reconciliation and Justice in Afghanistan.[26]

The AIHRC continues to work on documentation and data analysis in close collaboration with the ICTJ and UNAMA to develop an extensive database for recording the stories of survivors, a comprehensive list of atrocities, and where they were committed. It has divided the time frame of the continued conflict into three distinct categories: (i) 1978–92, the period of the communist regime; (ii) 1992–96, which was the time of the mujahedeen rule; and (iii) 1996–2001, when Afghanistan was under the control of the Taliban; however, a commissioner emphasized: "the documentation process is not a base for trial of anyone. Its aim is that no stories are left unrecorded. At a later stage there will be complimentary mechanisms to verify this. At this stage we are not judging. We are just listening and recording."[27]

Since its establishment, the Transitional Justice Unit of the AIHRC has been actively expanding the transitional justice constituency and the ownership of the transitional justice processes through conducting transitional justice workshops; awareness-raising meetings with civil society representatives, government officials, community and religious leaders; creating radio programs; publishing stories of survivors in newspapers as well as distributing copies of the Action Plan to rights activists, civil society organizations, and community-based groups in many parts of the country. With the discovery of mass graves, it began working with UNAMA and the Physicians for Human Rights (PHR) to train transitional justice staff, regional and provincial managers, and members of local NGOs on documentation and other essential forensic skills for conducting exhumations. It was also involved in constructing a monument in Kabul University to celebrate human rights and it has been involved in discussions to build a museum in Badakshan where a mass grave was discovered in 2007. Under Key Action 2 of the National Plan, the AIHRC also worked with the Afghan Civil Service Commission to review the human rights records for persons considered for appointment and encouraged the establishment of an Advisory Panel for the Appointments, which formulates rules and advises the president on senior political appointments.

In February 2009, a strategic coordination conference organized by the Commission, ICTJ, OSI, and UNAMA's Human Rights Unit created the Transitional Justice Coordination Group (TJCG), which today comprises of a loose network of 25 civil society organizations committed to, and working directly or indirectly on the issue of transitional justice and human rights.[28] The network faces multi-layered challenges, including internal issues about trust, heavy representation of civil society actors from Kabul, informality of membership that raises questions of security, allegations of heavy-handedness of some organizations for leadership roles over others, while operating in a political climate that fosters distrust of different ethnic groups and bitter competition for resources and even legitimacy. Nevertheless, the TJCG has been a remarkable initiative and the first of its kind committed to keeping the transitional justice question alive in Afghanistan. Using press statements and through organizing press conferences, the network has consistently reached out to the media and tries to keep the discussion alive in public forums. On May 9, 2010, the TJCG organized the Victims' Jirga, an alternative to Karzai's National Consultative Peace Jirga (NCPJ) that aimed to bring together representatives from across Afghanistan to discuss ways to move forward on issues of justice, peace, and reconciliation.[29] The NCPJ was heavily criticized for its marginalization of women, victims, and civil society actors who are critical of Karzai and for giving limited space for an honest discussion about accounting for the past and promoting reconciliation. The Victim's Jirga in contrast was an unprecedented event, bringing together more than 100 victims of the various wars from different parts of the country and providing a platform for them to share their experiences, their challenges, and their understandings of what constitutes "peace," "justice," and "reconciliation."[30]

As one of the most prominent members of TJCG, the AIHRC was heavily involved in the network's public outreach activities for the *Jirga*. It provided valuable office space for strategic meetings and offered logistical and administrative support to organize the event, relying heavily on its regional and provincial offices' networks to identify participants for the vent.

In sharp contrast, at the state level, since 2005 there has been very little discernible progress regarding transitional justice, and this has been further obscured by the discussions of reconciliation with the Taliban. President Karzai declared December 10 as the National War Victims Day, but no other progress has been made on the commitments made in the Action Plan, including the promise to build a national monument at *Pul-Charki* to pay tribute to the mass killings, mass arrests, and torture of students and political activists that occurred during the communist regime. The National Action Plan for Peace, Justice, and Reconciliation in Afghanistan expired in 2009.

The Nepal Human Rights Commission

In the early 1990s, Nepali human rights activists and some members of parliament began the long drawn out process of establishing a NHRI. In 1996, a few parliamentarians took a private bill to Parliament. Between 1995–6, various human rights organizations organized a series of seminars to explore the possibilities and implications of a National Human Rights Commission for Nepal (NHRC-N). Those seminars were instrumental in the growing recognition among those working on separate human rights issues that a human rights commission could support the work of the existing courts and other governmental agencies.

126   *National Human Rights Institutions*

In 1997, a Nepali Congress member tabled the Human Rights Commission Act in the National Assembly as a private member's bill.

The enactment of the Human Rights Commission Act in 1997 provided access to a wide range of rights for which individuals previously had no remedy and the search for which was a historically difficult and time-consuming process. But the NHRC-N was neither a substitute for the rights and remedies inherent in Articles 23 and 88, nor does it have any kind of appellate role. The Act cannot even by amendment, strip the Supreme Court of its jurisdiction, alter the role of the judiciary, or inquire in any matter "within the jurisdiction of the Military Act."[31] The intent of the Act, at most, is to secure governmental accountability in case of infringement of any fundamental rights of the people. Courts of law respond to the violation of human rights only after their jurisdiction is invoked and so the court's redress of injury to human rights is compensatory in nature. Article 132 of the Interim Constitutions, however, allows the NHRC-N to promote, protect, and respect human rights and ensure its effective enforcement. It is also structured to effectively deal with questions involving human rights with recourse to simple and inexpensive procedures. In May 2000, after years of delays and negotiations, the Commission was provided with basic facilities and space for its head office in Harihar Bhawan, Kathmandu.[32] Today, it has five operational divisions: (i) Legislative Assistance; (ii) Human Rights Promotion; (iii) Protection and Monitoring; (iv) Planning, Internal Monitoring and Evaluation; and (v) Operations. In addition, the office of the National Rapporteur on Trafficking in the NHRC Central Office functions as an important wing of the commission for preventing and controlling human trafficking.[33]

The NHRC quickly positioned itself to work on the emerging crisis in human rights. After two weeks of the first proclamation of emergency,[34] on December 11, 2001, it convened a meeting with the secretaries of security-related ministries to discuss human rights protection in times of emergency. The meeting resulted in measures that included establishing a temporary complaint registration unit and a commitment toward pushing the government to follow the rule of law in all its activities during the emergency. The monitoring activities focused on the emergency situation but was undergirded by the need to (i) monitor non-derogable rights under the International Convention on Civil and Political Rights (ICCPR) and the Nepalese Constitution; (ii) investigate the excessive use of force by the security forces under the pretext of the emergency; (iii) organize its leadership; (iv) interact with stakeholders to minimize human rights violations; and (v) educate people and policy makers on human rights. On June 14, 2002, the commission drew the attention of the government to the issue of sexual harassment of women and their arrest and detention without any observation of due process. It also conducted a short-term *Responding to Crisis Project* to monitor the human rights situation during the state of emergency.

Throughout the period of emergency, the NHRC received numerous complaints about human rights violations committed by both government and Maoist forces. Based on the volume of complaints filed with the NHRC, in 2003 the commission created a public list of all enforced disappearances and launched an appeal on behalf of the disappeared.[35] During this period, it also produced a string of investigative reports that highlighted the scale and type of human rights violations being committed by the armed and Maoist forces. Following the massacres in Doramba, it launched an investigation about the actual sequence of incidents and found that the Nepali armed forces perpetrated a series of human rights violations, including the extrajudicial execution of at least 19 suspected Maoists. In response, the armed forces questioned the validity of the commission's report and launched an internal investigation.[36] In its report on the Nagi Incident of July 5, 2003, the commission concluded that the Maoists were responsible for an explosion, which resulted in several deaths, and that the explosion had occurred "in contravention of the provision contained in Common Article Three of the Geneva Convention of 12 August 1949."[37] In particular, it raised concerns over the death of a non-combatant civilian.[38] Similarly, in its report on the Zeromile Incident of August 19, 2003, the commission identified actions constituting breaches of common Article 3 of the Geneva Conventions.[39] In 2008, in coordination with the NP and Nepalese and Finnish forensic experts, the NHRC monitored the Kapilavastu riots and its aftermath and carried out exhumations of the cremated ruins of 49 individuals in the Shivapuri National Park, who were detained by the army during the conflict.[40] It also provided recommendations to the government on compensations to victims and disciplinary actions against those who committed these crimes. In addition, with the commitments made to transitional justice mechanisms in the CPA, NHRC has been involved in the discussions surrounding the TRC, the COID, and the question of financial compensation to victims.[41]

These spaces in between: the dynamics between government and civil society

An overview of AIHRC and NHRC exposes their extent of influence, relationships, and challenges they face in their efforts to work on the transitional justice in particular, and human rights in general. The following section analyzes these tensions and the complex landscape of partnerships and rivalry that determine their level of success.

Multidimensionality of independence and coordination

Independence and accountability are simultaneously key objectives and challenges for NHRIs because they are critical components of their claims to credibility and their effectiveness. Independence poses a central theoretical and practical conundrum for such institutions, given that they are charged with multiple responsibilities: "'downwards' to their partners, beneficiaries, staff and supporters; and 'upwards' to their funders, parliaments and host governments."[42] Smith identifies four different levels of independence regarding the relationship of NHRIs with their respective governments: (i) legal and operational autonomy; (ii) financial autonomy; (iii) independence with regard to appointment and dismissal procedures; and (iv) independence concerning pluralism and composition.[43] In

128 *National Human Rights Institutions*

each of these areas, both the AIHRC and NHRC have experienced several tensions in trying to work closely with the Afghan and Nepali Governments while simultaneously trying to maintain the "independent" nature of their work.

AIHRC and the GoA

An increasing source of tension for the AIHRC has been that "despite being its constitutional obligation, the government has failed to provide any financial support to the AIHRC ever since its establishment."[44] Further, it has been criticized about the "independent" nature of its work and questioned by some in the Afghan society about its undue influence, despite the institution's own efforts to proceed with prudence in its working relationships, particularly with political parties. Consider the following example. The AIHRC has had a substantive relationship with the Constitutional Commission, the Civil Service Reform Commission, and the Judicial Reform Commission to further the aims of transitional justice; however the fact that the commissions were not fully independent stood in the way of their effective coordination in a complementary and reinforcing way.[45] Mani suggests: "the Constitutional Commission might have incorporated judicious measures into the constitution to ensure that certain types of people, particularly war criminals, never participate in government."[46] This, she continues, "would have had the legitimacy of *Shari'a law* and also Afghan tradition, as both have numerous injunctions that 'those with blood on their hands should stand in the back row' as much in the mosque as in government."[47]The Judicial Reform Commission also could have instituted systems of lawmaking and enforcement that acted as firm deterrents to war crimes and human rights violations. In both these cases, limitations caused by the lack of independence and the requisite power to implement such measures limited possibilities of action. The resultant missed opportunities for integration of local and international legal norms ultimately undermined people's confidence in state institutions of governance.

NHRC and the GoN

In Nepal, the NHRC has had a historically terse relationship with the question of independence. While the National Human Rights Commission Act came into force in 1997, because of government delays, the commission itself was not constituted until May 2000.[48] The political instability after the 1990 elections has been mainly attributed to the reason why there was hardly any official progress or government effort to establish the NHRC, but certain commentators saw this delay as evidence that the then government lacked any real intention to promote human rights in Nepal.[49] In the early days of the commission, the NHRC positioned itself as a serious investigative body, challenging both the Maoists as well as government forces on the issue of human rights violations. A former commissioner noted: "In 2000, when there were a lot of disappearances and killings, we were very mobilized to work on human rights…and a major turning point was the killings in Doramba. We investigated that…we dug up and exhumed the bodies…"[50]

In late 2003, the GoN announced its intention of establishing a Human Rights Promotion Center (HRPC), a move many allege was a direct consequence of the commission's stance on the Doramba incident.[51] The GoN, however, publicly insisted that the role of the center was to complement and assist the commission in the latter's efforts to promote and protect human rights, but it soon became evident that the center was an attempt to undermine the work of the commission through taking on many of its responsibilities.

The NHRC increasingly struggles with the notion of independence, despite its commendable past working on incidences such as the Doramba killings. When asked about the independent nature of the commission today, the question met with significant cynicism from all quarters of Nepal's civil society, both national and international, who point out that increasing politicization of the NHRC and the influence of the political parties have seriously derailed the efficacy of the institution. A representative from PD noted:

> NHRC is doing its little share in transitional justice, but it does not demonstrate any leadership...when criticized, it defends itself saying it is still in its infant stage. And since the government is not committed to human rights, it becomes very difficult for the Commission to work independently [due to] political interference by different political parties.[52]

Such criticisms, however, do not seem very fair to those working in the commission. A NHRC commissioner acknowledged the challenges facing NHRC but maintained:

> The human rights defenders may criticize the Commission, but they do not necessarily understand the kind of challenges we face. We are even limited by our rights within the Constitution – what process should we follow? What laws? There is much work to be done regarding the amendment of the bill itself.[53]

The NHRC has also continuously struggled with limited financial resources. Since it began operations in 2000, staff and advocates of the NHRC claimed that organizational effectiveness was consistently undermined by the lack of government funding.[54] The limited ability to pay sufficient wages contributed to a high staff turnover; and the People's War in particular exacerbated fears amidst already existing budget limitations that for security purposes the government would hold a percentage of its 2003–4 budget committed to the commission.[55] Foreign donors have therefore been an important source of funding for the NHRC. Specific projects such as the *Responding to Crisis Project* would not have been possible without external assistance.[56] Between 2001–4, the commission indirectly received significant international support through pooled funds to finance its Capacity Development Project (CDP), which aimed at providing the commission with technical support and strategic coordination advice under the auspices of the United Nations Development Programme (UNDP). The commission has also

130 *National Human Rights Institutions*

received financial and organizational assistance from a variety of governments, NGOs and intergovernmental organizations such as the UNDP, the OHCHR, the Danish Institute of Human Rights (DIHR), the German Technical Agency (GTZ), the Norwegian Refugees Council (NRC), and various other entities.[57] Overall, between the period 2004–8, 87 percent of its funding was calculated to be coming from external sources.[58]

Despite this diversity of foreign resources, the continuing struggle for adequate funding has irrevocably led to tangible problems for the commission. It has also been unable to deal with complaints efficiently, struggles to pay the wages of its existing personnel and cannot attract new staff.[59] The NHRC-N has acknowledged that up to 90 percent of complaints made since its establishment is still "in the process of investigation" and the US State Department reports that the figure may be as high as 94 percent.[60] These low efficiency levels may be due to the fact that the commission is not "acting vigorously in cases brought to its attention. Indeed…the vast majority of complaints received are not acted upon at all."[61]

The extensive dependence on foreign funding has inevitably meant that the NHRC has to abide by the conditions set by various donors. The 2004 Asia Pacific Human Rights Network (APHRN) report recognizes that such kinds of external influence results in a situation where instead of a comprehensive and coordination strategy, the commission's policy approach is perceived to be a collection of short-term, unconnected efforts.[62] This constant tension has led the NHRC to recognize the importance of securing "unconditional" external funds and to identify "impediments in the plans and programs run under the assistance of donor agencies."[63] However, even with the programs over which the commission has control – those funded by government grants – budgetary constraints have forced the NHRC to adopt a "short-term" and non-systematic approach to human rights policy. In short, the commission's position reflects the reality of donor aid: the need for external funds to supplement the government's inadequate funding, which in turn limits its independence and long-term planning and creates a culture of "donor dependency."

The commissions and the international community

The AIHRC occupies a unique position in Afghanistan with regard to its relationship with the international community. It relies heavily on the international community for its work and the international community in turn has found itself a reliable partner in pursuing work on human rights in Afghanistan. International actors interviewed about their assessment of AIHRC's involvement with transitional justice in particular and human rights work in general, were largely positive, with many pointing out the novelty of such a body functioning in a context of fragmented civil society activism in a climate dominated by serious security concerns and the heavy hand of warlords and militia commanders. A former HRW employee provided the following assessment:

> For the longest time the AIHRC was working as a real watchdog saying things other organizations weren't saying. Look at the Sherpur incident where

there was a land grab and people who had been living on the land for over 20 years was moved out by government officials mandated by Fahim. AIHRC produced a complete list of all of these people in the government who owned land...and [subsequently] the commissioners put themselves in a situation of vulnerability...yet they are criticized for not speaking out enough and being too close to the government. It's such a difficult context to work. Who is going to provide them security? What resources do they have? In a context where there is no rule of law, how far can these people go?[64]

The AIHRC and the UNAMA

The AIHRC and the UNAMA generally work in close consultation on a host of human rights issues, including special areas of concern. For example, the AIHRC has a special relationship with the United Nations Children's Fund (UNICEF) for their work on children's rights and with United Nations High Commission for Refugees (UNHCR) for their work on the internally displaced Afghans and for those who were deported from Pakistan and Iran. Fahim Rahimi, one of the commissioners with the AIHRC, stated:

> We do need their [UN] political support to do the work we do...but for matters of political sensitivity the UN has to take the first step. For example, the case of Abdur Rahman who was sentenced to death for his conversion to Christianity – this was a very sensitive issue for us. We could not have a very concrete stance because we would be immediately labeled as spies of the west, weak Muslims influenced by America, or be perceived as leftists or Maoists in our society.[65]

To counter the real possibility of being delegitimized or attacked for work on issues such as the Abdur Rahman incident, over time the AIHRC adopted a more strategic and non-provocative approach to some of the more sensitive cases.[66] A commissioner interviewed for this research conceded that the UNAMA has been "extremely supportive" in such instances; however, there still remains areas of contention between field staff and the UNAMA. The corresponding signing of Memorandums of Understanding (MoU) with the UN was a direct consequence of these tensions, aimed at avoiding competition between the field staff and UNAMA and [to establish] that the AIHRC is [generally] the leader for human rights protection and monitoring, and others have a supporting role.[67]

The NHRC and the UN Mission (OHCHR-N)

The NHRC has had different periods of tension with the international community, particularly with OHCHR-N. OHCHR's initial entry into Nepal was met with strong support from all elements of Nepali society and it was warmly welcomed by the NHRC; however, a public statement made by one of the commissioners in 2008 shed light into growing tensions between the two institutions. This was the

132   *National Human Rights Institutions*

inevitable outcome of both institutions working in the same space, having similar functions, developing partnerships with the same national and international actors and consequently competing against each other to prove their respective effectiveness. In 2009, there was strong national opposition to the renewal of the OHCHR-N's mandate as it expired. A government spokesperson told the media "a majority of stakeholders seem to be at odds with the request for extension."[68]

Amongst those opposing the renewal of the mandate were members of the current government, the NHRC, and some in the elite civil society. The commission's main opposition came from the belief that it was a capable enough institution to undertake the current responsibilities of OHCHR-N. In addition, it also believed that extending OHCHR-N's mandate was a way in which the government would try to weaken the commission itself. There were, however, key civil society actors who disagree with this assessment and believed that a strong NHRC–OHCHR collaboration could bring structural changes in the human rights situation in Nepal. Mandira Sharma of AF, for example, stressed that a complementary role for the NHRC and OHCHR-N is essential to address current human rights challenges:

> While the NHRC needs to explore ways to challenge cases that they have investigated in the national court, the OHCHR is in a position to provide technical inputs to investigations and litigations as they have access to international experts who have worked in international tribunals.[69]

Local civil society actors also emphasized the significance of the symbiotic relationship between the two institutions and their legacy. For OHCHR-N, an important indicator of its success would be how strong a national human rights institution that it leaves behind, as a resulting of its mentoring and collaborating activities, is. In turn, NHRC's challenge would be to strengthen its capacity in monitoring and human rights investigation while enhancing its understanding of the country's changing political dynamics. The need for both institutions is therefore clear – NHRC's responsibility to fight for human rights protection, and the OHCHR's supporting role in assisting the government's efforts to end impunity and strengthening the capacity of the NHRC.[70]

Legitimacy, accountability, and popularity among local actors

One of the most noteworthy features of NHRIs is the unique position they occupy between government on one hand and civil society on the other. Their public/popular accountability is the mainstay of their support. Such accountability helps members of the public to ascertain the independence of an NHRI and scrutinize its performance while allowing the institution to benefit from the experience and insight of local and international partners. By establishing these relationships, NHRIs can provide societal groups with effective channels to make their claims as "receptors" and "transmitters" in the cycle of human rights activity as they endeavor to implement international norms while simultaneously filtering information from civil society back to the state. "It is this conceptual space," Smith states, "which gives NHRIs a potentially distinctive role in society."[71] In an ideal setting, this leads to the expectation that such institutions interact actively with civil society and provide effective channels for their local partners to make their claims. Further, their unique status is expected to allow such entities to access information that NGOs may not be able to obtain, as well as allow for a closer engagement with government officials. Moreover, the working relationship between NHRIs and local civil society plays a critical role in generating its popularity and legitimacy. Ironically, these very advantages associated with being a formal institutionalized body with significant leverage could compromise NHRIs' relationship with local actors. Mertus acknowledges: "operating in a highly charged and deeply politicized atmosphere NHRIs not only are subject to manipulation by government actors but must also contend with the often conflicting agendas of the various segments of civil society."[72]

The AIHRC and local civil society

Mertus' observation about local politics, their influence on NHRIs and vice versa, rings true when observing the strained relationship between AIHRC and many local actors, who have in general tended to view the institution as being too "isolated," "elitist," "arrogant," "a monopolist of the human rights agenda," and one that is not interested in forging equitable partnerships with local partners. For several of the local actors interviewed, the AIHRC has also appeared to be one that is too close to the international community and is not enough of a "nuisance factor" for the government or the warlords. The existing gulf between local actors and the commission continues to be an issue of concern because it weakens the already fragile human rights community against mounting opposition to accountability and the rule of law. This gap between AIHRC and local actors has not evaded the notice of international actors, who also point out that the commission is in a "lose–lose" situation in a context where the weakness of actors determines the strength of effective partnerships.

The AIHRC, territoriality, and competition

The realities of donor dependency, resentment toward large NGOs "parachuting" in to monopolize the human rights and/or development agenda and the consequent turf wars between NGOs are not new phenomena in any developing or transitional society.[73] Afghanistan has not been an exception. In a context dictated by donor agencies, a fragmented civil society landscape, extreme political volatility, and marked tensions among and between local and/or central government, local NGOs appear and disappear overnight. Those that remain are largely uncoordinated and uninformed about each other's work. Under these circumstances, the issue of territoriality looms large while the constant climate of vying for resources and donor attention generates "distrust and suspicion of associations and competition over mandates."[74] Together, these factors create an environment that is highly non-conducive for creative interaction and cooperation. The AIHRC's special

134 *National Human Rights Institutions*

status in the Constitution, its early recognition by the international community, and its subsequent prominence in the Afghan human rights community have irrefutably meant that the commission has a monopoly over sources of funding. Further, because it has the mandate to work in issues of past and present human rights abuses, it has taken on a position that has generated significant resentment and a perception among local civil society actors and NGOs that it is "arrogant" and "egotistical."

The skepticism about the AIHRC is not limited to local actors, but is also present amongst the very people it tries to serve. There are anecdotes from several provinces where the local population alleges that its work in women's rights is "radical" and "Westernized," accusing the commission of encouraging divorce rates among women. Others do not hesitate to connect the commission's work to the communists and assert that it is far too politicized. One religious scholar interviewed alleged that one of the commissioners is connected to the Revolutionary Association of the Women of Afghanistan (RAWA),[75] and insisted that the commission takes the same highly radicalized position as RAWA in accusing "all mujahideen [of being] war criminals, which is a serious distortion of reality."[76] Some others held the perception that certain members of the commission have connections to political parties, which colors its agenda significantly.[77]

The AIHRC's relationship with the Afghan Government is also somewhat tenuous. Before its establishment, Karzai held up several of the appointments for the commissioners. Although originally supportive of the commission, increasingly the GoA has distanced itself from the institution, offering little support to the commission's human rights projects and to the more outspoken commissioners. Human rights monitors, for example, are often held up in their work and not given access to conduct their investigations. In the area of transitional justice particularly, it has been an uphill battle for the commission and other actors to keep the pressure on implementing any of the provisions of the Action Plan.[78] Individual commissioners who have been the most vocal about human rights and warlord accommodation not only do so with a personal risk to their lives, but also live with the real possibility of having their jobs terminated by President Karzai.[79] Ironically, tensions between the GoA and the AIHRC strengthen the commission's stand with the international community and even with local actors. For example, during 2007 demonstrations in support of the amnesty law, when warlords and their supporters chanted "Death to the Commission! Death to the infidels! Death to Simar Samar!"[80] international actors recognized that the strong opposition to the AIHRC was an indication that the commission has become a notable voice for the human rights community.

The commission acknowledges some of the criticisms that have been leveled against it over the years by local NGOs and civil society actors. A commissioner interviewed about the institution's unpopularity noted that:

> [S]ince the Commission enjoys a good level of support from the international community and is perceived as having a huge budget, but does not provide [local NGOs] financial support, some local NGOs feel that we are not

cooperating with civil society organizations. From our side, we do not wish to be seen as a donor agency responsible for funding and 'fixing' the problems of NGOs, but to be honest, this misunderstanding is a reflection that we still lack a vibrant visionary civil society in Afghanistan, even in Kabul.[81]

Criticisms about the AIHRC monopolizing the human rights doctrine, and the commission's demand that local actors need "to step up to the plate" have led to some back and forth about how they could work together more effectively. The recent establishment of the TJCG has been important development in this regard, providing the AIHRC a much-desired venue to exercise initiative, bringing together local actors and those in the international human rights arena to brainstorm ways of keeping the activism on transitional justice alive. "With the TJCG," remarked an international actor in confidence, "the AIHRC seems to have found a new lease of life…it can put aside the differences with other civil society actors, take a leadership role, and serve as the gathering point for mobilization on transitional justice."[82]

The NHRC and Nepal's civil society

The NHRC's relationship with local actors needs to be analyzed in terms of its relationship with (a) the army and (b) civil society actors. The commission's relationship with the military has been particularly contentious especially during the conflict years. At the height of its effectiveness, the commission encountered the military several times and was often obstructed in its human rights investigations. Such incidents were exacerbated when the armed forces refused to recognize that their actions constituted human rights abuses. This was clearly illustrated during the Mudbhara incident when the commission alleged that four school students were killed in an army operation and armed forces denied it[83] and refused to answer any of the commission's queries.[84] The Army's Human Rights Cells, with the specific objective of resolving human rights issues internally, allegedly followed up with its own inquiry into the incident, but the results of this inquiry were never made public.[85] Generally, a skeptical attitude towards human rights, and towards the commission, seems to pervade the armed forces. Brigadier BA Kumar Sharma of the NA was reported as having said that the Army "is surprised how biased the [Commission]…has been while monitoring human rights violations…how can I teach my soldiers that the [Commission] is an independent human rights watchdog body?"[86] The Human Rights Cells have also continued to generate criticism on the basis that the interests of justice and transparency are not served by internal disciplinary procedures.[87]

Numerous human rights violations, ranging from extrajudicial executions to torture to arbitrary arrest and detention, continue to be perpetrated by the armed forces and recorded by the commission and external monitors.[88] The military made certain claims that the armed forces had improved their human rights record, and investigations had been launched for specific cases of abuses. Indeed, in late January 2004, it announced that a number of armed forces troops had been

136 *National Human Rights Institutions*

court-martialed for human rights violations, and that 17 of those court-martialed were imprisoned.[89] Nevertheless, the lack of transparency of the internal procedures and results of alleged investigations by the military and the Human Rights Cells, and the clear absence of acknowledging many of the crimes committed by the NA during the period of the People's War continue to foster skepticism and distrust for the military amongst the NHRC and Nepal's civil society and human rights organizations.

The current commission also struggles with a poor public perception particularly among local civil society actors since 2005. That year, on the eve of the expiration of the commissioners' tenure, the then king amended the NHRC Act of 1997 and appointed new commissioners without recommendations from the committee, making the commission a "puppet" institution. While the current commission does not include all of the king's appointees, such types of political manipulation coupled with other limitations discussed previously has contributed to an overall NHRC that continues to be weakened by the absence of strong leadership and the loss of its reputation as an "independent" institution. Its current inability to take charge, to be creative, and to act as a strong partner for local NGOs have consolidated the perception that it is a *faux* human rights body with no teeth. A civil society actor stated:

> The NHRC is not that active and that is our main concern. They should be leading the efforts…they receive so many complaints which they should investigate and act on…after all it is in their mandate to do so and yet they seem to do nothing."[90]

Sushil Pyakurel, a former commissioner with the NHRC expressed a deep-seated frustration with the commission's current lack of leadership and commitment when he argued:

> The major problem with the NHRC is that it is not taking any proactive role… they are apathetically following an old prescription…they are not providing leadership but following civil society's lead…this is a time of transition and they have to take advantage of the current situation and creatively push for human rights and transitional justice…they have to mobilize civil society and the international community around the disappearance commission, the TRC, for transitional justice….if you have the courage to do, you can do it all.[91]

Pyakurel's disappointment with the current state of the NHRC emphasizes the decline of a promising institution that, during the period of the People's War, creatively interpreted its mandate to investigate, report, and publicize human rights atrocities and challenge both the GoN and the Maoists. The gap it left in the Nepali landscape has, to some extent, been filled by individual organizations such as the AF and INSEC. But as individual human rights NGOs can neither take on the responsibilities of an umbrella organization that connect the government to

National Human Rights Institutions 137

local concerns and actors, nor have a unique mandate, it remains the duty of the NHRC to reclaim its position and continue to build on its human rights legacy.

Conclusion: a voice for the voiceless

In transitional contexts, NHRIs such as the AIHRC and the NHRC face significant challenges in their efforts to establish human rights norms. The OHCHR recognizes six "effective factors" generally applicable to human rights institutions: independence, defined jurisdiction and adequate powers, accessibility, cooperation, operational efficiency, and accountability.[92] The AIHRC and NHRC struggle with trying to meet most of the six criteria. As they work to find their place in their respective civil society landscapes, they continue to struggle against being co-opted into largely government driven projects. Yet individual examples from AIHRC and NHRC have demonstrated that consistent negotiations, strong and committed leadership, and creative interpretations of respective mandates do create opportunities for such bodies to play critical roles in the human rights and transitional justice movement.

Lofty expectations of international actors and donors do not necessarily demonstrate sensitivity to the realities within which these bodies function. Commissions such as the AIHRC and the NHRC work in unique contexts defined by a very weak rule of law. In the absence of other institutions established to address questions of the past, NHRIs could also be left to take on the role of a truth commission and charged with the responsibility of documentation, while struggling to fulfill other core obligations. Finally, neither the international human rights community nor the norms by which such institutions are created reflect an understanding of the cultures and religious practices of the local contexts within which such institutions work.

Critics might argue that NHRIs should focus more on human rights education rather than devoting substantive resources to pursuing accountability for past atrocities. Some suggest AIHRC and NHRC should build strategic partnerships for change rather than delving into the past. Others, however, argue that such institutions have a unique position as a watchdog, and in the best of circumstances, can interpret their mandate to confront the government to perform better. From the beginning, the AIHRC has addressed several of these concerns through specific programming in fields as diverse as human rights education, women's rights, and rights of detainees and people with disabilities. But inevitably, it is its work in transitional justice that in some ways is cutting edge, demonstrating its creativity and commitment in using its mandate. The AIHRC's current work in documenting the deaths of civilians by indiscriminate US and NATO bombings, land grabs by warlords, and its interaction with local and religious civil society actors are examples of how it tries to position itself as both a coordinating body, and a bridge between grass-roots, national and international stakeholders on human rights, and transitional justice. Further, its unique role in shedding light on the continuing human rights abuses in Afghanistan emphasizes the continuity of past atrocities and current violations that fall within the purview of the transitional

138 *National Human Rights Institutions*

justice framework. Finally, its interactions with remote communities, who look to them to file their complaints, and with religious actors and informal civil society networks explore ways in which human rights issues can be raised in far-flung areas of the country.

The early years of NHRC clearly demonstrated its role as an *avant-garde* in Nepal's human rights movement because it investigated excesses of the army and the Maoists. Particularly, because transitional justice is not covered in its mandate, the role of certain commissioners in taking risks to challenge the government and expose the Maoists was proof that a national institution committed to human rights promotion and protection can use its mandate creatively and effectively. Its complaint mechanism, at least in theory, also provides a venue for victims of human rights abuses to formally file their experiences and establishes a state-level record-keeping process of rights abuses during and after war. The past legacy of its active and provocative role is certainly a model that the NHRC, under strong leadership, can look to in its fight to protect human rights in Nepal.

Finally and perhaps most importantly, both the AIHRC and the NHRC underscore that under conditions of impunity, there is little distinction between concerns for human rights and justice during "ordinary" times and during times of war. In fact, effective NHRIs have the pulse on increasing political turmoil that may result in war (e.g. NHRC) and the flagrant disregard for the law during hostilities (e.g. AIHRC). Nevertheless, such institutions are as good as the people who lead them and the networks that support them. Left to volatile environments, however, their struggles can overshadow their achievements and they constantly run the risk of becoming symbolic institutions rather than ones of practice.

7 Conclusion
Toward a theory of the "local"

Justice is a decidedly messy affair. In societies trying to emerge from conflict, issues pertaining to its necessity, scope, and feasibility become even more urgent, and far exceed what external and internal efforts promise to deliver. Recent efforts in post-conflict reconstruction packages have included the transitional justice toolkit, which consists of measures to generate an "accounting for the past" for the period of violent upheaval. While initially such packages comprised of punitive measures, today, they also include provisions for a truth and/or reconciliation commission, institutions of remembrance, acknowledgement of victims' sufferings, their right to compensation and reparation, as well as legal and security sector reform. In short, the multifaceted repercussions of conflict and the demands they generate – institutional, legal, historical, and political – have led to new transitional justice frameworks that take into account the criticisms of the earlier and narrower legalistic approaches to justice. They make some room for engaging with existing socioeconomic constraints, religion, and cultural practices in the context in question. But transitional justice has also become a lucrative cottage industry. It is a highly professionalized knee-jerk response to conflicts, ushering in well-founded criticisms about what constitutes "transition" and points out the limitations of individual criminal culpability highly influenced by the Western penological rationale, the shortcomings of importing mechanisms, such as the TRC, and, more broadly, exposes the neoliberal agenda from which it derives both its philosophy and its legitimacy.

Using a comparative study, this book takes into serious account such criticisms, particularly focusing on the tensions between the international approach and the local context, and well-founded critiques of TRCs. It draws attention to the need for a more critical and nuanced understanding of the "local" with which the international actors engage with in order to not only establish the parameters of transitional justice, but more broadly, of other post-conflict reconstruction packages. It essentially argues the urgent need to unpack the meaning and understanding of the "local" as is now accepted by international actors to expose the tensions and hierarchies of and within the local, and to question whose version of the "local" is actually prioritized in the transitional justice discourse and programming.

140 *Toward a theory of the "local"*

In its essence, however, this book is the story of transitional justice in Afghanistan and Nepal, examining how these two south Asian contexts, on a parallel trajectory to transition, are grappling with the question of "accounting for the past" in a context of highly weak and inadequate legal institutions, institutionalized impunity, and, as in the case of Afghanistan, a continuing war. While each chapter specifically looked into the transitional justice process and its struggles in each context, the issues they raised have far-reaching implications, both beyond the case studies and beyond South Asia. They informed four empirical research questions: to what extent have official commitments to seeking justice for those who have suffered the agonies of war ("local" consumers of justice processes) recognized and involved these actors and their communities? To what extent have these official commitments recognized, involved, and supported "local" actors and their communities who are meant to be the consumers of such mechanisms? What concept of the "local" has been harnessed in the transitional justice discussions and processes in Afghanistan and Nepal? And finally, how would the "local" understandings of justice compliment, challenge, and impact the existing discourse and framework of post-conflict justice?

This study's findings certainly provide a more nuanced understanding of what constitutes key components of the "local," long understood to primarily imply the primacy of religion and culture in a domestic context. It urges five specific areas which should also be considered critical components of what defines and informs the "local:" (i) the historical context within which "transitional justice" mechanisms are implemented; (ii) the legal dimensions of justice, including *de jure* impunity and the limitations of, and opportunities for, local legal systems in the context of transitional justice; (iii) the political process by which the transitional justice discourse is introduced in a context and the subsequent internal/domestic and international politicking that could limit and/or direct the justice question; (iv) survivors' demands in the context of socioeconomic and political realities; and (v) the domestic and institutional struggle for long-term justice, such as the establishment of NHRIs (or similar institutions), which try to link local voices to national and international platforms of decision-making and balance their role of advocating for present human rights, while looking into past instances of abuses.

Each of these observations requires further discussion. First, past legacies of experimentation with the different manifestations of "transitional justice," matter. The discussion of reconciliation in Afghanistan cannot only be conducted in cultural and religious terms; the historicity of such practices has relevance to current efforts. It follows then that reconciliation in Afghanistan is not just informed by *sulh*s and *jirgas*, but an overzealous focus on conciliation and appeasement and desperate bids to control terrain and political power, a cycle that is being repeated until today. Turning to Nepal's history of ineffectual commissions, it is small wonder that the current discussions of a disappearance commission or a TRC are looked upon with cynicism and distrust. For the ordinary Nepali citizen, these commissions fall in the same category as a long line of "paper institutions" that emerged and collapsed without any impact on the actual challenges in society or on people's lives. Transitional justice efforts to address wartime atrocities in such

Toward a theory of the "local" 141

contexts cannot, of course, rewrite the legacy of past failures, but perhaps need to be both cognizant and self-reflexive of the historical and political contexts in which they attempt to institutionalize promised mechanisms, and be humble about what the commitments they make.

A second assertion of this book regards the legal dimension of transitional justice, which brings *extraordinary* crimes to *ordinary* institutions. This has the deepest significance for ordinary laws because in many instances, they have to recalibrate their parameters of crimes and criminality. Moreover, in transitional instances, the struggle becomes centered on institutional change; the focus on rule of law reform is too often about the structures, and less about context. Even the most well-intentioned legal transformations, however, have to take into account not only the cultural, but the *contextual* historicity of legal/adjudication mechanisms and investigate how they have effectively addressed, or systematically marginalized the needs of the people. For example, while the different forms of *jirgas* in Afghanistan have been a viable source of dispute resolution and sometimes even an accounting mechanism, traditional decision-making processes on matters of justice and arbitration in Nepal have been extremely hierarchical and reflective of caste and power relationships in society. Traditional customary laws in both societies have been particularly inaccessible to marginalized communities, particularly women and people of other ethnic and/or caste groups. Further, even customary and traditional mechanisms have been subjected to political influences, challenging the assumption that such institutions are necessarily pristine, static entitities that have prevailed through the times without undue internal and external political influence.

Despite the challenges and complexities of the formal and informal legal landscape, law's position, particularly in a transitional context is both *retroactive* – underscoring the criminality of past excesses – and *proactive* justice i.e. creating new parameters for criminality. Law and legal institutions are seen both as regulatory mechanisms as well as opportunities to bring about societal change. In short, the blurring of the lines between past and present justice underscores that because law derives legitimacy from past events, it also inherits problems from the past. Despite this, it occupies a functionalist position, which assumes that more laws mean better justice. It is these functional assumptions around law that serves as a logical site of mobilization for rights-based actors in Afghanistan and Nepal to strengthen existing laws of criminality and, as in the latter case, minimize the scope of both *de jure* and de facto impunity. Ultimately, however, the immunity that emerging legal systems aim to address, through both institutional adjustments and through responding to the crisis of legal *lacunae*, does not fully capture the complexity of the societal transformations required for challenging de facto impunity.

Third, internal and external politicization of transitional justice processes have tremendous bearing on the mechanisms sought for seeking culpability for the past and establishing accountability for the future. Transitional justice mechanisms, in other words, do not take place in a vacuum; they are subject to contextual exigencies. These exigencies can mean calculations at the very top about what

142 *Toward a theory of the "local"*

can and should be deployed *at the expense* of the "local." In articulating their claims, survivors fundamentally assert the *universal* value of justice. This universal claim to "right the wrongs," seriously calls into question the legitimacy of the new trend within "transitional justice" of coating some of the most difficult questions (e.g. how to address the issue of perpetrators) facing societies in transition with the "dressings" of reconciliation (i.e. framing warlord/perpetrator bargaining as a process of reconciliation and claiming legitimacy from local customs and values). Serious questions about accountability and the power exerted by warlords and elites in political bargaining are therefore evaded with superficial measures. Succinctly, the question of "how does the local 'do' reconciliation" takes precedence over "how does the local want justice to be done." This kind of prioritization glosses over not only the structural and endemic practices, but also misses some of the opportunities to address questions of ongoing injustices.

Under these conditions, efforts at even political reconciliation and indeed the kind of concessions made to political actors could be seen as efforts mounting to appeasement. Moreover, while reconciliatory efforts at the grass-roots level between and among community members would be critical for a "closing of the books," the reality of such efforts taking place within a context of ongoing conflict, and perhaps even more importantly, under circumstances where illicit power structures have been consolidated, raises questions of whose reconciliation is in fact prioritized.

The current APRP builds off of the experiences of reintegrating and reconciling with the different antagonistic parties in the country since 2001. The APRP has received significant support and encouragement from the international community and by individuals associated with the Karzai administration; however, it continues to cause concerns among local civil society actors, particularly women's rights and human rights organizations, that the rights of minorities and media freedom will be sacrificed in political negotiations to accommodate the demands of the insurgency leadership. One possible scenario, feared by civil rights activists, is that verbal commitments from reconciled parties would allow Karzai to present himself as an effective leader, prompting the international community to laud the advances made in moving toward a peace settlement in Afghanistan, while in reality such a process could pave the way for Afghanistan to lose the modest gains made in human rights since 2001. Questions may also be raised about the extent to which "Afghan notions of reconciliation and forgiveness" have been exploited at the grass-roots levels to dissipate societal tensions, while raw demands of justice for the loss of family members, kidnappings, torture, sexual violence, illegal land seizures, and corruption continue to plague the every day lives of ordinary Afghans.

In a similar vein, while national elites and international stakeholders continue to discuss the need for "reconciliation" and the broader themes of civil and political rights in Nepal, victims' groups are increasingly becoming vulnerable to political groups. Simultaneously, there is a deepening sense of disenfranchisement by such networks because of what they perceive as marginalization and disinterest by international organizations, political elites, and civil society organizations in the capital. Specific mechanisms for transitional justice that have been proposed reflect their limitation in tackling impunity and socioeconomic inequity, which have existed prior to, during, and even after a decade-long conflict. The glaring incongruity of a TRC and its relevance in the Nepal context serves as a reminder that the practice of foreign implants, with acquiescence and support of certain aspects of the local (i.e. primarily those who wish to maintain the status quo of power and authority) continues to be a hallmark for transitional justice practices and a source of scepticism among local actors about the relevance of such an import. Kritz once lamented:

> Truth commissions have become almost routine…You have a transition and everybody immediately says we have to have a truth commission without any clear understanding as to why or what they are about. Except for some of the preliminary and good quality work …there is a real dearth of any serious empirical research on exactly what impact truth commissions actually have in any place, impact on victims, on perpetrators, on society as a whole…[1]

Emerging research on the efficacy of TRCs suggests that there is no empirical evidence that such commissions *alone* bring about any positive change in society, unless they are combined with other measures that ensure an end to impunity and consider the rights of victims seriously. Yet their preponderance in transitional justice activities underscore that because they do not make criminal punishment their main focus, they continue to be popular with the political elite in a transitional context.

Each of the factors outlined previously underscores the fourth assertion – that "local" still matters. While professionalized mechanisms are more relevant for external consumption i.e. for donors and those who support such measures, they often reflect little of the expectations in the local communities in question. It is then possible to argue that to the extent that the local is included in discussions of transitional justice, too often it is a *subjective* interpretation of the local, offered by local elite stakeholders, who may have their own interests in what approach is adopted in a transitional justice process. Furthermore, in transitional justice discourse and programming, the understanding of the local has been limited to a society's culture and traditions in its more static sense, which I define as the "static local" rather than taking into account the dynamic nature of the local, informed and influenced by constant engagement with external forces and grounded in its historical experiences. This study essentially argues that it is the focus on the static local and privileging of certain elite actors that simplifies the complex and kinetic nature of realities on the ground. Subsequently, this study urges that historicity, political negotiations and local politicking, and victims' demands are engaged with more extensively grasping the complexity and evolving nature of the "local."

Does the current trend create space for the dynamic local to become the center for debating and discussing the parameters of "transitional justice" rather than being at the margin of reference? Certainly, in non-Western societies, Baxi's

144 *Toward a theory of the "local"*

observation that "omniscience of western liberal thought in the design and propagation of human rights has led critics to identify 'rights' as having [strictly] a western derivative, motivated by western politics, used for furthering foreign policies and globalised through international law"[2] is still legitimate. Further, it is possible to concede that the "overall, human rights discursivity was and still remains, according to the narrative of origins, the patrimony of the West."[3] Certainly, several scholars have applied Baxi's logic to assert that, for example, prosecutorial measures against well-known perpetrators could have resulted in bringing to the forefront resentment and skepticism regarding Western legal norms, not only within Afghanistan but also among at least constituents of the Islamic world.[4] This view, however, does not capture the depth, complexity, and breadth of the multi-dimensional aspects of justice in contexts such as Nepal and Afghanistan. Rather, it allows for a reification of a singular "Muslim/Afghan" culture, and continually stresses the differences between "Western" paradigms of justice and of local contexts without focusing attention on certain universal claims of the "local." In asserting this, one can draw heavily on Drumbl's argument that there is limited benefit in revering the local to contain the dominant discourse and promoting a pluralistic discourse and seeing it as an end in itself.[5] Instead, perhaps the goal should be to identify and address some of these universal claims such that transitional justice packages do not remain intellectual and/or elite-controlled exercises far removed from local demands and realities.

Taking Baxi's argument seriously would also suggest that the very assumption that retributive measures would bring about anti-Western hysteria in Afghanistan and the Muslim world, has legitimized the "looking away" approach. This is particularly apparent regarding the questions of amnesties, carte blanche to the worst perpetrators, and contributed to the focus on the reconciliatory dimensions in the Afghan culture. It follows then that if the West has the monopoly of human rights and retribution, non-Western states are left with the reconciliatory dimension, which can be exploited in any transitional context. In other words, such an assumption suggests there are no cultural roots for accounting and penalizing in non-Western contexts. Carried to its logical extreme, the argument crudely boils down to: the West does justice, the East does reconciliation. Viewed in this light, the oversimplication of realities in transitional contexts where the "West" is pitted against the "East" under-serves developments in Afghanistan and in Nepal, or indeed in any country emerging from conflict. The demand for justice is raw, and it is real. It involves an end to impunity, punishment for perpetrators but also for social reconciliation, but only after people's basic needs have been met. Yet, in the statebuilding flurry that emerges after the official end of a conflict, the societal costs of amnesties and manipulated reconciliatory efforts have severe consequences, manifesting in increasing political instability, growing inconfidence of civilians in governance structures, and increasing fear and apprehension about personal security. In other words, the manifestations of McSherry and Mejía psychological impunity, brought about as a consequence of hierarchical and horizontal networks that emerge in a culture of *non*-accountability, become a collective experience.[6]

The components of a comprehensive transitional justice package does not begin and end with retributive punishment, nor with removing culpable individuals from the centers of power, or marginalizing their spheres of influence, or acknowledging the demands of survivors. It is a sum total of all these demands; however, the fluidity and non-linear period of transitions clearly indicate that these activities are not necessarily "closing the books" or "accounting for the past" but rather responding to the realities of the present. Perpetrators do not begin and end their reign with the beginning and end of a conflict. Socioeconomic realities of poverty, of gender discrepancies, and of lack of access to health, legal and political systems are not just products of war – in Afghanistan and Nepal, these are ongoing injustices and therefore constitute ongoing justice claims. This study argues that failure to deliver on these platforms matters because not only do they impact the efficacy of transitional justice promises, but they also give birth to a cycle of distrust and reflect failures of the international community and of the local elite to deliver on the promise of making that break between the past and the present.

Ultimately, this book urges a deeper understanding of what it identifies as the "dynamic local," such that current efforts to understand the local in transitional justice practices does not remain contained and restrained by the parameters of culture. While culture itself is an ever-evolving concept, its link to certain fundamental traditional practices allow current efforts to "consult the local" to remain limited within the sphere of cultural practices, particularly relating to issues of reconciliation. The findings of this study do not suggest a retraction of such efforts. Rather, it cautions against an overt reliance of a static understanding of cultural and traditional practices. It insists the dynamic dimensions of the "local" (relating to law, legal systems and legal customs; politicking and politicization around whose version of transitional justice and justice in general is prioritized and legitimized; and whose "voices in autistic isolation" i.e. "absent while in the middle of the action" remain sidelined) require even further exploration.[7] In such an examination the local should not be merely subjects of study, but should also become the venue through which scholarship continues to understand the depth and complexity of the aftermath of conflict.

The goals of "transitional justice" cannot be too lofty if they are meant to be effective. Certainly, the normative assumption that the past must be accounted for has some merit. Nevertheless, transitional justice remains the domain of the elite. Shaw, Lars and Waldorf argue, "[s]urvivors are in any case unlikely to get what they ask for if it contradicts international legal norms."[8] Going forward, however, perhaps this defeatism can be challenged. Certainly, all the demands of survivors have yet to be addressed and all may not be met, but neither should refuge be sought in doing too little, assuming that the justice question is too much. At the least, there should be greater introspection about whether reconciliation at the sake of justice is the right way forward, even if that reconciliation comes dressed in its cultural fineries. After all, the challenge is no longer simply to recognize the local, but to move beyond seeing it as a static entity contained by cultural, religious, and traditional practices, and to critically question whose interpretation of the local is infused in transitional justice packages, and to engage with it as the dynamic

146 Toward a theory of the "local"

center, influenced and shaped by historical experiences, external influences, and a diverse articulation of a complex set of demands. In short, there is a need to constantly grapple with the idea that culture matters, but context endures.

The question then should be how to do justice better, and better by victims' standards could perhaps open the next ground of analysis, debate, and scholarly research. Certainly, there needs to be an understanding and acknowledgement that transitional justice alone does not address questions of impunity. In fact, employing the rhetoric of reconciliation without engaging with all its dimensions, including that of justice claims or meeting the standards of political reconciliation, ultimately reinforces a culture of impunity. It is this endemic practice that constitutes the ultimate act of injustice against survivors. Until scholars, practitioners, and policy-makers are willing to truly engage with the hard questions of justice and assess areas of contention without necessarily either subduing or silencing them, particularly in the name of reconciliation and commissions, transitional justice will continue to be a distant goal – one that is too ambitious and, at times, could become dangerously irrelevant.

Glossary

Aasht-i-Milli: national reconciliation

Adalat: justice

Adat: customs

Afghaniyat: "Afghanhood"

Afwa: forgiveness

Ain Kausal: Law Council in the Nepali language

Al-Amr bi al-Ma'ruf wa al-Nahi 'an al- Munkir: Ministry of Enforcement of Virtue and Suppression of Vice in Afghanistan

Amir-ul Momineen: Commander of the Faithful

Amma: mother in the Nepali language

Amma samuha: mother's group

Arbab: mediator

Aungsa: ancestral property in the Nepali language

Badal: principle of revenge in Pushtunwali

Badghar: dispute resolution mechanism in Tharu communities in Nepal

Bahira rakeko: woman kept secretly and outside the home in the Nepali language

Bahudaliya janabad: multiparty people's democracy

Bahun Chhetris: the Brahman and Chhetri are the high Hindu castes in Nepal. Brahmans in Nepali are known as "Bahuns." Chhetri is the Nepali equivalent of Kshatriya, the warrior caste in Hinduism.

Bang: chief in Nepali indigenous communities

Bepatta Aayog: COID or the Disappearance Commission

Bhalmansa: mechanism through which Raji communities in Nepal seek to resolve disputes on justice and security

Bihe gareko: married woman in the Nepali language

Bihe nagareko: never married in the Nepali language

Brahmin: highest caste

Buhari: daughter-in-law in the Nepali language

Chaupadi: strict taboos concerning women's menstrual periods

Chetri: widely used term for Kshatriyas, the warrior caste within the Hindu caste system

Choho: members in indigenous communities in Nepal

148   *Glossary*

Chora hune: woman with sons in Nepali

Chora nahune: woman without sons in Nepali

CPN-M: Unified Communist Party of Nepal-Maoists, far-left faction whose central aim was to capture state power and establish new people's democracy

Dalit: the term Dalit refers to the lowest caste in the Hindu caste hierarchy, the Shudra. Historically, the Dalits were relegated to doing dirty, menial work and were considered "untouchable" by the higher castes. Traditionally, they have been subjected to socioeconomic marginalization including in the Civil Code of 1853. The New Civil Code of 1963 and the 1990 Constitution have banned untouchability and abolished discriminatory legal provisions, but socially, the Dalits continue to occupy the margins of Nepali society.

Dandahinta: closest term to mean impunity in Nepal

de facto: in practice, not necessarily ordained by law

de jure: concerning law

Dharmadhikara: the owner of justice

Diat: financial compensation in Pushtunwali

Divya Pariksha: Ordeal

Enteqam: see Badal

ex gratia: out of kindness

Ezzat: principle of honor in Pushtunwali

Fatwa: a ruling or opinion on a point by a recognized authority in Islam

Fiqh: Islamic jurisprudence

Gacaca: "grass courts" or local courts in the traditional justice system in Rwanda, employed as a method of justice after the Rwanda genocide of 1994, that created thousands of local courts to handle some genocide suspects accused of minor crimes, such as arson, as well as capital crimes.

Ghach: see Badal

Ghairat: principle of heroism/personal honor in Pushtunwali

Gomo tong: ritual of bending of the spears for reconciliation after fighting in Northern Uganda

Gono Andalon: people's movement

Gundi: principle of rivalry in Pushtunwali

Habeas corpus: A writ of habeas corpus is a judicial mandate to a prison official ordering that an inmate be brought to the court to determine whether or not that person is imprisoned lawfully and whether or not the person should be released from custody.

Hadith: sayings and actions of Prophet Muhammed

Hajj: religious pilgrimage to Mecca

Hamsaya: principle of protection of neighbors or outsiders living with a family or in a village in Pushtunwali

Hanafi: Jurisprudendence

Haqqul Ibad: The doctrine of Haqqul Ibad is based on the principle that in Islam, sins against men are forgivable only if the offended pardon the offender.

Haqqul Rab: The doctrine of Haqqul Rab is premised on committing sins against God, which may be forgiven if divine pardon is sought.

Glossary 149

Hazarajat: land of the Hazara people in Afghanistan

Hazarat: a regional name for the territory inhabited by the Hazara people. It is located in the central highlands of Afghanistan, among the Koh-i-Baba mountains and the western extremities of the Hindu Kush.

Hudd: Islamic crimes

Hudud: punishment restrictive prescriptions decided by the divine

Ijma: consensus of legal scholars of Islam on specific cases similar to opinio juris

Ijtihad: concept of individual conscience in Islam

Ipso facto: by the fact itself

Irsy: property compensation in Pushtunwali

Islamiyat: the study and practice of Islam

Ittihad Ittehad-e Islami bara-ye Azadi-ye Afghanistan: began as an attempt to bring unity amongst Islamist opposition forces in Afghanistan but it soon evolved as an independent entity led by Abdul Rasul Sayyaf and supported by financial aid from Saudi sources. Between 1993–94, it was one of the main actors, which participated in the fractional infighting for control over Kabul after the ousting of the PDPA government.

Jafariyya: school of jurisprudence

Jana Andalon: people's movement

Janajatis: the indigenous people of Nepal

Janayat-i-jang: crime of waging war

Jang salar: warlords

Jat: caste

Jihad: holy war in Islam

Jirga: Council

Jus cogens: Latin term for "compelling law" that must be followed by all countries

Kachahari: a village "court," traditionally presided over by the village elder(s)

Kanya: virgin in the Nepali language

KHAD Khidamati Ittila'at-i Dawlati/ State Information Service: the main security agency and intelligence agency of Afghanistan, which also served as the secret police during the Soviet occupation

Kipat: communal system of resource ownership among indigenous communities in Nepal

Kul: kin group

Linga: sex

Liyaeko: woman who has been brought but not formally married in the Nepali language

Loya Jirga: Grand Council. It is traditionally a gathering of male representatives selected by their local leadership from different tribes and factions in Afghanistan. The Loya Jirga discusses any important political and social issue important to the community.

150   *Glossary*

Madhab: private schools of jurists

Madhesis: those of Indian origin, considered to be more recent migrants and living predominantly in the plains of the Terai (the flat lands or plains). They constitute about 32 percent of the population of Nepal.

Majelisi Qawmi: circles of deliberation and consensus building where punishment forgiveness, and compensatory measures are discussed in the Hazara communities in Afghanistan

Marakchi: voluntary members of open forums at village levels in Afghanistan

Mata oput: ritual of drinking the bitter root for reconciliation in Northern Uganda

Maulana: honorific title for those who are formally trained in religion

Melmilap: reconciliation in Nepali

Meshrano Jirga: Council of Elders in Afghanistan

Muftis: jurists in Afghanistan

Mukhi: cleric in Afghanistan

Mukhiya: village leader in Nepal

Mullahs: clerics

Mutasibs: religious superintendents in Afghanistan

Namus: principle of protection of female family members and wealth in Pushtunwali

Nanawati: principle of forgiveness/harmony in Pushtunwali

Nang: see Ezzat

Naulo janabad: new people's democracy

Nepali Brihyat Sabdhakosh: root dictionary of the Nepali language

Newars: people in the Kathmandu Valley in Nepal

Nyaya: justice

Opinio juris: In customary international law, in addition to state practice opinio juris is necessary to establish a legally binding custom.

Panchayat: a South Asian political system, which literally translates to assembly (yat) of five (panch) wise and respected elders chosen and accepted by the village community

Pande, Pant, Bohara, Aryal, Khanal, and Rana: groups that constituted the Tharghar and were afforded the highest status in society and the premier posts of the state during the Shah period in Nepal

Pashtunwali: the code of conduct for the Pushtuns

Patna: principle of feud in Pushtunwali

Poar: blood money in Afghanistan's customary practices

Poila gaiyo: having eloped in the Nepali language

Proceay-i Tahkeem-i Sulha: the Strengthening Peace Program, or Peace and Reconciliation Commission, also known as the PTS established by presidential decree by President Karzai in May 2005 and headed by the first President of the Islamic Republic of Afghanistan

Pur: see Badal

Santan: family lineage

Glossary   151

Sibghatullah Mojaddedi: former president of the Islamic state of Afghanistan

Sulh: arbitration

Qadi: judge

Qanun: statute, law

Qassass/quisas: intentional crimes in Islamic jurisprudence

Qawm: principle of ethnicity, tribe, social network in Pushtunwali

Qawmi Taroon: principle of tribal binding in Pushtunwali

Qiyas: cases decided by analogical reasoning in Islamic jurisprudence

Ram Charit Manas: poet Goswami Tulsidas' epic sixteenth-century Hindu poem that chronicles the life of Ram, who is worshipped as an incarnation of the God Vishnu.

Sadhya: married, with a living husband in the Nepali language

Sankramankaalin Nyaya: the coined term for "transitional justice" in Nepali

Satya Dagaune: unfaithful woman in the Nepali language

Satya Nirupan Tatha Mil Milap Aayog: Nepali Truth and Reconciliation Commission

Seals, sanad, sawal, rokka, istihar: Components of the unified legal code of the Law Council appointed by Jung Bahadur Rana in Nepal in 1851.

Seyal: principle of equality in Pushtunwali

Seyali: principle of applying equality through competition in Pushtunwali

Shahids: martyrs

Sharm: principle of payment such as sheep for compensation in Pushtunwali

Shi'a: faction of Ali, Prophet Mohammad's cousin and son-in-law, who maintain that the most legitimate authorities in all matters are the Imams or select members of Prophet Mohammad's family, beginning with Ali ibn Abi Talib.

Shi'ite: adherents of the faction of Ali

Shura-e-ulema: councils of religious leaders

Shura-I-Islahi/Shura-Qawnii/ Majles-Eslahy/Jirgas, and Mookee Khans: practices of circles of deliberation and consensus building, punishment and forgiveness, compensatory measures among the people of Nuristan, and the ethnically diverse provinces of northern Afghanistan among the Tajiks, Uzbeks, Turkmen, and Arabs.

Shura-i-Jamaatkhana: gathering in a place or house amongst the Afghan Ismaili Shi'a communities to resolve disputes

Sindhur: red powder in married women's hair that denotes marriage

Stare decisis: Latin for judicial precedent

Sulh: arbitration

Sunni: strand of Islamic tradition whose name comes from the Arabic phrase meaning "the people of sunnah and the community of believers" who maintain that the most legitimate authorities in all matters are the Caliphs, leaders chosen initially by the consensus of community leaders on the basis of their experience and public reputation.

Taqqalli: transition

Tazir: discretionary punishment determined by the qadi

152 *Glossary*

Tharghar: comprising of the groups of Pande, Pant, Bohara, Aryal, Khanal, and Rana who were afforded the highest status in society and the premier posts of the state during the Shah period in Nepal

Tharus: a culturally and linguistically diverse ethnic category who live along the Indo–Nepal border. There are approximately 1.2 million Tharu in Nepal, and smaller numbers live in the adjacent areas of India.

Tsali: general principles and practices in Afghan law

Tukhum: dispute resolution body comprising of representatives from different lineages and other Pushtun clans in Afghanistan

Ucchrinkal: one who is unfettered by rules and discipline or out of control in Nepali

Uddhanda: one who seeks to exert control over others even with the use of force and does not fear retribution

Ulema: legal scholars in Islam

Vidhva: widowed in the Nepali language

Vidhva buhari: widowed daughter-in-law in Nepali

Wahdat: The Hizb-e-Wahdat (Party of Unity) was one of the main forces that emerged during the anti-Soviet resistance period in the 1980s. It was in response to a strong urge for unity among the Hazara leaders and the Shi'ite community.

Wakil: local government representative in Northern Afghanistan

Wolesi Jirga: People's Council

Zar: gold

Zamin: land

Zan: women

Notes

1 Introduction

1 Inter-state wars include the Bangladesh War of Independence with Pakistan 1971, and the Indo-Pakistan wars in 1947, 1965, 1971, and 1999; intra-state wars include the Tamil struggle for a separate homeland in Sri Lanka between 1983 and 2009, the contemporary Afghanistan wars between 1979–89, 1989–92, 1992–96, 1996–2001, and 2001 to the present, and the People's War in Nepal 1996–2006.

2 There was significant confusion about when exactly President Karzai signed the bill. According to some, Karzai signed the bill sometime in March 2007; however, interviews conducted in Kabul and Washington DC indicated that although the National Assembly approved the National Reconciliation Bill, the president actually did not sign it. The Constitution of Afghanistan (CoA) indicates that a president's signature is not required for the passage of a bill; however, if there is disagreement between the president and the National Assembly, he can send it back to the *Wolesi Jirga* within 15 days. Karzai made changes to the original bill allowing for victims' rights before sending it back to Parliament, and both the *Wolesi Jirga* and the *Meshrano Jirga* accepted these changes. According to the CoA, once the bill is returned to the president, it is considered endorsed and enforceable after 15 days, regardless of whether he actually signs the document. Several of the interviews conducted during the research revealed that, particularly for civil society, this confusion was not necessarily considered a bad thing. Instead, questions about the bill's legal status allowed the space for work to be done quietly around transitional justice. There was genuine fear that too many questions about the amnesty bill would bring the issue into the limelight, which in turn would negatively impact any movement on "transitional justice" activism.

3 E. Winterbotham, *The State of Transitional Justice in Afghanistan: Actors, Approaches and Challenges: A Discussion Paper* (Afghanistan Research and Evaluation Unit, April 2010), accessed April 30, 2010. http://www.areu.org.af/Uploads/EditionPdfs/1009E-The State of Transitional Justice in Afghanistan – Actors, Approaches and Challenges DP 2010 Final Web.pdf.

4 This list initially had appeared in Human Rights Watch, *Blood-Stained Hands: Past Atrocities in Kabul and Afghanistanís Legacy of Impunity* (New York, NY: Human Rights Watch, July 7, 2005), accessed January 5, 2007, http://www.hrw.org/en/reports/2005/07/06/blood-stained-hands.

5 The term "post-conflict" is irrefutably problematic, given that violence does not end with the signing of a peace agreement. In the case of Afghanistan, the label is inherently troubling, given that the war did not end in 2001 with the signing of the Bonn Agreement, or with the parliamentary and presidential elections that have taken place since. Instead, the escalation of violence in the country led to a troop surge in 2010. In May 2012, NATO leaders signed off on President Obama's exit strategy to end all

154 *Notes*

combat operations in 2013 and withdraw US-led international military force by the end of 2014.

6 A.L. George and A. Bennett, *Case Studies and Theory Development in the Social Sciences* (Cambridge, MA: MIT Press, 2005).

7 A. Przeworski and H. Teune, *Logic of Comparative Social Inquiry* (New York, NY: Wiley–Interscience, 1970), 153.

8 D. Backer, "Cross-National Comparative Analysis," in *Assessing the Impact of Transitional Justice: Challenges for Empirical Research,* ed. H. Merwe, V. Baxter, and A. Chapman (Washington DC: USIP Press, 2009).

9 H. Arendt, *The Human Condition* (Chicago, IL: University of Chicago Press, 1998), 241.

10 Ruti Teitel first coined the term "transitional justice" in her seminal work *Transitional Justice* (New York, NY: Oxford University Press, 2002). Other scholars have offered alternative terms to define the same processes and mechanisms. In this study, transitional justice is used synonymously with "closing the books," a term suggested by J. Elster in *Closing the Books: Transitional Justice in Historical Perspective* (Cambridge, MA: Cambridge University Press, 2004) and the commonly used term "accounting for the past."

11 According to J. Galtung, negative peace refers to the absence of violence or an end to conflict. See J. Galtung, "An Editorial," *The Journal of Peace Research* 1(1) (1964): 1–4.

12 P. Hazan, "Transitional Justice After September 11: A New Rapport with Evil," in *Localizing Transitional Justice: Interventions and Priorities After Mass Violence,* ed. R. Shaw, L. Waldorf, and P. Hazan, (Stanford, CA: Stanford University Press, 2010), 56.

13 Ibid., 57.

14 S.P. Huntington, *The Third Wave: Democratization in the Late Twentieth Century (Julian J. Rothbaum Distinguished Lecture Series)* (Norman, OK: University of Oklahoma Press, 1993).

15 D. Rustow, "Transitions to Democracy: Towards a Dynamic Model," *Comparative Politics* 2(3) (1970): 337–363.

16 E.D. Mansfield and J. Snyder, "Democratic Transitions, Institutional Strength, and War," *International Organization* 56(2) (2002): 301.

17 S. Stacey, "Political Theory and Transitional Justice" (PhD diss., Department of Politics, Princeton University, 2005), 3. Accessed January 10, 2011.

18 See, for example, V. Bunce, "Should Transitologists Be Grounded?" *Slavic Review* 54(1) (1995): 111–27; K. Jowitt, "Undemocratic Past, Unnamed Present, Undecided Future," *Demokrati-zatsiya* 4(3) (1996): 409–19; S.M. Terry, "Thinking About Post-Communist Transitions: How Different Are They? *Slavic Review* 52(2) (1993): 333–7; H.J. Wiarda, "Southern Europe, Eastern Europe, and Comparative Politics: Transitology and the Need for New Theory," *Eastern European Politics and Societies* 15(3) (2001): 485–501.

19 See, for example, M. Burawoy and K. Verdery, *Uncertain Transition: Ethnographies of Change in the Postsocialist World* (Lanham, MD: Rowman and Littlefield, 1999); D. Stark, "From System Identity to Organizational Diversity: Analyzing Social Change in Eastern Europe," *Contemporary Sociology* 21(3) (1992): 299–304.

20 J. Gans-Morse, "Searching for Transitologists: Contemporary Theories of Post-Communist Transitions and the Myth of a Dominant Paradigm," *Post-Soviet Affairs* 20(4) (2004): 320.

21 T. Carothers, "The End of the Transition Paradigm," *Journal of Democracy* 13(1) (2002): 5–21.

22 Ibid., 4.

23 J. Elster, "Coming to Terms with the Past: A Framework for the Study of Justice in the Transition to Democracy," *Archives Européennes de Sociologie* 39(1) (1998): 47.

Notes   155

24 Huntington, op. cit., 5.

25 For a discussion of the normative questions that face society, see P.B. Hayner, *Unspeakable Truths: Confronting State Terror and Atrocity* (New York, NY: Routledge, 2001), 210–234; E. Stover and H.M. Weinstein, "Introduction: Conflict, Justice and Reclamation," in *My Neighbor, My Enemy, Justice And Community In The Aftermath Of Mass Atrocity*, ed. E. Stover and H.M. Weinstein (New York, NY: Cambridge University Press, 2004), 1–26.

26 N. Scheper-Hughes, "Undoing Social Suffering and the Politics of Remorse in the New South Africa," *Social Justice* 25(4) (1998): 116.

27 For example, see J. Snyder and L. Vinjamuri, "Trials and Errors: Principles and Pragmatism in Strategies of International Justice," *International Security*, 28 (2003–2004): 5–44; P.C. McMahon and D.P. Forsythe, "The ICTY's Impact on Serbia: Judicial Romanticism Meets Network Politics," *Human Rights Quarterly* 30(2) (2008): 412–35.

28 See for example, M.C. Bassiouni and M.H. Morris "Accountability for International Crime and Serious Violations of Fundamental Human Rights," *Law And Contemporary Problems* 59(4) (1996): 5–230; D.F. Orentlicher, "Settling Accounts: The Duty to Prosecute Human Rights Violations of a Prior Regime," *The Yale Law Journal* 100(8) (1991): 2537–2615.

29 P. Lundy and M. McGovern, "Whose Justice? Rethinking Transitional Justice from the Bottom Up," *Journal of Law and Society* 35(2) (2008): 265–292.

30 E. Bertram, "Reinventing Governments: The Promise and Perils of United Nations Peace Building," *Journal of Conflict Resolution* 39(3) (1995): 398.

31 See Snyder and Vinjamuri, op. cit., 5–44.

32 See H. Cobban, *Amnesty after Atrocity? Healing Nations After Genocide and War Crimes* (Boulder, CO: Paradigm Publishers, 2007).

33 Greenwalt offers seven dimensions along which amnesties have varied historically: "(1) an amnesty may be blanket or limited, extended to all crimes committed within a particular period, or restricted to less serious crimes or to less responsible actors or both; (2) it may be automatic, covering all individuals within the classes named, or require applications by individuals; (3) for amnesties that require individual application, an individual may or may not have to disclose exactly what crimes he or she has committed. In South Africa, for example, individuals have to make 'full disclosure' of their violations of human rights; amnesty covered only crimes that were fully disclosed; (4) an amnesty may affect both criminal as well as civil liability, but (5) an amnesty may be total or partial. A partial amnesty is one that exempts those covered from the full measure of criminal and civil liability but would allow some lesser degree of punishment or liability for damages; (6) an amnesty may or may not protect persons from consequences other than legal liability; (7) an amnesty from civil liability may or may not be accompanied by some alternative scheme to compensate victims." See K. Greenwalt, "Amnesty's Justice," in *Truth v. Justice: The Morality of Truth Commissions,* ed. R.I. Rotberg and D. Thompson (Princeton, NJ: Princeton University Press, 2000), 189–210.

34 R.C. Slye, "Amnesty, Truth and Reconciliation: Reflections on the South African Amnesty Process," in Rotberg and Thompson, op cit., 170–88.

35 N. Roht-Arriaza and L. Gibson, "The Developing Jurisprudence on Amnesty," *Human Rights Quarterly* 20(4) (1998): 843.

36 M.P. Scharf and N. Rodley, "International Law Principles on Accountability," in *Post-Conflict Justice,* ed. M.C. Bassiouni (Ardsley, NY: Transaction Publishers, 2002), 89–96.

37 J.J. Moore, "Problems with Forgiveness: Granting Amnesty under the Arias Plan in Nicaragua and El Salvador," *Stanford Law Review* 43(3) (1991): 774.

38 C.L. Sriram, *Confronting Past Human Rights Violations: Justice vs Peace in Times of Transition* (New York, NY: Frank Cass, 2004), 10.

39 Snyder and Vinjamuri, op. cit., 6.

156 Notes

40 Ibid., 5–44.
41 L. Mallinder, *Amnesty, Human Rights and Political Transitions* (Orlando, FL: Hart Publishing, 2008).
42 M. Freeman, *Necessary Evils: Amnesties and the Search for Justice* (New York, NY: Cambridge University Press, 2009), 9.
43 A. Schaap, *Political Reconciliation* (New York, NY: Routledge, 2005), 71–81.
44 Teitel, op. cit., 52.
45 C. Bell, "The 'New Law' of Transitional Justice: Study 'Workshop 1 – From Mediation to Sustainable Peace'" (workshop organized by the Crisis Management Institute at the International Conference: Building a Future on Peace and Justice, Nuremberg, June 25–27, 2007). Accessed November 10, 2010. http://www.peace-justice-conference.info/download/WS1-Bell%20report.pdf.
46 Greenwalt, op. cit., 191.
47 Sriram, op. cit.. 11.
48 Slye, op. cit., 2000.
49 Ibid., 183.
50 See F.M. Afflito, "Victimization, Survival and the Impunity of Forced Exile: A Case Study from the Rwandan Genocide," *Crime, Law and Social Change* 34(1) (2000): 77–97. Also see J.P. McSherry and R.M. Mejía, "Confronting the Question of Justice in Guatemala," *Journal of Social Justice* 19(3) (1992): 1–28; M.M. Penrose, "Impunity-Inertia, Inaction and Invalidity: A Literature Review," *Boston University International Law Journal* 17(2) (1999): 241–68.
51 S. Opotow, "Reconciliation in Times of Impunity: Challenges for Social Justice," *Social Justice Research* 14(2) (2001): 150.
52 S. Opotow, "Psychology of Impunity and Injustice: Implications for Social Reconciliation," in *Post-Conflict Justice,* ed. M.C. Bassiouni (Ardsley, NY: Transaction Publishers, 2002), 205.
53 Ibid.
54 Ibid.
55 David Crocker quoting Leo Valladares, the Human Rights Commissioner of Honduras in D. Crocker, "Transitional Justice and International Civil Society: Toward a Normative Framework," *Constellations* 5(4) (1998): 506.
56 McSherry and Mejía, op. cit., 1–28.
57 Opotow, op. cit., 202.
58 McSherry and Mejía, op. cit., 14.
59 Ibid.
60 C.S. Nino, *Radical Evil on Trial* (New Haven, CT: Yale University Press, 1996), viii.
61 M. Aukerman, "Extraordinary Evil, Ordinary Crime: A Framework for Understanding Transitional Justice," *Harvard Human Rights Journal* 15(39) (2002): 41–2.
62 M.A. Drumbl, *Atrocity, Punishment and International Law* (New York, NY: Cambridge University Press, 2007), 3.
63 H. Arendt, "Letter from Hannah Arendt to Karl Jaspers (August 18, 1946)," in *Hannah Arendt, Karl Jaspers Correspondence 1926–1969,* ed. L. Kohler and H. Saner (San Diego, CA: Harcourt Brace and Company, 1992), 54.
64 Drumbl, op. cit., 3.
65 See D. Luban, "A Theory of Crimes Against Humanity," *The Yale Journal of International Law* 29(1) (2004): 85, 90.
66 Genocide, considered by many as the worst kind of violation of international humanitarian law, is defined by the "careful parsing of Articles II and III of the 1948 Convention of the Prevention and Punishment of Genocide." See R.I. Rotberg, *Mass Atrocity Crimes: Preventing Future Outrages* (Washington, DC: Brookings Institution Press, 2010), 3. Article II describes two elements of what constitutes genocide: "(1) the mental element, meaning the 'intent to destroy, in whole or in part, a national, ethnic, racial or religious group as such' and (2) the physical element, including killing members of group, causing serious or mental harm to members of

a group deliberately inflicting on a group conditions of life calculated to bring about its physical destruction, in whole or part, imposing measures intended to prevent births within a group and forcibly transferring children of one group to another." See Rotberg, op. cit., 3. For a war crime to be considered genocide, it must fulfill both these categories. Further, for a crime to be classified as genocide, it needs to prove intent and/or commission of the acts. Drumbl states: "The Rome Statute accords states the option of a seven year opt out period to the ICC's jurisdiction over war crimes but not for genocide and crimes against humanity." See Drumbl, op. cit., 34. This research does not address the question of genocide since in neither of the two contexts have the crimes committed been classified as genocidal acts.

67 A. Gerwith, "War Crimes and Human Rights," in *War Crimes and Collective Wrongdoing: A Reader,* ed. A. Jokic and A. Ellis (Malden, MA: Wiley-Blackwell, 2001), 49.

68 Gerwith, op. cit., 49.

69 Ibid., 48.

70 See for example, M.C. Bassiouni and E.M. Wise, *Aut Dedere Aut Judicare: The Duty To Extradite Or Prosecute In International Law* (Dordrecht, The Netherlands: Martinus Nijhoff Publishers, 1995), 51–69; M.C. Bassiouni, *International Criminal Law Conventions And Their Penal Provisions* (Irvington-on-Hudson, NY: Transaction Publishers, 1997), 451–54; M.C. Bassiouni, *Crimes Against Humanity In International Law* (New York, NY: Springer Publishing, 1992), 499–527; L. Hannikainen, *Peremptory Norms (Jus Cogens) In International Law: Historical Development, Criteria, Present Status* (University of Lapland Publications in Law, Series A1, Helsinki: Finnish Lawyers' Publishing Co, 1988), 713–18; G.A. Christenson, "Jus Cogens: Guarding Interests Fundamental to International Society," *Virginia Journal of International Law* 28 (1988): 585–648; K. Parker and L.B. Neylon, "Jus Cogens: Compelling the Law of Human Rights," *Hastings International and Comparative Law Review* 12 (1989): 429–35.

71 International Committee of the Red Cross, "National Measures To Repress Violations Of International Humanitarian Law" (Report of the Meeting on Experts, Geneva, September 23–25, 1997, by C. Pellandini), accessed May 12, 2009, http://www.icrc.org/eng/assets/files/other/report-icrc_002_0726.pdf.

72 See for example, M.C. Bassiouni, "International Crimes: 'Jus Cogens' and 'Obligatio Erga Omnes'," *Law And Contemporary Problems* 59(4) (1996): 63–74. Also see C.J. Tams, *Enforcing Obligations Erga Omnes in International Law* (New York, NY: Cambridge University Press, 2005), 17–94.

73 For a discussion on amnesties and war crimes, see Orentlicher, op. cit., 2537–2615; C. Douglass, "Lessons from the Americas: Guidelines for International Response to Amnesties for Atrocities," *Law and Contemporary Problems* 59(4) (1996): 197–230; N.J. Kritz (ed.), *Transitional Justice: How Emerging Democracies Reckon with Former Regimes*, vol. I (Washington DC: USIP Press, 1995), 155–334; N. Roht-Arriaza (ed.) *Impunity and Human Rights in International Law and Practice* (Oxford, UK: Oxford University Press, 1995), 3–13; R.G. Teitel, "Transitional Jurisprudence: The Role Of Law In Political Transformation," *Yale Law Journal* 106(7) (1997): 2009–80; J. Dugard, "Dealing With Crimes Of A Past Regime. Is Amnesty Still An Option?" *Leiden Journal of International Law* 12(4) (1999) 1001–15; S.R. Ratner and J.S. Abrams, *Accountability for Human Rights Atrocities in International Law: Beyond the Nuremburg Legacy*, 2nd ed. (Oxford, UK: Oxford University Press, 2001), 46–77. See also Bell, op. cit.

74 Huntington, op. cit.

75 See Teitel, op. cit. Also see UN Security Council (UNSC), *The Rule Of Law And Transitional Justice In Conflict And Post-Conflict Societies: Report of the Secretary-General*, by K. Annan, S/2004/616 (UN Security Council, August 23, 2004), accessed January 10, 2007, http://www.unrol.org/files/2004%20report.pdf.

158 *Notes*

76 A. Barahona de Brito, C. González-Enríquez, and P. Aguilar, ed., *The Politics of Memory: Transitional Justice in Democratizing Societies* (Oxford, UK: Oxford University Press, 2001), 315.

77 R. Teitel, "Theoretical and International Framework: Transitional Justice In A New Era," *Fordham International Law Journal* 26(4) (2003): 893–906.

78 M.C. Okello, "Afterward: Elevating Transitional Local Justice or Crystallizing Global Governance?" in Shaw, Waldorf and Hazan op. cit., 277.

79 L.S. Wiseberg, "Human Rights Nongovernmental Organizations: Questions for Reflection and Discussion," in *Human Rights in the World Community: Issues and Actions,* ed. R.P. Claude and B.H. Weston (Philadelphia, PA: University of Pennsylvania Press, 1992), 372–82. See also S. Cohen, "State Crimes of Previous Regimes: Knowledge, Accountability and the Policing of the Past," *Law and Social Inquiry* 20(1) (1995): 7–50.

80 D. Crocker, "Truth Commissions, Transitional Justice and Civil Society," in Rotberg and Thompson, op cit., 99–121.

81 K. McEvoy, "Letting Go Of Legalism: Developing A 'Thicker' Version Of Transitional Justice," *Journal Of Law And Society* 34(4) (2007): 412.

82 Teitel, op. cit., 893–906.

83 R. Nagy, "Transitional Justice as Global Project: Critical Reflections," *Third World Quarterly* 29(2) (2008): 277.

84 Teitel, op. cit., 213.

85 Nagy, op. cit., 277.

86 N. Roht-Arriaza, "The New Landscape in Transitional Justice," in *Transitional Justice in the Twenty-First Century: Beyond Truth Versus Justice,* ed. N. Roht-Arriaza and J. Mariezcurrena (New York, NY: Cambridge University Press, 2006), 2.

87 Ibid.

88 T.D. Olsen, L.A. Payne, and A.G. Reiter, *Transitional Justice in Balance: Comparing Processes, Weighing Efficacy* (Washington DC: USIP Press, 2010), 1.

89 R. Mani, *Beyond Retribution: Seeking Justice in the Shadows of War* (Malden, MA: Polity Press, 2002), 17.

90 Mani, op. cit., 2002.

91 C. Moon, "Beyond Retribution: Seeking Justice in the Shadows of War [book review]," *International Peacekeeping* 10(4) (2003): 149–151.

92 Mani, op. cit., 51.

93 Nagy, op. cit., 278.

94 R. Lui, "Beyond Retribution: Seeking Justice in the Shadows of War [book review]," *Australian Journal of Political Science* 38(3) (2003): 589–590.

95 B. Leebaw, "Transitional Justice, Conflict, and Democratic Change: International Interventions and Domestic Reconciliation," (prepared for APSA Task Force on Difference and Inequality in the Developing World, University of Virginia, Charlottesville, April 21–23, 2005), accessed January 10, 2010, http://www.apsanet.org/imgtest/TaskForceDiffIneqLebaw.pdf.

96 Y. Bar-Siman-Tov, "Israel–Egypt Peace: Stable Peace?" in *Stable Peace Among Nations,* ed. Y. Bar-Siman-Tov, A.M. Kacowicz, O. Elgström and M. Jerneck (Boulder, CO: Rowman Publishers, 2000), 220–38.

97 See J.P. Lederach, *Building Peace: Sustainable Reconciliation in Divided Societies* (Washington, DC: USIP Press, 1998).

98 L. Gardner-Feldman, *The Special Relationship Between West Germany and Israel* (Boston, MA: Allen and Unwin, 1984).

99 C. Villa-Vicencio, "A Different Kind Of Justice: the South African Truth and Reconciliation Commission," *Contemporary Justice Review* 1 (1998): 407.

100 M. Osiel, *Mass Atrocity, Collective Memory and the Law* (New Brunswick, Canada: Transaction Books, 1997), 17.

101 A. Gutmann and D. Thompson, "Why Deliberative Democracy is Different," *Social Philosophy and Policy* 17(1) (2000): 161–80.
102 T. Govier and W. Verwoerd, "Trust and the Problem of National Reconciliation," *Philosophy of the Social Sciences* 32(2) (2000): 200.
103 For a discussion on political reconciliation, see for example M.R. Amstutz, *Healing of Nations: The Promise and Limits of Political Reconciliation* (Lanham, MD: Rowmann and Littlefield Publishers, 2005), 66–90.
104 Schaap, op. cit., 84.
105 Ibid., 523.
106 See Hayner, op. cit. Also see M. Minow, *Between Vengeance and Forgiveness: Facing History after Genocide and Mass Violence* (Boston, MA: Beacon Press, 1998), 52–90.
107 Minow, op. cit., 1998.
108 Ibid.
109 Nagy, op. cit., 285–286.
110 Olsen, Payne, and Reiter, op. cit., 17.
111 For a discussion of the minimalist approach also see M.J. Osiel, "Why Prosecute? Critics for Punishment for Mass Atrocity," *Human Rights Quarterly* 22(1) (2000): 118–147. For a succinct discussion of the maximalist and minimalist positions as well as a discussion on moderate and holistic approaches, see Olsen, Payne, and Reiter, op. cit., 16–25.
112 Olsen, Payne, and Reiter, op. cit., 146.
113 Ibid.
114 Ibid., 153.
115 E. Wiebelhaus-Brahm, *Truth Commissions and Transitional Societies: The Impact on Human Rights and Democracy* (New York, NY: Routledge, 2010), 140.
116 The premises of restorative justice perhaps best define justice that goes beyond the punitive. Restorative justice recognizes the humanity of the offender as well as the dignity of the victim. It is most commonly expressed in the form of truth commissions. Since it is victim-centered and future-oriented, it can outline necessary reforms, allow victims to speak of their pain, provide acknowledgement of the past and keep abuses from happening in the future. Martha Minnow, an advocate for restorative justice and truth commissions, argues that promoting prosecutions ultimately foments more tensions and can deepen the schisms while commissions of inquiry promote catharsis for victims, perpetrators, and witnesses through the restorative power of speaking about trauma. Ultimately, restorative justice creates the space for true reconciliation and healing to take place. Hence, both justice is served and relationships are restored in the best-case scenario. For a deeper discussion on restorative justice, see E. Kiss, "Moral Ambitions Within and Beyond Political Constraints: Reflections on Restorative Justice," in Rotberg and Thompson, op. cit., 68–98.
117 A. Hutchinson provides various definitions in his book, *The Rule of Law: Ideal or Ideology?* (Piscataway, NJ: Transaction Publishers, 1987).
118 R. Mani, "Exploring the Rule of Law in Theory and Practice," in *Civil War and the Rule of Law: Security, Development and Human Rights,* ed. A. Hurwitz and R. Huang (Boulder, CO: Lynne Rienner Publishers, 2008), 21–46.
119 F. von Hayek, *The Road to Serfdom with the Intellectuals and Socialism,* 5th ed. (Chicago, IL: University of Chicago Press, 1994), 10.
120 Peacebuilding Initiative, *Defining Rule of Law, Introduction: Definitions & Conceptual Issues,* accessed March 1, 2011, http://www.peacebuildinginitiative.org/index.cfm?pageId=1843.
121 Mani, op. cit., 24.
122 Ibid., 25.
123 UNSC, *The Rule Of Law And Transitional Justice In Conflict And Post-Conflict Societies: Report of the Secretary-General,"* op. cit.

160   *Notes*

124 See Mani, op. cit.
125 Ibid., 25.
126 B.Z. Tamanaha, *On the Rule of Law: History, Politics, Theory* (New York, NY: Cambridge University Press, 2004), 91–102.
127 B. Rajagopal, "Invoking the Rule of Law in Post-Conflict Rebuilding: A Critical Examination," *William and Mary Law Review* 49(4) (2008): 1348.
128 See K. Pistor, "Advancing the Rule of Law: Report on the International Rule of Law Symposium Convened by the American Bar Association November 9–10, 2005," *Berkeley Journal of International Law* 25(1) (2007): 7–43.
129 D. Tolbert and A. Solomon, "United Nations Reform and Supporting the Rule of Law in Post-Conflict Societies," *Harvard Human Rights Journal* 19 (2006): 33.
130 Ibid.
131 Mani, op. cit., 71.
132 T. Carothers, *Promoting The Rule Of Law Abroad: The Problem of Knowledge.* Rule of Law Series, Democracy and Rule of Law Project No. 34, January 2003 (Washington DC: Carnegie Endowment for International Peace, 2003), accessed April 10, 2008, http://www.carnegieendowment.org/files/wp34.pdf.
133 Comparative scholars have taken to task the functionalist view that formally independent judiciaries always support the rule of law. See generally J.M. Maravall and A. Przeworski, ed., *Democracy And The Rule Of Law*, vol. 13, no. 11 (New York, NY: Cambridge University Press, 2003); R. Hirschl, "Juristocracy – Political, not Juridical," *The Good Society* 13(3) (2004): 6–11.
134 See for example E.H. Boyle and J.W. Meyer, "Modern Law as a Secularized and Global Model: Implications for the Sociology of Law," in *Global Prescriptions: The Production, Exportation, and Importation of a New Legal Orthodoxy,* ed. Y. Dezalay and B.G. Garth (Ann Arbor, MI: University of Michigan Press, 2002), 65–95.
135 See for example, C. Bell, *Peace Agreements and Human Rights* (Oxford, UK: Oxford University Press, 2000), 119–60; C. Bell, "Dealing with the Past in Northern Ireland," *Fordham International Law Journal* 26 (2003): 1095–147; C. Bell, "Negotiating Justice: Conflict Resolution and Human Rights," in *Human Rights and Conflict: Exploring the Links between Rights, Law, and Peacebuilding,* ed. J. Helsing, and J. Mertus (Washington DC: USIP Press, 2004), 345–74; C. Campbell, "Peace and the Law of War: The Role of International Humanitarian Law in the Post-Conflict Environment," *International Review of the Red Cross* 839 (2000): 627–52. C. Campbell and F. Ní Aoláin, "Local Meets Global: Transitional Justice in Northern Ireland," *Fordham International Law Journal* 24 (2003): 1201–23; C. Campbell, F. Ní Aoláin, and C. Harvey, "The Frontiers of Legal Analysis: Reframing the Transition in Northern Ireland," *Modern Law Review* 66 (2003): 317–45.
136 C. Bell, C. Campbell, and F. Ní Aoláin, "Justice Discourses in Transition," *Social & Legal Studies* 13(3) (2004): 305–28.
137 Bell, op. cit.
138 Bell, 306.
139 Campbell, op. cit.
140 See Anonymous, "Human Rights in Peace Negotiations," *Human Rights Quarterly* 18(2) (1996): 249–58. Also see P.H. Baker, "Conflict Resolution Versus Democratic Governance: Divergent Paths to Peace?" in *Turbulent Peace: The Challenges of Managing International Conflict,* ed. C.A. Crocker, F.O. Hampson, and P. Aall (Washington DC: USIP Press, 2001), 753–63.
141 Ibid.
142 Ibid.
143 For example, see O'Donnell, Schmitter, and Whitehead, op. cit.; Huntington, op. cit.; J. Zalaquett, "Confronting Human Rights Violations Committed by Former Governments: Principles Applicable and Political Constraints" in *Transitional Justice,* ed. N.J. Kritz (Washington DC: USIP Press, 1995), 3–31; D. Pion-Berlin,

"The Armed Forces and Politics: Gains and Snares in Recent Scholarship," *Latin American Research Review* 30(1) (1995): 147–162; Wilson, op. cit.; J. Zalaquett, "Balancing Ethical Imperatives and Political Constraints: The Dilemma of New Democracies Confronting Past Human Rights Violations," *Hastings Law Journal* 43 (1992): 1425–1438.

144 Snyder and Vinjamuri, op. cit., 6.
145 Okello, op. cit., 277.
146 A.L. Tsing, "From the Margins," *Cultural Anthropology* 9(3) (1994): 279–297.
147 D. Otto, R. Aponte-Toro and A. Farley, "The Third World and International Law: Voices from the Margins," *American Society of International Law* 94 (2000): 51.
148 In Nepal, its NHRI is actually referred to as the National Human Rights Commission (NHRC).

2 The legacy of past initiatives

1 The term is borrowed from A. Rashid's, *Descent into Chaos: The United States and the Failure of Nation Building in Pakistan, Afghanistan, and Central Asia* (New York, NY: Viking Press, 2008), 544.
2 Appeasement may be defined as "a policy of granting concessions in response to aggressive or hostile demands with the intent of gaining some a greater good or asset. [It] is usually portrayed as a willingness to accede to an immoral actor or entity. In extreme cases, practitioners may even be accused of cowardice." See C.E. Miller and M.E. King, ed., *A Glossary of Terms and Concepts in Peace and Conflict Studies,* 2nd ed. (Geneva, Switzerland: University for Peace, 2005), 15, accessed October 1, 2010. http://www.africa.upeace.org/documents/glossaryv2.pdf.
3 A conditional surrender or yielding of rights by a party engaged in a conflict, ibid.
4 PDPA, comprising of the Khalq and Pancham parties, was a small, Marxist–Leninist Party, strongly supported by the Soviet Union. On 27 April 1978, it instigated the coup d'état, which resulted in the overthrow and killing of President Muhammed Daoud Khan and most of his family members. The party then mobilized around what has come to be recognized as an ambitious and brutally ruthless campaign with the singular goal to transform Afghanistan into a modern socialist state. Soon after its take over, the PDPA split along internal lines, with the dominant Khalq faction purging leading members of the Parcham faction through an extensive campaign of arrests and executions of known opponents, targeted authorities, former government officials, religious and tribal leaders, and political activists. The Khalq-dominated PDPA also indiscriminately bombed pockets of resistance resulting in millions of Afghans pouring out of the country's borders. This was the largest outflow of refugees to Europe, the United States, Iran, and Pakistan. For a detailed discussion of the PDPA rule, see M. Ewans, *Afghanistan: A Short History of its People and Politics* (New York, NY: Harper Perennial, 2002). Also see P. Hokirk, *The Great Game: The Struggle for Empire in Central Asia* (New York, NY: Kodansha International, 1992).
5 The "Lion of Panjishir," Ahmed Shah Masood was a Tajik military commander and a leader of the anti-Soviet resistance. His loyal followers called him Āmir Sāhib-e Shahīd (Our Martyred Commander). Following the withdrawal of Soviet troops from Afghanistan and the collapse of the Soviet-backed Najibullah government, Masood served as the Defense Minister for President Rabbani's government. Masood also served as the military commander of the United Islamic Front for the Salvation of Afghanistan (UISFA), better known as the Northern Alliance against the Taliban since their rise to prominence in 1996.
6 M. Semple, *Reconciliation in Afghanistan* (Washington DC: USIP Press, 2009), 17.
7 Ibid.
8 Ibid.
9 Semple, op. cit., 2009.

162   *Notes*

10 This repression also resulted in the *mujahideen* growing in number supported by the United States and Saudi Arabia. Thousands of Muslim radicals from the Middle East, North Africa and other Muslim countries also joined the Pashtun factions including the Hizb- i Islami of Gulbuddin Hekmatyar and Osama bin Laden.

11 Human Rights Watch, *Afghanistan: The Forgotten War: Human Rights Abuses and Violations of the Laws of War Since the Soviet Withdrawal* (New York, NY: Human Rights Watch, February 1, 1991), accessed March 5, 2011, http://www.unhcr.org/ref-world/docid/45c9a5d12.html, 810.

12 For a more detailed discussion, see B.R. Rubin, *The Search For Peace in Afghanistan: From Buffer State to Failed State* (New Haven, CT: Yale University Press, 1995).

13 Afghanistan's first president.

14 Rabbani served as Afghanistan's president between 1992 and 1996. He was also the leader of Jamiat-e Islami Afghanistan (Islamic Society of Afghanistan) as well as the political head of the Northern Alliance.

15 The factionalization inside Kabul was mirrored outside the capital with commanders capturing territories, setting up *ad hoc* checkpoints, and operating by their own laws. See Afghanistan Justice Project, *Casting Shadows: War Crimes and Crimes against Humanity: 1978–2001: Documentation And Analysis Of Major Patterns Of Abuse In The War In Afghanistan* (Kabul, Afghanistan: Afghanistan Justice Project, 2005), accessed May 21, 2007, http://www.afghanistanjusticeproject.org/warcrime-sandcrimesagainsthumanity19782001.pdf, 62.

16 One of the most controversial rebel commanders in Afghanistan who allegedly committed some of the worst atrocities during the *mujahideen* wars. He was the founder and leader of the political party and paramilitary group, the Hizb-i-Islami and served as Prime Minister between 1993 and 1994.

17 Rubin, op. cit., 143.

18 See W. Maley, *The Afghanistan Wars*, 2nd ed. (New York, NY: Palgrave Macmillan, 2002); B.R. Rubin, *The Fragmentation of Afghanistan: State Formation and Collapse in the International System*, 2nd ed. (New Haven, CT: Yale University Press, 2002); A. Rashid, *Taliban: Militant Islam, Oil and Fundamentalism in Central Asia* (New Haven, CT: Yale Nota Bene Books, 2001); O. Roy, *Islam and Resistance in Afghanistan*, 2nd ed. (New York, NY: Cambridge University Press, 1990). Also see P. Gossman, "Afghanistan in the Balance," *Middle East Research and Information Project (MERIP)*, Winter (2001): 14, accessed October 1, 2010, http://www.merip.org/mer/mer221/afghanistan-balance.

19 Ibid.

20 A. Davis, "How the Taliban Became a Military Force," in *Fundamentalism Reborn? Fundamentalism and the Taliban*, ed. W. Maley, (New York, NY: New York University Press, 1998), 43; and Rashid, op. cit., 24–5.

21 See International Crisis Group, *Taliban Propaganda: Winning The War Of Words?* Report No. 158, July 24, 2008, accessed September 10, 2010, http://www.crisisgroup.org/~/media/Files/asia/south-asia/afghanistan/158_taliban_propaganda___winning_the_war_of_words.ashx.

22 Ibid., 23.

23 Semple, op. cit., 24.

24 The official name used by the US Government for the Afghanistan War together with three smaller military actions, under the umbrella of what President Bush declared as the "Global War on Terror."

25 See B.R. Rubin, "Transitional Justice and Human Rights in Afghanistan," *International Affairs* 79(3) (2003): 567–581. See also generally International Center for Transitional Justice, *Research Brief: Transitional Justice and DDR: The Case of Afghanistan*, by P. Gossman (International Center for Transitional Justice, June 2009), accessed January 9, 2010, http://ictj.org/sites/default/files/ICTJ-DDR-Afghanistan-ResearchBrief-2009-English.pdf, 1–4. Also see J.A. Thier, "The Politics of Peacebuilding, Year

One: From Bonn to Kabul," in *Nation-Building Unraveled? Aid, Peace and Justice in Afghanistan,* ed. A. Donini, N. Niland, and K. Wermester (West Hartford, CT: Kumarian Press, 2004), 39–60.

26 See Afghanistan Online, "Agreement on Provisional Arrangements in Afghanistan Pending the Re-Establishment of Permanent Government Institutions," (Bonn Agreement), accessed January 5, 2007, http://www.afghan-web.com/politics/bonn_agreement_2001.html.

27 Rubin, op. cit., 571.

28 Ibid.

29 Ibid., 570.

30 A peace agreement comprises of critical components of negotiated settlements between two formerly antagonistic parties, which include, but are not limited to, the formal designation of geopolitical borders, status or refugees, access to and apportioning resources, settlement of existing debts, new power-sharing arrangements, processes of addressing future disputes, defining and regulating behavior of state parties and opposition, outlining status and role of arms and armies, reapplication of existing treaties, the role of an interim administration, and increasingly, the question of how to address human rights atrocities committed during the period of conflict.

31 A. Suhrke, K.B. Harpviken, and A. Strand, "After Bonn: Conflictual Peace Building," *Third World Quarterly* 23(5) (2002): 876.

32 See Bonn Agreement.

33 In the 1980s, Sayyaf led the mujahideen faction of the Islamic Union for the Liberation of Afghanistan against the PDPA government. In his role, he also allegedly received patronage from Arab sources while mobilizing Arab volunteers to fight on behalf of the mujahideen. It was Sayyaf who allegedly was the first to invite Osama bin Laden to seek shelter in Afghanistan when the latter was expelled from Sudan in 1996. His crimes against humanity and involvement in war crimes are one of the best-documented in Afghanistan.

34 Rubin notes that there was also considerable conflict because of the paragraph that called for the disarmament, and demobilization and reintegration of unofficial armed groups was perceived to be a dishonorable demand placed on the *Mujahideen.* See Rubin, op. cit., 572.

35 T. Sajjad, "These Spaces in Between: The AIHRC and its Work on Transitional Justice," *The International Journal of Transitional Justice* 3(3) (2009): 442.

36 Rubin, op. cit. 573.

37 According to Thomas Ruttig, senior analyst of the Afghanistan Analyst Network (AAN), there were also suggestions how to define these Taliban more precisely using terms such as "pragmatic" or "politically thinking," see comments on the draft of T. Sajjad, *Peace At All Costs? Reintegration and Reconciliation in Afghanistan,* Issue Paper Series, Afghanistan Research and Evaluation Unit, October, 2010, accessed November 1, 2010, http://www.ecoi.net/file_upload/1788_1287995505_peace-at-all-costs-ip-2010-web.pdf, 7.

38 A.J. Tellis, *Reconciling with the Taliban? Toward an Alternative Grand Strategy in Afghanistan,* (Washington DC: Carnegie Endowment for Peace, April 2009), accessed July 2, 2010, http://www.carnegieendowment.org/files/reconciling_with_taliban.pdf.

39 "Afghan Truth Commission Requested," *Associated Press Online,* March 9, 2002, accessed May 7, 2010, http://www.freerepublic.com/focus/f-news/643825/posts.

40 Interview with Afghan researcher and former civil society actor, Washington DC, August 12, 2008.

41 "Karzai Sets Out Afghanistan Vision," BBC World News, June 14, 2002, accessed September 26, 2008, http://news.bbc.co.uk/2/hi/south_asia/2044337.stm.

42 *Loya Jirga,* or Grand Council, is traditionally a gathering of male representatives selected by their local leadership from different tribes and factions in Afghanistan. The *Loya Jirga* discusses any important political and social issue important to the

community. The Emergency *Loya Jirga* was held between June 10–16, 2002 (20–26 Jauza 1381) as per the Bonn Agreement to discuss Afghanistan's future and select members for a two-year interim government. For a deeper discussion of *jirgas*, see A. Wardak, *"Jirga* – A Traditional Mechanism of Conflict Resolution in Afghanistan," University of Glamorgan, UK: Centre for Criminology, 2003, accessed June 10, 2006, http://unpan1.un.org/intradoc/groups/public/documents/apcity/unpan017434. pdf, 1–20.

43 E.M. Lederer, "International Criminal Court Prosecutor Eyeing War Crimes In Afghanistan," *IJ Central*, September 9, 2009, accessed September 2, 2010, http:// ijcentral.org/blog/international_criminal_court_prosecutor_eyeing_war_crimes_in_ afghanistan.

44 The ICC is not mandated to investigate and prosecute cases prior to its establishment.

45 P. Gossman, "The Past As Present: War Crimes, Impunity And The Rule Of Law" (paper originally presented at State Reconstruction And International Engagement In Afghanistan, May 30–June 1, 2003, accessed September 15, 2010, http://eprints.lse. ac.uk/28365/1/Gossman_LSERO_version.pdf.

46 Human Rights Watch, *UN Rights Body in Serious Decline* (New York, NY: Human Rights Watch, April 26, 2003), accessed September 1, 2010, http://www.hrw.org/en/ news/2003/04/25/un-rights-body-serious-decline.

47 Gossman, op. cit.

48 A. Tarzi, "Recalibrating the Afghan Reconciliation Program," *Prism* 1(4) (2010): 68, accessed July 2, 2010, http://www.ndu.edu/press/lib/images/prism1-4/Prism_67-78_Tarzi.pdf.

49 Ibid.

50 Sajjad, op.cit.

51 A. Tarzi, "Afghanistan: Is Reconciliation With The Neo-Taliban Working?" *Eurasia Net Online*. June 1, 2005, accessed April 10, 2010, http://www.eurasianet.org/depart-ments/insight/articles/pp060205.shtml.

52 Ibid. Both Mojaddedi and Karzai have since backed off from those statements, and the issue of "reconciliation" was overshadowed by the international focus on the develop-ments in the Iraq war and a string of endeavors to disarm the insurgency and bring insurgents back to civilian life.

53 See, for example, Afghanistan News Centre, "Kabul Distances Itself From Claim of Amnesty for Mullah Omar," *Radio Free Europe/Radio Liberty*, May 10, 2005, accessed July 3, 2010, http://www.afghanistannewscenter.com/news/2005/may/ may102005.html.

54 These criticisms will be discussed in Chapter 4.

55 A detailed discussion of the findings of the report appears in Chapter 5.

56 The legal principle of universal jurisdiction in international public law requires that states can claim criminal jurisdiction over persons whose alleged crimes were com-mitted outside the boundaries of the prosecuting state, regardless of nationality, coun-try of residence, or any other relation with the prosecuting country.

57 Amidst allegations that he did not have ongoing legal assistance and that none of the prosecution witnesses presented direct evidence against him, the national security court sentenced him to death in 2006, raising questions about due process. As of writ-ing this research, his appeal is pending.

58 See Human Rights Watch, *Blood-Stained Hands: Past Atrocities in Kabul and Afghanistanis Legacy of Impunity* (New York, NY: Human Rights Watch, July 7, 2005), accessed January 5, 2007, http://www.hrw.org/en/reports/2005/07/06/blood-stained-hands.

59 Some stated that the report was never published and a few others recollected that the report was made public for a few days on the UN website before being taken down.

60 Interview with Dr P. Gossman, Washington DC, June 8, 2009.

61 According to Michael Semple, the PTS aimed to serve three important functions: (i) be a symbol of an official commitment to the president's public gestures and consistently stress on encouraging insurgents to lay down their arms and reintegrate; (ii) provide a vehicle for accommodating within the system and dispensing patronage to those directly associated with the leadership of the commission; and (iii) provide a public forum for welcoming back significant figures who have been reconciled through other channels, such as the National Security Council (NSC). See Semple, op. cit.

62 M. Waldman, "Golden Surrender: The Risks, Challenges, and Implications of Reintegration in Afghanistan," *Afghanistan Analyst Network* April 22, 2010, accessed April 22, 2010, http://aan-afghanistan.com/uploads/2010_AAN_Golden_Surrender.pdf.

63 This view was expressed in several interviews with various stakeholders and civil society actors in Kabul, Afghanistan, April 2010.

64 See the defection of Mullah Salam, a low-ranking commander in Musa Qala in Helmand Province in late 2007 in Congressional Research Service, *Afghanistan: Post-War Governance, Security, and US Policy*, by K. Katzman (Washington DC: Congressional Research Service, September 29, 2008), accessed July 3, 2010, http://fpc.state.gov/documents/organization/110749.pdf. It is notable that although some former high-ranking Taliban figures have been "reconciled," such as Mullah Zaeef or Mawlawi Wakil Ahamad Mutawakel, this was a condition of release from US or Afghan custody. See also J. Nathan, "A Review of Reconciliation Efforts in Afghanistan," *CTC Sentinel* 2(8) (2009): 11–13, accessed July 3, 2010, http://www.ctc.usma.edu/posts/a-review-of-reconciliation-efforts-in-afghanistan.

65 See UK Foreign and Commonwealth Office, "Information Relating to British Financial Help to Afghan Government in Negotiations with the Taliban," (released under Freedom of Information Act) September 27, 2007, accessed July 3, 2010, http://www.fco.gov.uk/resources/en/pdf/foi-releases/2008a/1.1-digest. Another example offered is that of Arshala Khan, who currently serves as a senator and who, in the past, used to work as the Ministry of Pilgrimage and during the Taliban worked as the vice president. Interview with PTS representative, Kabul, Afghanistan, April 29, 2010.

66 Sajjad, op. cit., 8.

67 The national reconciliation process referred to is the Proceay-i Tahkeem-i- Sulha (the Strengthening Peace Program, or Peace and Reconciliation Commission), which will be further discussed in the section on Afghanistan's past initiatives. As recently as 2010, Karzai launched a new program called the Afghanistan Peace and Reintegration Programme (APRP) which, in theory, draws on the lessons learned from the former initiatives launched in Afghanistan since 2001, including the PTS to end the war and make a transition to peace. The APRP has a two-pronged approach to the current conflict, aiming to integrate rank and file combatants and reconcile with the senior members of the leadership of insurgent forces. For an in-depth discussion on the APRP see Sajjad, op. cit.

68 Critics of the amnesty law contend that it is unconstitutional. They argue the amnesty law contradicts Kabul's obligations under international law to prosecute serious crimes such as torture, rape, war crimes, crimes against humanity, and genocide. Chapter 7, Article 6 of the Afghan Constitution states: "The Supreme Court upon request of the Government or the Courts can review compliance with the Constitution of laws, legislative decrees, international treaties, and international conventions, and interpret them, in accordance with the law." See Afghanistan Online, "Constitution of Afghanistan, 1382, Chapter 7, Article 6," accessed March 10, 2007, http://www.afghan-web.com/politics/current_constitution.html#chapterseven.

69 Afghanistan's legislative process requires that a draft law is first signed by the president, and then published in an official gazette before it takes effect. The actual process is sometimes far less transparent. A constitutional provision, however, allows any bill to become law within 60 days even without presidential approval.

166 *Notes*

70 See Human Rights Watch, *Afghanistan: Repeal Amnesty Law; Measure Brought into Force by Karzai Means Atrocities Will Go Unpunished* (New York, NY: Human Rights Watch, March 10, 2010), accessed January 19, 2011, http://www.hrw.org/en/news/2010/03/10/afghanistan-repeal-amnesty-law.

71 Phone interview with Afghan local civil society actor, Afghanistan, July 10, 2008.

72 E. Winterbotham, *The State of Transitional Justice in Afghanistan. Actors, Approaches and Challenges: A Discussion Paper,* Kabul, Afghanistan: AREU, April 2010, accessed April 30, 2010, http://www.areu.org.af/Uploads/EditionPdfs/1009E-The State of Transitional Justice in Afghanistan – Actors, Approaches and Challenges DP 2010 Final Web.pdf.

73 Interview with Scott Worden, USIP Rule of Law advisor, Washington DC, June 12, 2008.

74 Follow-up interview with Afghan civil society actor, Afghanistan, April 10, 2010.

75 *UN Security Council Resolution 1868*, Paragraph 30, March 23, 2009, accessed September 15, 2010, http://www.unhcr.org/refworld/docid/49c9f9992.html.

76 Londoño, E. "Key Afghan leader Rabbani killed in Kabul bombing," *The Washington Post*, September 20, 2011, accessed September 20, 2011, http://www.washingtonpost.com/world/key-afghan-peacemaker-rabbani-killed-in-kabul-bombing/2011/09/20/gIQAxlF9hK_story.html.

77 The *Panchayat* is a South Asian political system, which literally translates to assembly (yat) of five (panch) wise and respected elders chosen and accepted by the village community. Traditionally, these assemblies settled disputes between individuals and villages. In Nepal, each caste group system forms its own *panchayat*, or council of elders, that can expand to include neighboring districts or even function on a zonal basis. See Mongabay.com, "Nepal – The Panchayat System," accessed October 1, 2010, http://www.mongabay.com/reference/country_studies/nepal/GOVERNMENT.html.

78 The concept of "new democracy" can be traced to the writings of Mao Zedong, who in turn built his political philosophy borrowing heavily from the views of Lenin, Trotsky, and Stalin.

79 See International Crisis Group, *Nepalís Maoists: Their Aims, Structure and Strategy*, Asia Report No. 104, October 27, 2005, accessed October 5, 2010, http://www.crisisgroup.org/~/media/Files/asia/south-asia/nepal/104_nepal_s_maoists_their_aims_structure_and_strategy.ashx.

80 Ibid.

81 Ibid.

82 King Birendra and his family were massacred in 2001. His brother Gayendra took over the throne after the death of the *de jure* king, Dipendra, son of Birendra, who was allegedly responsible for the killings.

83 In August 2002, the state of emergency elapsed. The same year, the Terrorist and Disruptive Activities (Control and Punishment) Ordinance (TADO) was adopted into law by the parliament. When TADO elapsed, in the absence of a functioning parliament, it was re-promulgated repeatedly by royal decree; however, the ordinance was not renewed after it lapsed in September 2006 and is no longer in force.

84 See Asia Report No. 104, op. cit.

85 Cabinet decisions are not usually made public and therefore it is not publicly available. See also "Commission of Inquiry: Nepal 90," Truth Commissions Digital Collection, USIP Press, accessed October 20, 2010, http://www.usip.org/publications/commission-inquiry-nepal-90.

86 Interviews with civil society actors, Kathmandu, Nepal, April 2009.

87 T.L. Brown, *The Challenge to Democracy in Nepal*, 2nd ed. (New York, NY: Routledge, 2006), 148.

Notes 167

88 For a brief discussion of the Mallik Commission, see B. Bhattarai *et al.*, *Impunity In Nepal: An Exploratory Study* (Kathmandu, Nepal: The Asia Foundation, September 1999), accessed November 1, 2010, http://asiafoundation.org/resources/pdfs/nepal-impunity.pdf.

89 Brown, op. cit. 148.

90 Waiting for Justice: Unpunished Crimes from Nepal's Armed Conflict, Human Rights Watch, 2008, http://www.hrw.org/sites/default/files/reports/nepal0908web_0.pdf.

91 Ibid.

92 Human Rights Watch, *Waiting for Justice* (New York, NY: Human Rights Watch, September 11, 2008), accessed October 12, 2010, http://www.hrw.org/reports/2008/09/11/waiting-justice.

93 For a detailed discussion on the Doramba case, see Chapter 5.

94 UN Human Rights Council, *Report of the United Nations High Commissioner for Human Rights on the Human Rights Situation and the Activities of her Office Including Technical Cooperation in Nepal*, para 46, A/HRC/4/97 (January 17, 2007), accessed November 1, 2010, http://www.unhcr.org/refworld/docid/461e448c2.html.

95 Human Rights Watch, *Waiting for Justice: Unpunished Crimes from Nepalis Armed Conflict* (New York, NY: Human Rights Watch, September 11, 2008), accessed October 1, 2008, http://www.hrw.org/en/reports/2008/09/11/waiting-justice-0.

96 Ibid.

97 Ibid.

98 See *Report of the United Nations High Commissioner for Human Rights on the Human Rights Situation and the Activities of her Office Including Technical Cooperation in Nepal*, op. cit.

99 The dismissal was confirmed on 13 February 2005. See "Army Major Sacked Over Doramba Case," *The Rising Nepal,* February 14, 2005, accessed June 10, 2005, http://www.gorkhapatra.org.np/ pageloader.php? file=2005/02/14//topstories/main7.

100 Nepal's Peace Agreement: Making it Work, Asia Report N°126, International Crisis Group, December 2006, http://nepalconflictreport.ohchr.org/html/2006-12-15_report_icg_eng.html#.f194 (assessed January 10, 2009).

101 Departmental action was recommended against Home Minister Kamal Thapa and Information and Communication Ministers Shrish Shumsher Rana and Tanka Dhakal, incumbent Army chief Rukmangad Katuwal and the Armed Police Force chief.

102 See "Nepal King Blamed For Crackdown," *BBC World News*, November 20, 2006, accessed August 3, 2008, http://news.bbc.co.uk/2/hi/south_asia/6164298.stm.

103 International Center for Transitional Justice, *Negotiating Peace in Nepal: Implications for Justice*, by W. Farasat and P. Hayner (Brussels: Initiative for Peacebuilding, June 2009), accessed March 2, 2011, http://www.initiativeforpeacebuilding.eu/pdf/Negotiating_Peace_in_Nepal.pdf.

104 King Gayanendra sacked the Prime Minister, took over power and declared a state of emergency. For an in-depth detailed analysis, see International Crisis Group, *Nepalis Royal Coup: Making A Bad Situation Worse*, Asia Report No. 91, February 9, 2005, accessed February 9, 2008, http://www.crisisgroup.org/~/media/Files/asia/south-asia/nepal/091_nepal_royal_coup_making_a_bad_situation_worse.ashx.

105 Farasat and Hayner, op. cit. 100.

106 Ibid.

107 Interviews with local civil society actors, Kathmandu, Nepal, 2009.

108 Ibid.

109 Farasat and Hayner, op. cit. 101.

110 The coalition of seven political parties in Nepal, which led the Loktontro Andalon and aimed at ending the autocratic rule of King Gayendra.

111 5.2.3. Both sides also agree to make public within 60 days of signing of the agreement the real name, caste, and address of the people made "disappeared" or killed during the conflict and also inform the family members about it. 5.2.4. Both sides

168   *Notes*

agree to constitute a National Peace and Rehabilitation Commission and carry out works through it to normalize the adverse situation arising as a result of the armed conflict, maintain peace in the society, and run relief and rehabilitation works for the people victimized and displaced as a result of the conflict. 5.2.5. Both sides agree to set up a High-Level Truth and Reconciliation Commission as per the mutual consensus in order to probe about those involved in serious violation of human rights and crime against humanity in the course of the armed conflict and develop an atmosphere for reconciliation in the society. See *Comprehensive Peace Accord Concluded Between the Government of Nepal and The Communist Party of Nepal (Maoist),* November 21, 2006, accessed February 9, 2008, http://id.cdint.org/content/documents/Comprehensive_Peace_Agreement_of_2006.pdf.

112 *Comprehensive Peace Agreement 2006,* accessed February 9, 2008, http://www.satp.org/satporgtp/countries/nepal/document/papers/peaceagreement.htm.

113 War crimes in Nepal: UN urged to investigate Kapilavastu killings, Asian Center for Human Rights (ACHR), March 3, 2005, http://www.achrweb.org/press/2005/NEP0305.htm (accessed March 10, 2009).

114 The youth wing of the CPN-M.

115 See Human Rights Watch, *Children in the Ranks – The Maoists' Use of Child Soldiers in Nepal* (New York, NY: Human Rights Watch, February 2, 2007), accessed September 2, 2010, http://hrw.org/reports/2007/nepal0207/.

116 UN Resident and Humanitarian Coordinator's Office, *Nepal Peace and Development Strategy 2010–2015: A Contribution To Development Planning From Nepal's International Development Partners,* January 2011, accessed 6 February, 2011, http://nepal.um.dk/en/~/media/Nepal/Documents/Content%20English/Nepal-Peace-and-Development-Strategy.ashx, 45.

117 This is further illustrated in Chapter 5.

118 See Advocacy Forum, *Discrimination and Irregularities: A Painful Tale of Interim Relief in Nepal,* accessed October 1, 2010, http://www.advocacyforum.org/downloads/pdf/publications/Discriminations_and_Irregularities_A_painful_tale_of_Interim_Relief_in_Nepal.pdf. The different victims groups and human rights actors interviewed for this research also repeatedly emphasized this view.

119 Interview, civil society actor, Kathmandu, Nepal, July 7, 2009.

120 Advocacy Forum, *Review Of Implementation Of The Recommendations Made By The UN Working Group on Enforced or Involuntary Disappearances After Its Visit To Nepal In December 2004,* (September 2010), accessed October 10, 2010, http://www.advocacyforum.org/downloads/pdf/publications/af-briefing-series-1-disappearance.pdf.

121 Between late 2001 and the time of the ceasefire in January 2003, there were reports of at least 200 disappearances and widespread torture carried out by the security forces in Bardiya. The vast majority of victims were from the marginalized and disadvantaged Tharu community, who were particularly vulnerable to both Maoist intimidation and state abuse due to their weak links to human rights organizations and existing tensions with high-caste landowners as well Nepal's security forces.

122 Bhairabnath battalion of the RNA's 10th Brigade is held primarily responsible for the arbitrary arrests, torture of hundreds of people and at least 45 disappearances in Kathmandu between late 2003 and 2004. It is alleged that those who were detained and tortured were largely but not all active Maoists, many of them belonging to the party's student wing. The army still denies its role in the Bhairabnath case, despite existing extensive evidence about their role in the arrests, torture, and disappearances.

123 Interview with NHRC commissioner, Kathmandu, Nepal July 15, 2009.

124 Nepal Conflict Report: An analysis of conflict-related violations of international human rights law and international humanitarian law between February 1996 and 21 November 2006, Office of the High Commissioner for Human Rights (OHCHR), 2012, http://www.ohchr.org/Documents/Countries/NP/OHCHR_Nepal_Conflict_Report2012.pdf (accessed December 1, 2012).

Notes 169

125 Farasat and Hayner op. cit.
126 See also *OHCHR-Nepal Calls For Swift Implementation Of Supreme Court Ruling On Dhanusha Disappearance,* OHCHR-Nepal, Press Release, February 5, 2009, accessed March 2, 2009, http://nepal.ohchr.org/en/resources/Documents/English/pressreleases/Year%202009/Feb%202009/2009_02_05_Dhanusha_Diappearance_E.pdf.
127 See National Human Rights Commission (NHRC), *Ceasefire Report,* December 2006, accessed 6 May, 2009, http://www.internal-displacement.org/8025708F004CE90B/(httpDocuments)/944E0E93E66B48EFC125735C00513A04/$file/Ceasefire+report+NHRC+Dec06.pdf.
128 See Human Rights Watch, *Waiting for Justice: Unpunished Crimes from Nepal's Armed Conflict.* See also UN Office of the High Commissioner for Human Rights (OHCHR), "Conflict-Related Disappearances in Bardiya District," December 2008, accessed November 1, 2010, http://www.unhcr.org/refworld/docid/494ba58d2.html.
129 Interviews held in Kathmandu, Nepal, 2009. For a more detailed discussion of how the TRC appeared in the CPA, see Chapter 5.
130 Farasat and Hayner, op. cit.
131 Nepal's Supreme Court ruling included the following provisions: 1. To criminalize the act of disappearance and formulate law according to international standards and the ruling of the Supreme Court dated June 1, 2007. 2. To make known immediately the whereabouts of citizens forcibly disappeared during the armed conflict. 3. To make arrangements of relief, rehabilitation, compensation, and reparation for the citizens subjected to enforced disappearance. 4. To create an independent commission with all necessary authority to investigate incidents of disappearances. 5. To implement immediately the recommendations of the Supreme Court and National Human Rights Commission immediately. 6. To ratify the International Convention for the Protection of All Persons from Enforced Disappearance. See ICTJ, "Nepal: Enforced Disappearances Should Be Criminalized," (ICTJ, August 30, 2009), accessed January 15, 2010, http://www.ictj.org/en/news/press/release/3014.html.
132 See UN Office of the High Commissioner for Human Rights-Nepal (OHCHR-N), *Comments and Recommendations on draft Truth and Reconciliation Commission Bill,* August 6, 2007, accessed January 10, 2010, http://nepal.ohchr.org/en/resources/Documents/English/pressreleases/Year%202007/AUG2007/Comments%20on%20draft%20Truth%20and%20Reconciliation%20Bill_03_09_07.doc.pdf. In the interviews conducted in the course of this research, both national and international human rights activists and civil society actors voiced their criticisms and concerns about the TRC.
133 Ibid.
134 Ibid.
135 Nepal Secretariat of Legislative Parliament, A Bill Made for Making Provisions Related to a Truth and Reconciliation Commission, (unofficial translation), Registered December 2009, s. 25(4) (hereinafter TRC Bill).
136 ICTJ, *Navigating Amnesty and Reconciliation in Nepal's Truth and Reconciliation Commission Bill* (International Center for Transitional Justice-Nepal Briefing, November, 2011), accessed June 12, 2012, http://ictj.org/sites/default/files/20111208_Nepal_Amnesty_Reconciliation_bp2011.pdf.
137 Ibid.
138 TRC Bill, op. cit. 23. "(1) If a victim or a perpetrator files an application to the Commission for reconciliation, the Commission may have them reconcile. However, the absence of an application from victim or perpetrator will not prevent the Commission from undertaking collective reconciliation. (2) The Commission may, in relation to making reconciliation pursuant to Sub-section (1), ask the perpetrator to apologize to the victim for his/her past misdeeds. (3) The Commission shall, in relation to making reconciliation pursuant to Sub-section (1), make the perpetrator provide reasonable compensation for damages caused to the victim. (4) The

170 *Notes*

Commission may in relation to reconciling pursuant to Sub-section (1), carry out or cause to be carried out the following activities in order to motivate the victim and the perpetrator: (a) To organize reconciliation functions in conflict-ravaged areas by involving perpetrators and victims and their families, (b) To make arrangements for putting up statutes or memorials in memory of those who were killed during the armed conflict by involving the perpetrator, victim and his/her family in the process, (c) To publish various articles, essays, songs, art, etc. relating to reconciliation, (d) To increase social and societal harmony, (e)To carry out other appropriate tasks. (5) If a victim has already been killed or is a minor or is mentally impaired, according to this section, the Commission may reconcile such persons with his/her family-members and the perpetrator. (6) Not withstanding anything written in this section, there can be no reconciliation without the victim's consent. (7) If reconciliation is carried out between the victim and the perpetrator as per this Section, then no action shall be taken on any other issues except for the crimes mentioned under Section 25 (2)."

139 *Navigating Amnesty and Reconciliation in Nepal's Truth and Reconciliation Commission Bill*, op. cit.
140 TRC Bill, s.23 (3).
141 *Navigating Amnesty and Reconciliation in Nepal's Truth and Reconciliation Commission Bill*, op. cit.
142 Outside of the efforts of establishing a TRC, there have been a few quiet measures at the international level to debar Nepalese Army officers accused of serious violations from senior UN posts, peacekeeping missions, and military training.

3 Ordinary laws

1 M.A. Drumbl, *Atrocity, Punishment and International Law* (New York, NY: Cambridge University Press, 2007).
2 Ibid., 4.
3 See for example, M. Aukerman, "Extraordinary Evil, Ordinary Crime: A Framework for Understanding Transitional Justice," *Harvard Human Rights Journal* 15(39) (2002): 41–2; Drumbl, *Atrocity Punishment and International Law*; M.B. Harmon and F. Gaynor, "Ordinary Sentences for Extraordinary Crimes," *Journal of International Criminal Justice* 5(3) (2007): 683–712.
4 See for example, Drumbl, op. cit.; P. Akhavan, "The International Criminal Court in Context: Mediating the Global and the Local in the Age of Accountability," *The American Journal of International Law* 97(3) (2003): 712–21; P. Akhavan, "Beyond Impunity: Can International Criminal Justice Prevent Future Atrocities?" *The American Journal of International Law* 95(1) (2001): 7–31; J. Klabbers, "Just Revenge? The Deterrence Argument in International Criminal Law," *Finnish Yearbook of International Law* 12 (2001): 249–67. See also generally A. Cassese, "Reflections on International Criminal Justice," *Modern Law Review*, 61(1) (1998): 1–10.
5 See, for example, M. Tondini, *Statebuilding and Justice Reform: Post-Conflict Reconstruction in Afghanistan* (New York, NY: Routledge, 2010); International Legal Foundation, *The Customary Laws of Afghanistan* (New York, NY: International Legal Foundation, September 2004), accessed March 12, 2011, http://www.usip.org/files/file/ilf_customary_law_afghanistan.pdf, 7; B. Etling, *Legal Authorities in the Afghan Legal System (1964–1979)*, (Cambridge, MA: Harvard Law School, Islamic Studies Program, 2003), accessed March 20, 2011, http://www.law.harvard.edu/programs/ilsp/research/etling.pdf; M.H. Kamali, *Law in Afghanistan: A Study of the Constitutions, Matrimonial Law and the Judiciary*, vol. 36 (Leiden, The Netherlands: Brill Academic Publishers, 1985), 6–8; E. Meininghaus, *Legal Pluralism in Afghanistan – Working Paper Series 33, Amu Darya Series Paper No 8, December 2007* (Bonn, Germany: Center for Development

Research, University of Bonn), accessed March 12, 2011, http://131.220.109.9/file-admin/webfiles/downloads/projects/amudarya/publications/ZEF_Working_Paper_Meininghaus_33.pdf; N. Nojumi, D. Mazurana, and E. Stites, *Afghanistan's Systems of Justice: Formal, Traditional, and Customary* (Boston, MA: Feinstein International Famine Center, June 2004), accessed March 12, 2011, http://www.gmu.edu/depts/crdc/neamat1.pdf, 37; A. Suhrke and K. Borchgrevnik, "Negotiating Justice Sector Reform In Afghanistan," *Crime, Law and Social Change* 51(2) (2009): 211–230, accessed March 13, 2011, http://www.springerlink.com/content/n5147p5588k43362/fulltext.pdf; M.G. Weinbaum, "Legal Elites in Afghan Society," *International Journal of Middle East Studies* 12(1) (1980): 39–57; T. Barfield, *Afghan Customary Law and Its Relationship to Formal Judicial Institutions*, (Washington DC: USIP Press, June 26, 2003), accessed March 12, 2011, http://www.usip.org/files/file/barfield2.pdf.

6 M. Tondini, op. cit., 3.
7 Ibid.
8 Interviews held with international legal experts, in Kathmandu, Nepal 2009 and in Washington DC 2008 and 2010.
9 Interview with international legal expert, Kathmandu, Nepal, June 29, 2009.
10 Interview with an international rule of law consultant, Kathmandu, Nepal July 19, 2009.
11 Wardak explains: "*Shari'a* is an Arabic word, which means 'the path to follow'; it is also used to refer to legislation, legitimacy, and legality in modern Arabic literature; however, *Shari'a* in a jurisprudential context means Islamic Law. The primary sources of shari'a are the Qu'ran and the Sunnah." A. Wardak, "Building a Post-War Justice System in Afghanistan," *Crime, Law and Social Change* 41 (2004): 323.
12 K. Mendoza, *Islam and Islamism in Afghanistan*, (undated), accessed March 13, 2011, http://www.law.harvard.edu/programs/ilsp/research/mendoza.pdf.
13 W. Maley, "Political Legitimation in Contemporary Afghanistan," *Asian Survey* 27(6) (1987): 705–25 at 710.
14 Tondini, op. cit., 31.
15 Ibid., 32.
16 Legal pronouncement or ruling in Islam.
17 W.B. Hallaq, "'Muslim Rage' and Islamic Law," *Hastings Law Journal* 54 (2003): 1719.
18 F.E. Vogel, *Islamic Law and Legal System: Studies of Saudi Arabia* (Leiden, The Netherlands: Brill Publishers, 2000), 23.
19 Tondini, op. cit., 32.
20 L. Rosen, *The Justice of Islam: Comparative Perspectives on Islamic Law and Society* (New York, NY: Oxford University Press, 2000), 171.
21 Tondini, op. cit., 32.
22 J. Schacht, "Law and Justice," in *The Cambridge History of Islam*, vol. 2, ed. P.M. Holt, A.K.S. Lambton, and B. Lewis (Cambridge, UK: Cambridge University Press, 1977), 540.
23 Schacht states: "Islamic law being a doctrine and a method rather than a code...is by its nature incompatible with being codified, and every codification must subtly distort it." Cited in S.A. Jackson, *Islamic Law and the State: The Constitutional Jurisprudence of Shihab al-Din al-Qarafi, Studies in Islamic Law and Society* (Leiden, The Netherlands: Brill Publishers, 1996), xvii.
24 Tondini, op. cit., 33.
25 Ibid.
26 S. Zubaida, *Law and Power in the Islamic World* (London, UK: I.B. Tauris, 2005), 208.
27 Tondini, op. cit., 33.
28 K.M. Abou El Fadl, "Islam and the State: A Short History," in *Democracy and Islam in the New Constitution of Afghanistan*, ed. C. Bernard and N. Hachigian, (Santa Monica, CA: RAND Corporation, 2003), 13–16.

172 *Notes*

29 Tondini, op. cit., 33.
30 Ibid.
31 Ibid.
32 R. Owen, *State, Power and Politics in the Making of the Modern Middle East*, 3rd ed. (London, UK: Routledge, 2004).
33 Article 21 stated: all cases "will be decided in accordance with the principles of sharia and general civil and criminal law." See Afghanistan Online, *The Constitution of Afghanistan 1382*, Article 21, accessed March 10, 2011, http://www.afghan-web.com/politics/current_constitution.html.
34 Suhrke and Borchgrevnik, op. cit.
35 Article 14 stated no law must be repugnant to the principles of the sacred religion of Islam. Afghanistan Online, *The Constitution of Afghanistan 1964*, accessed March 10, 2011, http://www.afghan-web.com/history/const/const1964.html.
36 Suhrke and Borchgrevnik, op. cit.
37 Article 2, Afghanistan Online, *The Constitution of Afghanistan 1987*, accessed March 12, 2011, http://www.afghan-web.com/history/const/const1987.html.
38 Suhrke and Borchgrevnik, op. cit.
39 Article 3(1), The Constitution of Afghanistan 1382, accessed March 10, 2011, http://www.afghan-web.com/politics/current_constitution.html.
40 Suhrke and Borchgrevnik, op. cit.
41 Ibid.
42 Kamali, op. cit., 6–8.
43 F. Ahmed, "Afghanistan's Reconstruction, Five Years Later: Narratives of Progress, Marginalized Realities, and the Politics of Law in a Transitional Islamic Republic," *Gonzaga Journal of International Law* 10(3) (2007): 269–314.
44 T. Barfield, "Culture And Custom In Nation-Building: Law In Afghanistan," *Maine Law Review* 60(2) (2008): 351.
45 See "Afghanistan Demographics Profile 2012," accessed March 12, 2011, http://www.indexmundi.com/afghanistan/demographics_profile.html.
46 See *The Customary Laws of Afghanistan*, op. cit.
47 S. Miakhel, *Understanding Afghanistan: The Importance of Tribal Culture and Structure in Security and Governance*, (Washington DC: USIP Press, November 2009), accessed 12 March 12, 2011, http://www.pashtoonkhwa.com/files/books/Miakhel-ImportanceOfTribalStructuresInAfghanistan.pdf.
48 J.W. Spain, *The Way of the Pathans: The Pathan Borderland* (London, UK: Oxford University Press, 1972), 46.
49 T. Barfield, N. Nojumi, and J.A. Thier, *The Clash of Two Goods: State and Non-State Dispute Resolution in Afghanistan in Customary Justice and the Rule of Law in War-Torn Societies* (Washington DC: USIP Press, 2011), 165.
50 A. Zadran, "Socio–Economic and Legal–Political Processes in a Pashtun Village, Southeastern Afghanistan" (PhD diss., State University of New York, July 15, 1977): 205–07, on file with SUNY-Buffalo Library, 234.
51 Ibid.
52 Miakhel, op. cit.
53 Ibid.
54 Barfield, op. cit., 358.
55 Ibid.
56 Ibid.
57 Barfield, Nojumi, and Their, op. cit. 166.
58 For an in-depth discussion of how *Jirgas* function, see for example, *The Customary Laws of Afghanistan*," op. cit. Also see Meininghaus, op. cit.; Nojumi, Mazurana, and Stites, op. cit.; Barfield, op. cit.; Wardak, op. cit.
59 Barfield, Nojumi, and Thier, op. cit., 167.

60 Ibid.
61 Ibid.
62 Ibid.
63 Ibid.
64 Ibid., 169.
65 Ibid.
66 For an in depth discussion of the different manifestations of customary laws in Afghanistan, see *The Customary Laws of Afghanistan*, op. cit.
67 Barfield, Nojumi, and Thier, op. cit., 169.
68 Ibid., 170.
69 Ibid.
70 Nojumi, Mazurana, and Stites, op. cit.
71 Ibid.
72 Interviews with international and Afghan civil society actors, Washington DC and Kabul, Afghanistan, between 2008 and 2010. See also for example, Meininghaus, op. cit.
73 Kamali, op. cit., 5–6, 9.
74 For example, the three permanent legal institutions of the Afghan state – Ministry of Justice, Supreme Court, and Attorney General's office (the Saranwali) – are "coequal in stature and for a variety of political, personality and turf-consciousness have fractious relations with each other." See USIP, *Establishing the Rule of Law in Afghanistan: Special Report 117* (Washington DC: USIP Press, March 2004), accessed March 1, 2008, http://www.usip.org/files/file/sr117.pdf, 3. Others have observed there is a combative relationship that exists between the Ministry of Defense and the Ministry of Finance. For a discussion on this, see M. Sedra, *Security Sector Transformation in Afghanistan*, Working Paper 143 (Geneva Center for the Democratic Control of Armed Forces, August 2004), accessed March 10, 2011. http://www.dcaf.ch/_docs/WP143.pdf.
75 Weinbaum, op. cit., 39.
76 Ibid., 41.
77 J.A. Thier, "The Making of a Constitution in Afghanistan," (paper originally presented at State Reconstruction and International Engagement in Afghanistan – Panel IV: Re-Establishing a Legal System, Bonn, Germany, June 1, 2003), accessed March 12, 2008, http://eprints.lse.ac.uk/28380/1/Thier_LSERO_version.pdf.
78 See for example, J.A. Gardner, *Legal Imperialism: American Lawyers And Foreign Aid In Latin America* (Madison, WI: University of Wisconsin Press, 1980); D.M. Trubek, "The 'Rule of Law' in Development Assistance: Past, Present, and Future," in *The New Law and Economic Development: A Critical Appraisal*, ed. D.M. Trubek and A. Santos (Cambridge, UK: Cambridge University Press, 2006), 74–94; R.E. Brooks, "The New Imperialism: Violence, Norms, and the 'Rule of Law'," *Michigan Law Review* 101(7) (2003): 2275–340; R.E. Gordon and J.H. Sylvester, "Deconstructing Development," *Wisconsin International Law Journal*, 22(1) (2004): 1–98.
79 See for example Wardak, op. cit.
80 Ahmed, op. cit., 284.
81 Gardner, op. cit., 1980.
82 Ahmed, op. cit., 291.
83 See International Crisis Group, *Afghanistan: Judicial Reform and Transitional Justice*, Asia Report No. 45, January 28, 2003, accessed March 12, 2008, http://unpan1.un.org/intradoc/groups/public/documents/apcity/unpan016653.pdf.
84 Wardak, op. cit., 325.
85 Article 3, *Afghanistan Constitution 1964*.
86 Ibid., Article 32.
87 Ibid., Article 34.

174   *Notes*

88 Ibid., Article 28.

89 Ibid., Article 30.

90 The "New Democracy" period of the 1960s was led by Zahir Shah, who began the process of secularizing criminal, commercial, and general civil law.

91 See *Afghanistan: Judicial Reform and Transitional Justice*, op. cit.

92 B.R. Rubin, *The Fragmentation of Afghanistan: State Formation and Collapse in the International System,* 2nd ed. (New Haven, CT: Yale University Press, 2002), 39.

93 See *Afghanistan: Judicial Reform and Transitional Justice*, op. cit.

94 Rubin, op. cit., 116–7.

95 See *Afghanistan: Judicial Reform and Transitional Justice*, op. cit.

96 G. Dorronsoro, *Revolution Unending: Afghanistan: 1979 To The Present* (New York, NY: Cambridge University Press, 2005).

97 Suhrke and Borchgrevnik, op. cit.

98 See UN Commission On Human Rights (UNCHR), *Question of the Violation of Human Rights and Fundamental Freedoms in any Part of the World, with Particular Reference to Colonial and Other Dependent Countries and Territories: Final Report on the Situation of Human Rights in Afghanistan,* by C.-H. Paik, Special Rapporteur, submitted in accordance with UN Commission On Human Rights Resolution 1995/74, Fifty-second session, Item 10 Of The Provisional Agenda. E/CN.4/1996/64 (UN Commission On Human Rights, February 27, 1996), accessed March 12, 2011, http://www.unhchr.ch/Huridocda/Huridoca.nsf/TestFrame/d473d7cb72ece7b7802566f200 4d3d14?Opendocument; See also "Final Report on the Situation of Human Rights in Afghanistan," by C.-H. Paik, Special Rapporteur, submitted in accordance with UN Commission On Human Rights Resolution 1996/75 (UN Commission On Human Rights, E/CN.4/1997/59, February 20, 1997), accessed 12 March, 2011, http://www.unhcr.org/refworld/docid/3ae6b0d34.html.

99 Interviews with Afghan lawyers and international rule of law specialists, Afghanistan and Washington DC 2008 and 2010.

100 Ibid.

101 Ibid. Also see Suhrke and Borchgrevnik, op. cit.

102 Weinbaum, op. cit.

103 Tondini, op. cit., 660–673.

104 Suhrke and Borchgrevnik, op. cit.

105 Ibid.

106 The lack of activity for most of 2002 was not entirely Italy's fault; the long delay in establishing a functioning Judicial Commission – the logical partner in any reform effort – is partly to blame as were the obstacles posed by the political rivalries between the three main components of the justice system; however, as the 2003 ICG report notes, some of the activities that Italy could have initiated earlier, such as assessment of institutional and training needs in Afghanistan and the provincial centers, did not take place.

107 See International Crisis Group, *Reforming Afghanistan's Broken Judiciary*, Asia Report No. 195, November 17, 2010, accessed March 15, 2011, http://www.crisisgroup.org/~/media/Files/asia/south-asia/afghanistan/195%20Reforming%20 Afghanistans%20Broken%20Judiciary.ashx.

108 Suhrke and Borchgrevnik, op. cit. See also M.C. Bassiouni and D. Rothenberg, "An Assessment of Justice Sector and Rule of Law Reform in Afghanistan and the Need for a Comprehensive Plan" (paper presented at the Conference on the Rule of Law in Afghanistan, Rome, Italy, July 2, 2007, accessed September 10, 2008, http://www.law.depaul.edu/centers_institutes/ihrli/pdf/rome_conference.pdf.

109 Wardak, op. cit., 329.

110 *Afghanistan: Judicial Reform and Transitional Justice*, op. cit.

111 NATO Public Diplomacy Division, Press And Media Section Media Operations Centre, *Facts and Figures: Afghan National Police, June 2010* (Brussels: NATO

HQ, 2010), accessed July 12, 2010, http://www.nato.int/nato_static/assets/pdf/pdf_2010_06/20110310_100610-media-backgrounder-ANP.pdf.

112 R.M. Perito, "Afghanistan's Police: The Weak Link in Security Sector Reform," in *Revisiting Borders between Civilians and Military: Security and Development in Peace Operations and Post Conflict Situations,* ed. E. Hamann and A. Livingstone (Rio de Janeiro, Brazil: Viva Rio, 2009).

113 A. Wilder, "Cops or Robbers? The Struggle to Reform the Afghan National Police," Afghanistan Research and Evaluation Unit, July 1, 2007, accessed February 1, 2008, http://www.areu.org.af/Uploads/EditionPdfs/717E-Cops%20or%20Robbers-IP-print.pdf.

114 Afghanistan's Attorney General Sabbit's presentation at USIP, Washington DC, June 24, 2008.

115 M. Lau, "Islamic Law and the Afghan Legal System," (undated), accessed January 10, 2008, http://www.ag-afghanistan.de/arg/arp/lau.pdf.

116 Wardak, op. cit., 328.

117 See K.B. Thapa, "Religion and Law in Nepal," *Brigham Young University Law Review* 2010(3) (2010): 922. Historians classify Nepal into the phases of Ancient Nepal (which consists of the Kirata and Lichhavi periods), Medieval Nepal, and Modern Nepal. Particularly during the Kirata and Lichhavi periods, there was heavy reliance on customary laws, which in turn borrowed from traditional practices and socio–cultural values. During the Kirata period, the state's primary responsibility was the maintenance of peace and security. Violence was considered to be particularly sinful and those responsible for violence were dealt with harshly. Justice followed the principle of "an eye for an eye, a tooth for a tooth, a life for a life." Those who were responsible for the death of another were handed the death sentence. During the Medieval period, there was a complex intersection between crime and sin with classifications about what constituted the greatest sin. For example, Strihatya (killing of a woman) was considered as heinous as Brahmahatya (killing of Brahmin), Balhatya (infanticide), Gohatya (cow-slaughter), Guruhatya (killing of a teacher), and Gotra hatya (killing of a relative). See R.B. Pradhananga, *Homicide Law in Nepal; Concept, History and Judicial Practice* (Kathmandu, Nepal: Ratna Pustak Bhandar, 2001).

118 Thapa, op. cit., 921–930.

119 A. Riaz and S. Basu, "The State–Society Relationship and Political Conflicts in Nepal (1768–2005)," *Journal of Asian and African Studies* 42(2) (2007): 123–142.

120 Ibid.

121 J. Pfaff-Czarnecka, "Vestiges and Visions: Cultural Change and the Process of Nation-Building in Nepal," in *Nationalism and Ethnicity in a Hindu Kingdom: The Politics of Culture in Contemporary Nepal,* ed. D.N. Gellner, J. Pfaff-Czarnecka, and J. Whelpton (Newark, NJ: Harwood Academic Publishers, 1997), 421–429.

122 D.R. Regmi Jr., *Modern Nepal: Rise and Growth in the Eighteenth Century,* vol. I & II (Kathmandu, Nepal: Rupa Publishers, 1961), 294.

123 T. Riccadi, "The Royal Edicts of King Rama Shah of Gorkha," *Kailash* 5(1) (1977): 29–65.

124 Chetris is the widely used term for Kshatriyas, the warrior caste within the Hindu caste system.

125 See Advocacy Forum and the International Center for Transitional Justice, *Across the Lines: The Impact of Nepal's Conflict on Women,* (December 2010), accessed March 10, 2011, http://www.ictj.org/sites/default/files/ICTJ-Nepal-Across-Lines-2010-English.pdf.

126 S. Limbu, "Summary of a Comparative Study of the Prevailing National Laws Concerning Indigenous Nationalities in Nepal and ILO Convention No.169 on Indigenous and Tribal Peoples," (undated), http://www.ccd.org.np/pages/25%20Limbu%20Comparative%20Analysis.pdf.

176   *Notes*

127   K.K. Adhikari, "Criminal Cases And Their Punishments Before And During The Period Of Jang Bahadur," *Journal Of The Institute Of Nepal And Asian Studies* 3(1) (1976): 105–116.
128   A. Hofer, *The Caste Hierarchy and State in Nepal: A Study of the Muluki Ain of 1854* (Innsbruck, Austria: Universitatsverlag Wagner, 1979), 40.
129   Ibid.
130   Ibid.
131   Ibid.
132   Thapa, op. cit., 921–930.
133   R.B. Pradhananga and P. Shrestha, *Domestic Violence against Women in Nepal: Concept, History and Existing Laws* (undated), accessed October 15, 2010, http://www.childtrafficking.com/Docs/domestic_violence_0607.pdf.
134   Officially known as the *Manava-dharma-shas,* the *Manusmriti* is the most authoritative of the books of the Hindu code (Dharma-shastra). It is attributed to Manu, the legendary first man and lawgiver. The *Manusmriti* prescribes *dharma* i.e. that set of obligations incumbent upon a Hindu as a member of one of the four social classes (*varnas*) and engaged in one of the four stages of life (*ashramas*). It deals with cosmogony; the definition of the dharma; the sacraments (*samskaras*); initiation (*upanayana*) and study of the Vedas (the sacred texts of Hinduism); marriage, hospitality, dietary restrictions, pollution, and means of purification; the conduct of women and wives; and the law of kings. The last also reflects on issues of juridical interest. Further, it lays out principles and functions of donations, rites of reparation, the doctrine of karma, the soul, and hell. The text makes no categorical distinction between religious law and practices and secular law. The *Manusmriti* has been viewed as the work that has established the code of practical morality for Hindus.
135   A. de Sales, "The Kham Magar Country, Nepal: Between Ethnic Claims and Maoism," *European Bulletin Of Himalayan Research* 19 (2000): 41–71.
136   K. Gilbert, "Women and Family Law in Modern Nepal: Statutory Rights and Social Implications," *New York Journal of International Law and Politics* 24 (1992–1993): 736.
137   Limbu, op. cit.
138   Ibid. 5.
139   Thapa, op. cit., 927.
140   Ibid.
141   Pradhananga and Shrestha, op. cit.
142   Gilbert, op. cit., 729–758.
143   See S.K. Kuba and S. Thapalia, "A Probe into the Laws of Matrimonial Causes in Nepal," in *Readings In The Legal System Of Nepal*, ed S.P.S Dhungel, P.M Bajracharya, and B.B. Bajracharya (Delhi, India: LAWS Publishing, 1986), 103, 105–15.
144   The agnatic kin group consists of the husband's lineage: his father, himself, and his brothers. This lineage stretches back to include long-dead ancestors, as well as forward to include unborn male descendants.
145   Gilbert, op. cit., 733.
146   Ibid., 742.
147   Ibid., 733.
148   At the lowest tier, there were 4000 village assemblies (*gaun sabha*), which elected nine members of the village *panchayat*. They in turn elected a mayor (*sabhapati*). Each village *panchayat* sent a representative to one of 75 district (zilla) panchayat. Members of the district *panchayat* elected representatives to 14 zone assemblies (anchal sabha) for the National *Panchayat*, or *Rashtriya Panchayat*, in Kathmandu. Moreover, there were class organizations at village, district, and zonal levels for peasants, youth, women, elders, laborers, and ex-soldiers who elected their own representatives to assemblies. There were strict rules for the functioning of the *panchayat* system, including that the National Panchayat of about 90 members could not criticize

the royal government, debate the principles of partyless democracy, introduce budgetary bills without royal approval, or enact bills without approval of the King. The King was the supreme commander of the armed forces, appointed (and had the power to remove) members of the Supreme Court, appointed the Public Service Commission to oversee the civil service, and could change any judicial decision or amend the constitution at any time. For Nepali citizens, particularly amongst the poor and the uneducated, the King was also representative of the god Vishnu upholding *dharma* on earth. See "The Panchayat System under King Mahendra," accessed September 20, 2010, http://countrystudies.us/nepal/19.htm.

149 UN Development Programme (UNDP), *The Interim Constitution Of Nepal, 2063, (2007)*, Part 1, Article 3, accessed September 10, 2010, http://www.worldstatesmen.org/Nepal_Interim_Constitution2007.pdf.

150 *The Interim Constitution Of Nepal, 2063, (2007)*, Part 1, Article 4, accessed September 10, 2010, http://www.worldstatesmen.org/Nepal_Interim_Constitution2007.pdf.

151 P. Tamang, "Customary Law and Conservation in the Himalaya," (undated), accessed November 10, 2010, http://www.docstoc.com/docs/50524187/Customary-Law-and-Conservation-in-the-Himalaya-The-Case.

152 Tamang, op. cit.

153 Ibid., 3.

154 The practice of an accused undergoing a prescribed physical test to prove their guilt or innocence.

155 "Nepal: Justice in Transition," op. cit.

156 The Khas were rice-growing communities, thought to have been settled in the Karnali region since ancient times. These communities have maintained strong traditions, even to this day.

157 Antenna Foundation Nepal, Equal Access Nepal, Forum for Women Law and Development (FWLD), Institute for Human Rights and Communication Nepal (IHRICON), International Alert and Saferworld, *Security and Justice in Nepal: District Assessment Findings*, March 2010, accessed July 10, 2012, http://www.international-alert.org/sites/default/files/publications/Security%20and%20justice%20in%20Nepal_distirct%20assesment%20findings.pdf.

158 Ibid., 11.

159 Ibid., 29.

160 "Nepal: Justice in Transition," op. cit.

161 B. Bhattarai *et al.*, *Impunity In Nepal: An Exploratory Study* (Kathmandu, Nepal: The Asia Foundation, September 1999), accessed November 1, 2010, http://asiafoundation.org/resources/pdfs/nepalimpunity.pdf.

162 Ibid.

163 Interview with PD representatives, Kathmandu, Nepal, June 10, 2009.

164 Interview with member of FOHRID, Kathmandu, Nepal, July 12, 2009.

165 See Advocacy Forum, *Hope and Frustration: Assessing the Impact of Nepal's Torture Compensation Act – 1996* (June 26, 2008), accessed November 10, 2010, http://www.humansecuritygateway.com/documents/AF_Nepal_hopeandfrustration.pdf, 3.

166 R. Thapa, *Nepal's Failure to Address Torture: The Relevance of the UN Torture Convention*, Working Paper No. 5 (Paris, France: University of Notre Dame, Center for Civil and Human Rights, Winter 2008), accessed January 10, 2008, http://www.nd.edu/~ndlaw/cchr/papers/thapa_nepal_torture.pdf, 6.

167 UN Committee Against Torture (CAT), *Convention Against Torture and Other Cruel, Inhuman or Degrading Treatment or Punishment*, Article 2, accessed January 10, 2008, http://www.hrweb.org/legal/cat.html.

168 Ibid.

169 See UN Committee Against Torture (CAT), *Consideration of Reports Submitted by States Parties under Article 19 of the Convention*," CAT/C/16/Add.3,

178 *Notes*

December 16, 1993, accessed January 15, 2008, http://www.bayefsky.com/reports/nepal_cat_c_16_add.3_1993.php.

170 Ibid.
171 Ibid.
172 Interviews held with civil society actors in Kathmandu, Nepal, June–July 2009.
173 See Amnesty International, *Nepal: Make Torture a Crime*, ASA 31/002/2001, (Kathmandu, Nepal: Amnesty International, March 1, 2001), accessed January 10, 2008, http://www.unhcr.org/refworld/docid/3c29def4e.html, 5–7, 10.
174 See *Hope and Frustration: Assessing the Impact of Nepal's Torture Compensation Act – 1996*, op. cit.
175 See Human Rights Watch, *Waiting for Justice: Unpunished Crimes from Nepal's Armed Conflict*, (Human Rights Watch, September 11, 2008), accessed October 1, 2008, http://www.hrw.org/en/reports/2008/09/11/waiting-justice-0.
176 Ibid.
177 OHCHR-Nepal, *The April Protests Democratic Rights and the Excessive Use of Force: Findings of OHCHRNepal's Monitoring and Investigations*, (September 2006), accessed January 10, 2008, http://nepal.ohchr.org/en/resources/Documents/English/reports/IR/Year2006/2006_09_21_OHCHR-Nepal.Report%20on%20The%20April%20Protests.pdf.
178 See "Section 6(1), Local Administration Act, 2028 (1971)," accessed January 10, 2008, http://www.lawcommission.gov.np.
179 "Report of Parliamentary Probe Committee," as cited in *Waiting for Justice: Unpunished Crimes from Nepal's Armed Conflict*, op. cit.
180 "Article 5 J, Appendix III: Terrorist and Disruptive Activities (Control and Punishment) Ordinance, 2004: Extract and Comment," Article2.org, accessed January 10, 2008, http://www.article2.org/mainfile.php/0306/176.
181 "Police Act, Section 37" as cited in *Waiting for Justice: Unpunished Crimes from Nepal's Armed Conflict*, op. cit., 53.
182 Ibid.
183 "Army Act, 2106 (1959), Sections 97, 98 and 107," as cited in *Waiting for Justice: Unpunished Crimes from Nepal's Armed Conflict*, op. cit., 54.
184 The Maina Sunuwar case is discussed further in Chapter 5.
185 *Waiting for Justice: Unpunished Crimes from Nepal's Armed Conflict*, op. cit., 57.
186 Ibid.
187 Malla argues that police corruption starts from the very first day an individual enters into the force as a trainee. Recruitment officials, for example, demand substantial bribes from a candidate before they will allow them to pass their examination to enter into the police force. He further states that the amount of bribes for a Assistant Sub-Inspector ranges from NPR 300,000 to 500,000 (approximately US$ 4600 to 7700), and for a post of Inspector it ranges from NPR 500,000 to 700,000 (approximately US$ 7700 to 10,800). Bribes are also used by police personnel to their seniors for getting transfer approval or promotion. See S.P. Malla, *Rule of Law and Policing in Nepal, Policing in Nepal: A Collection of Essays* (London, UK: A Saferworld, September 2007), 28–33.
188 Patronage links are quickly established in the police force. Upon appointment of an Inspector General of Police or when police chiefs are posted to new districts, there is an immediate reorganization of departments to ensure that patronage links are firmly entrenched and the flow of illegal income in not impeded. Malla, op. cit.
189 Ibid.
190 See Malla, op. cit.
191 See International Crisis Group, *Nepal: Peace and Justice*, Asia Report No. 184, January 14, 2010, accessed January 12, 2009, http://www.crisisgroup.org/~/media/Files/asia/south-asia/nepal/184%20nepal%20peace%20and%20justice.ashx, 6.
192 Very recently, on September 13, 2009, the court ordered the army to suspend one of the accused and to submit all the documentation it has on the case.

Notes 179

193 See International Crisis Group, *Nepal's Faltering Peace Process*, Asia Report No. 163, February 19, 2009, accessed March 12, 2009, http://www.crisisgroup.org/~/media/Files/asia/south-asia/nepal/163_nepal_s_faltering_peace_process.ashx.
194 Interview with a spokesperson of the Public Relations of Nepali Army, Kathmandu Nepal, July 19, 2009.
195 Interview with a local civil society actor, Kathmandu, Nepal, June 30, 2009.
196 Interview with rule of law specialist, Asia Foundation, Kathmandu, Nepal, July 3, 2009.
197 Address by David Johnson, Officer-in-Charge, OHCHR-Nepal, *Accountability and the International Criminal Court*, (Kathmandu, Nepal: Nepal Bar Association, August 6, 2006), accessed March 20, 2011, http://nepal.ohchr.org/en/resources/Documents/English/statements/HCR/Year2006/2006_08_06_HCR_DJ_Speech_NBA.pdf.
198 J.J. Moore, "Problems with Forgiveness: Granting Amnesty under the Arias Plan in Nicaragua and El Salvador," *Stanford Law Review* 43(3) (1991): 733.

4 Through local lenses

1 The most prominent demands of Afghan and Nepali victims and survivors i.e. the "local voices," will be discussed in detail in Chapter 5.
2 International excitement about the most recent Peace Jirga held in 2010 was palpable among the international community and among the Washington DC community at the same time that Afghan local civil society actors were highly skeptical and critical of the process of the *jirga* and its outcomes because they predicted that real concerns about justice and peace would be avoided in the discussions between hand-picked participants and supporters of the Karzai administration.
3 Thousands of Afghans Rally in Support of Amnesty Bill, Radio Free Europe: Radio Liberty, February 23, 2007, http://www.rferl.org/content/article/1074886.html (accessed February 24, 2007).
4 Interview with Scott Worden, USIP Rule of Law Advisor, Washington DC, June 10, 2008.
5 Ibid.
6 Expressed in interviews held with international civil society actors in Washington DC and Afghanistan between 2008 and 2010.
7 Interview with Rina Amiri, Open Society Institute, New York, July 9, 2008.
8 Interview with an Afghan human rights activist, Washington DC, August 10, 2008.
9 See for example H. Abdulati, "The Islamic Perspective on Sin," *On Islam*, September 13, 2006, accessed March 8, 2008, http://www.onislam.net/english/shariah/refine-your-heart/it-is-never-too-late/441343-the-islamic-perspective-of-sin.html.
10 Ibid.
11 See the section on Justice as Marginalization, Chapter 5.
12 Phone interview with Afghan local civil society actor, Afghanistan, August 3, 2008.
13 Phone interview with Afghan human rights actor, Afghanistan, August 8, 2008.
14 Interview, Afghan human rights actor, Washington DC, September 12, 2008.
15 Views expressed in interviews held in Washington DC and Afghanistan between 2008 and 2010.
16 Follow-up interview with local Afghan civil society actor, Kabul, Afghanistan, April 3, 2010.
17 ICTJ, *Negotiating Peace in Nepal: Implications for Justice*, IFP Mediation Cluster: Country Case Study: Nepal, by W. Farasat, and P. Hayner (International Center for Transitional Justice, June 2009) accessed September 10, 2011, http://www.initiative-forpeacebuilding.eu/pdf/Negotiating_Peace_in_Nepal.pdf.
18 Ibid.
19 Interview with local civil society actor, Kathmandu, Nepal, July 14, 2009.
20 Interview with a prominent human rights actor, Kathmandu, Nepal, July 13, 2009.

180 *Notes*

21 Interview with Richard Bennett, head of OHCHR-N, Kathmandu, Nepal, July 17, 2009.
22 Interview with Nepal civil society actor, Kathmandu, Nepal, June 27, 2009.
23 Interview with representative of NTTP, Kathmandu, Nepal, June 27, 2009.
24 Interview with representative of Protection Desk, Kathmandu, Nepal, June 26, 2009.
25 Farasat and Hayner, op. cit., 1–28.
26 Interview, civil society actor, Kathmandu, Nepal, 2009.
27 Interview, civil society actor, Kathmandu, Nepal, 2009.
28 Interview with Senior MVA official, Kathmandu, Nepal, 2009.
29 "Conflict Victim's Committee (CVC): Nepal," Insight on Conflict, Peace Direct, accessed July 10, 2012, http://www.insightonconflict.org/conflicts/nepal/peacebuilding-organisations/conflict-victims-committee-cvc/.
30 R.K. Bhandari, "The Role Of Victims' Organizations In Transition From Conflict: Families Of The Disappeared" (Masters thesis, University of Hamburg, 2011).
31 Ibid.
32 Ibid., 77.
33 F. Bieber, "Aid Dependency in Bosnian Politics and Civil Society: Failures and Successes of Post-War Peacebuilding in Bosnia-Herzegovina," *Croatian International Relations Review* 8 (2002): 25–9; J. Mertus and T. Sajjad, "When Civil Society Promotion Fails State-Building," in *Subcontracting Peace: The Challenges of NGO Peacebuilding*, ed. O.P. Richmond and H.F. Carey (Farnham, UK: Ashgate Publishing Limited, 2005).
34 See, for example, M. Minow, *Between Vengeance and Forgiveness: Facing History after Genocide and Mass Violence* (Boston, MA: Beacon Press, 1998); See also A. Gutmann and D. Thompson, "The Moral Foundations of Truth Commissions," in *Truth v. Justice: The Morality of Truth Commissions,* ed. R.I. Rotberg and D. Thompson (Princeton, NJ: Princeton University Press, 2000), 22–44. M. Kaye, "The Role of Truth Commissions in the Search for Justice, Reconciliation and Democratization: The Salvadorean and Honduran Cases", *Journal of Latin American Studies* 29(3) (1997): 693–716.
35 R.G. Teitel, *Transitional Justice* (New York, NY: Oxford University Press, 2000), 82.
36 P.B. Hayner, *Unspeakable Truths: Confronting State Terror and Atrocity* (New York, NY: Routledge, 2001), 29.
37 See for example, M. Ensalaco, "Truth Commissions for Chile and El Salvador: A Report and Assessment," *Human Rights Quarterly* 16(4) (1994): 656–75; Minow, op. cit. See also D. Gairdner, *Truth In Transition: The Role Of Truth Commissions In Political Transition In Chile And El Salvador*, vol. 8, (Bergen, Norway: Chr. Michelsen Institute, 1999), accessed January 10, 2008, http://www.cmi.no/publications/1999/rep/r1999-8.pdf; Gutmann and Thompson, op. cit.; Kaye, op. cit.
38 E. Wiebelhaus-Brahm, *Truth Commissions and Transitional Societies: The Impact on Human Rights and Democracy* (New York, NY: Routledge, 2010), 24.
39 Phone interview with local Afghan human rights actor, Afghanistan, July 12, 2008.
40 Interview with representative of Protection Desk-Nepal, Kathmandu, Kathmandu, Nepal, June 27, 2009.
41 R.L. Jepperson, A. Wendt, and P.J. Katzenstein, "Norms, Identity, and Culture in National Security" in *The Culture of National Security*, ed. P.J. Katzenstein (New York, NY: Columbia University Press, 1996), 33–75.
42 M. Finnemore, *National Interests In International Society* (Ithaca, NY: Cornell University Press, 1996), 141; M. Lynch, *State Interests And Public Spheres: The International Politics Of Jordan's Identity* (New York, NY: Columbia University Press, 1999).
43 T. Bonacker, W. Form, and D. Pfeiffer, "Transitional Justice and Victim Participation in Cambodia: A World Polity Perspective," *Global Society* 25(1) (2011): 113.
44 See D.J. Frank and J.W. Meyer, "The Profusion of Individual Roles and Identities in the Postwar Period," *Sociological Theory* 20(1) (2002): 86–105.

Notes 181

45 E.A. Nadelmann, "Global Prohibition Regimes: The Evolution Of Norms In International Society," *International Organization* 44(4) (1990): 479–526.
46 W.R. Scott and J.W. Meyer, *Institutional Environments and Organizations: Structural Complexity and Individualism* (Thousand Oaks, CA: Sage Publications, 1994), 47.
47 Interview with Richard Bennett, head of OHCHR-N, Kathmandu, Nepal, July 17, 2009.
48 Interview with Hari Phuyel, constitutional lawyer and member of Accountability Watch, Kathmandu, Nepal, July 9, 2009.

5 A meaning of justice

1 See for example, USIP, *Establishing the Rule of Law in Afghanistan: Special Report 117*, (Washington DC: USIP Press, March 2004), accessed January 25, 2007, http://www.usip.org/files/file/sr117.pdf. Also see S. Ladbury and Cooperation for Peace and Unity, *Testing Hypotheses On Radicalization In Afghanistan: Why Do Men Join The Taliban And Hizb-I Islami? How Much Do Local Communities Support Them?* Independent Report for Department Of International Development (DFID), August 14, 2009), accessed March 15, 2010, http://d.yimg.com/kq/groups/23852819/1968355965/name/Drivers%20of%20Radicalisation%20in%20 Afghanistan%20Sep%2009.pdf.
2 See, for example, W.A. Byrd, *Responding to Afghanistan's Opium Economy Challenge: Lessons and Policy Implications from a Development Perspective* (The World Bank South Asia Region, Policy Research Working Paper 4545, March 2008), accessed February 10, 2009, http://www-wds.worldbank.org/servlet/WDSContentServer/WDSP/IB/2008/03/04/000158349_20080304082230/Rendered/PDF/wps4545.pdf. See also UN Office on Drugs and Crime, *Addiction, Crime and Insurgency, The Transnational Threat of Afghan Opium*, (October 2009), accessed January 5, 2010, http://www.unodc.org/documents/data-and-analysis/Afghanistan/Afghan_Opium_Trade_2009_web.pdf. For a critique of the UN report, see J. Mercille, "UN Report Misleading on Afghanistan's Drug Problem," *Global Research* (November 6, 2009), accessed January 5, 2010, http://www.globalresearch.ca/index.php?context=va&aid=15943.
3 F. Ahmed, "Afghanistan's Reconstruction: Five Years Later: Narratives of Progress, Marginalized Realities, and the Politics of Law in a Transitional Islamic Republic," *Gonzaga Journal of International Law* 10(3) (2007): 273.
4 Mohammad Qasim Fahim, a former defense minister and vice president in Karzai's Government, is allegedly linked to war crimes and serious human rights abuses committed in the 1990s. Arsala Rahmani, a former high-level in the Taliban's religious affairs ministry, and under whom, the Ministry of Enforcement of Virtue and Suppression of Vice (al- Amr bi al-Ma'ruf wa al-Nahi `an al-Munkir) imposed severe restrictions on basic freedoms, particularly on women. Sher Mohammed Akhunzada, currently governor of Helmand province, is linked to recent abuses committed by forces under his control, including in private prisons. Other prominent parliamentarians with some of the worst human rights records include Abdul Rabb al Rasul Sayyaf, Mohammed Qasim Fahim, Burhanuddin Rabbani, and Vice President Karim Khalili.
5 See Human Rights Watch, *Afghanistan on the Eve of Parliamentary and Provincial Elections*, (New York, NY: Human Rights Watch, September 15, 2005), accessed March 12, 2007, http://www.hrw.org/en/reports/2005/09/15/afghanistan-eve-parliamentary-and-provincial-elections. See also *Blood-Stained Hands Past Atrocities in Kabul and Afghanistan's Legacy of Impunity*, (New York, NY: Human Rights Watch, July 6, 2005, accessed January 5, 2007, http://www.hrw.org/en/node/11668.
6 Interview, international civil society actor, Washington DC June 13, 2008.

182   *Notes*

7 S.J. Stedman, "Spoiler Problems in Peace Processes," *International Security* 22(2) (1997): 6.

8 A. Krog, "The Choice for Amnesty: Did Political Necessity Trump Moral Duty?" in *The Provocations of Amnesty: Memory, Justice and Impunity,* ed. C. Villa-Vicencio and E. Doxtader (Trenton, NJ: Africa World Press, 2003), 115.

9 See National Human Rights Commission-Nepal, *Doramba Incident, Ramechhap: On-the-spot Inspection and Report of the Investigation Committee 2060 BS,* (Nepal National Human Rights Commission, 2003), accessed January 10, 2008, http://www. nhrcnepal.org/publication/doc/reports/Reprot_Doramba_R.pdf.

10 Ibid.

11 See Human Rights Watch, *Nepal: Human Rights Concerns for the 61st Session of the UN Commission on Human Rights* (New York, NY: Human Rights Watch, March 10, 2005), accessed January 15, 2008, http://www.hrw.org/node/83518.

12 See Amnesty International, *2005 UN Commission on Human Rights: An Important Opportunity To Address Human Rights Violations Whenever And Wherever They Occur,* (Amnesty International, March 10, 2005), accessed January 15, 2008, http:// www.amnesty.org/en/library/asset/IOR41/012/2005/en/6b7a7dd4-d512-11dd-8a23-d58a49c0d652/ior410122005en.html.

13 See International Crisis Group, *Nepal: Peace and Justice, Asia Report No. 184,* (International Crisis Group, January 14, 2010), accessed January 20, 2010, http://www. crisisgroup.org/~/media/Files/asia/south-asia/nepal/184%20nepal%20peace%20 and%20justice.pdf.

14 Ibid.

15 Ibid.

16 Ibid.

17 See OHCHR, *Report Of Investigation Into Arbitrary Detention, Torture And Disappearances at Maharajgunj RNA barracks in 2003–2004* (Kathmandu, Nepal: OHCHR, May 2006), accessed January 20, 2010, http://nepal.ohchr.org/en/resources/ Documents/English/reports/IR/Year2006/Pages%20from%202006_05_26_OHCHR-Nepal.Report%20on%20Disappearances%20linked%20to%20Maharajgunj%20 Barracks_Eng.pdf.

18 The court martial found the colonel and two captains involved guilty of "not following the standard procedures and orders." Each was sentenced to six months' imprisonment; however, because they were judged to already have spent that time when confined to barracks during the period of investigation, they were released. The two captains were ordered to pay NPR25, 000 (approx. US$335) and the colonel NPR50, 000 (US$670) as compensation. They were also ruled ineligible for promotion for one and two years, respectively. See UN Office of the High Commission for Human Rights, *The Torture And Death In Custody Of Maina Sunuwar: Summary Of Concerns* (UN Office of the High Commission for Human Rights (OHCHR-Nepal) December 2006), accessed January 20, 2010. http://nepal.ohchr.org/en/resources/ Documents/English/reports/IR/Year2006/2006_12_01_HCR%20_Maina%20 Sunuwar_E.pdf, 5.

19 The NA holds one of the officers in detention as of this writing.

20 Overall US military aid from October 2001 to October 2004 was over US$29 million. See R. Maitra, "US jittery over Nepal," *Asia Times,* March 16, 2005, accessed January 5, 2011, http://www.atimes.com/atimes/South_Asia/GC16Df01.html. US training expenditure increased steadily from the November 2001 state of emergency reaching its highest point from October 2002 to September 2003 at $1,470,892. See US Department of Defense and US Department of State Joint Report to Congress, *Foreign Military Training In Fiscal Years 2003 and 2004, Volume I* (US Department of Defense and US Department of State Joint Report to Congress, June 2004), accessed January 12, 2008, http://www.state.gov/t/pm/rls/rpt/fmtrpt/2004/. UK assistance was also substantial, some £8.9 million between April 2002 and April 2004 including helicopters. See also Human Rights Watch, *Nepal: Between a Rock and a Hard Place* (New York, NY:

Human Rights Watch, October 6, 2004), accessed February 1, 2008, http://www.hrw.org/en/node/11973/section/4, 89–91. India significantly stepped up its longstanding military assistance from late 2001, supplying the bulk of RNA weaponry and ammunition and being the first (after the Nepali Government) to brand the Maoists "terrorists."

21 The number of Nepali military observers, police, and troops deployed in peacekeeping operations was just under 1,000 from 2001 to September 2003. It nearly doubled in October and grew to over 2,200 in December 2003. By the end of 2004, the number was 3,400, making Nepal was the fourth-largest troop-contributing country in the world. It has maintained its fourth or fifth position since then and had approximately 4,300 people deployed in late 2009. See *Nepal: Peace and Justice*, op. cit.

22 See *Nepal: Peace and Justice*, op. cit.

23 A Call for Justice: *A Call for Justice – A National Consultation on past Human Rights Violations in Afghanistan*, Afghanistan Independent Human Rights Commission (AIHRC), January 25 2005, http://www.aihrc.org.af/Rep_29_Eng/rep29_1_05call4justice.pdf> (accessed 27 February, 2007).

24 Afghanistan Independent Human Rights Commission (AIHRC), *A Call for Justice: A National Consultation on Past Human Rights Violations in Afghanistan* (Kabul, Afghanistan: AIHRC, 2005), accessed February 27, 2007, http://www.aihrc.org.af/media/files/Reports/Thematic%20reports/rep29_1_05call4justice.pdf.

25 Ibid. 17.

26 Ibid. 21.

27 Ibid. 28.

28 Ibid. 18.

29 Ibid. 18.

30 International Center for Transitional Justice and the Advocacy Forum, *Nepali Voices: Perceptions of Truth, Justice Reconciliation, Reparations and the Transition in Nepal* (International Center for Transitional Justice and the Advocacy Forum, Kathmandu, Nepal, March 2008), accessed September 15, 2010, http://ictj.org/sites/default/files/ICTJ-Nepal-Voices-Reconciliation-2008-English.pdf, 23.

31 Ibid. 26.

32 Ibid. 27.

33 Ibid. 28.

34 Ibid. 43.

35 S. Robins, "Whose Voices? Understanding Victims' Needs In Transition. Review Essay of Nepali Voices: Perceptions of Truth, Justice, Reconciliation, Reparations and the Transition in Nepal," *Journal of Human Rights Practice* 1(2) (2009): 325.

36 P. Pham and P. Vinck, "Empirical Research and the Development and Assessment of Transitional Justice Mechanisms," *The International Journal of Transitional Justice* 1(2) (2007): 243. Also see Robins, op. cit., 320–331. The issue of exclusion of victims in the process of designing the research was also reiterated by several civil society members interviewed for this research.

37 The term *Janajati* generally refers to the indigenous people of Nepal constituting 35.6 percent of the total population.

38 *Madeshis* are those of Indian origin, considered to be more recent migrants and living predominantly in the plains of the Terai (the flat lands or plains). They constitute about 32 percent of the population of Nepal.

39 *Dalit* refers to the lowest caste in the Hindu caste hierarchy, the *Shudra*. Historically, the *Dalits* were relegated to doing dirty, menial work and were considered "untouchable" by the higher castes. Traditionally, they have been subjected to socioeconomic marginalization by the Civil Code of 1853. The New Civil Code of 1963 and the 1990 Constitution have banned untouchability and abolished discriminatory legal provisions, but socially, the *Dalits* continue to occupy the margins of Nepali society.

40 Robins, op. cit., 326.

184   *Notes*

41 See International Committee of the Red Cross, *Families Of Missing Persons In Nepal: A Study of Their Needs* (Kathmandu, Nepal: International Committee of the Red Cross, June 30, 2009), accessed September 15, 2010, http://www.icrc.org/eng/resources/documents/report/nepal-missing-persons-report-300609.htm.

42 Phone interview with Islamic scholar and former delegate of two Loya Jirgas, Afghanistan, June 12, 2008.

43 The abbreviation AW-N is being used only in this book to differentiate it from Afghan Women's Network (AWN).

44 Interview with Hari Phuyel, constitutional lawyer and member of Accountability Watch, Kathmandu, Nepal, July 9, 2009.

45 See for example, P. Zyl, "Dilemmas of Transitional Justice: The Case of South Africa's Truth and Reconciliation Commission," *Journal of International Affairs* 52(2) (1999): 647–667; S. Landsman, "Alternative Responses to Serious Human Rights Abuses: Of Prosecution and Truth Commissions," *Law and Contemporary Problems* 59(4) (1996): 81–92.

46 M.J. Aukerman, "Extraordinary Evil, Ordinary Crime: A Framework for Understanding Transitional Justice," *Harvard Human Rights Journal* 15(39) (2002): 39–97.

47 J. Elster, "Coming to Terms with the Past: Framework for the Study of Justice in the Transition to Democracy," *European Journal of Sociology* 39(1) (1998): 37.

48 Aukerman, op. cit., 39–97.

49 See Zyl, op. cit., 647, 651.

50 Ibid. 146.

51 M.A. Drumbl, *Atrocity, Punishment and International Law* (New York, NY: Cambridge University Press, 2007), 9.

52 Ibid. 7.

53 C. Douglass, "Why We Need the International Criminal Court," *Christian Century* 116(15) (1999): 532–36.

54 Former Ugandan President Idi Amin was one of the most brutal military dictators in post-independence Africa. He seized power in 1971 and after eight years of power left the country a legacy of extreme repression, killings, and economic mismanagement. The death toll during the Amin regime will never be accurately known. The ICJ in Geneva estimates that the numbers of dead could be between 80,000 and, most likely, 300,000. Exile organizations supported by AI put the number killed at 500,000.

55 D.F. Orentlicher, "Settling Accounts: The Duty to Prosecute Human Rights Violations of a Prior Regime," *Yale Law Journal* 100(8) (1991): 2542.

56 N.J. Kritz, "Coming to Terms with Atrocities: A Review of Accountability Mechanisms for Mass Violations of Human Rights," *Law and Contemporary Problems* 59(4) (1996): 129.

57 Minow, op. cit., 66.

58 K. Sikkink, *The Justice Cascade: How Human Rights Prosecutions are Changing World Politics,* (New York, NY: W.W. Norton & Company, 2011), 149.

59 Ibid.

60 T.D. Olsen, L.A. Payne, and A.G. Reiter, *Transitional Justice in the Balance: Comparing Processes, Weighing Efficacy* (Washington DC: USIP Press 2010).

61 This was a sentiment expressed by the vast majority of national interviewees.

62 International Center for Transitional Justice, *Vetting Lessons for the 2009–10 Elections in Afghanistan*, by F. Ayub, A. Deledda, and P. Gossman (New York, NY: International Center for Transitional Justice, January 2009), accessed January 5, 2011, http://ictj.org/sites/default/files/ICTJ-Afghanistan-Vetting-Lessons-2009-English.pdf.

63 Ibid.

64 Ibid.

65 Ibid.

66 Interview with Afghan civil society actor, Washington DC, June 30, 2008.

Notes   185

67 Interview with independent international actor, Washington DC, June 28, 2008.
68 Afghanistan's Attorney General Sabbit's presentation at USIP, Washington DC, June 24, 2008.
69 Interview with local and international civil society actors, Kathmandu, Nepal, 2009.
70 Several of the human rights organizations and civil society actors interviewed echoed the criticism that the UN did not effectively negotiate for a stronger platform, which would have allowed it to lay down some terms of engagement and guidelines for the decisions being taken by the various stakeholders in the negotiations. This observation is based on the recurring discussions with local as well as international actors in Kathmandu, Nepal regarding OHCHR's limited mandate.
71 Interview with local human rights actor, Kathmandu, Nepal, July 2, 2009.
72 Interview with a prominent local civil society actor, Kathmandu, Nepal, June 22, 2009.
73 Phone interview with an international Afghanistan analyst, Afghanistan, June 30, 2008.
74 Interview with independent Afghanistan analyst, Washington DC July 13, 2008.
75 C. Haviland, "Parallel Justice, Maoist Style," *BBC World News*, October 14, 2006, accessed January 10, 2011, http://news.bbc.co.uk/2/hi/south_asia/6048272.stm.
76 K. Frank, "Nepal Maoists Reactivate People's Courts," *Himalaya Times*, February 17, 2010, accessed January 11, 2011, http://southasiarev.wordpress.com/2010/02/20/nepal-maoists-reactivate-peoples-courts; See also D.R. Pant, "Maoist People's Court Harassing Politicos, Civilians," *Kantipur Online*, July 30, 2010, accessed January 11, 2011, http://www.hotelnepal.com/nepal_news.php?id=2460.
77 Ministry of Local Development, and Ministry of Women, Children and Social Welfare, and Japan International Cooperation Agency, *Gender Mainstreaming and Social Inclusion Project (GEMPSIP): Inception Report*, Ministry of Local Development, and Ministry of Women, Children and Social Welfare, and Japan International Cooperation Agency (JICA), May 2009, accessed September 23, 2012, http://www.gemsip.org.np/pdf/IC-R%20Draft.pdf.
78 Absolute poverty level is interpreted as the inability to attain basic consumption levels.
79 See W. Schabas, "Reparation Practices in Sierra Leone and the Truth and Reconciliation Commission," in *Out of the Ashes: Reparations for Victims of Gross and Systematic Human Rights Violations*, eds. K. Feyter, S. Parmentier, M. Bossuyt and P. Lemmens (Antwerp, Belgium: Intersentia, 2006), 289–308.
80 R. Mani, *Beyond Retribution: Seeking Justice in the Shadows of War* (Malden, MA: Polity Press, 2002).
81 E.-C. Gillard, "Reparation For Violations Of International Humanitarian Law," *International Committee of the Red Cross* 85(851) (2003): 529–553, accessed January 12, 2011, http://www.icrc.org/eng/assets/files/other/irrc_851_gillard.pdf.
82 See UN Sub-Commission on the Promotion and Protection of Human Rights *Study Concerning The Right To Restitution, Compensation And Rehabilitation For Victims Of Gross Violations Of Human Rights And Fundamental Freedoms: Final Report,* E/CN.4/Sub.2/1993/8, by T. von Boven, Special Rapporteur, (UN Sub-Commission on the Promotion and Protection of Human Rights, July 2, 1993), accessed January 10, 2011, http://www.unhcr.org/refworld/docid/3b00f4400.html; See also R.E. Goodin, "Theories of Compensation," *Oxford Journal of Legal Studies* 9(1) (1989): 56–75.
83 Minow, op. cit.
84 Campaign for Innocent Victims in Conflict (CIVIC), *Losing The People: The Costs and Consequences of Civilian Suffering in Afghanistan,* by E.L. Gaston (Washington DC: CIVIC, 2009), accessed March 15, 2011, http://reliefweb.int/sites/reliefweb.int/files/resources/0EA38479D95508AF49257561000AFF3C-Full_Report.pdf.
85 Interviews with PRT participants and international actors, Kabul, Afghanistan, 2010.
86 For more detailed information, see United States Army Combined Arms Center (CAC), *Chapter 4: Commander's Emergency Response Program, Commander's Guide to Money as a Weapons System Handbook: Tactics, Techniques and Procedures,*

186   *Notes*

no. 09–27 (United States Army CAC, April 2009), accessed January 2, 2011, http://usacac.army.mil/cac2/call/docs/09-27/09-27.pdf, 13–22.

87 See Department for International Development (DFID), *Quick Impact Projects: A Handbook For The Military*, (London, UK: DFID), accessed December 10, 2010, http://webarchive.nationalarchives.gov.uk/+/http:/www.dfid.gov.uk/pubs/files/qip/booklet.pdf.

88 Interview with Afghan civil society actors, Kabul, Afghanistan, April 2010. Also see Gaston, op. cit.

89 Ibid.

90 Gaston, op. cit.

91 See International Organization for Migration Afghanistan, *Afghan Civilian Assistance Program (ACAP)*, (International Organization for Migration Afghanistan, September 2008), accessed December 10, 2010, http://www.iom.int/jahia/webdav/shared/shared/mainsite/activities/countries/docs/afghanistan/acap_factsheet_sept08.pdf. Also see United States Agency for International Development, *Afghan Civilian Assistance Program: USAID Audit Report, Audit Report No. 5-306-10-004-P* (United States Agency for International Development (USAID), December 15, 2009), accessed December 10, 2010, http://oig.usaid.gov/sites/default/files/audit-reports/5-306-10-004-p.pdf.

92 Gaston, op. cit.

93 Interviews with national and international actors in Kabul, Afghanistan, April 2010. See also Gaston, op. cit.

94 Ibid.

95 Interview with Patrick Duplat, Refugees International, Washington DC June 10, 2008. This concern was also raised in interviews with civil society actors and international analysts in interviews conducted between 2008 and 2010 in Afghanistan and Washington DC. For a deeper discussion on changing nature of the military in conflict zones and criticisms of militarized humanism, see T.G. Weiss, "Military–Civilian Humanitarianism: The 'Age of Innocence' is Over," *International Peacekeeping* 2(2) (1995): 157–74; T.J. Farer, "Humanitarian Intervention Before And After 9/11: Legality And Legitimacy" in *Humanitarian Intervention: Ethical, Legal, and Political Dilemmas,* eds. J.L. Holzgrefe and R.O. Keohane (Cambridge, UK: Cambridge University Press, 2003), 53–90. See also M. Duffield, *Global Governance and the New Wars: The Merger of Development and Security* (London, UK: Zed Books, 2001), 304.

96 *Waiting for Justice* op. cit., 45.

97 Ibid.

98 Army men at Belbari, Morang District, killed six people and injured approximately 60 others in April 2006 when people were protesting against rape and subsequent killing of Sapana Gurung. See Conflict Study Center, *Nepal's Peace Process at the Crossroads: Situation Update 2* (Conflict Study Center, August 2, 2006), accessed March 3, 2008, http://www.ssronline.org/edocs/situation_update_2.pdf.

99 Measures for financial support and relief for conflict victims pursuant to cabinet decision, April 25, 2008; "Guidelines For Providing Relief to Beneficiary of a Deceased Person Pursuant to Cabinet Decision, October 5, 2008," and "Guidelines For Providing Relief To The Beneficiary Of A Disappeared Person Pursuant To Cabinet Decision, January 12, 2009," in *From Relief To Reparations: Listening to the Voices of Victims*, (International Center for Transitional Justice and United Nations Human Rights Office of the High Commissioner, 2011), accessed June 10, 2012, http://ictj.org/sites/default/files/ICTJ-NPL-Relief-to-Reparations-Report-2011-English.pdf, 6.

100 Ibid.

101 Ibid.

Notes 187

102 See Terms of Reference of Local Peace Committees, Section 4.1, accessed June 12, 2012, http://www.peace.gov.np/uploads/Publication/LPC-ToR-Eng-%202065-10-20. pdf.
103 See *From Relief To Reparations*. This was also raised in several of the interviews conducted in Nepal.
104 Phone interview, Nepal, February 2012.
105 Interviews with national and international actors in Kathmandu, Nepal in 2009. See R. Kshetry, "Civil War Victims Await Compensation," *IPS News Agency*, October 6, 2008, accessed March 5, 2011, http://www.ipsnews.net/2008/10/nepal-civil-war-victims-await-compensation/; "Nepal: Relief Distribution Affected By False Claims – Home Ministry," *Relief Web*, October 23, 2008, accessed October 23, 2008, http://reliefweb. int/node/284515. See also *Discrimination and Irregularities: A Painful Tale of Interim Relief in Nepal*, (Kathmandu, Nepal: Advocacy Forum, 2010), accessed October 1, 2010, http://www.advocacyforum.org/downloads/pdf/publications/Discriminations_ and_Irregularities_A_painful_tale_of_Interim_Relief_in_Nepal.pdf.
106 Interview with local civil society actor, Kathmandu, Nepal, July 15, 2009.
107 D. Aguirre and I. Pietropaoli, "Gender Equality, Development and Transitional Justice: The Case of Nepal," *International Journal of Transitional Justice* 2(3) (2008): 356–377.
108 Ibid.
109 C. Deschamps and A. Roe, *Land Conflict in Afghanistan: Building Capacity to Address Vulnerability,* Issues Paper Series, (Kabul, Afghanistan: AREU, April 2009), accessed March 2, 2011, http://www.ecoi.net/file_upload/1226_1242042724_land-conflict-layout-web.pdf.
110 See L.A. Wily, D. Chapagain, and S. Sharma, *Land Reform In Nepal: Where Is It Coming From And Where Is It Going?,* (UK Department for International Development (DFID), April 2009), accessed 2 March, 2011, http://www.landcoali-tion.org/publications/land-reform-nepal-where-it-coming-and-where-it-going.
111 See Community Self Reliance Centre (CSRC), Land Watch Asia, and Asian NGO Collation for Agrarian Reform and Rural Development, *Land and Land Tenure Security in Nepal*, (Kathmandu, Nepal: CSRC, March 2009), accessed March 1, 2011, http://www.csrcnepal.org/CSRC%20_Ebulliten/Land%20and%20Land%20 Tenure%20Security%20in%20nepal.pdf.
112 See "Nepal: Land tenure reforms 'urgently needed,'" *IRIN News*, December 8, 2010, accessed May 12, 2012, http://www.irinnews.org/Report/91313/NEPAL-Land-tenure-reforms-urgently-needed.
113 Interview with international actor, Kathmandu, Nepal, July 17, 2009.
114 P. de Greiff, "Justice and Reparation," in *The Handbook of Reparations,* ed. P. de Greiff (New York, NY: Oxford University Press, 2006), 451–77.
115 E. Verdeja, "Normative Theory Of Reparations In Transitional Democracies," *Metaphilosophy,* 37(3–4) (2006): 457.
116 H. Arendt, *Origins of Totalitarianism* (New York, NY: Harcourt Brace, 1973), 423.
117 Gaston, op. cit.
118 Ibid.
119 Interview with victims' group representative, outskirts of Kathmandu, Nepal, July 16, 2009.
120 R. Copelon, "Women and War Crimes," *St John's Law Review* 69 (1995): 61–8.
121 C. Bell and C. O'Rourke, "Does Feminism Need a Theory of Transitional Justice," *International Journal of Transitional Justice* 1(1) (2007): 23–44.
122 Ibid.
123 See for example, Robins, "Whose Voices," op. cit., 320–331. See also, S. Robins, "Towards Victim-Centred Transitional Justice: Understanding the Needs of Families of the Disappeared in Postconflict Nepal," *International Journal of Transitional*

188   *Notes*

Justice 5 (2011): 75–98; S. Robins, "Transitional Justice as an Elite Discourse: Human Rights Practice between the Global and the Local in Postconflict Nepal," (paper presented at the annual International Studies Association convention, New Orleans, LA, February 17, 2010); Aguirre and Pietropaoli, op. cit., 356–377; Advocacy Forum and International Center for Transitional Justice, *Across the Lines: The Impact of Nepal's Conflict on Women* (Advocacy Forum and International Center for Transitional Justice, Kathmandu, December 2010), accessed January 10, 2011, http://ictj.org/sites/default/files/ICTJ-Nepal-Across-Lines-2010-English.pdf.

124 International Center for Transitional Justice, *Addressing Gender-Specific Violations in Afghanistan,* by F. Ayub, S. Kouvo, and Y. Sooka, (International Center for Transitional Justice, February 2009), accessed March 15, 2011, http://ictj.org/sites/default/files/ICTJ-Afghanistan-Gender-Violations-2009-English.pdf, 15.

125 See Human Rights Watch, *The 'Ten-Dollar Talib' and Women's Rights: Afghan Women and the Risks of Reintegration and Reconciliation* (New York, NY: Human Rights Watch, July 13, 2010), accessed March 10, 2011, http://www.hrw.org/en/reports/2010/07/13/ten-dollar-talib-and-women-s-rights, 16.

126 See for example, Human Rights Watch, *Humanity Denied: Systematic Violations of Women's Rights in Afghanistan* (New York, NY: Human Rights Watch, October 2001), accessed March 8, 2008, http://www.hrw.org/legacy/reports/2001/afghan3/, 3, 6, 12–20.

127 The Afshar Operation was a military operation led by Burhanuddin Rabbani's Islamic State of Afghanistan Government forces against Gulbuddin Hekmatyar's Hezb-i Islami and Hezb-i Wahdat forces. The Afshar-based Iran-controlled Hezb-i Wahdat in coordination with the Pakistani-backed Hezb-i Islami of Hekmatyar heavily shelled the densely populated areas in Kabul. In response, the Islamic State forces attacked Afshar in order to capture Wahdat's position and their leader Abdul Ali Mazari and consolidate parts of the city controlled by the government. For a detailed description of the Afshar Operation see Afghanistan Justice Project, *Casting Shadows: War Crimes and Crimes against Humanity: 1978–2001: Documentation And Analysis Of Major Patterns Of Abuse In The War In Afghanistan* (Afghanistan Justice Project, Kabul, Afghanistan 2005), accessed May 21, 2007, http://www.afghanistanjustice-project.org/warcrimesandcrimesagainsthumanity19782001.pdf.

128 *Ittehad-e Islami bara-ye Azadi-ye Afghanistan* began as an attempt to bring unity amongst Islamist opposition forces in Afghanistan but it soon evolved as an independent entity led by Abdul Rasul Sayyaf and supported by financial aid from Saudi sources. Between 1993–94, it was one of the main actors, which participated in the fractional infighting for control over Kabul after the ousting of the PDPA government.

129 The Hizb-e-Wahdat (Party of Unity) was one of the main forces that emerged during the anti- Soviet resistance period in the 1980s. It was in response to a strong urge for unity among the Hazara leaders and the Shi'ite community.

130 See Afghanistan Justice Project, *Addressing the Past: The Legacy of War Crimes and the Political Transition in Afghanistan,* (Afghanistan Justice Project, 2005), accessed January 8, 2007, http://66.116.195.23/blog/wp-content/uploads/2006/05/AfghJusticeReport.pdf, 12.

131 Interview with international analyst, Washington DC, 2008. This issue was raised in subsequent interviews held both in Afghanistan and Washington DC between 2008 and 2010.

132 See UN Entity for Gender Equality and the Empowerment of Women, *UNIFEM Afghanistan – Fact Sheet 2007,* (UNIFEM, 2007), accessed March 10, 2011, http://www.unifem.org/afghanistan/docs/pubs/08/UNIFEM_factsheet_08_EN.pdf.

133 See Human Rights Watch, *Human Rights Watch Letter to President Barack Obama on Afghanistan,* (New York, NY: Human Rights Watch, March 26, 2009), accessed

March 10, 2011, http://www.hrw.org/en/news/2009/03/26/human-rights-watch-letter-president-barack-obama-afghanistan.

134 See for example, "Disgrace to Humanity: Afghan Girls on Sale for 100kg Wheat," *The News International*, February 10, 2002, accessed June 10, 2012, http://www.rawa.org/girlsale.htm. Also see M. Kaufman, "Afghan Poor Sell Daughters as Brides," *MSNBC*, February 23, 2003, accessed January 2011, http://www.rawa.org/brides.htm.

135 M.A. Drumbl, "Rights, Culture, and Crime: The Role of Rule of Law for the Women of Afghanistan," *Columbia Journal of Transnational Law* 42(2) (2004): 349–81.

136 See Z. Coursen-Neff and J. Sifton, "Afghan Regression: Falling Back to Taliban Ways with Women: An Editorial," *New York Times*, January 21, 2003, accessed June 10, 2010, http://www.nytimes.com/2003/01/21/opinion/21iht-edzama_ed3_.html.

137 D.B. Edwards, *Before Taliban: Genealogies of the Afghan Jihad* (Berkeley, CA: University of California Press, 2002).

138 See K. Brulliard, "Afghan Women Fear Loss Of Hard-Won Progress," *The Washington Post*, March 16, 2010, accessed March 16, 2010, http://www.washingtonpost.com/wp-dyn/content/article/2010/03/15/AR2010031503669.html.

139 The London Conference was held on January 28, 2010. The conference aimed to move the international effort forward in three key areas: (i) security; (ii) governance; and (iii) development with regional support and garnered international support for a formalization of a reintegration strategy with financial backing, resulting in a preliminary commitment of approximately US$160 million. For details, see UK Government, "Communiqué of 'Afghanistan: The London Conference'." (paper presented at the International Conference on Afghanistan, London, UK, January 28, 2010), accessed February 5, 2010, http://www.isaf.nato.int/images/stories/File/factsheets/Documents_Communique%20of%20London%20Conference%20on%20Afghanistan.pdf.

140 Conducted by Afghan Women's Network (AWN) with the support of UNIFEM Afghanistan Country Office and the Institute for Inclusive Society and held on January 23–24, 2010.

141 "Afghan Women Civil Society Leaders Meet in Dubai to Discuss Peace and Security for Afghanistan in the Context of the London Conference," January 28, 2010, accessed March 12, 2011, http://peacewithjustice4afghanistan.blogspot.com/2010/01/afghan-women-civil-society-leaders-meet.html.

142 Poet Goswami Tulsidas' epic sixteenth century Hindu poem that chronicles the life of Ram, who is worshipped as an incarnation of the God Vishnu as cited in *Across the Lines,* op. cit.

143 Ibid.

144 L. Bennett, "Gender, Caste And Ethnic Exclusion In Nepal: Following The Policy Process From Analysis To Action" (paper presented at the World Bank Conference, Arusha, December 12–15, 2005), accessed December 12, 2010, http://siteresources.worldbank.org/INTRANETSOCIALDEVELOPMENT/Resources/Bennett.rev.pdf, 24–25.

145 Interview with Executive Director of FEDO, Kathmandu, Nepal, July 10, 2009.

146 Sexual violence and rape was widely reported in the decade-long People's War, with a majority of these crimes being committed by state security forces i.e. the RNA. Women were raped when accused of supporting the CPN-M or having some affiliation with them. In many instances, women were targeted because their husbands or family members had joined the CPN-M. According to the 2010 report *Across the Lines*, released by AF and ICTJ, "female CPN-M cadres were subjected to particularly brutal forms of sexual violence by security forces, and research findings indicate that rape was a common practice adopted by the RNA to punish female CPN-M cadres and sympathizers for their rebelliousness against the state and defiance of their traditional roles. See *Across the Lines*, op. cit.

190   *Notes*

147 See "40 Points Demand," *United People's Front*, February 4, 1996, accessed March 12, 2011, http://www.satp.org/satporgtp/countries/nepal/document/papers/40points.htm.
148 See Aguirre and Pietropaoli, op. cit., 356–377. Women and human rights organizations, however, claim that particular practices such as the chaupadi was not eliminated solely because of the Maoists because such groups and civil society organizations had long mobilized and advocated for such changes. They do recognize that the Maoist ban on chaupadi and other social practices went a long way to try to eradicate such discriminatory practices.
149 Aguirre and Pietropaoli, op. cit., 356–377.
150 See *Across the Lines*, op. cit.
151 Ibid.
152 Ibid.
153 Interview with local human rights actor, Kathmandu, Nepal, June 27, 2009.
154 Truth and Reconciliation Bill 2009 2 (j) as cited in *Across the Lines,* op. cit.
155 *Across the Lines,* op. cit.
156 See "Nepal: Women Raped by Security Personnel During Conflict Demand Compensation," *Nepal News*, June 22, 2010, accessed June 22, 2010, http://www.nepalnews.com/home/index.php/news/19/7005-women-raped-by-security-personnel-during-conflict-demand-compensation.html.
157 Ibid.
158 Ibid.
159 S. Opotow, "Psychology of Impunity and Injustice: Implications for Social Reconciliation," in *Post-Conflict Justice,* ed. M.C. Bassiouni (Ardsley, NY: Transaction Publishers, 2002), 201–216.
160 Phone interview with local civil society actor, Afghanistan, September 3, 2008.

6 Negotiating narrow spaces

1 "Civil Society Should Find Means of Implementing Transitional Justice," *Armanshahr Newsletter*, Year 1, Issue 6, February–March 2010, accessed February 10, 2011, http://www.scribd.com/doc/56631763/Newsletter-6-English.
2 In Nepal, the NHRI is actually known as the NHRC.
3 The following contains excerpts from T. Sajjad, "These Spaces in Between: The AIHRC and its Work on Transitional Justice," *International Journal of Transitional Justice* 3(3) (2008): 424–444.
4 J. Mertus, *Human Rights Matters: Local Politics and National Human Rights Institutions* (Stanford, CA: Stanford University Press, 2009).
5 M. Kjærum, *National Human Rights Institutions Implementing Human Rights* (Danish Institute for Human Rights, Martinus Nijhoff Publishers, 2003), accessed February 10, 2008, http://w.nhri.net/pdf/NHRI-Implementing%20human%20rights.pdf.
6 The Paris Principles were defined at the first International Workshop on National Institutions for the Promotion and Protection of Human Rights in Paris on October 7–9, 1991, and adopted by the UN Human Rights Commission Resolution 1992/54 of 1992 and the General Assembly Resolution 48/134 of 1993. The Paris Principles relate to the status and functioning of national institutions for the protection and promotion of human rights.
7 See UN, *Fifty-Third Session of the UN Commission on Human Rights, Item 9 of the provisional agenda, National Institutions for the Promotion and Protection of Human Rights – Report of the Secretary-General, submitted in accordance with the Commission on Human Rights resolution 1996/50, Economic and Social Council*, E/CN.4/1997/41. (United Nations, February 5, 1997), accessed March 5, 2008, http://daccess-dds-ny.un.org/doc/UNDOC/GEN/G97/104/46/PDF/G9710446.pdf?OpenElement.
8 S. Cardenas, *Adaptive States: The Proliferation Of National Human Rights Institutions*, Carr Center for Human Rights Policy, Working Paper (Cambridge, MA: Harvard

University, 2004), accessed February 10, 2007, http://www.hks.harvard.edu/cchrp/Web%20Working%20Papers/Cardenas.pdf, 53.

9 International Council on Human Rights Policy, *Performance & Legitimacy: National Human Rights Institutions* (International Council on Human Rights Policy, Versoix, Switzerland, 2004), http://www.ichrp.org/files/reports/17/102_report_en.pdf.

10 C. Bell, *Peace Agreements and Human Rights* (New York, NY: Oxford University Press, 2000), 198.

11 UN Office of High Commissioner for Human Rights, *Guidance Note on National Human Rights Institutions and Transitional Justice*, UN Office of High Commissioner for Human Rights, September 27, 2008, accessed February 10, 2007, http://nhri.ohchr.org/EN/Themes/Portuguese/DocumentsPage/NHRIs_Guidance%20Note%20TJ_Oct%2008.pdf.

12 Ibid.

13 Ibid.

14 See, for example, the works of the Historical Enquiries Team in Northern Ireland, the Human Rights Consultative Council (CCDH) in Morocco, and the Commission on Human Rights of the Philippines (CHRP) in the Philippines.

15 Cardenas, op. cit., 1.

16 R. Mani, *Ending Impunity and Building Justice in Afghanistan* (Kabul, Afghanistan: AREU, December 2003), accessed February 18, 2008, http://unpan1.un.org/intradoc/groups/public/documents/apcity/unpan016655.pdf, 23.

17 Interview with AIHRC commissioner, Washington DC, June 1, 2008.

18 Mani, op. cit. 1–46.

19 Article 11, *Constitution of Afghanistan, 1382*.

20 UN Development Programme, *United Nations Development Programme in Afghanistan* (Kabul, Afghanistan: UNDP, 2005), accessed 10 February, 2007, http://www.undp.org.af/publications/KeyDocuments/UNDP_in_Afghanistan_2005.pdf, 9.

21 Ibid.

22 Phone interview with Qader Rahimi, AIHRC Regional Manager, Afghanistan, August 17, 2008.

23 Phone interview with AIHRC staff, August 20, 2008.

24 AIHRC, *Transitional Justice: Challenging Injustice, Meeting Accountability* (Kabul, Afghanistan: AIHRC, undated), accessed January 10, 2007, http://www.aihrc.org.af/tra_jus.htm.

25 *Transitional Justice: Challenging Injustice* op. cit.

26 For more information, see AIHRC, *Peace, Reconciliation and Justice in Afghanistan Action Plan of the Government of the Islamic Republic of Afghanistan* (Kabul, Afghanistan, AIHRC, 2005), accessed 5 January, 2007, http://www.constitutionnet.org/files/Peace%20Reconciliation%20and%20Justice%20in%20Afghanistan.pdf.

27 Interview with AIHRC commissioner, Washington DC, June 1, 2008.

28 TJCG comprises of self-identified victims' groups, organizations that work with victims and/or ones that advocate for their rights, and those that work on transitional justice.

29 For detailed discussion about the 2010 Peace *Jirga*, see Sajjad, op. cit., 1–41.

30 For a detailed discussion of the Victims' *Jirga*, see S. Kouvo and D. Mazoori, "Reconciliation, Justice and Mobilization of War Victims in Afghanistan," *International Journal of Transitional Justice* 5(3) (2011): 492–503.

31 By way of contextualization, it should be noted that the Military Act, enacted in 1959–60, has not been updated to accord with the principles contained in the Constitution of Nepal of 1990; under the Military Act's provisions, effective command of the military is vested in the King rather than in civilian government. The Military Act has been described as "one of the most obsolete laws needing urgent democratization." See K.K. Adhikari, "Nepal: Human Rights and Inhuman Wrongs," *Spotlight,*

192   *Notes*

23(19) December 5, 2003, accessed February 12, 2008, http://www.nepalnews.com.np/contents/englishweekly/spotlight/2003/dec/dec05/perspective.htm.

32 The Commission currently shares a building with the Ministry of General Administration of the then King's Government.

33 *Strategic Plan – 2008–2010* (Kathmandu, Nepal: National Human Rights Commission, 2010).

34 On November 26, 2001, a state of emergency was declared for the first time in Nepal following the Maoists' first attack on the army after the breakdown of peace talks. The state of emergency was renewed every three months by the parliament until it lapsed on August 25, 2002. Since May 2002, when parliament was dissolved, the emergency was extended through an ordinance. After a gap of nearly two and a half years, another state of emergency was declared on February 1, 2005. This political reality was a new experience for the newly established Commission, which did not have the experience to deal with human rights issues that emerged during that period.

35 See National Human Rights Commission, *Nepal: National Human Rights Commission – 'An Appeal'* (Kathmandu, Nepal: National Human Rights Commission, 2004), accessed March 12, 2010, http://www.rghr.net/mainfile.php/0642/810/.

36 "Doramba Killings Were 'Cold-Blooded'," *The Kathmandu Post*, September 19, 2003.

37 National Human Rights Commission, *Human Rights in Nepal: A Status Report 2003* (Kathmandu, Nepal: National Human Rights Commission, 2003), accessed January 28, 2008, http://nhrcnepal.org/nhrc_new/doc/newsletter/HumanRights_Status_ReportEng_03Full.pdf, 10.

38 Ibid. 10.

39 Ibid. 12.

40 The violent riots in Kapilavastu began after the September 2007 death of a local landowner. The violence claimed 14 lives, displaced thousands of people, and caused extensive destruction.

41 Elite civil society actors and international and local human rights organizations have called into question the extent to which NHRC has been actively involved and taken on a leadership position. These criticisms will be addressed in greater detail in the rest of the chapter.

42 A. Smith, "The Unique Position of National Human Rights Institutions: A Mixed Blessing?," *Human Rights Quarterly* 28(4) (2006): 906.

43 Ibid, 904–946.

44 Interview with AIHRC commissioner, Washington DC September 15, 2007. Other commissioners interviewed in the course of this research also expressed this opinion.

45 Sajjad, op. cit., 435.

46 Mani, op. cit., 1–46.

47 Ibid.

48 For a more detailed discussion of the delays, see Asia Pacific Human Rights Network, *Human Rights Commission of Nepal: A Long Road to Nirvana* (New Delhi, India: APHRN, 2002), 94.

49 For more information see SAHRDC, *National Human Rights Institutions in the Asia Pacific Region: Report of the Alternate NGO Consultation on the Second Asia – Pacific Regional Workshop on National Human Rights Institutions* (New Delhi, India: South Asia Human Rights Documentation Center (SAHRDC), March 1998).

50 Interview with former commissioner of NHRC, Kathmandu, Nepal, July 22, 2009.

51 See Asian Centre for Human Rights (ACHR), *Nepal Urged Not To Set Up The Cover Up Commission,* (New Delhi, India: ACHR, November 14, 2003), accessed March 14, 2008, http://www.achrweb.org/press/2003/November2003/NEP011103.htm.

52 Interview with representative of Protection Desk, Kathmandu, Nepal, July 18, 2009.

53 Interview with current NHRC commissioner Gauri Prasad, Kathmandu, Nepal, July 19, 2009.

Notes 193

54 Adhikari, op. cit.

55 Ibid.

56 See *Study on Insurgency Related Torture and Disability: Human Rights Violations in the Context of Maoist Insurgency* (Kathmandu, Nepal: National Human Rights Commission, 2003). The British Embassy in Nepal funded the project. The Responding to the Crisis Project is currently jointly funded by British, Danish, and Norwegian development agencies.

57 See, for example, National Human Rights Commission-Nepal, *The National Human Rights Commission Annual Report 2000–2001*, (Kathmandu, Nepal: National Human Rights Commission, 2001), accessed March 12, 2008, http://nhrc.nic.in/ar00_01.htm. See also *Human Rights in Nepal: NHRC Summary of Annual Report*, (Kathmandu, Nepal: National Human Rights Commission, 2003), 6, 10.

58 See National Human Rights Commission, *National Human Rights Commission Strategic Plan 2004–2008* (Kathmandu, Nepal: National Human Rights Commission, 2008), accessed March 15, 2011, http://europeandcis.undp.org/news/show/8036F990-F203-1EE9-B7365BC8C2C28F82, 32.

59 Interview with NHRC commissioner, Kathmandu, Nepal, July 10, 2009.

60 The NHRC estimated that as of December 2002, 969 of the 1,072 complaints were still in the process of investigation as cited in Asia Pacific Human Rights Network, *National Human Rights Commission Of Nepal: Government Launches Operation Scuttle* (New Dehli, India: Asia Pacific Human Rights Network, February 2004), accessed 15 March, 2011, http://www.asiapacificforum.net/about/annual-meetings/8th-nepal-2004/downloads/ngo-statements/ngo_nepal.pdf. The US State Department estimated that 805 out of 861 complaints remained in the process of investigation as of March 2003. See US Department of State, *Nepal: Country Reports on Human Rights Practices* (Washington DC: US State Department, 2002), accessed March 12, 2008, http://www.state.gov/g/drl/rls/hrrpt/2002/18313.htm.

61 See International Commission of Jurists, *Human Rights and Administration of Justice: Obligations Unfulfilled: Fact-Finding Mission to Nepal*, (International Commission of Jurists, June 2003, accessed March 12, 2008, http://icj.concepto.ch/dwn/database/Report_Nepal_SUMMARY.pdf, paragraph 137.

62 See *National Human Rights Commission Strategic Plan 2004–2008*, op. cit. 8.

63 Ibid. See also *Human Rights in Nepal, NHRC Summary of Annual Report*, Nepal Human Rights Commission, 2003, 5.

64 Interview with independent Afghanistan analyst, July 10, 2008.

65 Interview with commissioner Fahim Rahimi, USIP, Washington DC, June 1, 2008.

66 Rahman, a father of two, was arrested in 2006 and brought to trial for converting to Christianity, a crime of apostasy according to the Afghan constitution, which is based on the Shari'a. On March 26, 2006, under heavy pressure from foreign governments, the court returned his case to prosecutors, citing "investigative gaps." The next day he was released in the custody of his family. He currently lives in Italy after being offered asylum by the Italian Government.

67 Interview with commissioner Fahim Rahimi, USIP, Washington DC, June 1, 2008.

68 *Doramba Killings Were 'Cold Blooded'*, op. cit.

69 Interview with Executive Director Mandira Sharma of Advocacy Forum, June 10, 2009.

70 J. Poudyal, "OHCHR's Challenge in Nepal, (ACHR)," *Asian Centre for Human Rights Weekly Review*, November 25, 2008, accessed March 9, 2010, http://www.indigenousportal.com/Human-Rights/OHCHR-s-challenge-in-Nepal.html.

71 Smith, op. cit., 905.

72 Mertus, op. cit., 3.

73 See for example, A. Fowler, "Authentic Partnerships in the New Policy Agenda for International Aid: Dead End or Light Ahead?" *Journal of Development and Change*

194 *Notes*

29(1)(1998): 137–59; F. Bieber, "Aid Dependency in Bosnian Politics and Civil Society: Failures and Successes of Post-War Peacebuilding in Bosnia-Herzegovina," *Croatian International Relations Review* 8 (2002): 25–29; C.E. Welch, *NGOs and Human Rights: Promise and Performance* (Philadelphia, PA: University of Pennsylvania Press, 2000); J. Mertus and T. Sajjad, "When Civil Society Promotion Fails State-Building," in *Subcontracting Peace: The Challenges of NGO Peacebuilding*, eds. O.P. Richmond and H.F. Carey (Farnham, UK: Ashgate Publishing Limited, 2005), 119–130; G. Hancock, *The Lords of Poverty: The Power, Prestige, and Corruption of the International Aid Business* (London, UK: Atlantic Monthly Press, 1989).

74 Expressed in interviews with international analysts and civil society actors conducted in Washington DC in 2008.

75 RAWA is a women's organization in Afghanistan that promotes women's rights and secular democracy. The organization aims to involve women of Afghanistan in political and social activities aimed at acquiring human rights for women and continuing the struggle against the government of Afghanistan based on democratic and secular principles and in which women can participate fully. RAWA has faced criticism from conservative quarters over the years for being a "radical" organization that undermines the role of Islamic practices and principles in society.

76 Phone interview with local civil society actor and former Loya *Jirga* representative, Afghanistan, July 8, 2008.

77 This kind of criticism is easy to level at an institution that is required to work closely with political parties on several issues on the human rights agenda.

78 It must be noted that the Ministry of Justice has been a general exception in this regard, relying on the commission's research and recommendations on issues of prisoners and the state of detention centers to protect the rights of the incarcerated.

79 The current political climate has been increasingly hostile to the AIHRC and to commissioners such as Nader Nadery who has long been a strong advocate for transitional justice. As of writing this manuscript, there are serious allegations that Karzai is under strong pressure to terminate his position and any others who have been critical of the GoA and warlords.

80 Dr Sima Samar is the chairperson for AIHRC.

81 Interview with an AIHRC commissioner, Washington DC, May 13, 2008.

82 Follow-up interview with international civil society actor in Kabul, Afghanistan, April 10, 2010.

83 "NHRC Empowerment: An Editorial," *The Kathmandu Post*, November 26, 2003.

84 Ibid.

85 Ibid.

86 Comments of Sharma from *The Himalayan Times*, August 25, 2003 reported in the International Commission of Jurists' open letter to the King of Nepal of October 10, 2003 as cited in Asia Pacific Human Rights Network, *National Human Rights Commission Of Nepal: Government Launches Operation Scuttle*, op. cit.

87 See *National Human Rights Commission Strategic Plan 2004–2008*, op. cit. See also *Nepal Should Abandon Plans for Civilian Militias: International Commission of Jurists Statement*, (International Commission of Jurists, November 13, 2003), accessed 15 March, 2011 http://icj.concepto.ch/dwn/database/Nepal_militias_13.11.03.pdf.

88 The Act restricts the Commission's jurisdiction over the armed forces; however, the absence of any other recourse often forced the Commission to report abuses committed by the armed forces when investigating a violation. See Asia Pacific Human Rights Network, *National Human Rights Commission Of Nepal: Government Launches Operation Scuttle*, op. cit.

89 See "Nepalese Army Court Martials 23 Soldiers," *The Hindu*, January 30, 2004. See also S. Sharma, "Nepal Soldiers Jailed For Abuses," *BBC World News*, January 29, 2004, accessed May 15, 2010, http://news.bbc.co.uk/1/hi/world/south_asia/3440639.stm.

90 Interview with local civil society actor, Kathmandu, Nepal, July 13, 2009.
91 Interview with Sushil Pyakurel, former NHRC commissioner and head of Accountability Watch-Nepal, Kathmandu, Nepal, July 22, 2009.
92 See UN Office of the High Commissioner for Human Rights, *National Human Rights Institutions. A Handbook on the Establishment and Strengthening of National Institutions for the Promotion and Protection of Human Rights*, Professional Training Series No. 4, 1995.

7 Conclusion

1 N. Kritz, "Empirical Research Methodologies of Transitional Justice Mechanismî (conference report presented at AAAS Science and Human Rights Program Conference, Stellenbosch, South Africa, November 18–20, 2002).
2 U. Baxi, *The Future of Human Rights,* 3rd ed. (New Delhi, India: Oxford University Press, 2002), 24.
3 Ibid.
4 A. An-Na'im, *Towards an Islamic Reformation: Civil Liberties, Human Rights and International Law*, (Syracuse, NY: Syracuse University Press, 1990); D.A. Westbrook, "Islamic International Law And Public International Law: Separate Expressions Of World Order," *Virginia Journal of International Law* 33 (1993): 819–832; N. Hilmy, "Historical Development Of Human Rights And Its Influence On Some Aspects Of Islamic Law," *Africa Legal Aid Quarterly* (2000) 14–17.
5 M.A. Drumbl, *Atrocity, Punishment and International Law* (New York, NY: Cambridge University Press, 2007), 13.
6 P. McSherry and R.M. Mejía, "Confronting the Question of Justice in Guatemala," *Journal of Social Justice* 19(3) (1992): 1–28.
7 D. Otto, R. Aponte-Toro, and A. Farley, "The Third World and International Law: Voices from the Margins," *American Society of International Law* 94 (2000): 51.
8 R. Shaw, L. Waldorf, and P. Hazan, *Localizing Transitional Justice: Interventions and Priorities after Mass Violence* (Stanford, CA: Stanford University Press, 2010), 4.

Bibliography

"40 Points Demand." *United People's Front*, February 4, 1996. http://www.satp.org/satporgtp/countries/nepal/document/papers/40points.htm (accessed March 12, 2011).

Abdulati, H. "The Islamic Perspective on Sin." *On Islam*, September 13, 2006. http://www.onislam.net/english/shariah/refine-your-heart/it-is-never-too-late/441343-the-islamic-perspective-of-sin.html (accessed March 8, 2008).

Abou El Fadl, K.M. "Islam and the State: A Short History." In *Democracy and Islam in the New Constitution of Afghanistan*, edited by C. Bernard and N. Hachigian, 13–6. Santa Monica, CA: RAND Corporation, 2003.

Adhikari, K.K. "Criminal Cases And Their Punishments Before And During The Period Of Jang Bahadur." *Journal Of The Institute Of Nepal And Asian Studies* 3(1) (1976): 105–16.

———. "Nepal: Human Rights and Inhuman Wrongs." *Spotlight* 23(19) (2003). http://www.nepalnews.com.np/contents/englishweekly/spotlight/2003/dec/dec05/perspective.htm (accessed February 12, 2008).

Advocacy Forum. *Discrimination and Irregularities: A Painful Tale of Interim Relief in Nepal*. Kathmandu, Nepal: Advocacy Forum. http://www.advocacyforum.org/downloads/pdf/publications/Discriminations_and_Irregularities_A_painful_tale_of_Interim_Relief_in_Nepal.pdf (accessed October 1, 2010).

———. *Hope and Frustration: Assessing the Impact of Nepal's Torture Compensation Act – 1996*. Kathmandu, Nepal: Advocacy Forum, June 26, 2008. http://www.humansecuritygateway.com/documents/AF_Nepal_hopeandfrustration.pdf (accessed November 10, 2010).

———. *Review Of Implementation Of The Recommendations Made By The UN Working Group on Enforced or Involuntary Disappearances After Its Visit To Nepal In December 2004*. Kathmandu, Nepal: Advocacy Forum, September 2010. http://www.advocacyforum.org/downloads/pdf/publications/af-briefing-series-1-disappearance.pdf (accessed October 10, 2010).

Advocacy Forum and International Center for Transitional Justice. *Across the Lines: The Impact of Nepal's Conflict on Women* (December 2010). http://www.ictj.org/sites/default/files/ICTJ-Nepal-Across-Lines-2010-English.pdf (accessed March 10, 2011).

Afflito, F.M. "Victimization, Survival and the Impunity of Forced Exile: A Case Study from the Rwandan Genocide." *Crime, Law and Social Change* 34(1) (2000): 77–97.

"Afghan Truth Commission Requested." *Associated Press Online*, March 9, 2002. http://www.freerepublic.com/focus/f-news/643825/posts (accessed May 7, 2010).

"Afghan Women Civil Society Leaders Meet in Dubai to Discuss Peace and Security for Afghanistan in the Context of the London Conference." January 28, 2010. http://

peacewithjustice4afghanistan.blogspot.com/2010/01/afghan-women-civil-society-leaders-meet.html (accessed March 12, 2011).

"Afghanistan Demographic Profile 2012." http://www.indexmundi.com/afghanistan/demographics_profile.html (accessed March 12, 2011).

Afghanistan Independent Human Rights Commission (AIHRC). *A Call for Justice: A National Consultation on Past Human Rights Violations in Afghanistan.* Kabul, Afghanistan: AIHRC, 2005. http://www.aihrc.org.af/media/files/Reports/Thematic%20reports/rep29_1_05call4justice.pdf (accessed February 27, 2007).

———. *Peace, Reconciliation and Justice in Afghanistan Action Plan of the Government of the Islamic Republic of Afghanistan.* Kabul, Afghanistan: AIHRC, 2005. http://www.constitutionnet.org/files/Peace%20Reconciliation%20and%20Justice%20in%20Afghanistan.pdf (accessed January 5, 2007).

———. *Transitional Justice: Challenging Injustice, Meeting Accountability.* Kabul, Afghanistan: AIHRC, undated. http://www.aihrc.org.af/tra_jus.htm (accessed January 10, 2007).

Afghanistan Justice Project. *Casting Shadows: War Crimes and Crimes against Humanity: 1978–2001: Documentation And Analysis Of Major Patterns Of Abuse In The War In Afghanistan.* Kabul, Afghanistan: Afghanistan Justice Project, 2005. http://www.afghanistanjusticeproject.org/warcrimesandcrimesagainsthumanity19782001.pdf (accessed May 21, 2007).

———. *Addressing the Past: The Legacy of War Crimes and the Political Transition in Afghanistan.* Kabul, Afghanistan: Afghanistan Justice Project, 2005. http://66.116.195.23/blog/wp-content/uploads/2006/05/AfghJusticeReport.pdf (accessed January 8, 2007).

Afghanistan News Center. "Kabul Distances Itself From Claim of Amnesty for Mullah Omar." *Radio Free Europe/Radio Liberty,* May 10, 2005. http://www.afghanistannews-center.com/news/2005/may/may102005.html (accessed July 3, 2010).

Afghanistan Online. "Agreement on Provisional Arrangements in Afghanistan Pending the Re-Establishment of Permanent Government Institutions." (Bonn Agreement). http://www.afghan-web.com/politics/bonn_agreement_2001.html (accessed January 5, 2007).

———. "Constitution of Afghanistan 1382, Chapter 7, Article 6." http://www.afghan-web.com/politics/current_constitution.html#chapterseven (accessed March 10, 2007).

———. "The Constitution of Afghanistan 1382." http://www.afghan-web.com/politics/current_constitution.html (accessed March 10, 2011).

———. "The Constitution of Afghanistan 1964." http://www.afghan-web.com/history/const/const1964.html (accessed March 10, 2011).

———. "The Constitution of Afghanistan 1987." http://www.afghan-web.com/history/const/const1987.html (accessed February 10, 2008).

Aguirre, D., and I. Pietropaoli. "Gender Equality, Development and Transitional Justice: The Case of Nepal." *International Journal of Transitional Justice* 2(3) (2008): 356–77.

Ahmed, F. "Afghanistan's Reconstruction, Five Years Later: Narratives of Progress, Marginalized Realities, and the Politics of Law in a Transitional Islamic Republic." *Gonzaga Journal of International Law* 10(3) (2007): 269–314.

Akhavan, P. "Beyond Impunity: Can International Criminal Justice Prevent Future Atrocities?" *The American Journal of International Law* 95(1) (2001): 7–31.

———. "The International Criminal Court in Context: Mediating the Global and the Local in the Age of Accountability." *The American Journal of International Law* 97(3) (2003): 712–21.

198 *Bibliography*

Amnesty International. *Nepal: Make Torture a Crime.* ASA 31/002/2001. Kathmandu, Nepal: Amnesty International, March 1, 2001. http://www.unhcr.org/refworld/docid/3c29def4e.html (accessed January 10, 2008).

———. *2005 UN Commission on Human Rights: An Important Opportunity to Address Human Rights Violations Whenever and Wherever They Occur.* Kathmandu, Nepal: Amnesty International, March 10, 2005. http://www.amnesty.org/en/library/asset/IOR41/012/2005/en/6b7a7dd4-d512-11dd-8a23-d58a49c0d652/ior410122005en.html (accessed November 10, 2010).

Amstutz, M.R. *Healing of Nations: The Promise and Limits of Political Reconciliation.* Lanham, MD: Rowmann and Littlefield Publishers, 2005.

An-Na'im, A. *Towards an Islamic Reformation: Civil Liberties, Human Rights and International Law.* Syracuse, NY: Syracuse University Press, 1990.

Anonymous. "Human Rights in Peace Negotiations." *Human Rights Quarterly* 18(2) (1996): 249–58.

Antenna Foundation Nepal, Equal Access Nepal, Forum for Women Law and Development (FWLD), Institute for Human Rights and Communication Nepal (IHRICON), International Alert, and Saferworld. *Security and justice in Nepal: District Assessment Findings*, March 2010. http://www.international-alert.org/sites/default/files/publications/Security%20and%20justice%20in%20Nepal_distirct%20assesment%20findings.pdf (accessed July 10, 2012).

Arendt, H. *Origins of Totalitarianism.* New York, NY: Harcourt Brace, 1973.

———. "Letter from Hannah Arendt to Karl Jaspers (August 18, 1946)." In *Hannah Arendt, Karl Jaspers Correspondence 1926–1969,* edited by L. Kohler and H. Saner, 54. San Diego, CA: Harcourt Brace and Company, 1992.

———. *The Human Condition.* Chicago, IL: University of Chicago Press, 1998.

"Army Major Sacked Over Doramba Case." *The Rising Nepal,* February 14, 2005. http://www.gorkhapatra.org.np/ pageloader.php? file=2005/02/14//topstories/main7 (accessed June 10, 2005).

Article 2.Org. *Article 5 J, Appendix III: Terrorist and Disruptive Activities (Control and Punishment) Ordinance, 2004: Extract and Comment.* http://www.article2.org/mainfile.php/0306/176 (accessed January 10, 2008).

Asia Pacific Human Rights Network (APHRN). *Human Rights Commission of Nepal: A Long Road to Nirvana.* New Delhi, India: APHRN, 2002.

———. *National Human Rights Commission Of Nepal: Government Launches Operation Scuttle.* New Dehli, India: APHRN, February 2004. http://www.asiapacificforum.net/about/annual-meetings/8th-nepal-2004/downloads/ngo-statements/ngo_nepal.pdf (accessed March 15, 2011).

Asian Centre for Human Rights (ACHR). *Nepal Urged Not To Set Up The Cover Up Commission.* New Delhi, India: ACHR, November 14, 2003. http://www.achrweb.org/press/2003/November2003/NEP011103.htm (accessed March 14, 2008).

Aukerman, M.J. "Extraordinary Evil, Ordinary Crime: A Framework for Understanding Transitional Justice." *Harvard Human Rights Journal* 15(39) (2002): 41–2.

Backer, D. "Cross-National Comparative Analysis." In *Assessing the Impact of Transitional Justice: Challenges for Empirical Research,* edited by H. Merwe, V. Baxter, and A. Chapman. Washington DC: United States Institute of Peace Press, 2009.

Baker, P.H. "Conflict Resolution Versus Democratic Governance: Divergent Paths to Peace?" In *Turbulent Peace: The Challenges of Managing International Conflict,* edited by C.A. Crocker, F.O. Hampson, and P. Aall, 753–63. Washington, DC: United States Institute of Peace Press, 2001.

Bibliography 199

Barahona de Brito, A., González-Enríquez, C., and Aguilar, P. *The Politics of Memory: Transitional Justice in Democratizing Societies.* Oxford, UK: Oxford University Press, 2001.

Barfield, T. *Afghan Customary Law and Its Relationship to Formal Judicial Institutions.* Washington DC: United States Institute of Peace Press, June 26, 2003. http://www.usip. org/files/file/barfield2.pdf (accessed March 12, 2011).

_____. "Culture And Custom In Nation-Building: Law In Afghanistan." *Maine Law Review* 60(2) (2008): 351.

Barfield T., N. Nojumi, and J.A. Thier. *The Clash of Two Goods: State and Non-State Dispute Resolution in Afghanistan in Customary Justice and the Rule of Law in War-Torn Societies.* Washington DC: United States Institute of Peace Press, 2011.

Bar-Siman-Tov, Y. "Israel–Egypt Peace: Stable Peace?" In *Stable Peace Among Nations,* edited by Y. Bar-Siman-Tov, A.M. Kacowicz, O. Elgström and M. Jerneck, 220–38. Boulder, CO: Rowman Publishers, 2000.

Bassiouni, C.M. *Crimes Against Humanity In International Law.* New York, NY: Springer Publishing, 1992.

_____. "International Crimes: 'Jus Cogens' and 'Obligatio Erga Omnes'." *Law And Contemporary Problems* 59(4) (1996): 63–74.

_____. *International Criminal Law Conventions And Their Penal Provisions.* Irvington-on-Hudson, NY: Transaction Publishers, 1997.

Bassiouni, C.M. and E.M. Wise. *Aut Dedere Aut Judicare: The Duty To Extradite Or Prosecute In International Law.* Dordrecht, The Netherlands: Martinus Nijhoff Publishers, 1995.

Bassiouni, C.M. and M.H. Morris. "Accountability for International Crime and Serious Violations of Fundamental Human Rights." *Law And Contemporary Problems* 59(4) (1996): 5–230.

Bassiouni, C.M. and D. Rothenberg. "An Assessment of Justice Sector and Rule of Law Reform in Afghanistan and the Need for a Comprehensive Plan." Paper presented at the Conference on the Rule of Law in Afghanistan, Rome, Italy, July 2, 2007. http://www. law.depaul.edu/centers_institutes/ihrli/pdf/rome_conference.pdf (accessed September 10, 2008).

Baxi, U. *The Future of Human Rights,* 3rd ed. New Delhi, India: Oxford University Press, 2002.

Bell, C. *Peace Agreements and Human Rights.* Oxford, UK: Oxford University Press, 2000.

_____. "Dealing with the Past in Northern Ireland." *Fordham International Law Journal* 26 (2003): 1095–147.

_____. "Negotiating Justice: Conflict Resolution and Human Rights." In *Human Rights and Conflict: Exploring the Links between Rights, Law, and Peacebuilding,* edited by J. Helsing and J. Mertus, 345–74. Washington DC: United States Institute of Peace Press, 2004.

_____. "The 'New Law' of Transitional Justice: Study 'Workshop 1 – From Mediation to Sustainable Peace'." Workshop organized by the Crisis Management Institute at the International Conference: Building a Future on Peace and Justice, Nuremberg, June 25–27, 2007. http://www.peace-justice-conference.info/download/WS1-Bell%20report. pdf (accessed November 10, 2010).

Bell, C. and C. O'Rourke. "Does Feminism Need a Theory of Transitional Justice." *International Journal of Transitional Justice* 1(1) (2007): 23–44.

Bell, C., C. Campbell, and F. Ní Aoláin. "Justice Discourses in Transition." *Social Legal Studies* 13(3) (2004): 305–28.

Bennett, L. "Gender, Caste and Ethnic Exclusion in Nepal: Following the Policy Process from Analysis to Action." Paper presented at the World Bank Conference, Arusha, December

200 Bibliography

12–15, 2005. http://siteresources.worldbank.org/INTRANETSOCIALDEVELOPMENT/Resources/Bennett.rev.pdf (accessed December 12, 2010).

Bertram, E. "Reinventing Governments: The Promise and Perils of United Nations Peace Building." *Journal of Conflict Resolution* 39(3) (1995): 398.

Bhandari, R.K. "The Role Of Victims' Organizations In Transition From Conflict: Families Of The Disappeared." Masters thesis, University of Hamburg, 2011.

Bhattarai, B., M. Mainali, J. Ghimere, and A. Upadhyay. *Impunity In Nepal: An Exploratory Study*. Kathmandu, Nepal: The Asia Foundation, September 1999. http://asiafoundation.org/resources/pdfs/nepalimpunity.pdf (accessed November 1, 2010).

Bieber, F. "Aid Dependency in Bosnian Politics and Civil Society: Failures and Successes of Post-War Peacebuilding in Bosnia-Herzegovina." *Croatian International Relations Review* 8 (2002): 25–9.

Bonacker, T., W. Form, and D. Pfeiffer. "Transitional Justice and Victim Participation in Cambodia: A World Polity Perspective." *Global Society* 25(1) (2011): 113.

Boyle, E., and J.W. Meyer. "Modern Law as a Secularized and Global Model: Implications for the Sociology of Law." In *Global Prescriptions: The Production, Exportation, and Importation of a New Legal Orthodoxy,* edited by Y. Dezalay and B.G. Garth, 65–95. Ann Arbor, MI: University of Michigan Press, 2002.

Brooks, R.E. "The New Imperialism: Violence, Norms, and the 'Rule of Law'." *Michigan Law Review* 101(7) (2003): 2275–340.

Brown, T.L. *The Challenge to Democracy in Nepal*, 2nd ed. New York, NY: Routledge, 2006.

Brulliard, K. "Afghan Women Fear Loss Of Hard-Won Progress." *The Washington Post,* March 16, 2010. http://www.washingtonpost.com/wp-dyn/content/article/2010/03/15/AR2010031503669.html (accessed March 16, 2010).

Bunce, V. "Should Transitologists Be Grounded?" *Slavic Review* 54(1) (1995): 111–27.

Burawoy, M., and K. Verdery. *Uncertain Transition: Ethnographies of Change in the Postsocialist World*. Lanham, MD: Rowman and Littlefield, 1999.

Byrd, W.A. *Responding to Afghanistan's Opium Economy Challenge: Lessons and Policy Implications from a Development Perspective*. The World Bank South Asia Region, Policy Research Working Paper 4545, March 2008. http://www-wds.worldbank.org/servlet/WDSContentServer/WDSP/IB/2008/03/04/000158349_20080304082230/Rendered/PDF/wps4545.pdf (accessed February 10, 2009).

Campaign for Innocent Victims in Conflict (CIVIC). *Losing The People: The Costs and Consequences of Civilian Suffering in Afghanistan.* By E.L. Gaston. Washington DC: CIVIC, 2009. http://reliefweb.int/sites/reliefweb.int/files/resources/0EA38479D95508AF49257561000AFF3C-Full_Report.pdf (accessed March 15, 2011).

Campbell, C. "Peace and the Law of War: The Role of International Humanitarian Law in the Post-Conflict Environment." *International Review of the Red Cross* 839 (2000): 627–52.

Campbell, C. and F. Ní Aoláin. "Local Meets Global: Transitional Justice in Northern Ireland." *Fordham International Law Journal* 24 (2003): 1201–23.

Campbell, C., F. Ní Aoláin, and C. Harvey. "The Frontiers of Legal Analysis: Reframing the Transition in Northern Ireland." *Modern Law Review* 66 (2003): 317–45.

Cardenas, S. *Adaptive States: The Proliferation Of National Human Rights Institutions.* Carr Center for Human Rights Policy Working Paper T-01-04. Cambridge, MA: Harvard University, 2004. http://www.hks.harvard.edu/cchrp/Web%20Working%20Papers/Cardenas.pdf (accessed February 10, 2007).

Carothers, T. "The End of the Transition Paradigm." *Journal of Democracy* 13(1) (2002): 5–21.

_____. *Promoting The Rule Of Law Abroad: The Problem of Knowledge*. Rule of Law Series, Democracy and Rule of Law Project No. 34, January 2003. Washington DC: Carnegie Endowment for International Peace. http://www.carnegieendowment.org/files/wp34.pdf (accessed April 10, 2008).

Cassese, A. "Reflections on International Criminal Justice." *Modern Law Review* 61(1) (1998): 1–10.

Christenson, G.A. "Jus Cogens: Guarding Interests Fundamental to International Society." *Virginia Journal of International Law* 28 (1988): 585–648.

"Civil Society Should Find Means of Implementing Transitional Justice." *Armanshahr Newsletter*, Year 1, Issue 6, February–March 2010. http://www.scribd.com/doc/56631763/Newsletter-6-English (accessed February 10, 2011).

Cobban, H. *Amnesty after Atrocity? Healing Nations after Genocide and War Crimes*. Boulder, CO: Paradigm Publishers, 2007.

Cohen, S. "State Crimes of Previous Regimes: Knowledge, Accountability and the Policing of the Past." *Law and Social Inquiry* 20(1) (1995): 7–50.

Community Self Reliance Centre (CSRC), Land Watch Asia, and Asian NGO Collation for Agrarian Reform and Rural Development. *Land and Land Tenure Security in Nepal*. Kathmandu, Nepal: CSRC, March 2009. http://www.csrcnepal.org/CSRC%20_Ebulliten/Land%20and%20Land%20Tenure%20Security%20in%20nepal.pdf (accessed March 1, 2011).

"Comprehensive Peace Accord Concluded Between the Government of Nepal and The Communist Party of Nepal (Maoist)." November 21, 2006. http://id.cdint.org/content/documents/Comprehensive_Peace_Agreement_of_2006.pdf (accessed February 9, 2008).

"Comprehensive Peace Agreement 2006." http://www.satp.org/satporgtp/countries/nepal/document/papers/peaceagreement.htm (accessed February 9, 2008).

Conflict Study Center (CSC). *Nepal's Peace Process at the Crossroads: Situation Update 2*. Kathmandu, Nepal: CSC, August 2, 2006. http://www.ssronline.org/edocs/situation_update_2.pdf (accessed March 3, 2008).

Congressional Research Service. *Afghanistan: Post-War Governance, Security, and US Policy*. By K. Katzman. Washington DC: Congressional Research Service, September 29, 2008. http://fpc.state.gov/documents/organization/110749.pdf (accessed July 3, 2010).

Copelon, R. "Women and War Crimes." *St John's Law Review* 69 (1995): 61–8.

Coursen-Neff, Z., and J. Sifton. "Afghan Regression: Falling Back to Taliban Ways with Women: An Editorial." *New York Times*, January 21, 2003. http://www.nytimes.com/2003/01/21/opinion/21iht-edzama_ed3_.html (accessed June 10, 2010).

Crocker, D. "Transitional Justice and International Civil Society: Toward a Normative Framework." *Constellations* 5(4) (1998): 506.

_____. "Truth Commissions, Transitional Justice and Civil Society." In *Truth v. Justice: The Morality of Truth Commissions,* edited by R.I. Rotberg and D. Thompson, 99–121. Princeton, NJ: Princeton University Press, 2000.

Davis, A. "How the Taliban Became a Military Force." In *Fundamentalism Reborn? Fundamentalism and the Taliban,* edited by W. Maley, 24–5. New York, NY: New York University Press, 1998.

Deschamps, C., and A. Roe, *Land Conflict in Afghanistan: Building Capacity to Address Vulnerability,* Issues Paper Series. Kabul, Afghanistan: Afghanistan Research and Evaluation Unit, April 2009. http://www.ecoi.net/file_upload/1226_1242042724_land-conflict-layout-web.pdf (accessed March 2, 2011).

202 *Bibliography*

Department for International Development (DFID). *Quick Impact Projects: A Handbook For The Military.* London, UK: DFID. http://webarchive.nationalarchives.gov.uk/+/http://www.dfid.gov.uk/pubs/files/qip/booklet.pdf (accessed December 10, 2010).

"Disgrace to Humanity: Afghan Girls on Sale for 100kg Wheat." *The News International,* February 10, 2002. http://www.rawa.org/girlsale.htm (accessed June 10, 2012).

"Doramba Killings Were 'Cold Blooded'." *The Kathmandu Post,* September 19, 2003.

Dorronsoro, G. *Revolution Unending: Afghanistan: 1979 To The Present.* New York, NY: Cambridge University Press, 2005.

C. Douglass, "Lessons from the Americas: Guidelines for International Response to Amnesties for Atrocities." *Law and Contemporary Problems* 59(4) (1996): 197–230.

_____. "Why We Need the International Criminal Court." *Christian Century* 116(15) (1999): 532–36.

Drumbl, M.A. "Rights, Culture, and Crime: The Role of Rule of Law for the Women of Afghanistan." *Columbia Journal of Transnational Law* 42(2) (2004): 349–81.

_____. *Atrocity, Punishment and International Law.* New York, NY: Cambridge University Press, 2007.

Dugard, J. "Dealing With Crimes Of A Past Regime. Is Amnesty Still An Option?" *Leiden Journal of International Law* 12(4) (1999) 1001–15.

Duffield, M. *Global Governance and the New Wars: The Merger of Development and Security.* London, UK: Zed Books, 2001.

Edwards, D.B. *Before Taliban: Genealogies of the Afghan Jihad.* Berkeley, CA: University of California Press, 2002.

Elster, J. "Coming to Terms with the Past: A Framework for the Study of Justice in the Transition to Democracy." *Archives Européennes de Sociologie* 39(1) (1998): 47.

_____. *Closing the Books: Transitional Justice in Historical Perspective.* Cambridge, MA: Cambridge University Press, 2004.

Ensalaco, M. "Truth Commissions for Chile and El Salvador: A Report and Assessment." *Human Rights Quarterly* 16(4) (1994): 656–75.

Etling, B. *Legal Authorities in the Afghan Legal System (1964–1979).* Cambridge, MA: Harvard Law School, Islamic Studies Program, 2003. http://www.law.harvard.edu/programs/ilsp/research/etling.pdf (accessed March 20, 2011).

Ewans, M. *Afghanistan: A Short History of its People and Politics.* New York, NY: Harper Perennial, 2002.

Farer, T.J. "Humanitarian Intervention Before And After 9/11: Legality And Legitimacy." In *Humanitarian Intervention: Ethical, Legal, and Political Dilemmas,* edited by J.L. Holzgrefe and R.O. Keohane, 53–90. Cambridge, UK: Cambridge University Press, 2003.

Finnemore, M. *National Interests In International Society.* Ithaca, NY: Cornell University Press, 1996.

Fowler, A. "Authentic Partnerships in the New Policy Agenda for International Aid: Dead End or Light Ahead?" *Journal of Development and Change* 29(1) (1998): 137–59.

Frank, D.J., and J.W. Meyer. "The Profusion of Individual Roles and Identities in the Postwar Period." *Sociological Theory* 20(1) (2002): 86–105.

Frank, K. "Nepal Maoists Reactivate People's Courts." *Himalaya Times,* February 17, 2010. http://southasiarev.wordpress.com/2010/02/20/nepal-maoists-reactivate-peoples-courts (accessed January 11, 2011).

Freeman, M. *Necessary Evils: Amnesties and the Search for Justice.* New York, NY: Cambridge University Press, 2009.

Bibliography 203

Gairdner, D. *Truth In Transition: The Role Of Truth Commissions In Political Transition In Chile And El Salvador,* vol. 8. Bergen, Norway: Chr. Michelsen Institute, 1999. http://www.cmi.no/publications/1999/rep/r1999-8.pdf (accessed January 10, 2008).

Galtung, J. "An Editorial." *The Journal of Peace Research* 1(1) (1964): 1–4.

Gans-Morse, J. "Searching for Transitologists: Contemporary Theories of Post-Communist Transitions and the Myth of a Dominant Paradigm." *Post-Soviet Affairs* 20(4) (2004): 320.

Gardner, A. *Legal Imperialism: American Lawyers And Foreign Aid In Latin America.* Madison, WI: University of Wisconsin Press, 1980.

Gardner-Feldman, L. *The Special Relationship Between West Germany and Israel.* Boston, MA: Allen and Unwin, 1984.

George, A.L., and A. Bennett. *Case Studies and Theory Development in the Social Sciences.* Cambridge, MA: MIT Press, 2005.

Gerwith, A. "War Crimes and Human Rights." In *War Crimes and Collective Wrongdoing: A Reader,* edited by A. Jokic and A. Ellis, 49. Malden, MA: Wiley-Blackwell, 2001.

Gilbert, K. "Women and Family Law in Modern Nepal: Statutory Rights and Social Implications." *New York Journal of International Law and Politics* 24 (1992–1993): 736.

Gillard, E.-C. "Reparation For Violations Of International Humanitarian Law." *International Committee of the Red Cross* 85(851) (2003): 529–553. http://www.icrc.org/eng/assets/files/other/irrc_851_gillard.pdf accessed January 12, 2011).

Goodin, R.E. "Theories of Compensation." *Oxford Journal of Legal Studies* 9(1) (1989): 56–75.

Gordon, R.E., and J.H. Sylvester. "Deconstructing Development." *Wisconsin International Law Journal* 22(1) (2004): 1–98.

Gossman, P. "Afghanistan in the Balance." *Middle East Research and Information Project (MERIP),* Winter (2001): 14. http://www.merip.org/mer/mer221/afghanistan-balance (accessed October 1, 2010).

_____. "Truth, Justice and Stability in Afghanistan." In *Transitional Justice in the Twenty-First Century: Beyond Truth Versus Justice,* edited by N. Roht-Arriaza and J. Mariezcurrena. New York, NY: Cambridge University Press, 2006.

_____. "The Past As Present: War Crimes, Impunity And The Rule Of Law." Paper originally presented at State Reconstruction And International Engagement In Afghanistan, May 30–June 1, 2003. http://eprints.lse.ac.uk/28365/1/Gossman_LSERO_version.pdf (accessed September 15, 2010).

Govier, T., and W. Verwoerd. "Trust and the Problem of National Reconciliation." *Philosophy of the Social Sciences* 32(2) (2000): 200.

Greenwalt, K. "Amnesty's Justice." In *Truth v. Justice: The Morality of Truth Commissions,* edited by R.I. Rotberg and D. Thompson, 189–210. Princeton, NJ: Princeton University Press, 2000.

de Greiff, P. "Justice and Reparation." In *The Handbook of Reparations,* edited by P. de Greiff, 451–77. New York, NY: Oxford University Press, 2006.

Gutmann, A. and D. Thompson. "The Moral Foundations of Truth Commissions." In *Truth v. Justice: The Morality of Truth Commissions,* edited by R.I. Rotberg and D. Thompson, 22–44. Princeton, NJ: Princeton University Press, 2000.

_____. "Why Deliberative Democracy is Different." *Social Philosophy and Policy* 17(1) (2000): 161–80.

Hallaq, W.B. "'Muslim Rage' and Islamic Law." *Hastings Law Journal* 54 (2003): 1719.

Hancock, G. *The Lords of Poverty: The Power, Prestige, and Corruption of the International Aid Business.* London, UK: Atlantic Monthly Press, 1989.

204 Bibliography

Hannikainen, L. *Peremptory Norms (Jus Cogens) In International Law: Historical Development, Criteria, Present Status*. University of Lapland Publications in Law, Series A1, Helsinki: Finnish Lawyers' Publishing Co, 1988.

Harmon, M.B, and F. Gaynor. "Ordinary Sentences for Extraordinary Crimes." *Journal of International Criminal Justice* 5(3) (2007): 683–712.

Haviland, C. "Parallel Justice, Maoist Style." *BBC World News*, October 14, 2006. http://news.bbc.co.uk/2/hi/south_asia/6048272.stm (accessed January 10, 2011).

von Hayek, F. *The Road to Serfdom with the Intellectuals and Socialism*, 5th ed. Chicago, IL: University of Chicago Press, 1994.

Hayner, P.B. *Unspeakable Truths: Confronting State Terror and Atrocity*. New York, NY: Routledge, 2001.

Hazan, P. "Transitional Justice After September 11: A New Rapport with Evil." In *Localizing Transitional Justice: Interventions and Priorities After Mass Violence,* edited by R. Shaw, L. Waldorf, and P. Hazan, 56. Stanford, CA: Stanford University Press, 2010.

Hilmy, N. "Historical Development Of Human Rights And Its Influence On Some Aspects Of Islamic Law." *Africa Legal Aid Quarterly* (2000) 14–17.

Hirschl, R. "Juristocracy – Political, not Juridical." *The Good Society* 13(3) (2004): 6–11.

Hofer, A. *The Caste Hierarchy and State in Nepal: A Study of the Muluki Ain of 1854*. Innsbruck, Austria: Universitatsverlag Wagner, 1979.

Hokirk, P. *The Great Game: The Struggle for Empire in Central Asia*. New York, NY: Kodansha International, 1992.

Human Rights Watch (HRW). *Afghanistan: The Forgotten War: Human Rights Abuses and Violations of the Laws of War Since the Soviet Withdrawal*. New York, NY: Human Rights Watch, February 1, 1991. http://www.unhcr.org/refworld/docid/45c9a5d12.html (accessed March 5, 2011).

———. *Humanity Denied: Systematic Violations of Women's Rights in Afghanistan.* New York, NY: Human Rights Watch, October 2001. http://www.hrw.org/legacy/reports/2001/afghan3/ (accessed March 8, 2008).

———. *UN Rights Body in Serious Decline*. New York, NY: Human Rights Watch, April 26, 2003. http://www.hrw.org/en/news/2003/04/25/un-rights-body-serious-decline (accessed September 1, 2010).

———. *Nepal: Between a Rock and a Hard Place*. New York, NY: Human Rights Watch, October 6, 2004. http://www.hrw.org/en/node/11973/section/4 (accessed February 1, 2008).

———. *Nepal: Human Rights Concerns for the 61st Session of the UN Commission on Human Rights*. New York, NY: Human Rights Watch, March 10, 2005. http://reliefweb.int/node/168284 (accessed January 15, 2008).

———. *Blood-Stained Hands: Past Atrocities in Kabul and Afghanistan's Legacy of Impunity*. New York, NY: Human Rights Watch, July 7, 2005. http://www.hrw.org/en/reports/2005/07/06/blood-stained-hands (accessed January 5, 2007).

———. *Afghanistan on the Eve of Parliamentary and Provincial Elections*. New York, NY: Human Rights Watch, September 15, 2005. http://www.hrw.org/en/reports/2005/09/15/afghanistan-eve-parliamentary-and-provincial-elections (accessed March 12, 2007).

———. *Children in the Ranks – The Maoists' Use of Child Soldiers in Nepal*. New York, NY: Human Rights Watch, February 2, 2007. http://hrw.org/reports/2007/nepal0207/ (accessed September 2, 2010).

———. *Waiting for Justice*. New York, NY: Human Rights Watch, September 11, 2008. http://www.hrw.org/reports/2008/09/11/waiting-justice (accessed October 12, 2010).

Bibliography   205

_____. *Waiting for Justice: Unpunished Crimes from Nepal's Armed Conflict.* New York, NY: Human Rights Watch, September 11, 2008. http://www.hrw.org/en/reports/2008/09/11/waiting-justice-0 (accessed October 1, 2008).

_____. *Human Rights Watch Letter to President Barack Obama on Afghanistan.* New York, NY: Human Rights Watch, March 26, 2009. http://www.hrw.org/en/news/2009/03/26/human-rights-watch-letter-president-barack-obama-afghanistan (accessed March 10, 2011).

_____. *The 'Ten-Dollar Talib' and Women's Rights: Afghan Women and the Risks of Reintegration and Reconciliation.* New York, NY: Human Rights Watch, July 13, 2010. http://www.hrw.org/en/reports/2010/07/13/ten-dollar-talib-and-women-s-rights (accessed March 10, 2011).

_____. *Afghanistan: Repeal Amnesty Law; Measure Brought into Force by Karzai Means Atrocities Will Go Unpunished.* New York, NY: Human Rights Watch, March 10, 2010. http://www.hrw.org/en/news/2010/03/10/afghanistan-repeal-amnesty-law (accessed January 19, 2011).

Huntington, S. *The Third Wave: Democratization in the Late Twentieth Century (Julian J. Rothbaum Distinguished Lecture Series).* Norman, OK: University of Oklahoma Press, 1993.

Hutchinson, A. *The Rule of Law: Ideal or Ideology?* Piscataway, NJ: Transaction Publishers, 1987.

Insight on Conflict, "Conflict Victim's Committee (CVC): Nepal." Peace Direct. http://www.insightonconflict.org/conflicts/nepal/peacebuilding-organisations/conflict-victims-committee-cvc/ (accessed July 10, 2012).

International Center for Transitional Justice (ICTJ). *Nepal: Enforced Disappearances Should Be Criminalized.* New York, NY: International Center for Transitional Justice, August 30, 2009. http://www.ictj.org/en/news/press/release/3014.html (accessed January 15, 2010).

_____. *Research Brief: Transitional Justice and DDR: The Case of Afghanistan.* By P. Gossman. New York, NY: International Center for Transitional Justice, June 2009. http://ictj.org/sites/default/files/ICTJ-DDR-Afghanistan-ResearchBrief-2009-English.pdf (accessed January 9, 2010).

_____. *Negotiating Peace in Nepal: Implications for Justice.* IFP Mediation Cluster: Country Case Study: Nepal. By W. Farasat, and P. Hayner. Brussels: Initiative for Peacebuilding, June 2009. http://www.initiativeforpeacebuilding.eu/pdf/Negotiating_Peace_in_Nepal.pdf (accessed September 10, 2011).

_____. *Vetting Lessons for the 2009–10 Elections in Afghanistan.* By F. Ayub, A. Deledda, and P. Gossman. New York, NY: International Center for Transitional Justice, January 2009. http://ictj.org/sites/default/files/ICTJ-Afghanistan-Vetting-Lessons-2009-English.pdf (accessed January 5, 2011).

_____. *Addressing Gender-Specific Violations in Afghanistan.* By F. Ayub, S. Kouvo, and Y. Sooka. New York, NY: International Center for Transitional Justice, February 2009. http://ictj.org/sites/default/files/ICTJ-Afghanistan-Gender-Violations-2009-English.pdf (accessed March 15, 2011).

_____. *Navigating Amnesty and Reconciliation in Nepal's Truth and Reconciliation Commission Bill.* New York, NY: International Center for Transitional Justice, November 2011. http://ictj.org/sites/default/files/20111208_Nepal_Amnesty_Reconciliation_bp2011.pdf (accessed November 1, 2011).

_____., and the Advocacy Forum, *Nepali Voices: Perceptions of Truth, Justice Reconciliation, Reparations and the Transition in Nepal.* International Center for Transitional Justice and

206   *Bibliography*

the Advocacy Forum, March 2008. http://ictj.org/sites/default/files/ICTJ-Nepal-Voices-Reconciliation-2008-English.pdf (accessed September 15, 2010).

_____., and UN Human Rights Office of the High Commissioner, "Guidelines For Providing Relief To The Beneficiary Of A Disappeared Person Pursuant To Cabinet Decision, January 12, 2009." In *From Relief To Reparations: Listening to the Voices of Victims*. International Center for Transitional Justice and UN Human Rights Office of the High Commissioner, 2011. http://ictj.org/sites/default/files/ICTJ-NPL-Relief-to-Reparations-Report-2011-English.pdf (accessed June 10, 2012).

International Commission of Jurists. *Human Rights and Administration of Justice: Obligations Unfulfilled: Fact-Finding Mission to Nepal*. Geneva, Switzerland: International Commission of Jurists, June 2003. http://icj.concepto.ch/dwn/database/Report_Nepal_SUMMARY.pdf, paragraph 137 (accessed March 12, 2008).

_____. *Nepal Should Abandon Plans for Civilian Militias: International Commission of Jurists Statement*. Geneva, Switzerland: International Commission of Jurists, November 13, 2003. http://icj.concepto.ch/dwn/database/Nepal_militias_13.11.03.pdf (accessed March 12, 2011).

International Committee of the Red Cross. *National Measures To Repress Violations Of International Humanitarian Law*. Report of the Meeting on Experts, Geneva, September 23–25, 1997 by C. Pellandini. http://www.icrc.org/eng/assets/files/other/report-icrc_002_0726.pdf (accessed May 12, 2009).

_____. *Families Of Missing Persons In Nepal: A Study of Their Needs*. Kathmandu, Nepal: International Committee of the Red Cross, June 30, 2009. http://www.icrc.org/eng/resources/documents/report/nepal-missing-persons-report-300609.htm   (accessed September 15, 2010).

International Council on Human Rights Policy, *Performance & Legitimacy: National Human Rights Institutions*. Versoix, Switzerland: International Council on Human Rights Policy, 2004. http://www.ichrp.org/files/reports/17/102_report_en.pdf.

International Crisis Group. *Afghanistan: Judicial Reform and Transitional Justice*. Asia Report No. 45. Brussels: International Crisis Group, January 28, 2003. http://unpan1.un.org/intradoc/groups/public/documents/apcity/unpan016653.pdf (accessed March 12, 2008).

_____. *Nepal's Royal Coup: Making A Bad Situation Worse*. Asia Report No. 91. Brussels: International Crisis Group, February 9, 2005. http://www.crisisgroup.org/~/media/Files/asia/south-asia/nepal/091_nepal_royal_coup_making_a_bad_situation_worse.ashx (accessed February 9, 2008).

_____. *Nepal's Maoists: Their Aims, Structure and Strategy*. Asia Report No. 104. Brussels:International Crisis Group, October 27, 2005. http://www.crisisgroup.org/~/media/Files/asia/south-asia/nepal/104_nepal_s_maoists_their_aims_structure_and_strategy.ashx (accessed October 5, 2010).

_____. *Taliban Propaganda: Winning The War Of Words?* Asia Report No. 158. Brussels: International Crisis Group, July 24, 2008. http://www.crisisgroup.org/~/media/Files/asia/south-asia/afghanistan/158_taliban_propaganda___winning_the_war_of_words.ashx (accessed September 10, 2010).

_____. *Nepal's Faltering Peace Process*. Asia Report No. 163. Brussels: International Crisis Group, February 19, 2009. http://www.crisisgroup.org/~/media/Files/asia/south-asia/nepal/163_nepal_s_faltering_peace_process.ashx (accessed March 12, 2009).

_____. *Nepal: Peace and Justice*. Asia Report No. 184. Brussels: International Crisis Group, January 14, 2010. http://www.crisisgroup.org/~/media/Files/asia/south-asia/nepal/184%20nepal%20peace%20and%20justice.pdf (accessed January 12, 2009).

Bibliography 207

_____. *Reforming Afghanistan's Broken Judiciary*. Asia Report No. 195. Brussels: International Crisis Group, November 17, 2010. http://www.crisisgroup.org/~/media/Files/asia/south-asia/afghanistan/195%20Reforming%20Afghanistans%20Broken%20Judiciary.ashx (accessed March 15, 2011).

International Legal Foundation. *The Customary Laws of Afghanistan*. New York, NY: International Legal Foundation, September 2004. http://www.usip.org/files/file/ilf_customary_law_afghanistan.pdf (accessed March 12, 2011).

International Organization for Migration Afghanistan. *Afghan Civilian Assistance Program (ACAP)*. Afghanistan: International Organization for Migration, September 2008. http://www.iom.int/jahia/webdav/shared/shared/mainsite/activities/countries/docs/afghanistan/acap_factsheet_sept08.pdf (accessed December 10, 2010).

Jackson, S.A. *Islamic Law and the State: The Constitutional Jurisprudence of Shihab al-Din al-Qarafi, Studies in Islamic Law and Society*. Leiden, The Netherlands: Brill Publishers, 1996.

Jepperson, R.L., A. Wendt, and P.J. Katzenstein. "Norms, Identity, and Culture in National Security." In *The Culture of National Security*, edited by P.J. Katzenstein, 33–75. New York, NY: Columbia University Press, 1996.

Jowitt, K. "Undemocratic Past, Unnamed Present, Undecided Future." *Demokrati-zatsiya* 4(3) (1996): 409–19.

Kamali, M.H. *Law in Afghanistan: A Study of the Constitutions, Matrimonial Law and the Judiciary*, vol. 36. Leiden, The Netherlands: Brill Academic Publishers, 1985.

"Karzai Sets out Afghanistan Vision." *BBC World News,* June 14, 2002. http://news.bbc.co.uk/2/hi/south_asia/2044337.stm (accessed September 26, 2008).

Kaufman, M. "Afghan Poor Sell Daughters as Brides." *MSNBC,* February 23, 2003. http://www.rawa.org/brides.htm (accessed January 2011).

Kaye, M. "The Role of Truth Commissions in the Search for Justice, Reconciliation and Democratization: The Salvadorean and Honduran Cases." *Journal of Latin American Studies* 29(3) (1997): 693–716.

Kiss, E. "Moral Ambitions Within and Beyond Political Constraints: Reflections on Restorative Justice." In *Truth v. Justice: The Morality of Truth Commissions,* edited by R.I. Rotberg and D. Thompson, 68–98. Princeton, NJ: Princeton University Press, 2000.

Kjærum, M. *National Human Rights Institutions Implementing Human Rights.* Danish Institute for Human Rights, Martinus Nijhoff Publishers, 2003. http://w.nhri.net/pdf/NHRI-Implementing%20human%20rights.pdf (accessed February 10, 2008).

Klabbers, J. "Just Revenge? The Deterrence Argument in International Criminal Law." *Finnish Yearbook of International Law* 12 (2001): 249–67.

Kouvo, S., and D. Mazoori. "Reconciliation, Justice and Mobilization of War Victims in Afghanistan." *The International Journal of Transitional Justice* 5(3) (2011): 492–503.

Kritz, N.J. *Transitional Justice: How Emerging Democracies Reckon with Former Regimes*, vol. I. Washington DC: United States Institute of Peace Press, 1995.

_____. Coming to Terms with Atrocities: A Review of Accountability Mechanisms for Mass Violations of Human Rights." *Law and Contemporary Problems* 59(4) (1996): 129.

_____. "Empirical Research Methodologies of Transitional Justice Mechanism." Conference report presented at AAAS Science and Human Rights Program Conference, Stellenbosch, South Africa, November 18–20, 2002.

Krog, A. "The Choice for Amnesty: Did Political Necessity Trump Moral Duty?" In *The Provocations of Amnesty: Memory, Justice and Impunity,* edited by C. Villa-Vicencio and E. Doxtader, 115. Trenton, NJ: Africa World Press, 2003.

208   Bibliography

Kshetry, R. "Civil War Victims Await Compensation." *IPS News Agency*, October 6, 2008. http://www.ipsnews.net/2008/10/nepal-civil-war-victims-await-compensation/ (accessed March 5, 2011).

Kuba, S.K., and S. Thapalia. "A Probe into the Laws of Matrimonial Causes in Nepal." In *Readings In The Legal System Of Nepal*, edited by S.P.S Dhungel, P.M Bajracharya, and B.B. Bajracharya, 105–15. Delhi, India: LAWS Publishing, 1986.

Ladbury, S., and Cooperation for Peace and Unity (CPAU). *Testing Hypotheses On Radicalization In Afghanistan: Why Do Men Join The Taliban And Hizb-I Islami? How Much Do Local Communities Support Them?* Independent Report for Department Of International Development (DFID), August 14, 2009. http://d.yimg.com/kq/groups/23852819/1968355965/name/Drivers%20of%20Radicalisation%20in%20 Afghanistan%20Sep%2009.pdf (accessed March 15, 2010).

Landsman, S. "Alternative Responses to Serious Human Rights Abuses: Of Prosecution and Truth Commissions." *Law and Contemporary Problems* 59(4) (1996): 81–92.

Lau, M. "Islamic Law and the Afghan Legal System." (Undated). http://www.ag-afghanistan.de/arg/arp/lau.pdf (accessed January 10, 2008).

Lederach, J. *Building Peace: Sustainable Reconciliation in Divided Societies*. Washington, DC: United States Institute of Peace Press, 1998.

Lederer, E.M. "International Criminal Court Prosecutor Eyeing War Crimes In Afghanistan." *IJ Central*, September 9, 2009. http://ijcentral.org/blog/international_criminal_court_prosecutor_eyeing_war_crimes_in_afghanistan (ccessed September 2, 2010).

Leebaw, B. "Transitional Justice, Conflict, and Democratic Change: International Interventions and Domestic Reconciliation." Paper prepared for APSA Task Force on Difference and Inequality in the Developing World, University of Virginia, Charlottesville, April 21–23, 2005. http://www.apsanet.org/imgtest/TaskForceDiffIneqLebaw.pdf (accessed January 10, 2010).

Limbu, S. *Summary of a Comparative Study of the Prevailing National Laws Concerning Indigenous Nationalities in Nepal and ILO Convention No.169 on Indigenous and Tribal Peoples*. (Undated). http://www.ccd.org.np/pages/25%20Limbu%20Comparative%20 Analysis.pdf.

Londoño, E. "Key Afghan leader Rabbani killed in Kabul bombing." *The Washington Post*, September 20, 2011. http://www.washingtonpost.com/world/key-afghan-peacemaker-rabbani-killed-in-kabul-bombing/2011/09/20/gIQAxlF9hK_story.html (accessed September 20, 2011).

Luban, D. "A Theory of Crimes Against Humanity." *The Yale Journal of International Law* 29(1) (2004): 85, 90.

Lui, R. "Beyond Retribution: Seeking Justice in the Shadows of War [book review]." *Australian Journal of Political Science* 38(3) (2003): 589–90.

Lundy, P., and M. McGovern. "Whose Justice? Rethinking Transitional Justice from the Bottom Up." *Journal of Law and Society* 35(2) (2008): 265–92.

Lynch, M., *State Interests And Public Spheres: The International Politics Of Jordan's Identity*. New York, NY: Columbia University Press, 1999.

Maitra, R. "US jittery over Nepal." *Asia Times*, March 16, 2005. http://www.atimes.com/atimes/South_Asia/GC16Df01.html (accessed January 5, 2011).

Maley, W. "Political Legitimation in Contemporary Afghanistan." *Asian Survey* 27(6) (1987): 705–25.

———. *The Afghanistan Wars*, 2nd ed. New York, NY: Palgrave Macmillan, 2002.

Malla, S.P. *Rule of Law and Policing in Nepal, Policing in Nepal: A Collection of Essays.* London, UK: A Saferworld, September 2007.

Mallinder, L. *Amnesty, Human Rights and Political Transitions*. Orlando, FL: Hart Publishing, 2008.

Mani, R. *Beyond Retribution: Seeking Justice in the Shadows of Wa*r. Malden, MA: Polity Press, 2002.

_____. "Exploring the Rule of Law in Theory and Practice." In *Civil War and the Rule of Law: Security, Development and Human Rights,* edited by A. Hurwitz and R. Huang. Boulder, CO: Lynne Rienner Publishers, 2008.

———. *Ending Impunity and Building Justice in Afghanistan.* Kabul, Afghanistan: Afghanistan Research and Evaluation Unit, December 2003. http://unpan1.un.org/intradoc/groups/public/documents/apcity/unpan016655.pdf (accessed February 18, 2008).

Mansfield, E.D., and J. Snyder. "Democratic Transitions, Institutional Strength, and War." *International Organization* 56(2) (2002): 301.

Maravall, J.M., and A. Przeworski. *Democracy And The Rule Of Law*, vol. 13, no. 11. New York, NY: Cambridge University Press, 2003.

McEvoy, K. "Letting Go Of Legalism: Developing A 'Thicker' Version Of Transitional Justice." *Journal Of Law And Society* 34(4) (2007): 412.

McMahon, P., and D.P. Forsythe. "The ICTY's Impact on Serbia: Judicial Romanticism Meets Network Politics." *Human Rights Quarterly* 30(2) (2008): 412–35.

McSherry, P., and R.M. Mejía. "Confronting the Question of Justice in Guatemala." *Journal of Social Justice* 19(3) (1992): 1–28.

Meininghaus E. *Legal Pluralism in Afghanistan – Working Paper Series 33, Amu Darya Series Paper No. 8, December 2007*. Bonn, Germany: Center for Development Research, University of Bonn. http://131.220.109.9/fileadmin/webfiles/downloads/projects/amudarya/publications/ZEF_Working_Paper_Meininghaus_33.pdf (accessed March 12, 2011).

Mendoza, K. *Islam and Islamism in Afghanistan*. (Undated). http://www.law.harvard.edu/programs/ilsp/research/mendoza.pdf (accessed March 13, 2011).

Mercille. J. "UN Report Misleading on Afghanistan's Drug Problem." *Global Research* (November 6, 2009). http://www.globalresearch.ca/index.php?context=va&aid–15943 (accessed January 5, 2010).

Mertus, J. *Human Rights Matters: Local Politics and National Human Rights Institutions*. Stanford, CA: Stanford University Press, 2009.

_____., and T. Sajjad. "When Civil Society Promotion Fails State-Building." In *Subcontracting Peace: The Challenges of NGO Peacebuilding*, edited by O.P. Richmond and H.F. Carey. Farnham, UK: Ashgate Publishing Limited, 2005.

Miakhel, S. *Understanding Afghanistan: The Importance of Tribal Culture and Structure in Security and Governance*. Washington DC: United States Institute of Peace Press, November 2009. http://www.pashtoonkhwa.com/files/books/Miakhel-ImportanceOfTribalStructuresInAfghanistan.pdf (accessed March 12, 2011).

Miller, C.E., and M.E. King. *A Glossary of Terms and Concepts in Peace and Conflict Studies,* 2nd ed. Geneva, Switzerland: University for Peace, 2005. http://www.africa.upeace.org/documents/glossaryv2.pdf (accessed October 1, 2010).

Ministry of Local Development, and Ministry of Women, Children and Social Welfare, and Japan International Cooperation Agency. *Gender Mainstreaming and Social Inclusion Project (GEMPSIP): Inception Report*. Ministry of Local Development, and Ministry of Women, Children and Social Welfare, and Japan International Cooperation Agency, May 2009. http://www.gemsip.org.np/pdf/IC-R%20Draft.pdf (accessed September 23, 2012).

210 Bibliography

Minow, M. *Between Vengeance and Forgiveness*: *Facing History after Genocide and Mass Violence*. Boston, MA: Beacon Press, 1998.

Mongabay.com. "Nepal – The Panchayat System." http://www.mongabay.com/reference/country_studies/nepal/GOVERNMENT.html (accessed October 1, 2010).

Moon, C. "Beyond Retribution: Seeking Justice in the Shadows of War [book review]." *International Peacekeeping* 10(4) (2003): 149–51.

Moore, J.J. "Problems with Forgiveness: Granting Amnesty under the Arias Plan in Nicaragua and El Salvador." *Stanford Law Review* 43(3) (1991): 774.

Nadelmann, E. "Global Prohibition Regimes: The Evolution Of Norms In International Society." *International Organization* 44(4) (1990): 479–526.

Nadery, A.N. "Peace or Justice? Transitional Justice in Afghanistan." *International Journal of Transitional Justice* 1(1) (2007): 173–79.

Nagy, R. "Transitional Justice as Global Project: Critical Reflections." *Third World Quarterly* 29(2) (2008): 277.

Nathan, J. "A Review of Reconciliation Efforts in Afghanistan." *CTC Sentinel* 2(8) (2009): 11–3. http://www.ctc.usma.edu/posts/a-review-of-reconciliation-efforts-in-afghanistan (accessed July 3, 2010).

National Human Rights Commission (NHRC). *The National Human Rights Commission Annual Report 2000–2001*. Kathmandu, Nepal: Human Rights Commission, 2001. http://nhrc.nic.in/ar00_01.htm (accessed March 12, 2008).

_____. *Study on Insurgency Related Torture and Disability: Human Rights Violations in the Context of Maoist Insurgency*. Kathmandu, Nepal: National Human Rights Commission, 2003.

_____. *Human Rights in Nepal: NHRC Summary of Annual Report*. Kathmandu, Nepal: National Human Rights Commission, 2003.

_____. *Human Rights in Nepal: A Status Report 2003*. Kathmandu, Nepal: National Human Rights Commission, 2003. http://nhrcnepal.org/nhrc_new/doc/newsletter/HumanRights_Status_ReportEng_03Full.pdf (accessed January 28, 2008).

_____. *Doramba Incident, Ramechhap: On-the-Spot Inspection and Report of the Investigation Committee 2060 BS*. Kathmandu, Nepal: National Human Rights Commission, 2003. http://www.nhrcnepal.org/publication/doc/reports/Reprot_Doramba_R.pdf (accessed January 10, 2008).

_____. *Nepal: National Human Rights Commission – "An Appeal."* Kathmandu, Nepal: National Human Rights Commission, 2004. http://www.rghr.net/mainfile.php/0642/810/ (accessed March 12, 2010).

_____. *Ceasefire Report*. Kathmandu, Nepal: National Human Rights Commission, December 2006. http://www.internal-displacement.org/8025708F004CE90B/(httpDocuments)/944E0E93E66B48EFC125735C00513A04/$file/Ceasefire+report+NHRC+Dec06.pdf (accessed May 6, 2009).

_____. *National Human Rights Commission Strategic Plan 2004–2008*. Kathmandu, Nepal: National Human Rights Commission, 2008. http://europeandcis.undp.org/news/show/8036F990-F203-1EE9-B7365BC8C2C28F82 (accessed March 15, 2011).

_____. *Strategic Plan 2008–2010*. Kathmandu, Nepal: National Human Rights Commission, 2010.

NATO Public Diplomacy Division, Press And Media Section Media Operations Centre. *Facts and Figures: Afghan National Police, June 2010*. Brussels: NATO HQ, 2010. http://www.nato.int/nato_static/assets/pdf/pdf_2010_06/20110310_100610-media-backgrounder-ANP.pdf (accessed July 12, 2012).

Bibliography 211

"Nepal King Blamed For Crackdown." *BBC World News,* November 20, 2006. http://news.bbc.co.uk/2/hi/south_asia/6164298.stm (accessed August 3, 2008).

"Nepal: Land tenure reforms 'urgently needed'." *IRIN News,* December 8, 2010. http://www.irinnews.org/Report/91313/NEPAL-Land-tenure-reforms-urgently-needed (accessed May 12, 20120.

"Nepal: Relief Distribution Affected By False Claims – Home Ministry." *Relief Web,* October 23, 2008. http://reliefweb.int/node/284515 (accessed October 23, 2008).

"Nepal: Women Raped by Security Personnel During Conflict Demand Compensation." *Nepal News,* June 22, 2010. http://www.nepalnews.com/home/index.php/news/19/7005-women-raped-by-security-personnel-during-conflict-demand-compensation.html (accessed June 22, 2010).

"Nepalese Army Court Martials 23 Soldier." *The Hindu,* January 30, 2004.

Niland, N. "Justice Postponed." In *Nation-Building Unraveled? Aid, Peace and Justice in Afghanistan,* edited by A. Donini, N. Niland, and K. Wermester. Hartford, CT: Kumarian Press, 2004.

Nino, C.S. *Radical Evil on Trial.* New Haven, CT: Yale University Press, 1996.

"NHRC Empowerment Editorial." *The Kathmandu Post,* November 26, 2003.

Nojumi N., D. Mazurana, and E. Stites. *Afghanistan's Systems of Justice: Formal, Traditional, and Customary.* Boston, MA: Feinstein International Famine Center, June 2004. http://www.gmu.edu/depts/crdc/neamat1.pdf (accessed March 12, 2011).

Okello, M. "Afterward: Elevating Transitional Local Justice or Crystallizing Global Governance?" In *Localizing Transitional Justice: Interventions and Priorities After Mass Violence,* edited by R. Shaw, L. Waldorf, and P. Hazan, 277. Stanford, CA: Stanford University Press, 2010.

Olsen, T.D., L.A. Payne, and A.G. Reiter. *Transitional Justice in Balance: Comparing Processes, Weighing Efficacy.* Washington DC: United States Institute of Peace Press, 2010.

Opotow, S. "Reconciliation in Times of Impunity: Challenges for Social Justice." *Social Justice Research* 14(2) (2001): 150.

_____. "Psychology of Impunity and Injustice: Implications for Social Reconciliation." In *Post-Conflict Justice,* edited by M.C. Bassiouni, 205. Ardsley, NY: Transaction Publishers, 2002.

Orentlicher, D. "Settling Accounts: The Duty to Prosecute Human Rights Violations of a Prior Regime." *The Yale Law Journal* 100(8) (1991): 2537–615.

Osiel, M. *Mass Atrocity, Collective Memory and the Law.* New Brunswick, Canada: Transaction Books, 1997.

_____. "Why Prosecute? Critics for Punishment for Mass Atrocity." *Human Rights Quarterly* 22(1) (2000): 118–47.

Otto, D., R. Aponte-Toro, and A. Farley. "The Third World and International Law: Voices from the Margins." *American Society of International Law* 94 (2000): 51.

Owen R. *State, Power and Politics in the Making of the Modern Middle East,* 3rd ed. London, UK: Routledge, 2004.

Pant, D.R. "Maoist People's Court Harassing Politicos, Civilians." *Kantipur Online,* July 30, 2010. http://www.hotelnepal.com/nepal_news.php?id=2460 (accessed January 11, 2011).

Parker, K., and L.B. Neylon. "Jus Cogens: Compelling the Law of Human Rights." *Hastings International and Comparative Law Review* 12 (1989): 429–35.

Pasipanodya, T. "A Deeper Justice: Economic and Social Justice as Transitional Justice in Nepal." *International Journal of Transitional Justice* 2(3) 2008: 378–97.

212 *Bibliography*

Peacebuilding Initiative. "Defining Rule of Law, Introduction: Definitions & Conceptual Issue." http://www.peacebuildinginitiative.org/index.cfm?pageId=1843 (accessed March 1, 2011).

Penrose, M. "Impunity-Inertia, Inaction and Invalidity: A Literature Review." *Boston University International Law Journal* 17(2) (1999): 241–68.

Perito, R. "Afghanistan's Police: The Weak Link in Security Sector Reform." In *Revisiting Borders between Civilians and Military: Security and Development in Peace Operations and Post Conflict Situations,* edited by E. Hamann and A. Livingstone. Rio de Janeiro, Brazil: Viva Rio, 2009.

Pfaff-Czarnecka, J. "Vestiges and Visions: Cultural Change and the Process of Nation-Building in Nepal." In *Nationalism and Ethnicity in a Hindu Kingdom: The Politics of Culture in Contemporary Nepal,* edited by D.N. Gellner, J. Pfaff-Czarnecka, and J. Whelpton, 421–29. Newark, NJ: Harwood Academic Publishers, 1997.

Pham, P., and P. Vinck. "Empirical Research and the Development and Assessment of Transitional Justice Mechanism." *The International Journal of Transitional Justice* 1(2) (2007): 243.

Pion-Berlin, D. "The Armed Forces and Politics: Gains and Snares in Recent Scholarship." *Latin American Research Review* 30(1) (1995): 147–62.

Pistor, K. "Advancing the Rule of Law: Report on the International Rule of Law Symposium Convened by the American Bar Association November 9–10, 2005." *Berkeley Journal of International Law* 25(1) (2007): 7–43.

Poudyal, J. "OHCHR's Challenge in Nepal, (ACHR)." *Asian Centre for Human Rights Weekly Review,* November 25, 2008. http://www.indigenousportal.com/Human-Rights/OHCHR-s-challenge-in-Nepal.html (accessed March 9, 2010).

Pradhananga, R.B. *Homicide Law in Nepal; Concept, History and Judicial Practice.* Kathmandu, Nepal: Ratna Pustak Bhandar, 2001.

Pradhananga, R.B. and P. Shrestha. *Domestic Violence against Women in Nepal: Concept, History and Existing Laws.* (Undated). http://www.childtrafficking.com/Docs/domestic_violence_0607.pdf (accessed October 15, 2010).

Przeworski, A., and H. Teune. *Logic of Comparative Social Inquiry.* New York, NY: Wiley–Interscience, 1970.

Rajagopal, B. "Invoking the Rule of Law in Post-Conflict Rebuilding: A Critical Examination." *William and Mary Law Review* 49(4) (2008): 1348.

Rashid, A. *Taliban: Militant Islam, Oil and Fundamentalism in Central Asia.* New Haven, CT: Yale Nota Bene Books, 2001.

_____. *Descent into Chaos The United States and the Failure of Nation Building in Pakistan, Afghanistan, and Central Asia.* New York, NY: Viking Press, 2008.

Ratner, S.R., and J.S. Abrams. *Accountability for Human Rights Atrocities in International Law: Beyond the Nuremburg Legacy,* 2nd ed. Oxford, UK: Oxford University Press, 2001.

Regmi, D.R. *Modern Nepal: Rise and Growth in the Eighteenth Century,* vol. I & II. Kathmandu, Nepal: Rupa Publishers, 1961.

Riaz, A., and S. Basu. "The State–Society Relationship and Political Conflicts in Nepal (1768–2005)." *Journal of Asian and African Studies* 42(2) (2007): 123–42.

Riccadi, T. "The Royal Edicts of King Rama Shah of Gorkha." *Kailash* 5(1) (1977): 29–65.

Robins, S. "Whose Voices? Understanding Victims' Needs In Transition. Review Essay of Nepali Voices: Perceptions of Truth, Justice, Reconciliation, Reparations and the Transition in Nepal." *Journal of Human Rights Practice* 1(2) (2009): 325.

_____. "Towards a Victim-Centred Transitional Justice: Understanding the Needs of Families of the Disappeared in Post-Conflict Nepal." *The International Journal of Transitional Justice* 5(1) (2011): 75–98.

_____. "Transitional Justice as an Elite Discourse: Human Rights Practice Between the Global and the Local in Post-Conflict Nepal." *Critical Asian Studies* 44(1) (2012): 3–30.

Roht-Arriaza, N. *Impunity and Human Rights in International Law and Practice*. Oxford, UK: Oxford University Press, 1995.

_____. "The New Landscape in Transitional Justice." In *Transitional Justice in the Twenty-First Century: Beyond Truth Versus Justice,* edited by N. Roht-Arriaza and J. Mariezcurrena, 2. New York, NY: Cambridge University Press, 2006.

Robins, S. and L. Gibson. "The Developing Jurisprudence on Amnesty." *Human Rights Quarterly* 20(4) (1998): 843.

Rosen, L. *The Justice of Islam: Comparative Perspectives on Islamic Law and Society*. New York, NY: Oxford University Press, 2000.

Rotberg, R.I. *Mass Atrocity Crimes: Preventing Future Outrages*. Washington, DC: Brookings Institution Press, 2010.

Roy, O. *Islam and Resistance in Afghanistan,* 2nd ed. New York, NY: Cambridge University Press, 1990.

Rubin, B.R. *The Search For Peace in Afghanistan: From Buffer State to Failed State*. New Haven, CT: Yale University Press, 1995.

_____, *The Fragmentation of Afghanistan: State Formation and Collapse in the International System,* 2nd ed. New Haven, CT: Yale University Press, 2002.

_____. "Transitional Justice and Human Rights in Afghanistan." *International Affairs* 79(3) (2003): 567–81.

Rustow, D. "Transitions to Democracy: Towards a Dynamic Model." *Comparative Politics* 2(3) (1970): 337–63.

Sajjad, T. "These Spaces in Between: The AIHRC and its Work on Transitional Justice." *The International Journal of Transitional Justice* 3(3) (2009): 442.

_____. *Peace At All Costs? Reintegration and Reconciliation in Afghanistan."* Issues Paper Series. Kabul, Afghanistan: Afghanistan Research and Evaluation Unit, October 2010. http://www.ecoi.net/file_upload/1788_1287995505_peace-at-all-costs-ip-2010-web.pdf (accessed November 1, 2010).

de Sales, A. "The Kham Magar Country, Nepal: Between Ethnic Claims and Maoism." *European Bulletin Of Himalayan Research* 19 (2000): 41–71.

Schaap, A. *Political Reconciliation.* New York, NY: Routledge, 2005.

Schabas, W. "Reparation Practices in Sierra Leone and the Truth and Reconciliation Commission." In *Out of the Ashes: Reparations for Victims of Gross and Systematic Human Rights Violations*, edited by K. Feyter, S. Parmentier, M. Bossuyt and P. Lemmens, 289–308. Antwerp, Belgium: Intersentia, 2006.

Schacht, J. "'Law and Justice." In *The Cambridge History of Islam*, vol. 2, edited by P.M. Holt, A.K.S. Lambton, and B. Lewis, 540. Cambridge, UK: Cambridge University Press, 1977.

Scharf, M., and Rodley, N. "International Law Principles on Accountability." In *Post-Conflict Justice,* edited by M.C. Bassiouni, 89–96. Ardsley, NY: Transaction Publishers, 2002.

Scheper-Hughes, N. "Undoing Social Suffering and the Politics of Remorse in the New South Africa." *Social Justice* 25(4) (1998): 116.

Scott, W.R., and J.W. Meyer. *Institutional Environments and Organizations: Structural Complexity and Individualism*. Thousand Oaks, CA: Sage Publications, 1994.

214 *Bibliography*

Sedra, M. *Security Sector Transformation in Afghanistan,* Working Paper 143. Geneva Center for the Democratic Control of Armed Forces, August 2004. http://www.dcaf. ch/_docs/WP143.pdf (accessed March 10, 2011).

Semple, M. *Reconciliation in Afghanistan.* Washington DC: United States Institute of Peace Press, 2009.

Sharma, S. "Nepal Soldiers Jailed For Abuses." *BBC World News,* January 29, 2004. http:// news.bbc.co.uk/1/hi/world/south_asia/3440639.stm (accessed May 15, 2010).

Shaw, R., L. Waldorf, and P. Hazan. *Localizing Transitional Justice: Interventions and Priorities after Mass Violence.* Stanford, CA: Stanford University Press, 2010.

Sikkinki, K. *The Justice Cascade: How Human Rights Prosecutions are Changing World Politics.* New York, NY: W.W. Norton & Company, 2011.

Slye, R. "Amnesty, Truth and Reconciliation: Reflections on the South African Amnesty Process." In *Truth v. Justice: The Morality of Truth Commissions,* edited by R.I. Rotberg and D. Thompson, 170–88. Princeton, NJ: Princeton University Press, 2000.

Smith, A. "The Unique Position of National Human Rights Institutions: A Mixed Blessing?" *Human Rights Quarterly* 28(4) (2006): 906.

Snyder, J., and L. Vinjamuri. "Trials and Errors: Principles and Pragmatism in Strategies of International Justice." *International Security* 28(3) (2003/2004).

South Asia Human Rights Documentation Center (SAHRDC). *National Human Rights Institutions in the Asia Pacific Region: Report of the Alternate NGO Consultation on the Second Asia–Pacific Regional Workshop on National Human Rights Institutions.* New Delhi, India: South Asia Human Rights Documentation Center, March 1998.

Spain, J.W. *The Way of the Pathans: The Pathan Borderland.* London, UK: Oxford University Press, 1972.

Sriram, C.L. *Confronting Past Human Rights Violations: Justice vs Peace in Times of Transition.* New York, NY: Frank Cass, 2004.

Stacey, S. "Political Theory and Transitional Justice." PhD diss., documentation no. 305387486, Department of Politics, Princeton University, 2005 (accessed January 10, 2011).

Stark, D. "From System Identity to Organizational Diversity: Analyzing Social Change in Eastern Europe." *Contemporary Sociology* 21(3) (1992): 299–304.

Stedman, S. "Spoiler Problems in Peace Processes." *International Security* 22(2) (1997): 6.

Stover, E., and H.M. Weinstein. "Introduction: Conflict, Justice and Reclamation." In *My Neighbor, My Enemy, Justice And Community In The Aftermath Of Mass Atrocity,* edited by E. Stover and H.M. Weinstein, 1–26. New York, NY: Cambridge University Press, 2004.

Suhrke, A., and K. Borchgrevink. "Negotiating Justice Sector Reform In Afghanistan." *Crime, Law and Social Change* 51(2) (2009): 211–30. http://www.springerlink.com/ content/n5147p5588k43362/fulltext.pdf (accessed March 13, 2011).

_____, K.B. Harpviken, and A. Strand. "After Bonn: Conflictual Peace Building." *Third World Quarterly* 23(5) (2002): 876.

Tamanaha, B.Z. *On the Rule of Law: History, Politics, Theory.* New York, NY: Cambridge University Press, 2004.

Tamang, P. "Customary Law and Conservation in the Himalaya." (Undated). http://www. docstoc.com/docs/50524187/Customary-Law-and-Conservation-in-the-Himalaya-The-Case (accessed November 10, 2010).

Tams, C. *Enforcing Obligations Erga Omnes in International Law.* New York, NY: Cambridge University Press, 2005.

Bibliography   215

Tarzi, A. "Afghanistan: Is Reconciliation With The Neo-Taliban Working?" *Eurasia Net Online*, June 1, 2005. http://www.eurasianet.org/departments/insight/articles/pp060205.shtml (accessed April 10, 2010).

———. "Recalibrating the Afghan Reconciliation Program." *Prism* 1(4) (2010): 68. http://www.ndu.edu/press/lib/images/prism1-4/Prism_67-78_Tarzi.pdf (accessed July 2, 2010).

Teitel, R.G. "Transitional Jurisprudence: The Role Of Law In Political Transformation." *Yale Law Journal* 106(7) (1997): 2009–80.

———. *Transitional Justice*. New York, NY: Oxford University Press, 2002.

———. "Theoretical and International Framework: Transitional Justice In A New Era." *Fordham International Law Journal* 26(4) (2003): 893–906.

Tellis, A.J. *Reconciling with the Taliban? Toward an Alternative Grand Strategy in Afghanistan*. Washington DC: Carnegie Endowment for Peace, April 2009. http://www.carnegieendowment.org/files/reconciling_with_taliban.pdf (accessed July 2, 2010).

"Terms of Reference of Local Peace Committees, Section 4.1." http://www.peace.gov.np/uploads/Publication/LPC-ToR-Eng-%202065-10-20.pdf (accessed June 12, 2012).

Terry, S. "Thinking About Post-Communist Transitions: How Different Are They?" *Slavic Review* 52(2) (1993): 333–7.

Thapa, K.B. "Religion and Law in Nepal." *Brigham Young University Law Review* 2010(3) (2010): 922.

Thapa, R. *Nepal's Failure to Address Torture: The Relevance of the UN Torture Convention*. Working Paper No. 5. Paris, France: University of Notre Dame, Center for Civil and Human Rights, Winter 2008. http://www.nd.edu/~ndlaw/cchr/papers/thapa_nepal_torture.pdf (accessed January 10, 2008).

"The Panchayat System under King Mahendra." http://countrystudies.us/nepal/19.htm (accessed September 20, 2010).

Thier, J.A. "The Making of a Constitution in Afghanistan." Paper originally presented at State Reconstruction and International Engagement in Afghanistan – Panel IV: Re-Establishing a Legal System, Bonn, Germany, June 1, 2003. http://eprints.lse.ac.uk/28380/1/Thier_LSERO_version.pdf (accessed March 12, 2008).

———. "The Politics of Peacebuilding, Year One: From Bonn to Kabul." In *Nation-Building Unraveled? Aid, Peace and Justice in Afghanistan,* edited by A. Donini, N. Niland, and K. Wermester, 39–60. West Hartford, CT: Kumarian Press, 2004.

Tolbert, D., and A. Solomon. "United Nations Reform and Supporting the Rule of Law in Post-Conflict Societies." *Harvard Human Rights Journal* 19 (2006): 33.

Tondini, M. *Statebuilding and Justice Reform: Post-Conflict Reconstruction in Afghanistan*. New York, NY: Routledge, 2010.

Trubek, D. "The 'Rule of Law' in Development Assistance: Past, Present, and Future." In *The New Law and Economic Development: A Critical Appraisal*, edited by D.M. Trubek and A. Santos, 74–94. Cambridge, UK: Cambridge University Press, 2006.

Tsing, A.L. "From the Margins." *Cultural Anthropology* 9(3) (1994): 279–97.

UK Foreign and Commonwealth Office. *Information Relating to British Financial Help to Afghan Government in Negotiations with the Taliban*. Released under Freedom of Information Act, September 27, 2007. http://www.fco.gov.uk/resources/en/pdf/foi-releases/2008a/1.1-digest (accessed July 3, 2010).

UK Government. "Communiqué of 'Afghanistan: The London Conference'." Paper presented at the International Conference on Afghanistan, London, UK, January 28, 2010. http://www.isaf.nato.int/images/stories/File/factsheets/Documents_Communique%20of%20London%20Conference%20on%20Afghanistan.pdf (accessed February 5, 2010).

216   *Bibliography*

United Nations. *Fifty-Third Session of the UN Commission on Human Rights, Item 9 of the provisional agenda, National Institutions for the Promotion and Protection of Human Rights – Report of the Secretary-General, submitted in accordance with the Commission on Human Rights resolution 1996/50, Economic and Social Council.* E/CN.4/1997/41. February 5, 1997. http://daccess-dds-ny.un.org/doc/UNDOC/GEN/G97/104/46/PDF/G9710446.pdf?OpenElement (accessed March 5, 2008).

UN Commission On Human Rights (UNCHR). *Question of the Violation of Human Rights and Fundamental Freedoms in any Part of the World, with Particular Reference to Colonial and Other Dependent Countries and Territories: Final Report on the Situation of Human Rights in Afghanistan.* By C.-H. Paik, Special Rapporteur. Submitted in accordance with Commission On Human Rights Resolution 1995/74, Fifty-second session, Item 10 Of The Provisional Agenda. E/CN.4/1996/64. February 27, 1996. http://www.unhchr.ch/Huridocda/Huridoca.nsf/TestFrame/d473d7cb72ece7b7802566f2004d3d14?Opendocument (accessed March 12, 2011).

_____. *Final Report on the Situation of Human Rights in Afghanistan.*" By C.-H. Paik, Special Rapporteur. Submitted in accordance with UN Commission On Human Rights Resolution 1996/75. E/CN.4/1997/59. February 20, 1997. http://www.unhcr.org/refworld/docid/3ae6b0d34.html (accessed March 12, 2011).

UN Committee Against Torture (CAT). *Convention Against Torture and Other Cruel, Inhuman or Degrading Treatment or Punishment.* Article 2. http://www.hrweb.org/legal/cat.html (accessed January 10, 2008).

_____. *Consideration of Reports Submitted by States Parties under Article 19 of the Convention.* CAT/C/16/Add.3. December 16, 1993. http://www.bayefsky.com/reports/nepal_cat_c_16_add.3_1993.php (accessed January 15, 2008).

UN Development Programme (UNDP). *United Nations Development Programme in Afghanistan.* Kabul, Afghanistan: UNDP, 2005. http://www.undp.org.af/publications/KeyDocuments/UNDP_in_Afghanistan_2005.pdf (accessed February 10, 2007).

_____. *The Interim Constitution Of Nepal, 2063, (2007).* Part 1, Article 3. http://www.worldstatesmen.org/Nepal_Interim_Constitution2007.pdf (accessed September 10, 2010).

_____. *The Interim Constitution Of Nepal, 2063, (2007).* Part 1, Article 4. http://www.worldstatesmen.org/Nepal_Interim_Constitution2007.pdf (accessed September 10, 2010).

UN Entity for Gender Equality and the Empowerment of Women (UNIFEM). *UNIFEM Afghanistan – Fact Sheet 2007.* UNIFEM, 2007. http://www.unifem.org/afghanistan/docs/pubs/08/UNIFEM_factsheet_08_EN.pdf (accessed March 10, 2011).

UN Human Rights Council (UNHRC). *Report of the United Nations High Commissioner for Human Rights on the Human Rights Situation and the Activities of her Office Including Technical Cooperation in Nepal.* Para 46, A/HRC/4/97. January 17, 2007. http://www.unhcr.org/refworld/docid/461e448c2.html (accessed November 1, 2010).

_____. *Report of the United Nations High Commissioner for Human Rights on the Human Rights Situation and the Activities of her Office Including Technical Cooperation in Nepal.* A/HRC/13/73. February 5, 2010. http://www.unhcr.org/refworld/docid/4bc585ca2.html (accessed November 1, 2010).

UN Office on Drugs and Crime. *Addiction, Crime and Insurgency, The Transnational Threat of Afghan Opium.* October 2009. http://www.unodc.org/documents/data-and-analysis/Afghanistan/Afghan_Opium_Trade_2009_web.pdf (accessed January 5, 2010).

UN Office of the High Commissioner for Human Rights (OHCHR). *National Human Rights Institutions. A Handbook on the Establishment and Strengthening of National Institutions for the Promotion and Protection of Human Rights.* Professional Training Series No. 4, 1995.

Bibliography   217

_____. *Guidance Note on National Human Rights Institutions and Transitional Justice.* September 27, 2008. http://nhri.ohchr.org/EN/Themes/Portuguese/DocumentsPage/ NHRIs_Guidance%20Note%20TJ_Oct%2008.pdf (accessed February 10, 2007).

_____. "Conflict-Related Disappearances in Bardiya District – December 2008." http:// www.unhcr.org/refworld/docid/494ba58d2.html (accessed November 1, 2010).

UN Office of the High Commissioner for Human Rights-Nepal (OHCHR-Nepal). *Report of Investigation into Arbitrary Detention, Torture and Disappearances at Maharajgunj RNA barracks in 2003–2004.* Kathmandu, Nepal: Office of the High Commissioner for Human Rights-Nepal, May 2006. http://nepal.ohchr.org/en/resources/Documents/ English/reports/IR/Year2006/Pages%20from%202006_05_26_OHCHR-Nepal. Report%20on%20Disappearances%20linked%20to%20Maharajgunj%20Barracks_ Eng.pdf (accessed January 20, 2010).

_____. *Accountability and the International Criminal Court.* Kathmandu, Nepal: Nepal Bar Association. August 6, 2006. http://nepal.ohchr.org/en/resources/Documents/ English/statements/HCR/Year2006/2006_08_06_HCR_DJ_Speech_NBA.pdf (accessed March 20, 2011).

_____. *The April Protests Democratic Rights and the Excessive Use of Force: Findings of OHCHRNepal's Monitoring and Investigations.* September 2006. http://nepal.ohchr.org/ en/resources/Documents/English/reports/IR/Year2006/2006_09_21_OHCHR-Nepal. Report%20on%20The%20April%20Protests.pdf (accessed January 10, 2008).

_____. *The Torture And Death In Custody Of Maina Sunuwar: Summary Of Concerns.* December 2006. http://nepal.ohchr.org/en/resources/Documents/English/reports/IR/ Year2006/2006_12_01_HCR%20_Maina%20Sunuwar_E.pdf (accessed January 20, 2010).

_____. *Comments and Recommendations on draft Truth and Reconciliation Commission Bill.* August 6, 2007. http://nepal.ohchr.org/en/resources/Documents/English/press-releases/Year%202007/AUG2007/Comments%20on%20draft%20Truth%20and%20 Reconciliation%20Bill_03_09_07.doc.pdf (accessed January 10, 2010).

_____. *OHCHR-Nepal Calls For Swift Implementation Of Supreme Court Ruling On Dhanusha Disappearance.* February 5, 2009. http://nepal.ohchr.org/en/resources/ Documents/English/pressreleases/Year%202009/Feb%202009/2009_02_05_ Dhanusha_Diappearance_E.pdf (accessed March 2, 2009).

UN Resident and Humanitarian Coordinator's Office. *Nepal Peace and Development Strategy 2010–2015: A Contribution To Development Planning From Nepal's International Development Partners.* January 2011. http://nepal.um.dk/en/~/media/ Nepal/Documents/Content%20English/Nepal-Peace-and-Development-Strategy.ashx (accessed February 6, 2011).

UN Security Council (UNSC). *The Rule Of Law And Transitional Justice In Conflict And Post-Conflict Societies: Report of the Secretary-General.* By K. Annan, S/2004/616. August 23, 2004. http://www.unrol.org/files/2004%20report.pdf (accessed January 10, 2007).

_____. *United Nations Security Council Resolution 1868.* Paragraph 30. March 23, 2009. http://www.unhcr.org/refworld/docid/49c9f9992.html (accessed September 15, 2010).

UN Sub-Commission on the Promotion and Protection of Human Rights. *Study Concerning The Right To Restitution, Compensation And Rehabilitation For Victims Of Gross Violations Of Human Rights And Fundamental Freedoms: Final Report.* By T. von Boven, Special Rapporteur. E/CN.4/Sub.2/1993/8. UN Sub-Commission on the Promotion and Protection of Human Rights, July 2, 1993. http://www.unhcr.org/ref-world/docid/3b00f4400.html (accessed January 10, 2011).

Bibliography

US Agency for International Development (USAID). *Afghan Civilian Assistance Program: USAID Audit Report, Audit Report No. 5-306-10-004-P.* US Agency for International Development, December 15, 2009. http://oig.usaid.gov/sites/default/files/audit-reports/5-306-10-004-p.pdf (accessed December 10, 2010).

US Army Combined Arms Center (CAC). (April 2009) *Chapter 4: Commander's Emergency Response Program – Commander's Guide to Money as a Weapons System Handbook: Tactics, Techniques and Procedures, no. 09–27.* United States Army CAC, April 2009. http://usacac.army.mil/cac2/call/docs/09-27/09-27.pdf (accessed January 2, 2011).

US Department of Defense and US Department of State Joint Report to Congress (June 2004), *Foreign Military Training In Fiscal Years 2003 and 2004, Volume I.* Washington DC: US Department of Defense and US Department of State, June 2004. http://www.state.gov/t/pm/rls/rpt/fmtrpt/2004/ (accessed January 12, 2008).

US Department of State. *Nepal: Country Reports on Human Rights Practices.* Washington DC: US State Department, 2002. http://www.state.gov/g/drl/rls/hrrpt/2002/18313.htm (accessed March 12, 2008).

United States Institute of Peace (USIP). *Establishing the Rule of Law in Afghanistan: Special Report 117.* Washington DC: United States Institute of Peace Press, March 2004. http://www.usip.org/files/file/sr117.pdf (accessed March 1, 2008).

———. "Commission of Inquiry: Nepal 90." Truth Commissions Digital Collection. http://www.usip.org/publications/commission-inquiry-nepal-90 (accessed October 20, 2010).

Verdeja, E. "Normative Theory of Reparations in Transitional Democracies." *Metaphilosophy* 37(3–4) (2006): 457.

"A Different Kind Of Justice: the South African Truth and Reconciliation Commission." *Contemporary Justice Review* 1 (1998): 407.

Villa-Vicencio, C. and E. Doxtader. *The Provocations of Amnesty: Memory, Justice and Impunity.* Trenton, NJ: Africa World Press, 2003.

Vogel, F.E. *Islamic Law and Legal System: Studies of Saudi Arabia.* Leiden, The Netherlands: Brill Publishers, 2000.

Waldman, M. "Golden Surrender: The Risks, Challenges, and Implications of Reintegration in Afghanistan." Afghanistan Analyst Network, April 22, 2010. http://aan-afghanistan.com/uploads/2010_AAN_Golden_Surrender.pdf (accessed April 22, 2010).

Wardak, A. "Building a Post-War Justice System in Afghanistan." *Crime, Law and Social Change* 41 (2004): 323.

———. *Jirga – A Traditional Mechanism of Conflict Resolution in Afghanistan.* University of Glamorgan, UK: Centre for Criminology, 2003. http://unpan1.un.org/intradoc/groups/public/documents/apcity/unpan017434.pdf (accessed June 10, 2006).

Weinbaum, M. "Legal Elites in Afghan Society." *International Journal of Middle East Studies* 12(1) (1980): 39–57.

Weiss, T.G. "Military–Civilian Humanitarianism: The 'Age of Innocence' is Over." *International Peacekeeping* 2(2) (1995): 157–74.

Welch, C.E. *NGOs and Human Rights: Promise and Performance.* Philadelphia, PA: University of Pennsylvania Press, 2000.

Westbrook, D.A. "Islamic International Law and Public International Law: Separate Expressions of World Order." *Virginia Journal of International Law* 33 (1993) 819–32.

Wiarda, H.J. "Southern Europe, Eastern Europe, and Comparative Politics: Transitology and the Need for New Theory." *Eastern European Politics and Societies* 15(3) (2001): 485–501.

Wiebelhaus-Brahm, E. *Truth Commissions and Transitional Societies: The Impact on Human Rights and Democracy*. New York, NY: Routledge, 2010.

Wilder, A. *Cops or Robbers? The Struggle to Reform the Afghan National Police*. Kabul, Afghanistan: Afghanistan Research and Evaluation Unit, July 1, 2007. http://www.areu.org.af/Uploads/EditionPdfs/717E-Cops%20or%20Robbers-IP-print.pdf (accessed February 1, 2008).

Wily, L.A., D. Chapagain, and S. Sharma. *Land Reform In Nepal: Where Is It Coming From And Where Is It Going?* London, UK: Department for International Development, April 2009. http://www.landcoalition.org/publications/land-reform-nepal-where-it-coming-and-where-it-going (accessed March 2, 2011).

Winterbotham, E. *The State of Transitional Justice in Afghanistan. Actors, Approaches and Challenges: A Discussion Paper.* Kabul, Afghanistan: Afghanistan Research and Evaluation Unit April 2010. http://www.areu.org.af/Uploads/EditionPdfs/1009E-The State of Transitional Justice in Afghanistan-Actors, Approaches and Challenges DP 2010 Final Web.pdf (accessed April 30, 2010).

Wiseberg, L. "Human Rights Nongovernmental Organizations: Questions for Reflection and Discussion." In *Human Rights in the World Community: Issues and Action,* edited by R.P. Claude and B.H. Weston, 372–82. Philadelphia, PA: University of Pennsylvania Press, 1992.

Zadran, A. "Socio–Economic and Legal–Political Processes in a Pashtun Village, Southeastern Afghanistan." PhD diss., State University of New York, July 15, 1977 (on file with SUNY-Buffalo Library).

Zalaquett, J. "Balancing Ethical Imperatives and Political Constraints: The Dilemma of New Democracies Confronting Past Human Rights Violations." *Hastings Law Journal* 43 (1992): 1425–38.

_____. "Confronting Human Rights Violations Committed by Former Governments: Principles Applicable and Political Constraints." In *Transitional Justice,* edited by N.J. Kritz, 3–31. Washington DC: United States Institute of Peace Press, 1995.

Zubaida, S. *Law and Power in the Islamic World*. London, UK: I.B. Tauris, 2005.

Zyl, P. "Dilemmas of Transitional Justice: The Case of South Africa's Truth and Reconciliation Commission." *Journal of International Affairs* 52(2) (1999): 647–67.

Index

A Call for Justice (report) 32, 33, 95–8, 102, 112, 123
Aasht-i-Milli (national reconciliation) 27
accountability 75, 77, 88–9, 98, 121, 132–3
adalat (justice) 104–5
Adams, Brad 34
AF-N (Asia Foundation-Nepal) 71, 99, 117
Afghanistan: Justice for War Criminals Essential to Peace (report) 2
AIHRC (Afghanistan Independent Human Rights Commission): *A Call for Justice* (report) 32, 33, 95–8, 102, 112, 123; established 30, 31, 122; mandate of 123–4; and National Action Plan 1; role of 120, 137–8; and Rome Statute 72; socio-political relationships 127–8, 130–1, 133–5; and TJCG 124–5, 135; and women's rights 114
AJP (Afghanistan Justice Project) 31
Akbari, Ustad 29
Amanullah, King 48, 51, 56
Amiri, Rina 78
amnesties: and Bonn Agreement 30; and human rights 8; literature on 8–10; and justice 96, 98; and Nepalese commissions 43–4; and reconciliation 15, 144 ; and Shari'a law 78
'amnesty law' (National Reconciliation and Stability Law) 1–2, 30, 34–5, 77, 78
Amnesty International (AI) 68
Amnesty, Human Rights and Political Transitions (book) 8
ANP (Afghan National Police) 37, 61
Aponte-Toro, R. 22
arbab (mediator) 54
Arendt, H. 3, 11–12, 111
AREU (Afghanistan Research and Evaluation Unit) xi, 34–5, 60, 110
Army Act (1959) 69

atrocities x–xi, 1–2, 46, 93–5
Aukerman, M. J. 11, 100
'autistic isolation' 22
AW (Afghanistan Watch) 72
Awami League (AL) x
AW-N (Accountability Watch-Nepal) 99

Baluwatar Accord (2006) 40
Bangladesh Nationalist Party (BNP) x
Barahona de Brito, A. 13
Barfield, T. 52, 54
Bassiouni, Cherif 59
Baxi, U. 143–4
Bell, C. 9, 19–20, 112, 121
Bennett, Richard 82, 89
Bertram, E. 7
Bhattarai, Krishna Prasad 37
Birendra, King 36
Blood-Stained Hands (report) 33, 34
Bonn Agreement (2001) 20, 29–30, 59, 122
Borchgrevink, K. 51
Brahimi, Lakhdar 29–30
Brahmanic laws 61–2

Campbell, C. 19–20
Carothers, T. 6, 19
caste system (Nepal) 61–2, 105–6, 110–11
CAT (Convention Against Torture) 67–8
CERP (Commander's Emergency Response Program) 107
'change producers' 20
Cobban, H. 7
COID (Commission Inquiry on Conflict-Related Disappearances) 2, 41–2, 83
collective responsibility 65
compensation 53–4, 107–11
Confronting the Truth: Truth Commissions and Societies in Transition (documentary) 88

CPA (Comprehensive Peace Agreement):
and increase in negotiated settlements
20; launched 2, 37, 40; negotiations for
39–40; and 'shadow justice' 105; and
terming 'transitional justice' 83; and
TRCs 81; and women's rights 112
CPN-M (Unified Communist Party of
Nepal-Maoists) 36, 69, 84–5, 108
culture of impunity 9, 10, 16, 39, 146
culture of rights/responsibility 13
customary laws 52–6, 61, 64–6, 141
CVC (Conflict Victims' Committee) 85
CVSJ (Conflict Victim Society for Justice)
85–6

Daoud, King 51, 57
Dayton Peace Accords (1995) 121
DDR (Disarmament, Demobilization,
and Reintegratation) 13
de Beer, Anja 111
de Greiff, Pablo 111
'democratic reciprocity' 15
democratic transition 5–7
deontological constraint 9
deterrence theory 100
Deuba, Sher Bahadur 38
dispute resolution 64–6
Divya Pariksha (Ordeal) 65
*Does Feminism Need a Theory of
Transitional Justice?* (book) 112
Doramba massacre 94, 99, 128–9
DPKO (Department of Peacekeeping
Operations) 95
Drumbl, M. A. 11, 100, 144
'dynamic local' 5, 21, 25, 45, 143–4, 145

ECCC (Extraordinary Chambers in the
Courts of Cambodia) 22, 46
elite monopolization of 'transitional
justice' 88, 89–90
Elster, J. 6
evil 11–12
extraordinary crimes 11–12, 46–7, 141

Farley, A. 22
fatwas 51
FEDO (Feminist Dalit Organization) 115
findings of study 140–2
Fiqh (Islamic jurisprudence) 50, 51, 56–8
FIRs (First Information Reports) 67,
70–1, 99
Freeman, M. 8

Galtung, J. 14
Gardner, James A. 57
Gardner-Feldman, L. 15
Gayenendra, King 38
gender justice 92, 97, 105, 112–17, 118–19
Geneva Accords (1988) 27–8
Gerwith, A. 12
Gilbert, K. 63
goals of transitional justice 145–6
Gono Andalon (people's movements) 36–7
Gossman, Dr 31
Govier, T. 15
Greenwalt, K. 9
Gutman, A. 15

Hallaq, Dr Wael 49
Hayek, F. von 17–18
Hayner, P. 16, 87
Hazarat customary laws 54–5
Hekmatyar, Gulbuddin 28, 34
Hesam, Hesamuddin 33
Hinduisation 61
HRPC (Human Rights Promotion Center)
129
HRW (Human Rights Watch) 2, 33, 34,
37–8, 69,
Hudd (Islamic crimes) 50
human rights: and amnesties 8; and
amnesty bill 34–5; and atrocities x–xi,
1–2; and Bonn Agreement 30; defining
xiii; and democracy 7, 17; and impunity
92–5; institutions *see* NHRIs; and
justice 95–7; and marginalization of
perpetrators 101–2; and National Action
Plan 32; and Nepalese commissions
37–43; and Nepalese legal system
66–70; and retributive punishment
98–100; and Rome Statute 72; and
rule of law 8–9, 17–18, 20–1, 48; and
socioeconomic demands 109–10; and
terming 'transitional justice' 77–80, 83;
in transitional justice literature 13–14;
and TRCs 17; and war crimes 12, 31,
33; and women's rights 112–17
Hussein, Saddam 2

ICC (International Criminal Court) 31,
46, 72
ICCPR (International Convention on Civil
and Political Rights) 101, 126
ICG (International Crisis Group) 70, 94
ICTJ (International Center for Transitional
Justice) 4, 96–8, 102, 112, 117

222 *Index*

ICTR (International Criminal Tribunal for Rwanda) 46
ICTY (International Criminal Tribunal for Former Yugoslavia 46
IDP (Internally Displaced Peoples) 96–7
IHCHRP (International Council on Human Rights Policy) 121
IMF (International Military Forces) 30
impunity: contextualizing 92–5; culture of 9, 10, 16, 39, 146; and elite monopolization of 'transitional justice' 89–90; literature on 10–11; and marginalization of perpetrators 102–4, 118; and NHRIs 121; and 'shadow justice' 104–5; and violence 11
International War Crimes Tribunal Act (1972) x
IRP (Interim Relief Program) 109
ISA (Islamic State of Afghanistan) 28
Islamabad Accord (1993) 28

Jackson, Robert 99
Jahangir, Asma 31
Jalalzoy, Habibullah 33
Jamaat-e-Islami (JI) x
Jana Andalon (people's movement, Nepal) 37, 38, 69
Jirgas (open forums) 54, 55–6, 73, 141

kachahari system 65
Kamal, Babrak 27
Kamali, Dr Mohammed Hashim 52
Kant, I. 3, 4, 11
Karzai, Hamid: and Afghan legal system 59; and amnesty bill 34–5; and impunity 93; and National Action Plan 34; and NHRIs 125, 134; and reconciliation 31–2, 34, 142; and war crimes 30–1; and women's rights 114–15
KGB (Soviet secret police) 27
KHAD (Soviet secret police, Afghanistan) 27, 33
Kipat system 64
Kritz, N. J. 100, 143
Kutuwal, General 104

Land Act (1964) 110
land disputes 110–11
Lederach, J. 14–15
Leebaw, B. 14
legal reform 19
Lessons Learnt and Reconciliation Commission (LLRC) 1
Liberation War (1971) x

literature on transitional justice xi–xii, 12–14
Local Administration Act (LAA, 1971) 69
Local Self-Governance Act (LSGA, 1999) 66
Lomé Peace Agreement (1999) 121
LPCs (Local Peace Committees) 41, 109
Lundy, P. 7

MA (Muluk Ain) 62–3, 70
MacGovern, M. 7
Malego Committee (2004) 38
Mallik Commission (1990–1991) 37, 39
Mallinder, L. 8
Mani, R. 14, 18, 128
Mansfield, E. D. 5
Marakchi (elders) 54
marginalization of perpetrators 92, 101–4, 118
Masood, Ahmad Shah 26–7, 28
Mazurana, D. 55
McEvoy, K. 13
McSherry, P. 10–11, 144
Mejía, R. M. 10–11, 144
Mertus, J. 133
methodology of study 2–4
Meyer, J. W. 89
Ministry of Enforcement of Virtue and Suppression of Vice 58, 113
Minow, M. 16, 106
mobilization 71–3
Mojaddedi, Sibghatullah 32, 33
MoLSAMD (Ministry of Social Affairs, Labor, Martyrs, and Disabled) fund 107–8
MoPR (Ministry of Peace and Reconstruction) 41, 43, 84, 109
Mudbhara incident 135
Mujahideen 26, 27–9, 113
MVA (Maoists' Victims' Association) 85, 86

Nagy, R. 13, 16
Najibullah 27
National Action Plan: expiration of 34–5, 125; launched 1, 32; and socioeconomic demands 106–7, 108; and terming 'transitional justice' 76, 77; and women's rights 112
National Human Rights Commission Act (1997) 126, 128, 136
National Reconciliation and Stability Law see 'amnesty law'
NATO (North Atlantic Treaty Organization) 31
naulo janabad (new people's democracy) 36

Index   223

NC (Nepali Congress) 43
NCICC (National Coalition for the International Criminal Court) 72–3
NCPJ (National Consultative Peace Jirga) 125
NEFAD (Network of Families of the Disappeared and the Missing) 86
negative peace 14
negotiated settlements 20
neoliberalism xii, 5, 13, 16, 79, 139
Nepali Voices (study) 96–8, 112
NGO's (nongovernmental organizations): and circulation of information 4; and CPA negotiations 39; and dispute resolution 66; influence of 89; and NHRIs 133–4; strategies of x–xi; and transitional justice toolkits 13; and victims' networks 84–7
NHRC (National Human Rights Commission): and atrocities 94; influence of 120; role of 125–7, 137–8; socio-political relationships 127–30, 131–2, 135–7
NHRIs (National Human Rights Institutions): and AIHRC 122–5; influence of 120; and NHRC 125–7; role of 120–1, 137–8; socio-political relationships 127–37
Ningarhar Shura (1993) 28
Nojumi, N. 54, 55
'norm mergers' 20
Northern Ireland Peace Agreement (1998) 121
NP (Nepal Police) 70–1
NPRC (National Peace and Rehabilitation Commission) 2, 40–1
NTTP (Nepal's Transition to Peace) 39

O'Rourke, C. 112
OEF (Operation Enduring Freedom) 29
Official Gazette (Afghanistan) 1
OHCHR-N (Office of the High Commissioner for Human Rights-Nepal) 38, 131–2
OIC (Organization of Islamic Countries) 28
Olsen, T. D. 16–17, 101
Omar, Mullah Mohammad 28, 32, 34
Omar, Wahid 120
ongoing injustice 75–6, 103, 145
Opotow, S. 10–11, 117
ordinary crimes 11–12
ordinary laws/justice: and Afghan legal system 47–61; and atrocities 46; and extraordinary crimes 46–7, 141; and

mobilization 71–3; and Nepalese legal system 61–71; and 'shadow justice' 105; and Shari'a law 47; and transitional justice 23, 24, 95–6
Orentlichter, D. 9, 100
Osiel, M. 15
Otto, D. R. 22
outline of study 23–4, 140

Panchayat system (Nepal) 36, 37
Pashtunwali (code of conduct) 52–4, 55, 74
Payne, A. 16–17, 101
PDPA (People's Democratic Party) 26–7, 57–8
Peshawar Accords (1992) 28
Pham, P. 97
PHR (Physicians for Human Rights) 124
Phuyel, Hari 89–90, 99
PLA (People's Liberation Army) 94
Plato 4
Poar (blood money) 53, 54
political reconciliation 15–16
positive peace 14
poverty 106, 110–12
proactive justice 47, 73, 141
PRTs (Provincial Reconstruction Teams) 107, 108
Przeworski, Adam 3
PTS (Strengthening Peace Program) 33–4
Public Security Act (PSA, 1989) 69

Rabbani, Burhanuddin 28, 35
'radical evil' 3, 11
Rahimi, Fahim 131
Rahmani, Mullah Arsala 35, 114–15
Rana system 62
Rana, Jung Bahadur 62
rape 112, 113–17
RAWA (Revolutionary Association of the Women of Afghanistan) 134
Rayamajhi Commission (2006) 38–9
Rayamajhi, Krishna Jung 38
reconciliation: and amnesties 144; and appeasement 25; and history of Afghanistan's conflicts 26–9, 45; and justice 75–6, 80–1, 83–4, 142; literature on 14–17; and marginalization of perpetrators 102; modern Afghani commitments 29–36
Reiter, A. G. 16–17, 101
retributive punishment 92, 98–101, 118, 145
retroactive justice 7, 47, 141
revenge 53

224 *Index*

RNA (Royal Nepal Army) 36, 38, 42, 69, 94–5
RNP (Royal Nepal Police) 37
Robins, S. 97
Roht-Arriaza, N. 13–14
Rome Statute 72
Rubin, Barnett 29–30
rule of law: and Afghan legal system 59–60, 71; and amnesties 8; definitions of 17–18; formulaic prescriptions of 73; and human rights 8–9, 17–18, 20–1, 48; location in the state 17–19; and Nepalese legal system 71; and reconciliation 16; and transitional justice literature 13–14, 19–21
Rustow, D. 5

Sabbit, Attorney General 60, 103
Samar, Dr Sima 122
Sarwary, Assadullah 33
Saur Revolution (1978) 26
Sayyaf, Abd-al-Rabb al-Rasul 30, 31
SCA (State Cases Act) 68
Schaap, A. 8–9, 15–16
Scheper-Hughes, N. 6
Scott, W. R. 89
secular/Western legal systems 56–8, 61
Security and Justice in Nepal Districts (study) 97–8
selective immunity 9
sexual violence 112, 113–17
'shadow justice' 104–5
Shah, Prithivi Narayan 61
Shari'a (Islamic law): and Afghan legal system 48–52, 56–9; and customary laws 55–6; and emergence of Taliban 28; and NHRIs 128; and ordinary laws 47; and secular/Western legal systems 56–8; and terming 'transitional justice' 78–80; and women's rights 113–14
Sharma, Mandira 99
Shaw, R. 145
Shura-y-Nazar 26
Siebert, H. 39, 81
Sikkink, K. 100–1, 118
Sitoula, Krishna 38
Smith, A. 132–3
Snyder, J. 5, 21
SOCAJ (Solidarity Campaign for Justice) 86
socioeconomic demands 92, 97–8, 106–12, 118–19
SoFAD (Society of Families Disappeared by the State) 84–5, 86
Solomon, A. 19

Splinter, Peter 94
'spoiler syndrome' 93
Sriram, C. L. 8, 9
Stacey, S. 5
'static local' 5, 21
Stedman, S. 93, 95
Stites, E. 55
strategic impunity 10
structural impunity 11
successive justice 73
Suhrke, A. 51
Sunuwar, Maina 69, 70, 94–5
'swift' justice 104

TADO (Terrorist and Disruptive Activities Ordinance) 36, 69
Taliban: and Afghan legal system 58; and Bonn Agreement 29–30; emergence of 28; and history of Afghanistan's conflicts 26, 28–9; and reconciliation efforts 31–2, 33–4, 35; and 'shadow justice' 104–5; and war crimes 31; and women's rights 113, 115
Tamil Tigers (LTTE) xiii
Teitel, R. G. 13, 20
terming 'transitional justice' 76–81, 83, 90
Teune, Henry 3
Thapa, General 104
Thapa, K. B. 61
The 'New Law' in Transitional Justice (book) 9
The Justice Cascade (book) 100–1
The Logic of Comparative Social Inquiry (book) 3
Thier, J. A. 54
Thompson, D. 15
TJCG (Transitional Justice Coordination Group) 124–5, 135
Tolbert, D. 19
Tondini, M. 47–8
toolkits 13, 139
Torture Compensation Act (TCA, 1996) 68
transformational politics 8
Transition to Democracy (book) 5
Transitional Justice as Global Project: Critical Reflections (book) 13
Transitional Justice in the Balance (book) 16–17, 101
Transitional Justice in the Twenty-First Century (book) 13–14
transitology 5–6
TRCs (Truth and Reconciliation Commissions): as CPA provision 2; effectiveness of 87–90; and human

Index   225

rights 17; Nepalese commissions established 42–4; and reconciliation 16; scepticism towards xiv, 83, 139, 140–1, 143; South African model 81–2, 90; and women's rights 117
Treaty Act (1990) 67
Truth Commissions and Transitional Societies (book) 17
Tutu, Desmond 83

ulema (legal scholars) 49–50, 51–2, 58
UN Commission on Human Rights (2003) 31
UNAMA (United Nations Assistance Mission in Afghanistan) 33, 76, 77, 122–4, 131
UNDP (United Nations Development Program) 122–3, 129–30
USIP (United States Institute of Peace) 4, 88–9

Verwoerd, W. 15
Vice and Virtue Patrol 114
'Victims' Jirga' 102, 125
victims' networks 84–7, 90, 108–9, 142–3
Vinck, P. 97
Vinjamuri, L. 8, 21
violence 11

Waiting for Justice (report) 37–8, 69
Waldorf, L. 145
war crimes 12, 29–31, 33–4, 46
'war on terror' 4, 20
WDO (Women's Development Office) 66
Weinbaum, M. 56
WGEID (Working Group for Enforced and Involuntary Disappearances) 38, 41
Whose Justice? Rethinking Transitional Justice from the Bottom Up (book) 7
women's rights 92, 97, 105, 112–17, 118–19, 134
Worden, Scott 77
World Bank (WB) 4, 41, 108

Zahir Shah, King 26, 57
Zalaquett, Jose 93
Zardad, Faryadi 33

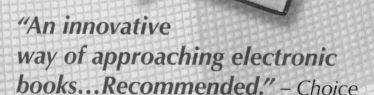

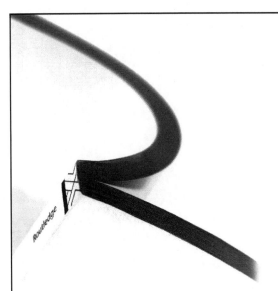

Routledge Paperbacks Direct

Bringing you the cream of our hardback publishing at paperback prices

This exciting new initiative makes the best of our hardback publishing available in paperback format for authors and individual customers.

Routledge Paperbacks Direct is an ever-evolving programme with new titles being added regularly.

To take a look at the titles available, visit our website.

www.routledgepaperbacksdirect.com